Musical Theatre

Musical Theatre

by Seth Rudetsky

Afternoon host of On Broadway on SIRIUSXM®

WITH **Ryan M. Prendergast**

Bill Jenkins

Musical Theatre For Dummies®

Published by: **John Wiley & Sons, Inc.**, 111 River Street, Hoboken, NJ 07030-5774, www.wiley.com

Copyright © 2023 by John Wiley & Sons, Inc., Hoboken, New Jersey

Media and software compilation copyright © 2023 by John Wiley & Sons, Inc. All rights reserved.

Published simultaneously in Canada

For general information on our other products and services, please contact our Customer Care Department within the U.S. at 877-762-2974, outside the U.S. at 317-572-3993, or fax 317-572-4002. For technical support, please visit https://hub.wiley.com/community/support/dummies.

Wiley publishes in a variety of print and electronic formats and by print-on-demand. Some material included with standard print versions of this book may not be included in e-books or in print-on-demand. If this book refers to media such as a CD or DVD that is not included in the version you purchased, you may download this material at http://booksupport.wiley.com. For more information about Wiley products, visit www.wiley.com.

Library of Congress Control Number: 2023930258

ISBN: 978-1-119-88950-2 (pbk); ISBN 978-1-119-88951-9 (ebk); ISBN 978-1-119-88952-6 (ebk)

SKY10044256_031123

Contents at a Glance

Introduction 1

Part 1: Getting Started with Musical Theatre 5

CHAPTER 1: Before the Curtain Rises: Just the Basics about Musical Theatre 7
CHAPTER 2: The History of Musical Theatre (in "only" 100 pages!) 19
CHAPTER 3: Finally . . . the Anatomy of a Musical 123
CHAPTER 4: Oklahoma, Chicago, Avenue Q: Where Musical Theatre
Takes Place 139
CHAPTER 5: Experiencing the Magic of Musical Theatre 167

**Part 2: The People Who Make Musical
Theatre Happen** 189

CHAPTER 6: Making the Musical — The Creators 191
CHAPTER 7: Creating the Big Picture — "The Room Where It Happens" 217
CHAPTER 8: Delivering the Details — The Creatives 231
CHAPTER 9: "Being Alive" — The Performers 249
CHAPTER 10: Introducing the People Who Work the Show Night after Night 271

Part 3: The Blood, Sweat, and Tears of Theatre Life 295

CHAPTER 11: Understanding How an Idea Becomes Broadway Gold 297
CHAPTER 12: "Hi-Ho, the Glamorous Life" (of a Broadway Performer) 319
CHAPTER 13: Landing a Role (Paying or Not!) 339

Part 4: The Part of Tens 363

CHAPTER 14: Ten (Plus) Songs You Didn't Realize Came from Musical Theatre 365
CHAPTER 15: Ten Celebs Who Started in Musical Theatre 369

Index 375

Table of Contents

INTRODUCTION 1

About This Book. 1

Foolish Assumptions. 2

Icons Used in This Book 3

Beyond This Book 3

Where to Go from Here 4

PART 1: GETTING STARTED WITH MUSICAL THEATRE 5

CHAPTER 1: **Before the Curtain Rises: Just the Basics about Musical Theatre** 7

"What Is This Thing Called Love*?" 8

Music. 9

Lyrics 9

Book. 10

Dance 10

Recognizing the Types of Musicals 12

Musical comedies 12

Golden Age musicals. 12

Jukebox musicals. 13

Rock musicals. 13

Sung-thru musicals 13

Identifying the Important People That Make Musicals Happen 14

Behind the scenes. 14

Onstage. 15

Test Your Broadway Knowledge 16

CHAPTER 2: **The History of Musical Theatre (in "only" 100 pages!)** 19

"Let's Start at the Very Beginning" — Before Show Boat Sailed to Broadway 20

A lighter shade of opera. 20

The crowd pleasers 23

It's a musical-ish. 25

The Birth of the Musical As It's Known Today 28

Music + lyrics + book = musical. 28

Music + lyrics + book + dance = Oklahoma!. 31

Shining the Spotlight on the Golden Age 31

What made this age so golden 32

The shows that defined the Golden Age 32

Moving into a New Era — The Post Golden Years (the 1960s) 42
How the '60s changed musical theatre 42
The shows that defined the '60s 43
Please Hello! The '70s and the Rise of Sondheim. 56
Identifying the new sound of Broadway 56
The shows that defined the '70s 56
Cor Blimey! The British Invasion of the 1980s. 69
From musical to MEGA-musical. 70
The shows that defined the '80s 76
525,6000 minutes of the 1990s 83
The shows that defined the '90s 84
Revivals — Everything old is still old again 88
Disney is here to stay 93
Looking Closer at Musical Theatre in the 21st Century 96
The film turned musical 97
The jukebox hits of the 2000s 103
Musicals not based on a film or full of songs from a jukebox . . .105
"A Whole New World" — 2010s 109
Not Hamilton — Other musical greats of the 2010s 109
Hamilton (2015) 118
Covid Hits: The Great Shutdown of 2020. 120
Defying Covid — 2021 to Now. 122

CHAPTER 3: **Finally . . . the Anatomy of a Musical** 123
Act One — Telling the First Part of the Story. 123
The overture — Y'all! The show's starting! 124
The opening number — Introducing the show's theme 126
"I want" song — Stating the quest. 126
"I am" song — Revealing a character's traits 127
"In one" song — Obscuring the activity behind the drop 128
Scene change music — Covering a small set change. 128
Dance break — Give them a chance in their wooly
jazz pants! 129
Underscoring — Adding emotion to a scene. 129
Uptempos and ballads — Expressing emotions on both
ends of the spectrum 130
Duets, trios, quartets . . . Not a solo, not a group number 131
Group numbers — Mixing up the singing with most
of the cast. 132
Finale of Act One — Ending on a high note! 132
Intermission! Time to Stand Up and Stretch (or Go to the
Restroom). 133
Act Two — Answering the Burning Questions 134
Entr'acte — Welcome back to the world of make believe 134
Reprise — Repeating a song for a new reason 135

11 o'clock number — Preparing to wrap things up 135
Finale of Act Two— Wrapping it up. 136
Bows — Accepting the audience's adoration 137
The megamix — Singing and dancing along 137
Exit music — So long, farewell. 137

CHAPTER 4: **Oklahoma, Chicago, Avenue Q: Where Musical Theatre Takes Place** 139
Identifying the World Capitals of Theatre 140
Broadway in New York City 140
Elsewhere in the United States 143
The West End in London. 143
Europe. 145
Asia 147
South America 149
Africa 149
Australia 149
Introducing the Pros in Your Hometown. 150
Preparing for a Broadway run — Out-of-town tryouts 150
Taking a show on the road — Touring productions. 153
Providing professional talent to locals — Regional theatre 155
"We Open in Venice" (California) — Summer stock 156
Combining a show and food — Dinner theatre 158
Mixing thrills with song — Theme parks 159
"Sit Down, You're Rocking the Boat" — Cruise ships 159
Meeting the Thespians in Your Neighborhood. 161
Shining the spotlight on local performers — Community theatre. 161
Training tomorrow's Broadway stars — University productions 162
Teaching students the ways of theatre — K-12 school productions 164
Showcasing outside-the-mainstream productions — Fringe events. 165

CHAPTER 5: **Experiencing the Magic of Musical Theatre**. 167
Overture — What Happens before the Curtain Rises 168
"This Is All Very New to Me" 168
"Far from the Home I Love" 168
"Food, Glorious Food" 169
"Put on Your Sunday Clothes" 170
"Days and Days" 171
Understanding the Inside of a Theatre —Stage and Seating 172
Considering the type of stage 172
Identifying the best seats in the house 175

Getting Tickets to the Hottest Show in Town .179
    Planning in advance: At the theatre's website or box office 179
    Taking a chance: At a TKTS booth 179
    Playing the lottery and winning big. 181
    Buying from a reseller: When ya just gotta see it 182
    A friend of a friend: Grabbing house seats 182
Knowing What to Expect When You Arrive at the Theatre 183
    Getting in the door 183
    Ticketing 101 184
    Heading to the restroom 184
    Checking out the lobby and the merch .185
    Going into the theatre proper 185
    Remembering important do's and don'ts 186

PART 2: THE PEOPLE WHO MAKE MUSICAL THEATRE HAPPEN 189

CHAPTER 6: **Making the Musical — The Creators** 191
"Mr. Cellophane" — the Librettist 192
    The librettist — The script writer. 192
    Identifying the best-ist librettist(s) 194
"I Feel a Song Coming On" — The Composer 197
"Words! Words! Words!" — The Lyricist 199
    Focusing on what a lyricist does 199
    Giving characters the words to sing and express
    their feelings. 200
Recognizing the Very Best 201
    Composer/lyricist teams. 202
    Composers with various partners. 206
    The composer/lyricist 212

CHAPTER 7: **Creating the Big Picture — "The Room Where It Happens"** 217
Finding the Talent — The Casting Director .218
Leading the Creative Vision — The Director 220
    Collaborating with everyone 220
    Figuring out what a show needs and making it happen 223
"Dancing through Life" — Choreographers. 223
Handling the Money and So Much More — Producers 225
    Money Makes the World Go Round 225
    Crafting the idea and assembling the players. 226
    Making the plan to get on Broadway 228
"The Music of the Night" — The Music Team 228

CHAPTER 8: **Delivering the Details — The Creatives**...........231

Who Are You Wearing? — Costume Designers...................232

    Recognizing what costume designers do.................233

    Identifying memorable costume moments in Broadway history...............234

Making the Physical Scenery — Set Designers 236

    Eyeing the different types — From painted backdrops to mechanized sets................236

    Spotting what set designers do.......................237

Illuminating the Stage — What Lighting Designers Do 240

"The Sweetest Sounds" — Sound Designers.....................243

    Comprehending what sound designers do................243

    Making sound board magic..........................244

Coifing the Do — Hair Designers............................245

    Knowing what hair designers do......................246

    Peeking behind the lace-front curtain 247

CHAPTER 9: **"Being Alive" — The Performers** 249

Naming the Leads and Featured Performers in Lights 250

    Identifying the lead(s).............................250

    Being a lead or featured performer 252

Introducing the Ensemble — Side by Side.....................258

    "So many people in the world" (of a musical) 258

    Recognizing who's in the ensemble 259

When the Show Must Go On: Understudies, Standbys, and More 260

    Understudies — "I know it! I can go on!" 260

    Standbys — The Vera Charles of understudies ("I was never in the chorus") 262

    Alternates — Guaranteed two shows a week 264

    Swings — So many parts!..........................265

    Orchestral and backstage understudies 267

CHAPTER 10: **Introducing the People Who Work the Show Night after Night** 271

"Another (Almost) Hundred People" — The Backstage Crew 272

    Keeping track of props — The prop crew 272

    The Sound of Music — The sound crew and sound board operator 273

    Shining the spot — The spotlight operator 274

    Handling set changes — On- and offstage crew members......275

    Flying in lights, scenery, and more — The fly rail crew 275

    Odd crew job example 1: Onstage 276

    Odd crew job examples 2 and 3: Under the stage 277

    Odd crew job example 4: Side of stage 278

"Go into Your Dance" — The Dance Captain .279
"Dress Has Always Been My Strongest Suit" — The
Costumes Crew 280
Taking care of show underwear and cleanings. 281
Helping with the quick change 281
Dressing the star 283
"Long Beautiful Hair" —The Hair Supervisor and Hairdressers 284
"You Can Always Count on Me" — The Stage Manager 286
Introducing the stage managers. 286
Managing everything during rehearsals 287
Keeping to the director's vision 289
Setting the Performance's Tone — The Conductor 290
Keeping track of cues 290
Setting the tempo 291
"76 Trombones" — The Orchestra 291
Wearing all black in the pit. 292
Living in the pit. 293
Being in a community. 293

PART 3: THE BLOOD, SWEAT, AND TEARS
OF THEATRE LIFE 295

CHAPTER 11: **Understanding How an Idea Becomes
Broadway Gold** 297
Finding Inspiration for Musicals 298
The Bible — Talk about old school 298
Shakespeare. 299
Other plays. 299
Films and TV shows. 300
Mythology and fairy tales. 300
History and biographies 301
Books. 302
Jukeboxes 303
Illustrations (cartoons and animation) .304
Moving from the Page to the Stage — The Birthing of a Show. 305
Readings — "I See Possibilities". 305
Workshops — Much more than readings 306
Labs — A new (controversial) version of workshops 307
The post-reading, pre-Broadway world 307
Finding a Theatre. 309
Narrowing down theatre options 310
Picking the right time to open 311
Recognizing What Happens Way before Opening Night 311
Auditions — Finalizing the cast 312

Offers — Negotiating . . . and signing on the dotted line 313
Rehearsing for six to eight weeks. 313
Tech rehearsal — Working in the actual theatre 314
The run-through — Including everything. 315
Previews — Having a live audience. .315
Being Ready — Right before Opening 316
Freezing a show. 316
Preparing for critics. 317
Finally, opening night 317

CHAPTER 12: **"Hi-Ho, the Glamorous Life" (of a Broadway Performer)**. 319
Rehearsal Makes Perfect 320
Diving deeper into the nitty-gritty of rehearsals. 320
Brushing up — "Put 'Em Back The Way They Was". 321
"Welcome to Our House on Maple Avenue" — Put-ins 321
Focusing on the understudies. 323
Arriving for the Big Show 325
Showing up — Half-hour call. 325
Rehearsing the fisticuffs — Fight call 326
Getting all dolled up — wig/makeup call 326
Setting That Alarm for TV Appearances .327
Participating in One-Night-Only Events .329
The Red Bucket Follies/The Easter Bonnet Competition. 329
MCC's Miscast. 330
Concert versions of musicals. 330
Waiting on Pins and Needles for Awards Season. 330
The Tony. 331
Olivier 333
Obie 334
Outer Critics/Drama Desk 334
Drama League 335
The Grammy. 335
The Pulitzer Prize. 336
Legacy Robe 337

CHAPTER 13: **Landing a Role (Paying or Not!)** 339
Identifying Skills You Need to be Onstage. 339
"The Music of the Night" — Singing (Yes! You can sing!) 340
"Doin' What Comes Natur'lly" — Acting (There's a reason why it's called a play) 343
"I Could Have Danced All Night" — Dancing (Don't skip!) 345
"I Hope I Get It" — Auditioning. 346
Being nice — The most important skill. 351

Talking like an Insider 352
"I'm the Greatest Star" — How Broadway Actors Become Stars 353
Getting a degree 354
Is Broadway the only place I can make "Money
Money Money"? 355
"Another Opening, Another Show" — Performing
for the Love of Theatre 359
Joining community theatre. 359
Putting together a cabaret act. 359
Reading through scripts with friends 359
Volunteering at your local fill-in-the-blank. 360
Going Pro 360
Getting an agent 360
Becoming a member of Equity 361
Working a side job 362

PART 4: THE PART OF TENS 363

CHAPTER 14: **Ten (Plus) Songs You Didn't Realize Came
from Musical Theatre** 365
"My Funny Valentine" 365
"All the Things You Are" 366
"Edelweiss" 366
"As Time Goes By" 366
"I'll Never Fall in Love Again" 366
"And I Am Telling You" 367
"Send in the Clowns" 367
"Aquarius"/"Let the Sunshine In" 368
"Come Rain or Come Shine" 368
"Til There Was You" . . . and a Few More 368

CHAPTER 15: **Ten Celebs Who Started in Musical Theatre** 369
Nancy Walker. 369
Valerie Harper 370
Christian Slater. 370
Sara Ramirez 371
Sarah Jessica Parker 371
John Travolta 372
Ariana Grande 373
Nick Jonas 373
Hair: The Show, Not a Performer 373
Fun Reveal: An Almost Was 374

INDEX 375

Introduction

You know that expression that people who love cocktails used to encourage day drinking? They pour themselves a drink at 11 a.m. and toast the air saying, "It's 5 o'clock somewhere!" I've repurposed that saying to be about musical theatre, and here it is:

> *No matter what time of day it is where you are, there is a musical being performed somewhere in the world.*

Yes, musicals are an American art form, but they're beloved all around the world. Well, not *all* around the world. There are definitely some places where musicals aren't performed.

Yet.

You see, I'm hoping musicals will eventually be performed in every city, town, and village the world over. Think how much safer the world would be! What do I mean by that? Well, my friend Kristine Zbornik said it best in her show *Ball of Confusion* during the opening number entitled "Show Tune" (written by Jason Robert Brown). She'd say, "I believe it is physically impossible to commit a violent act while singing a show tune." People would laugh because she was obviously exaggerating . . . but was she? Hmm. I say you and I try it first and then decide. Yes! We can see what happens if the people of the world spend the bulk of their day singing show tunes. *That*, my friends, is what this book is for! To spread the love of musical theatre. Globally. And also, hopefully, to impart some knowledge. And *definitely*, to give you some fun inside stories directly from the mouths of people who perform on Broadway! This book is for people who know every little thing about Broadway, *and* it's for people who have never heard of *Cats*, *Wicked*, or *Hamilton*.

Like musical theatre, this book is for everyone.

About This Book

Why read this book? Well, you can use it to discover historical information about how musicals have developed over time, or to figure out if you want some kind of career in theatre, or to read some fun stories about your favorite musical or favorite star. *Musical Theatre For Dummies* can help you brush up on theatre terms before you start rehearsal for your next show. It's also a way to take a break from the outside world and get lost in all things musicals.

And why was I asked to write this book? Well, I've been working on Broadway since the early 1990s, so I have ye olde "street cred*. I began as a pianist in the orchestra (the original Broadway run of Les Misérables), graduated to conducting, then to acting on Broadway, and then to co-writing my own musical as well. (*The street is Broadway.)

And throughout all those years, I've been chatting with stars and creators and everyone else who works on Broadway in the various talk shows I've done. First, in my weekly talk show at Don't Tell Mama that raised money for Broadway Cares/Equity Fights AIDS called Seth's Broadway Chatterbox, and then in my weekly talk show on SiriusXM radio called Seth Speaks. I've heard countless tales of bizarre auditions, hilarious mishaps onstage, last-minute ideas that saved a musical, wrong choices that doomed a show, costume failures, wig debacles, and so much more! And I've put all that knowledge that's been floating around my head for years into this book.

Full disclosure: If you like (stuffy) academic writing, this probably isn't the book for you. However, if you want information about musical theatre directly from the people who create it and/or are part of it eight times a week, this book *is* for you!

Foolish Assumptions

Are you at a bookstore right now flipping through this book and thinking "Hm . . . am I interested? Or should I spend this money on a latte?" Well, my therapist always tells me I project, so here are some of the assumptions I'm pretty sure you might be making right now:

>> YOU'RE THINKING: You don't know anything about musical theatre, and this book will be all inside information and theatre sayings and you won't know what the H is happening.

ASSUMPTION BUSTER: I wrote this book so someone unfamiliar with musical theatre can discover the basics about it and enjoy stories about some universal hilarious situations.

>> YOU'RE THINKING: You know everything about musical theatre, and you don't need to read a whole book about stuff you yourself could teach at a university.

ASSUMPTION BUSTER: Even if you have a PhD in musical theatre, this book has stories you've never heard before. Why? Because some of them were only told to me! Yes, I admit I'm breaking some boundaries and revealing inside stories so you can be entertained!

>> YOU'RE THINKING: I want to do musicals one day, but I'm too old/overweight/clumsy/short/tall/<insert adjective here>.

ASSUMPTION BUSTER: This book will give you confidence to pursue your dream.

>> YOU'RE THINKING: I hear Seth on the radio all the time, and his voice gives me a *splitting* headache.

ASSUMPTION BUSTER: Guess what? This book is made up of the written word, so you can hear it in your head in any voice you want. Why not imagine the dulcet tones of Meryl Streep reading it . . . in one of the millions of accents she's perfected.

Icons Used in This Book

In the margins of the book, you'll find these icons, and here's why they're there.

This means that it's a fun, possibly tangential, story. These are the kind of stories with which you'll want to regale your musical theatre pals!

This icon appears next to insider tidbits that are good to know, so you can throw them around at cocktail parties.

Sometimes I really want to emphasize the point I'm making, and this icon helps me do that.

Beyond This Book

If you're a musical theatre freak like me and want to know as much as you can about the goings-on on Broadway and more, check out the following:

>> **Cheat Sheet:** You can find the Cheat Sheet, complete with additional nuggets of information, for this book by going to www.dummies.com and searching for "Musical Theatre For Dummies Cheat Sheet." Save it in your bookmarks and refer to it whenever you need a quick refresh.

>> **My website SethRudetsky.com:** This has info on all my upcoming performances all over the world . . . many with Broadway stars who I mention in this book! It also has info on my Broadway Cruise. Yes, it's a super fun vacation to sail

on a fabulous boat to delicious destinations, but it's also a place where you can see some of the Broadway stars I mention in this book in performance up close and personal! *And* you can apply all the knowledge you've read in this book to some of my many Broadway trivia games on the boat. Or use it to impress one of the stars! Walk up to Audra McDonald and tell her "I heard your wig fell off in *Ragtime* at the end of Act One"! She'll be a combination impressed by your insider knowledge and furious at me for telling that story. P.S. If you like to perform, you can even take one of the master classes that are taught by me and a star! And if you're nervous about singing in front of a star, just remember: What happens in the middle of the Atlantic, stays in the middle of the Atlantic.

My website www.SethRudetsky.com also has links to tons of Broadway books that I've read and *loved* (plus links to all the other books I've written).

>> **YouTube:** You can find so many incredible Broadway performances on YouTube. I recommend searching for "Tony Awards" or "The Ed Sullivan Show" or "The Rosie O'Donnell Show" or just the name of one your favorite stars or musicals. The Internet has really made Broadway performances accessible to everyone, so take advantage of it.

I also have my own YouTube channel where you can watch tons of filmed performances of me showcasing some amazing Broadway singers plus my signature deconstructions. Take a gander at www.youtube.com/SethTV.

>> **SiriusXM 77:** There's only one satellite Broadway radio station and it's on SiriusXM, broadcasting 24 hours a day. You can listen at SiriusXM 77 and hear nonstop Broadway music plus my fabulous co-hosts! Christine Pedi is on in the morning, I'm on in the afternoon, and John Tartaglia is every Sunday. Who needs to listen to today's pop hits when you can hear five different versions of "Rose's Turn" (Ethel Merman, Angela Lansbury, Tyne Daly, Bernadette Peters, and Patti LuPone)?

Where to Go from Here

I wrote this book so you can flip to a section that interests you and read it, or you can start from the beginning and read all the way through. Or you can read the entire thing backward a la *Merrily We Roll Along.** (If you know, you know.) *For movie fans, a la *Eternal Sunshine of the Spotless Mind.*

If you're not sure where to start, flip to the Table of Contents or Index, find a topic that piques your interest, turn to that chapter, and start reading.

My point is, read it however you want! All right, everyone. Time to start. As Zach says in *A Chorus Line* "a 5, 6, 7, 8!"

1

Getting Started with Musical Theatre

IN THIS PART . . .

Gain an appreciation for the history of musical theatre during the past 100 years or so.

Look at the different parts of Act One, starting with the overture and ending with intermission.

Find out what happens through Act Two until the exit music.

Recognize the many places in the world you can enjoy musical theatre, beginning obviously with Broadway.

Discover how to find the best-value tickets for Broadway.

Know how to behave like a respectful veteran Broadway patron.

Chapter 1

Before the Curtain Rises: Just the Basics about Musical Theatre

You picked up your tickets at the box office, and you're about to enter the theatre. Ugh! Why did you bring a bag with you? Now, the security guard has to look inside it with a flashlight to see if you have anything forbidden — a weapon, a giant recording device, a sticker that says *I LOVE CATS! NOW AND FOREVER*.

*Just kidding**.

**Not really.

Phew! You're cleared and now you show your tickets to the usher who hands you a Playbill and escorts you to your seat. *Nice!* Eighth row aisle. *Ugh!* Why does there have to be a tall person sitting in front of you. *Down in front!* Oh, wait. That's Tommy Tune*. *Hi, Mr. Tune. Huge fan of your work! So . . . you're 6' 6", correct? Cool. What a wonderfully bold choice for you to wear a top hat. I'm sure I can see around it.*

*This really happened to me!

You flip through the Playbill. Ooh! You didn't realize this show had so-and-so. How exciting! You're a huge fan! You hear the announcement to turn off all cellphones and other noise-making devices. You put your Playbill on your lap. The lights dim. The orchestra is about to play the overture and . . . *curtain up!*

That's the Broadway musical version of you seeing this book in the bookstore (or online), buying it, planting yourself in a comfortable seat, and opening the cover.

This chapter serves as your jumping-off point to the joyous journey of discovering anything and everything related to Broadway musicals. Here I give you an overview of the miracle that is musical theatre.

"What Is This Thing Called Love*?"

*Musical theatre!

Fair question. What is musical theatre? Well, the most basic answer is that musical theatre is a type of performance that has music. And yet, some theatrical productions that have music are *not* musicals. Back in the 1990s, I conducted a show on Broadway called *An Inspector Calls.* I was playing the piano as well as conducting and there were also drums and strings and percussion and brass . . . and yet it wasn't a musical. *An Inspector Calls* was a play that had scenes underscored with music.

REMEMBER

So musicals must have music and lyrics that are sung. *Wait a minute*, you're wondering. Broadway had that production of *Swan Lake* that featured men dancing the roles of the swans and princes. It was all music, but there was no singing in it at all. And yet it was nominated for a Tony Award as Best Musical. And what about *Contact*? That show had dialogue and dancing, but no live singing! And it *won* the Tony Award for Best Musical.

FINE! Can I just give an answer that is 99 percent applicable? *Most* musicals have music, lyrics, a *book* (the script or libretto), and dancing. And the songs usually advance the plot. You can find permutations and exceptions to that rule, but that's the basic answer.

A musical combines scenes, songs, and dances to tell a story. Here I delve a little deeper.

Music

Yes, Broadway musicals must have music. Does that mean the music has to be in a *Broadway style*? Well, let me ask you: What *is* a Broadway style? Is it the old timey Irving Berlin/Cole Porter American Songbook style? Sure it is!

But is it also *Best Little Whorehouse In Texas* country style? You got it!

But what about rock 'n' roll *Hair* style? You bet!

And how about *Porgy and Bess* operatic style. Is that Broadway? Of course!

So, you're also saying *Hamilton* music is Broadway style?

Well, it's on Broadway, isn't it?

My point is, there is *no specific type of music* that has to be in a Broadway musical. The show just has to have music and be in a Broadway theatre.

What's your favorite Broadway song by the way? You may not remember the lyrics, but you undoubtably remember the melody. Broadway musicals must have music and, as I'm sure you know, *good* Broadway musicals have songs that stay with you forever.

Lyrics

The music in musical theatre must have lyrics. And those lyrics help define characters and situations as well as advance the plot. *And*, the most amazing part, those lyrics have to rhyme. Yes, some false rhymes have certainly hit Broadway (especially in the last 20 years! Don't get me started), but the majority of Broadway lyrics rhyme and, boy, that takes skill!

What's your favorite Broadway lyric? I have a lot, but I especially love the Sondheim lyrics from "Another Hundred People." There's one section that shows perfectly how busy New Yorkers are always looking for the next, best thing and not fully committing to anything. You know, *there may be something better out there so better not lock down a plan.*

> "Did you get my message cause I looked in vain?
>
> Can we see each other Tuesday if it doesn't rain?
>
> Look, I'll call you in the morning, or my service will explain . . .".

(P.S. *Service* refers to answering services. In 1970, people didn't have answering machines.) Think about *your* favorite lyric! Aren't you impressed the lyricist can get that thought across *and* make it rhyme?

Book

The *book* is also called the *libretto* or the *script* (See Chapter 2 for many more details about the book, as well as the music and lyrics). The book is vitally important to so many musicals, *yet* (twist ending) not all musicals have them. Meaning not all musicals have spoken dialogue, but 99 percent have a story and the story is *also* considered the book.

For example, the show *Falsettos* is entirely sung. It has no dialogue, but the story is very detailed. So, the music/lyrics are credited to William Finn, and the book is credited to William Finn and James Lapine, even though there's no spoken dialogue. They wrote the book (that is, the story) together.

Let me explain why I said that 99 percent of musicals have a book. That's because some musicals are *revues* — nearly identical to a musical but without the story/plot; those types of Broadway musicals aren't as common as book musicals. And often, they're not as successful. Probably the most successful was *Ain't Misbehavin'*, which was a revue of Fats Waller music and not only ran for years but also won the Tony Award for Best Musical! How incredible is that? Those five performers were simply riveting at performing Fats Waller songs that their show won Best Musical over scripted musicals like *On the Twentieth Century*.

Dance

The term *choreography* refers to the creation of dance. Most of you probably know that term, but maybe not everyone does. That's why when a musical wins a Tony Award for Best Choreography, it sometimes has a banner outside its theatre reading "Best Dancing!"

Unlike music, not every musical has dancing in it. Let me clarify: Not every musical has lots of dancing or big dance numbers in them, but 99 percent of musicals have some form of dancing. In fact, any type of specific movement that's a song is a form of dancing. So some musicals have lots of dance numbers like *Some Like It Hot* and some have smaller dance moments like *Dear Evan Hansen*.

Having dancing during a song can make it much more exciting. Listen to the song "America" from *West Side Story* with its wonderfully clever lyrics and hummable melody. Notice that within the song are three sections of just instruments playing — no singing. That fabulous Leonard Bernstein orchestral section is enjoyable to listen to on the recording with its drum and trumpet accents, right? Listen at www.youtube.com/watch?v=zI5c8qCff2w.

WHY DO SOME PEOPLE *HATE* MUSICAL THEATRE???

Short answer: They're idiots.

Yep. Some people love making sweeping statements. "I just don't like musicals." *Really*, I respond? *What musicals have you seen?*

The answer is always something along the lines of, "I've seen a few (*but they can't actually name them*)" or "I've never seen an entire musical" (*then on what are you basing your opinion?*), or they mention some movie musicals they've seen (*that isn't the same as a stage musical!*).

Anyhoo, my advice is to not engage with them. That type of person isn't clamoring to see a show, which means it's a little easier for you to get tickets to the latest hit, and they can sit home and watch the latest reality show. (And, as a veteran of a few reality shows, let me tell you; they're not actually reality!)

Longer answer: Here are other possible reasons:

- *Reason number one:* They've formed their opinion on the few bad productions they've seen. Let me be honest. A show can be brilliant, but if it's a bad production, it's hard to see what all the hoopla is about. And I don't even mean bad acting/singing/dancing that can ruin a show. I'm also talking about something like bad sound. I've seen a few Broadway shows I didn't really enjoy, but then I listened to the album and realized, "*That's* what they were singing? Now I love the show!"

- *Reason number two:* They don't realize how many different types of musicals there are. When I was young, I definitely didn't like old-school musicals. I wasn't interested in *Kismet*, but I was obsessed with *Chicago* and *A Chorus Line*. If I hadn't been exposed to different types of show, I would have thought that all musicals had the type of operatic singing as in *Kismet*, and I would have said I didn't like musicals. What's amazing about musicals is that you can find *so many different types!*

So, if someone tells you they don't like musicals, they maybe have only seen a certain type that just isn't their style.

Now watch a YouTube performance with Debbie Allen and the same instrumental accents you heard on the recording accompanied by dance moves. It makes a fabulous song that much more fabulous! Watch www.youtube.com/watch?v=6m9T-usMGH0.

P.S. Dancing not only makes a song more enjoyable but can also help tell the story or make an emotional point. Here's another example: In the song "Side by Side" in *Company*, each couple does a cute dance routine — first one spouse and then the other. The last person to do the dance break is the unmarried Bobby. He does part of the dance — followed by silence. It makes the point that he's alone. Watch www.youtube.com/watch?v=Rqspo5XK6S8.

I discuss choreographers in greater detail in Chapter 7.

Recognizing the Types of Musicals

Chapter 2 dives into the history of musicals, from the earliest shows to the most recent, and everything in between. I describe individual performances, define various terms, and leave very few stones unturned. (Make sure you're good and comfy when you start that chapter and have some food nearby . . . probably breakfast, lunch, and, quite frankly, dinner — it's a long chapter!). Here I give you the quick-and-dirty rundown of the *types* of musicals I discuss.

Musical comedies

When people who aren't familiar with musical theatre think "musical," they usually think of musical comedies. You know, light-hearted and laugh-filled shows like *Guys and Dolls, Kiss Me, Kate, Spamalot,* and *The Producers.* However, that's just one type of musical. There are plenty of musicals that are *not* musical comedies.

Yes, most musicals have comedy within them at certain points, like *West Side Story*'s brilliantly comedic "Gee, Officer Krupke," but any musical that has three tragic deaths decidedly *isn't* a comedy. So, the takeaway is that a musical comedy is a musical, but not all musicals are musical comedies.

Golden Age musicals

Golden Age musicals are the classics from the 1940s to the 1960s. *Oklahoma!, My Fair Lady, West Side Story, Kiss Me, Kate,* and so on. They were written by the early masters of musical theatre like Cole Porter, Leonard Bernstein, Alan Jay Lerner and Frederick Loewe (known as Lerner and Loewe), and the duo who started the Golden Age: Richard Rodgers and Oscar Hammerstein II (known simply as Rodgers and Hammerstein).

These shows are revived on Broadway and produced and performed all over the world in regional theatre, community theatre, colleges and high schools, and if you're from my Long Island hometown, synagogues.

Jukebox musicals

Don't you love pop songs? Everyone loves the songs they grew up listening to on the radio, and you can hear so many (well . . . there are *some*) amazing popular songs being written today. A *jukebox musical* takes these pop hits and puts them into a Broadway musical. I'm talking *Jersey Boys, Mamma Mia!, On Your Feet, Ain't Too Proud, Moulin Rouge,* and so many more.

TIP

If you know someone who "hates" musicals, start with a jukebox musical because they can go *in* humming the score! Refer to Chapter 11 for more details about jukebox musicals.

Rock musicals

Rock musicals are very similar to jukebox musicals in terms of the songs sounding like songs you can hear on the radio. But, instead of the score consisting of already existing songs, they're actually all original songs written for the show. *Hair* is considered the first rock musical; the genre then went on to include hits like *Jesus Christ Superstar* and *Chess* — and short runs like *Marlowe, Got Tu Go Disco,* and *Via Galactica.*

Interestingly, *Rock of Ages* has rock in its title, but it's not a true rock musical because the songs are all hits from the radio. It's considered a jukebox musical.

And *Almost Famous* has original songs by Tim Kitt and Cameron Crowe that were written in the style of '70s rock, but it also incorporates famous songs (like "Tiny Dancer") within the show, so that show is a hybrid!

Sung-thru musicals

Operas have always been *sung-thru,* meaning they have only music and lyrics with no dialogue between them. As I discuss in Chapter 2, musical theatre is derived from opera. *Yet* sung-thru musicals didn't come into vogue until the 1970s, many decades after the first Broadway musicals. Before the '70s, musicals always had a spoken script and songs in between (except *The Most Happy Fella*, which was an anomaly. P.S. An amazing show!).

Andrew Lloyd Webber and Tim Rice started the sung-thru musical trend with *Joseph and the Amazing Technicolor Dreamcoat, Jesus Christ Superstar*, and *Evita*. Other hit sung-thru shows include *Les Misérables, Miss Saigon, Falsettos*, and the current superhit *Hamilton!*

Identifying the Important People That Make Musicals Happen

A musical takes a lot of people: Those who create all aspects of it and those who do the show eight times a week onstage, backstage, and under the stage. Here is a sneak at who these professionals are. Part 2 discusses all of them in greater detail.

Behind the scenes

A multitude of professionals are involved with a musical before the curtain rises. Here are most of the people behind the scenes:

>> **Producer(s):** They're in charge of the whole shebang. They raise the money and (usually) have the last word on the creative team, the casting, the advertising, the marketing, when to open, when to close, and so on.

>> **The composer, lyricist, and book writer:** Sometimes three different people, sometimes the same person. They write the show (the music, lyrics, and book).

>> **The director:** They're in charge of picking the cast and often the creative team. The show is their vision, meaning they sign off on the costumes, the lights, the sound, and all the other details. They're the last word (except for the producer).

>> **General manager:** The GM creates the budget and the producer approves it. The GM also has to decide how the money is allocated for the show.

>> **The choreographer:** They're in charge of any dancing onstage. Often, they're in charge of any *movement* at all during musical numbers even if it's not what you'd think is literal dancing.

>> **The music director/conductor, vocal arranger, orchestrator:** This music team works with the composer to bring the music to life.

- The music director rehearses the singers and is present throughout rehearsal to shape the show musically . . . and often conducts the orchestra every night.

- The vocal arranger creates the harmonies that people sing in the show.

- The orchestrator turns the composer's initial version of the music, usually written on the piano, into a score played by the whole orchestra.

>> **The lighting/set/costume designer:** Each of them is responsible for what the audience sees onstage, including the costumes that every performer wears, the set that the performers move around in onstage, and the lights that illuminate the entire show.

>> **Hair/makeup:** Not always in every show, they create the hairstyles or wigs (think of shows that take place yesteryear where hairstyles were very specific) as well as someone who creates the makeup (think of the *Phantom*'s disfigured face).

>> **The stage manager:** They're in charge of everyone who works on the show daily. They call all the cues (lighting and sound), take acting notes, run understudy rehearsal — basically they keep the show in the same shape as it was on opening night.

>> **The company manager:** They handle all the cast's needs, including pay negotiation, transportation, dressing room assignments, and so on.

>> **Publicists and marketing teams:** They're in charge of deciding how and where the show should be advertised and the creative ideas used to sell tickets.

>> **The orchestra:** These musicians accompany all the songs in the show. They're usually located under the stage in the pit, and the conductor stands with their back to the audience so they can face the orchestra and the singers onstage.

>> **The crew:** It consists of *many* people who are charge of various things like handling props, moving the set, running the lights, running the sound, and so on.

Onstage

The audience sees these people onstage — the ones who bring the show to life:

>> **The leads:** Sometimes one person, sometimes two. These are the people around whom the story revolves.

>> **The featured actors:** These are the secondary characters, usually comedic.

>> **The ensemble:** These people play everyone else in the show. They usually sing and dance and often play small roles as well as understudy bigger roles.

>> **Understudies/standbys/swings:** These people define "The show must go on." They cover every single person on the stage. If someone can't make it for an evening's performance, someone out of these folks can go on so the show can continue.

Test Your Broadway Knowledge

Consider this section your pre-test to gauge what you know about musical theatre and Broadway.

1. Which of these women *didn't* star as Mama Rose in *Gypsy* on Broadway?

(A) Ethel Merman

(B) Angela Lansbury

(C) Tyne Daly

(D) Donna Murphy

(E) Linda Lavin

(F) Bernadette Peters

(G) Patti LuPone

2. Which Stephen Sondheim musical wasn't originally directed by Hal Prince?

(A) *Company*

(B) *Pacific Overtures*

(C) *Into the Woods*

(D) *Follies*

3. What is considered the first modern-day musical?

(A) *Oklahoma!*

(B) *My Fair Lady*

(C) *Anything Goes*

(D) *West Side Story*

4. Fill in the famous composing team name:

(A) Kander and _____

(B) Flaherty and _____

(C) Lerner and _____

(D) Pasek and _____

5. Who are the Tony Awards named after?

(A) Tony Randall

(B) Anthony Quinn

(C) Antoinette Perry

(D) Lucia Tony

Answers: 1. D, 2. C, 3. A, 4. A. Ebb, B. Ahrens, C. Loewe, D. Paul, 5. C.

TEN ACTORS WHO DEBUTED ON BROADWAY IN LEAD ROLES

You get a theatre degree, you pound the pavement, you get some shows out of town, you do chorus work for years, you understudy some parts, you replace in a featured role, and finally after years on Broadway in the ensemble, an understudy or a replacement, you debut on Broadway in a leading role. Many people have followed that path, but here are some lucky peeps who debuted on Broadway in a leading role:

- **Gavin Creel:** Jimmy in *Thoroughly Modern Millie* (Tony Award nomination for Best Actor in a Musical)

- **Bonnie Milligan:** Princess Pamela in *Head Over Heels*

- **Julie Andrews:** Polly in *The Boyfriend* (the show before she played Eliza in *My Fair Lady*)

- **Idina Menzel:** Maureen in *Rent* (Tony Award nomination for Best Featured Actress in a Musical)

- **Vanessa Williams:** The Spider Woman in *Kiss of the Spider Woman*

(continued)

(continued)

- **Andrea McArdle:** Annie in *Annie* (Tony Award nomination for Best Actress in a Musical)

- **Lea Salonga:** Kim in *Miss Saigon* (Tony Award for Best Actress in a Musical)

- **Adam Pascal:** Roger in *Rent*

- **Wilson Jermaine-Heredia:** Angel in *Rent* (Tony Award for Best Featured Actor in a Musical)

- **Sandy:** The doggie in *Annie* (was in a shelter beforehand! #Arf)

IN THIS CHAPTER

» Identifying the types of shows that led to modern-day musicals

» Highlighting the Golden Age of Broadway

» Looking at decade-by-decade hit shows

» Recognizing that the British are coming

» Bringing back shows — The revival becomes popular

» Appreciating Broadway in the 21st century

Chapter **2**

The History of Musical Theatre (in "only" 100 pages!)

An entire book can be written about every musical, whether flop, hit, or somewhere in between. Every show, no matter how successful, has great stories about the conception, the creation, the money raised, the casting, the previews, the opening, the run, the closing, and so much more. However, if you want to discover more about the genre of musical theatre, you need a delicious dose of knowledge about every show that made an impact on Broadway.

While reading this chapter, identify any particular show that piques your interest and then go online to read more. You're bound to find lots of articles about the show, as well as photos, recordings, and even videos.

This chapter gives an overview of how musical theatre evolved and highlights the shows you need to know about if you want to chat musical theatre at your local piano bar.

"Let's Start at the Very Beginning" — Before Show Boat Sailed to Broadway

Most Broadway fans can name most musicals playing on Broadway today. And most can confidently say that these types of musicals all derive from the writing of Oscar Hammerstein. Yet, some call Hammerstein's *Show Boat* the first modern-day musical because if combined the plot and the songs seamlessly and some call Hammerstein's *Oklahoma!* the first modern-day musical because it combined plot, songs, *and* dance. For the sake of stopping an argument before it begins, I'm going to create new verbiage and call *Show Boat* the grandparent of modern-day musicals and *Oklahoma!*, the parent.

Ah. I just averted a musical theatre scholar fistfight.

And in terms of leading to modern-day musicals, if you saw a production of *Show Boat* today, it wouldn't immediately make you think of *Hamilton*. You'd probably feel it was old-timey in terms of the style of the songs (similar to light opera) and dialogue, but it definitely laid the groundwork for today's musicals. P.S. It should be known that *Show Boat* wasn't the first musical ever performed. Plenty of shows and styles of shows led to *Show Boat,* and I delve into them in the following sections. (I discuss *Show Boat* in greater detail in the section, "The Birth of the Musical As It's Known Today," later in this chapter.)

A lighter shade of opera

Operas have been around since the late 1500s, and they were the great-great granparents to today's musical theatre. In many ways, operas and musicals don't differ much; they both involve people onstage who sing to advance the plot. The difference is in music versus lyrics. In opera, music is *the* most important aspect. Yes, music is often what makes people want to see musicals, of course, but the words in a musical are much more important than the words in an opera. Basically, the melodies of operas are beloved, but the music and lyrics *combined* are what's beloved in musicals.

THE BEGGAR'S OPERA (THE *MAMMA MIA* OF THE 1700S?)

In 1728, John Gay created *The Beggar's Opera* using the genre of what was called the *ballad opera*. If you had a ticket to *The Beggar's Opera* back in jolly olde England (see the upcoming figure), you wouldn't have been surrounded only by the typical opera audiences of nobles and the upper class. You'd see that *all* classes were in the audience.

Archivist/Adobe Stock

The Beggar's Opera was the *The Phantom Of The Opera* of its time. No, it didn't run for more than 30 years, but it ran an unprecedented 62 nights. *The Beggar's Opera* is considered a predecessor to today's musicals because instead of the opera's signature sung dialogue (*recitative*), it had speaking parts. And instead of composing highfalutin music, Gay used popular songs. Some were from operas, but they were the very well-known arias, plus he used church hymns and folk songs. The result was that the audience was able to sing along and/or leave the theatre singing the tunes. Sound familiar? Yes, it was basically the first jukebox musical! (Chapter 11 discusses jukebox musicals in greater detail.)

Another big difference: Opera has no spoken dialogue. Conversation or monologues between songs that are spoken in a musical are instead sung in opera in what's known as *recitative*. *Note:* Some musicals do have recitative (those musicals are called *sung through* or *through sung*), but they are the exception, rather than the rule.

Operettas

Operetta is the Italian diminutive term for opera. Operettas, sometimes called *light opera*, are clearly the predecessors to musicals. Even though everything is sung in an opera, operettas often contain spoken dialogue between songs, like in most musicals. Plus, one of the most popular genres of musicals is the musical *comedy*, and operettas are often comedic or satirical. While the United States can claim to have created musical theatre, the creation of the operetta was in France, around 1850.

The most famous operetta is *Die Fledermaus* by German composer Johann Strauss II (libretto by Karl Haffner and Richard Genée). *Fledermaus* means bat in German, but this operetta shouldn't be confused with the frightening Bat Boy, a half man/half bat who, according to the *Weekly World News*, terrorized people in the 1980s. (The story of this half man/half bat was musicalized in *Bat Boy*, a fantastic Off-Broadway musical, which I discuss in the book's Cheat Sheet at www.dummies.com — just search for "Musical Theatre For Dummies Cheat Sheet"). The operetta eventually made its way to England, where two brilliant gentlemen wrote lots of them. Many are still performed all over the world, especially in American colleges and universities. Yes, I'm talking about . . .

Gilbert & Sullivan (or, as insiders/nerds call them, G&S)

W. S. Gilbert (book/lyrics) and Arthur Sullivan collaborated on 14 comic operettas in the late 1800s. The audiences for theatre in England was growing at this time, and one of the reasons was street lighting. Why? Because it made it safer to travel home after a show!

Interestingly, safety was a reason that musicals changed start times on Broadway. Back in the Golden Age of Broadway, curtain time was usually 8:30 p.m. When the 1970s began, Times Square became more dangerous, so shows moved their start times to earlier to save patrons from wandering around 42nd Street late at night. Now Times Square is safe again, but many people prefer the earlier curtain times so the 8:30 curtain never came back into vogue.

Back to G&S: Of the 14 comic operettas they collaborated on, their most famous are *The Mikado, Pirates of Penzance,* and *H.M.S. Pinafore.* Sullivan's music is extremely tuneful, but it's the brilliant Gilbert lyrics that make their work closer to musicals than opera because, as I mention in the section, "A lighter shade of opera," earlier in this chapter, the lyrics in opera take a backseat. Gilbert's lyrics (and Sullvan's music) still hold up today. A 1980s Broadway production of *Pirates of Penzance* starred Rex Smith, Kevin Kline, George Rose, and Linda Rondstadt and was a huge hit. If you missed it, you can check out the film version.

SETH SPEAKS

Maureen McGovern took over for Linda Rondstadt. Maureen was a pop star first known for belting the Oscar-winning theme to *The Poseidon Adventure.* How did the producers know she could sing the operatic role of Mabel? Well, Maureen hit the pop charts again with *Different Worlds,* the theme to the TV show *Angie.* At the end, she hits some high notes, and Maureen told me that the powers-that-be from the production of *Pirates of Penzanze* heard the song on the radio and knew she had the chops to sing high soprano!

The crowd pleasers

Before there were fully scripted musicals, people still gathered for live musical theatre adjacent performances. These shows had singing, dancing, and lots of comedy, but they didn't have a throughline. Aspects of these types of show were incorporated into modern-day musicals.

THE SAD HISTORY OF MINSTREL SHOWS

Minstrels were racist "entertainment" that disparagingly depicted people of African descent, usually played by white people in blackface. Also called *minstrelsy,* they were the most popular musical stage shows of the early and mid-19th century. Minstrel shows had dancing and singing and "comedy" that depicted African-Americans as slow-witted, lazy, and buffoonish. Worst of all, they portrayed the enslaved as happy with their enslavement.

After the Civil War, all-Black minstrel shows became the only way Black performers could earn a living with their talent. The famous blues singers Ma Rainey and Bessie Smith began their careers in minstrel shows, but eventually they were able to become stars outside the confines of a minstrel show. The all-minstrel shows lost popularity by the early 1900s, but, sadly, performing in blackface remained and was incorporated in certain vaudeville shows.

The musical *The Scottsboro Boys,* with a book by David Thompson and a score by John Kander and Fred Ebb, used the framework of a minstrel show with an all-Black (except for one) cast to tell the story of nine Black teenagers, falsely accused of raping two white women aboard a train near Scottsboro, Alabama. The idea was to use what was a form of racist entertainment to tell the story of a racist crime. The Broadway production garnered 12 Tony nominations and then had a very successful run in London.

Once I was a schleppa . . . The rise of burlesque

To *burlesque* something means to spoof it. Even though the majority of people nowadays think of burlesque as strip shows, burlesque actually began as comedy spoofs of famous operas, plays, and even politics; burlesque shows started around 1840 and lasted all the way to the 1960s. These shows were an early version of the Carol Burnett show's movie parodies or *SNL's Weekend Update* and were similar to the vaudeville shows (which I discuss in the next section) in terms of them being filled with music and comedy. The difference was the focus: women. Specifically, women's bodies. Burlesque rose to popularity during the Victorian era when the fashion was for women to disguise their natural shape with hoops and bustles. Burlesque shows revealed their natural form and that sold tickets.

After *The Black Crook* (which featured women in revealing outfits) played in the Broadway theatre Niblo's Garden (refer to the section, "Before *Cats*, there was *The Black Crook*," later in this chapter), the next hit to play there was the burlesque *Ixion*. It spoofed mythology and featured women in, you guessed it, revealing tights. Another difference between vaudeville and burlesque is that vaudeville strove to maintain clean family entertainment; burlesque had ribald, sexually tinged humor. The hilarious 1970s musical *Sugar Babies* that starred Ann Miller and Mickey Rooney is an homage to burlesque songs and slightly dirty jokes. Here's a classic example:

> Hotel guest: "I can't get any sleep! There's a lady next door who loves candy bars. All night long she keeps yelling, 'Oh, Henry! Oh, Henry!'"

By the 1920s, audiences were mostly turning to vaudeville, film, and radio for entertainment. Revealing tights weren't enough to draw 'em in, so burlesque hauled out something none of the others had: stripping! Arguably, the two most famous strippers were Sally Rand and her fan dance and Gypsy Rose Lee, known to Broadway audiences as the subject of *Gypsy*. Going to burlesque strip shows was the only way men could see an (almost) naked woman. Burlesque was able to keep slogging along until nudity began to appear in theatre (the all-nude *Oh! Calcutta!* is one example, among others), which also coincided with the rise of pornographic films. Interestingly, even though vaudeville wound up being more popular at the time, there are no more vaudeville shows . . . but shows in the burlesque style still continue to be produced around the world.

There I was in Mr. Orpheum's office

Vaudeville was popular all across America from the 1880s to the 1930s and was basically a big variety show. Picture *America's Got Talent* without commercial breaks or the Golden Buzzer. Vaudeville shows consisted of a series of unrelated acts: singers, dancers, comedians, popular and classical musicians, ventriloquists, strongmen, animal acts, male/female impersonators, jugglers, mind-readers, clowns, acrobats, escape artists, short plays, and later on, short movies.

Plenty of amazingly talented people were in vaudeville, but performing talent wasn't required . . . if you were famous. Non-performers like baseball legend Hank Aaron and the inspirational Helen Keller appeared. Sometimes, *a la* Velma Kelly and Roxie Hart in *Chicago,* an actual murderess would be in the mix! Vaudeville troupes traveled around the country to perform in chains of vaudeville theatres (like the Orpheum Circuit). These were the early versions of Broadway show national tours, and the common two-a-day show schedule was retained on Broadway with Wednesday and Saturday matinées.

Mr. Ziegfeld! Mr. Ziegfeld!

The Ziegfeld Follies began on Broadway in 1907 and ended in 1936. These spectacles had the variety show elements of vaudeville with comics such as W. C. Fields and Bob Hope, singers like Helen Morgan, and dancers like Gilda Gray (who popularized the shimmy), but the Follies were much grander than a vaudeville show. Beautiful sets and lavish costumes were *de riguer.* Borrowing from burlesque, beautiful women were one of the key attractions of the Follies: The so-called Ziegfeld Girls would parade up and down stairs in elaborate attire.

The musical *Funny Girl* is all about real-life singer/comedienne Fanny Brice becoming a Ziegfeld star. On a side note, there was once a production with a star playing Fanny who had the singing chops but not much else. Insiders noted her distinct lack of comedic chops by renaming the production; instead of *Funny Girl,* they referred to as simply *Girl.* #ShowBizIsHarsh

It's a musical-ish

These next types of shows have lots of the essence of modern-day musicals, but they're still missing key elements. Think of them as the bridge between the operettas of yesteryear and the Broadway of today.

Before Cats, there was The Black Crook

What main thing is *Cats* known for? Yes, it's known for the song "Memory." Yes, the so-called cat fur on the costumes is made from yaks. Yes, an audience member sued the actor playing Rum Tum Tugger for leaping on her seat and "gyrating his pelvis." But the main thing? The tag line was "Now and Forever." And for a while, it looked like that would be true. On June 19, 1997, it became the longest-running show on Broadway (eventually surpassed by *The Phantom of the Opera*).

Back in the 1800s a show called *The Black Crook* consisted of adaptions of well-known songs, plus a few new ones thrown in, ran for a record-breaking 474 performances — not as many as *Cats* total performances of 7,485, *but* it played a theatre that sat 3,200 people . . . more than double the size of The Winter Garden where *Cats* ran.

The Black Crook was a romantic comedy, heavy on the melodrama. Apparently, its main attraction wasn't so much plot as the scantily dressed women. However, because there was a semblance of a plot as well as singing and dancing (despite the fact that most of it was thrown together haphazardly), some who study musical theatre see it as having all the elements of a modern-day musical — not at the level of *Show Boat*, but definitely a releative of today's shows. A *distant* relative. Whatever it was, it was *long*. Not just in terms of the 474 performances, but also in terms of the actual length people sat at the show: five and a half hours! I'm assuming this was the inspiration for the invention of adult diapers.

Give your regards to George M. Cohan

George M. Cohan was the Lin-Manuel Miranda of the early 1900s, meaning he was an overachieving multi-hyphenate. Playwright, composer, lyricist, actor, singer, dancer, and theatrical producer. He published more than 300 songs and wrote more than 50 shows, three dozen of which ran on Broadway! He not only is credited for helping develop the script-driven musical, but also using dance to further the plot. Though his shows are now considered too corny to be performed, many of his songs are still well-known today: "Over There," "The Yankee Doodle Boy," "You're a Grand Old Flag," and, most appropriately, "Give My Regards to Broadway." His statue stands in the heart of Times Square — the only statue of an actor on Broadway. And he's been portrayed in film by James Cagney and Mickey Rooney and on Broadway by Joel Grey.

The Gershwins . . . making America sing

George and Ira Gershwin were brothers who teamed up to produce some of the most beloved classics in what's known as the American Songbook. Though these songs are commonly thought of as simply popular music from back in the day, they actually came from Broadway musicals. "Fascinating Rhythm" comes from 1924's *Lady Be Good*, "Someone to Watch over Me" from 1926's *Oh, Kay!*, and "S' Wonderful" from *Funny Face*.

To demonstrate how the Gershwins were a link to modern musical theatre, it's important to note that their musicals aren't revived on Broadway. Why? Because their scripts are too silly for modern tastes. However, their songs are constantly being put, *as is*, into new shows. Yes, a new script is needed for an audience of today, but the melody and lyrics require no changes. The Gershwins may only have had original Broadway musicals in the early-mid 1900s, but they've had many current day musicals built around their songbook: *My One and Only, Crazy for You, Nice Work If You Can Get It, Fascinatin' Rhythm, An American in Paris.* Top *that*, Cole Porter!

Shuffle Along — a forgotten hit

Most Broadway fans had never heard of the 1921 musical *Shuffle Along* until the 2016 musical called *Shuffle Along, or the Making of the Musical Sensation of 1921 and All That Followed,* which, as the title suggests, told the story of the 1921 musical. *Shuffle Along* was extremely noteworthy because not only did it run for a lengthy 524 performances, but it also was the first hit Broadway musical to be written *and* produced by African Americans and both Black *and* white audiences flocked to the theatre.

This musical not only launched the careers of Josephine Baker and Paul Robeson, but it was credited with changing public perception that Black performers could only be in burlesque-type roles. The score had lyrics by Noble Sissie and music by Eubie Blake and proved so popular that Harry S. Truman used one of the tunes as his campaign anthem, a song still known today: "I'm Just Wild about Harry."

SETH SPEAKS

The cast of *Shuffle Along or the Making of the Musical Sensation of 1921 and All That Followed* performed on the 2016 Tony Awards (see Figure 2-1) and right before their number ended, there was a kick to the side that everyone does in unison. Audra McDonald, however, kicked her gam *high* up to the heavens! When I saw her afterward, I immediately asked her what was up with the incredible flexibility. Well, she was pregnant during the production and told me that because of her pregnancy, she had been having knee issues. On the morning of the Tony Awards, she had to have a lot of fluid drained out of her right knee. The doctor told her she couldn't do the show *and* the Tony Awards on the same day because her leg had to recuperate. The *Shuffle Along* producers told her that they wanted her on the Tonys, and she needed to take off the matinée. That night during the big production number at the Tonys, Audra was dancing and singing, and when she got to the part of the dance where she kicks, she used the same power she always used eight times a week. However, this time, all the liquid in her knee was gone so her leg was *much* lighter. When she hauled it up off the ground, it sailed all the way up to her ear! Not only was I stunned watching from home, but she said *she* was completely shocked when the leg took off! Watch it on YouTube at www.youtube.com/watch?v=jMUgUc8vqAA!

FIGURE 2-1:
Audra McDonald (center), Billy Porter (right), and the cast performing on the 70th Annual Tony Awards.

Theo Wargo/Getty Images

The Birth of the Musical As It's Known Today

If you're a Broadway fan, many of the shows that I mentioned previously are probably show titles you've heard of but shows you've never seen. Many of those musicals aren't likely to be performed today because the musical form has evolved, and getting audiences to come to see a show like *Lady Be Good* would be difficult, unless they were interested in researching dusty chestnuts. But all of the musicals in the following sections are still being performed. Why? Because they all combine the three elements that make modern day musicals.

Music + lyrics + book = musical

When operettas began, lyrics began to have more focus and soon they were on par with music. But the *libretto* (script) didn't receive equal weight until the late 1920s when the first modern-day musical was born. The following sections discuss noteworthy musicals from each decade.

Show Boat (1927)

Jerome Kern wrote the music and Oscar Hammerstein II the libretto and lyrics. Yes, that's the same Hammerstein who teamed up with Richard Rodgers later to create a string of Broadway hits. *Show Boat* was the first time he changed musical theatre (the second was *Oklahoma!*). As opposed to the light-hearted fare of the shows in the previous sections, *Show Boat* dealt with dark subject matters, such as racism and alcoholism — issues never before seen in a Broadway musical. And these real-life issues were presented with depth and feeling in a script that was equal to the beautiful melodies and intelligent lyrics of the score. Yes, all three elements were equal, making *Show Boat* the grandparent of the modern-day musical.

Proof that this musical was different from its predecessors is the fact that it's still being performed around the world to this day. Even if you've never seen the show, you've probably heard some of the music, such as the soaring anthemic "Ol' Man River" or the sweet love song "Bill."

Girl Crazy (1930)

This Gershwin show is noteworthy not because of the trend of the libretto being equal to the score. The score definitely surpassed the script. No, *Girl Crazy* will go down in history because it was the debut of the first lady of the Broadway musical!

Yes, the clarion tones of Ethel Agnes Zimmerman first rang out on October 14, 1930, making her an overnight star. Ethel Zimmerman was a secretary who dropped the "Zim" from her last name when she hit Broadway. The newly named Ethel *Merman* made her Broadway debut in *Girl Crazy* singing the now classic "I Got Rhythm" featuring a sustained "AH!" on a belted C. She began the trend of high belting that continues today on Broadway with *Wicked* and *Hamilton*.

SETH SPEAKS

Because Ethel Merman (see Figure 2-2) was known as a singer, people nowadays don't neccesarily think of her as an actress as well. However, the late, great Harvey Evans took over the role of Tulsa during the original run of *Gypsy* and told me that Ethel was a wonderful actress. He remembered watching her dramatic scene near the end of Act Two and how she'd have tears in her eyes. Then, he'd see her come offstage and tell *the* dirtiest joke. That's versatility!

Of Thee I Sing (1931)

The musical *Of Thee I Sing*, with a score by the Gershwins and libretto by George S. Kaufman and Morrie Ryskind, is noteworthy for two reasons:

>> It was the longest-running musical of the 1930s (441 performances).

>> It demonstrates how the librettos of musicals were now becoming on par with the music and lyrics. How? Because *Of Thee I Sing* was the first musical to win the Pulitzer Prize for Drama. The distinguished Pulitzer Prize had always been awarded to plays, but *Of Thee I Sing* changed that, proving a musical could be considered a dramatic work of art, not just an entertaining bonbon.

FIGURE 2-2:
Ethel Merman in
*Annie, Get
Your Gun.*

Bettmann/Getty Images

That first Pulitzer for a musical paved the way for future musical winners, such as *How To Succeed . . .*, *Next to Normal*, *Rent*, *Hamilton*, and *A Strange Loop*. Although the show is rarely revived, you can watch a film version of *Of Thee I Sing* from the early 1970s on YouTube starring three TV stars with musical theatre chops: Michele Lee from *Falcon Crest*, Cloris Leachman from *The Mary Tyler Moore Show*, and Carroll O'Connor from *All in the Family*. If you watch it, you'll see that musicals still had more development to go in terms of dialogue and plot, but it's certainly an entertaining piece of history. Hearing the great voice of Mary Richards's hilariously self-involved neighbor (Phyllis Lindstrom) is also quite fun!

SETH SPEAKS

I did Kathy Griffin's wonderful reality show *My Life on the D-List*, and one of the guest stars was Cloris. What many people don't know is that, for a short time period, Cloris starred in *South Pacific*! She auditioned for the national tour, and Rodgers and Hammerstein (R&H) offered her the role in New York, London, or the national tour, and then gave her four weeks on Broadway so she could see what it was like. Cloris wound up just doing the four-week Broadway run so she could pursue other opportunities (leading to her Academy Awards!). When I asked her about playing Nelly Forbush, she got teary-eyed, describing how, after her first performance, Oscar Hammerstein's wife came backstage and told Cloris it was as if she had been standing right behind Hammerstein the whole time he was writing the show. What a compliment!

Anything Goes (1934)

Anything Goes is noteworthy because it's the most produced musical from the 1930s era. A very successful London production in 2021, which starred Sutton Foster (reprising her 2011 Tony Award–winning performance) and Robert Lindsay, was a hit on the West End and filmed as well. The comedy about mistaken identities aboard a transatlantic ocean liner gave audiences the classic songs, "You're the Top," "I Get a Kick out of You," and, of course, "Anything Goes."

Cole Porter wrote the music and lyrics, and he had more hit shows in the 1930s than any other songwriter and continued to have hits through the 1950s. The original leading lady was Merman, but her understudy wound up becoming one of the biggest TV stars in history. Yes, before she was Ethel Mertz on *I Love Lucy*, Vivian Vance trod the boards and covered the role of Reno Sweeney on Broadway.

Music + lyrics + book + dance = Oklahoma!

Since *Show Boat*, musicals began to give equal weight to music, lyrics, and the script . . . but dance? Dance was there for enjoyment, and if you missed a dance sequence for a quick bathroom break, you certainly wouldn't miss any aspect of the plot. Then *Oklahoma!* came along. With music by Rodgers and lyrics and libretto by Hammerstein, *Oklahoma!* changed the rules in many ways, one of which was using dance to advance the plot.

How does one show that Laurie is in love with the handsome cowboy Curly, but subconsciously drawn to the dangerous farmhand Jud? Why, do a 17-minute dream ballet! To explore such deep emotional issues through dance was a first for Broadway and thus fully integrated the score, the script, and the choreography, starting the Golden Age of musical theatre.

Shining the Spotlight on the Golden Age

If you ever have the option of using a time machine to relive the time when Broadway churned out hit after hit after hit, set those dials to the late 1940s and set your return date for the end of the 1950s. When you open your chamber door, you'll be entering into what's known as Broadway's Golden Age.

After *Oklahoma!*, the hits just kept coming. Musicals that opened during these years are *still* being done all over the world — regionally and in summer stock, community theatre, high schools, and so on. And they're often revived on Broadway. *Gypsy* (1959) has had five Broadway productions!

Read on to find out why all the elements were right for the most fertile time in Broadway history and overviews of some of the most popular productions from this era.

What made this age so golden

The Golden Age came into its stride after World War II because of three main reasons:

>> **A bustling economy:** Many Americans had money to spend on entertainment such as Broadway shows. Travel to New York City was easier, so tourists from across the United States and around the world could see Broadway shows, guaranteeing a steady stream of audience members.

>> **Broadway on TV:** *The Ed Sullivan Show,* which consistently featured long segments featuring Broadway musicals, brought Broadway shows into people's living rooms every week. It's one thing to have heard the title of the new R&H musical, and perhaps bought the album out of curiosity, but it was another to see the original cast perform three songs with full staging, whetting your appetite to order tickets and see the entire production.

>> **Better quality:** Broadway shows had reached a level not seen before; American tastes coincided with what Broadway was producing.

The shows that defined the Golden Age

Shows of the Golden Age had many differences yet the bones of them were the same:

>> They were different because they took place in various locations (Siam, New York City, Napa Valley, London), different time periods (modern day, the 1920s, the 1930s, the 1800s, the early 1900s), and had different styles of music (classical, tin pan alley, jazz, swing).

>> They were all similar in terms of having an overture, an intermission, a chorus, multiple leads, big and small moments of comedy, dancing, and more.

However different or similar, the following Golden Age musicals are all musical theatre classics and are the result of the most fertile time on Broadway in terms of hit shows.

On the Town (1944)

When *Oklahoma!* opened in 1943, three audience members were poised to have their own musical smash just a year later. On that fateful opening night, composer Leonard Bernstein and lyricist/librettists Betty Comden and Adolph Green apparently were on the street and offered tickets to *Oklahoma!* By 1944, they had their own hit musical called *On the Town.* The three not only wrote it, but Comden and Green also starred in two of the six main roles!

On the Town was the debut of those three creative geniuses, and it also marked the debut of a titan of Broadway musicals, choreographer Jerome Robbins. Robbins later became a director/choreographer, but this production was his first foray into Broadway. *On the Town*, the story of three sailors on leave in New York City, was made into a film and revived on Broadway three times.

Fun Fact: The original production not only had Comden and Green, but also future TV star Nancy Walker (Rhoda's mother on *The Mary Tyler Moore Show* and *Rhoda*). And, speaking of future TV stars, the 1998 revival featured the Broadway debut of future *Modern Family* star, Jesse Tyler Ferguson.

Kiss Me, Kate (1948)

Cole Porter had a smash with *Anything Goes* in the 1930s, but *Kiss Me, Kate* proved to be his longest-running hit. The show lasted for more than 1,000 performances on Broadway, was made into a film, and was revived on Broadway in the late 1990s and again in 2019. The show-within-a-show concept centered around two former lovers (who fall in love again) playing the leads in a musical version of *The Taming of the Shrew*, and Porter churned out a bunch of hit songs like "Too Darn Hot," "Wunderbar," and "So in Love."

Porter's brilliant sexual double entendres were apparent throughout the show, as well. My personal anatomical favorite is within the song "Brush Up Your Shakespeare," where two gangsters inform the audience that being familiar with Shakespeare will get you in good with your loved one. And if not . . .

> "If she says your behavior is heinous . . .
>
> Kick her right in the *Corialanus*."

Hilarious!

South Pacific (1949)

R&H continued their successful partnership with this musical based on James Michener's *Tales of the South Pacific*. You probably know this show is filled with beautiful songs like "Some Enchanted Evening," "This Nearly Was Mine," "Younger Than Springtime," and "Bali Ha'i," and charming uptempos like "Cock-eyed Optimist," and "Wonderful Guy." But did you know it also has a strong progressive and anti-racism message? R&H got a lot of pushback for their song, "You've Got to be Carefully Taught," which explains that racism is passed down from generation to generation, but they insisted the song stay in the show.

Guys and Dolls (1950)

Guys and Dolls was composer/lyricist Frank Loesser's second hit Broadway musical (his first was 1948 *Where's Charley?* based on the play *Charley's Aunt*) and was called "The greatest American Musical of all time" by Bob Fosse. Based on two short stories by Damon Runyon, the musical centers around two couples in New York:

>> Nathan Detroit, who's having trouble finding a space for his illegal crap games, and his fiancé, performer Miss Adelaide to whom he's been engaged for 13 years and is getting fed up waiting.

>> Miss Sarah from the Salvation Army who's intent on saving sinners like gamblers, and Sky Masterson, a high stakes gambler who bets he can take Miss Sarah to Cuba on a date, but ultimately falls in love with her.

The show was a smash on Broadway, a successful film, and had an enormously successful revival in the 1990s, winning Faith Prince a Best Actress in a Musical Tony Award for her show-stopping performance as Miss Adelaide. "Luck Be a Lady Tonight" and "I've Never Been in Love Before" are just two of the hit songs from *Guys and Dolls*.

The musical is also responsible for naming one of Broadway's most famous actors: Joe Lane was about to join Equity, the Actors Union, but there was *another* Joe Lane, so he had to have a different professional name. He was starring in a local production of *Guys and Dolls* at the time and took on the first name of his character. And thus was born . . . *Nathan Lane!*

The King and I (1951)

One of R&H's most enduring musicals, *The King and I* has been a Hollywood film and revived on Broadway three times. It continues to play all over the world. The musical is based on the novel *Anna and the King of Siam*, which was based on the memoirs of Anna, an actual British governess who went to Siam (now Thailand) to be a governess for the King's children. The show won numerous Tony Awards including Best Musical and introduced the now classic R&H tunes, like "I Whistle a Happy Tune," "Hello, Young Lovers," and "Something Wonderful." Original leads Gertrude Lawrence and Yul Brenner both won Tony Awards for their performances of Anna and the King, respectively. *Note:* Although Brenner played the King of Siam, he was actually Russian, French, and Swiss.

As a matter of fact, in the original and subsequent productions (including the film), many of the Asian characters were played by actors *not* of Asian descent. This was an unfortunate trait of Broadway that, thankfully, began to be corrected in later years. Starting in the 1990s, the Asian roles in *The King and I* began being cast only with Asian actors. Leading roles that had been cast with white actors in the original production were given to those of Asian descent, such as the King being played by Lou Diamond Phillips (1996 Broadway) and Ken Watanabe (2018 Broadway), and Ruthie Ann Miles who won a Tony Award for her portrayal of Lady Thiang in the 2018 revival.

Yul Brenner (see Figure 2-3) continued to play the role of the King for more than 30 years and had very clear opinions on how the show should be performed. During his final national tour, a young boy playing Anna's son joined the cast in the middle of the run. It was none other than future *Rent* star, Anthony Rapp! Anthony told me his first performance was in a huge theatre; he remembers performing the final scene where the King is dying in bed. Anthony spoke his line, "Mother — it's the boat" and immediately heard someone speaking. It was a male voice. *That's odd because the King is supposed to be almost dead,* Anthony thought. *Why is he talking?* Well, let me just say it was less the King and more Yul. Yes, right after Anthony spoke, he heard the King tell him from his death bed, "LOUDER!" That line is *not* in the script, but apparently it was necessary that night.

FIGURE 2-3:
Yul Brenner.

Luis Dalvan/Archive Photos/Getty Images

Can-Can (1953)

Porter struck gold again with this musical set in Paris. *Can-Can* is filled with beautiful songs, like "C'est Magnifique," "It's All Right with Me," and "I Love Paris." This show is also noteworthy because it launched the career of one of Broadway's most famous triple threats: Gwen Verdon. She played the second female lead, Claudine, and was featured in the second act's Apache dance.

According to the late, great Harvey Evans who danced with Verdon numerous times, Verdon finished her dance on opening night to riotous applause and headed back to her dressing room for a costume change. The applause kept going so choreographer Michael Kidd ran from the audience to her dressing room and told her to come out for another bow. She wasn't fully dressed so theatre lore is she ran back out for another bow wearing just a towel. And a star was born! *Note:* In the ensemble of *Can-Can* was a young woman who had left ballet to pursue a career on Broadway. A few years later, she was starring in *West Side Story*. Yes, Chita Rivera was a chorus dancer in *Can-Can* before becoming a two-time Tony Award–winning star.

The Pajama Game (1954)

The Pajama Game has a libretto by George Abbott and a score by newcomers Richard Adler and Jerry Ross; it's a truly enjoyable show featuring the often recorded "Hey, There" and, one of my personal favorites, "I'm Not at All in Love." This musical also boasts the Broadway debut of two theatrical titans *and* the launchpad of a movie star. *The Pajama Game* was the very first show produced by the man who won more Tony Awards than anyone else, Hal Prince!

The Pajama Game is about pajama factory workers who want a raise and the female head of the union grievance committee who faces off against the new factory superintendent while they fall in love. That's the basic plot of the book *Seven-and-a-Half Cents,* and when Hal Prince read the book review, he decided it could be a musical. He optioned it and convinced veteran Golden Age director George Abbott to direct.

Hal also hired Fosse to choreograph, starting Fosse's ascension as one of the most famous choreographers (and later director) on Broadway. Carol Haney played the role of Gladys and got rave reviews dancing and singing the lead in the trio "Steam Heat." No one ever thought she'd miss a show, but she had no choice when she hurt her ankle. Her understudy went on (without rehearsal) and because a film agent was in the audience, she wound up signing a five-year Hollywood contract. The understudy was Shirley MacLaine, and that story has given hope to understudies ever since.

Kelli O'Hara told me she had a few auditions for the Broadway revival of *The Pajama Game* and, after her final callback, she was walking down the street when her phone rang. She answered and heard a deep male voice who simply said, "Hey, Babe . . ." *How dare–?* Was this the beginning of an obscene phone call? She hung up in a fury! She soon found out the call was from Harry Connick, Jr.! This was his way of telling her she had the role. He addressed her as the character's name — *Babe!*

Damn Yankees (1955)

The next musical that contained a score by Adler and Ross was *Damn Yankees*. Again, produced by Prince with choreography by Fosse, this show cemented the stardom of Verdon who played Lola, a woman who sold her soul to the devil in order to be beautiful. The plot involves Joe Hardy who temporarily sells his soul to the devil so his beloved baseball team, The Washington Senators, can beat those "damn Yankees" and the Devil wants Lola to use her skills so he can own Joe's soul permanently.

This musical is notable because *Damn Yankees* is one of the only Broadway musicals to feature sports throughout the show. Also, it allowed Verdon to join the very small club of Broadway stars who got to recreate their roles onscreen. Sadly, this was the last musical with a score by Adler and Ross because a few months after the opening of *Damn Yankees*, Ross died at the age of 29 from a lung ailment.

The Most Happy Fella (1956)

The Most Happy Fella contains deep and multilayered themes. The main plot is about a young waitress who finds a kind note and an amethyst tie pin from a customer named Tony whom she then starts to communicate with via mail. He's an Italian immigrant who nicknames her Rosabella, and she eventually arrives at his Napa Valley grape farm to marry him but discovers he sent a photo of a young, handsome worker instead of a photo of himself. Turns out, Tony is much older than Rosabella. On his way to pick her up from the station, he's critically injured in a car accident and, out of pity for him, she marries him . . . but he survives.

As the show progresses, they start to fall in love despite their outward differences. But then she realizes she's pregnant from a one night stand she had with the young handsome worker from the photo on the night she arrived. Her pregnancy leads to a beautiful exploration of the show's themes: shame, forgiveness, and love.

The lush score is by Frank Loesser and ranges in style from barbershop quartet to operatic. Tony was played by opera singer Robert Weede. Rosabella was played by Jo Sullivan, and she eventually became Jo Sullivan Loesser. Yes, she married the composer! Unlike other Golden Age musicals, the show is almost all completely sung. An album was released with the main songs, and — thrillingly for theatre fans — a two-album set has the *entire* show recorded.

My Fair Lady (1956)

The longest running musical of the 1950s was *My Fair Lady*. Based on George Bernard Shaw's *Pygmalion*, the show has a score by Alan Jay Lerner and Frederick Loewe and contains hit songs, like "I Could Have Danced All Night," "I've Grown

Accustomed to Her Face," and "On the Street Where You Live." The record was near the top of the charts for years and was the first LP album to sell one million copies. It made a star out of Julie Andrews, the flower girl who's taught to speak "proper" English. However, she wasn't enough of a star, according to producer Jack Warner, to be cast in the film, so the role went to Audrey Hepburn.

Luckily for Andrews, she was cast as Mary Poppins the same year as *My Fair Lady*. She then got sweet revenge when Hepburn wasn't nominated for an Oscar and, not only was Andrews nominated, but she also won! And for trivia buffs, her co-star, Rex Harrison, who played Professor Henry Higgins and teaches Eliza, joined the *very* slim list of actors who originated a role on Broadway as well as played it on the West End *and* in the film version.

SETH SPEAKS

Hepburn acted the role of Eliza Doolittle in the film version, but her singing voice was actually the voice of Marni Nixon. Marni also provided the singing voice of Deborah Kerr in the film version of *The King and I* and Natalie Wood in *West Side Story*. Marni's legacy is cemented forever recorded in those films. And her legacy also extends to TV. Her son was singer/songwriter Andrew Gold whom you might know because he wrote (and sang) the haunting "Oh, What a Lonely Boy." And TV fans have loved his work for years when they've enjoyed and sung along with his song at the beginning of every *Golden Girls*. Yes, Marni's son wrote "Thank You for Being a Friend"!

Jamaica (1957)

Jamaica is important in the evolution of Broadway because it was one of the few Golden Age musicals to have a Black leading lady. Harold Arlen and Yip Harburg (who composed the music and lyrics to *The Wizard of Oz*) wrote a score for *Jamaica* using the style of calypso music made popular by Harry Belafonte. The musical was actually written *for* Belafonte, but when he became unavailable, the lead character was changed to a woman so Lena Horne could star. This role led to Horne being the first Black woman to be nominated for a Tony Award! And in the 1980s, she won a special Tony for *Lena Horne: The Lady and Her Music*. In 2022, the Brooks Atkinson Theatre was renamed the Lena Horne Theatre, making her the first Black female performer to have her name on a Broadway theatre.

Jamaica also featured Ossie Davis and, in the chorus, future dance icon, Alvin Ailey. The leading man is perhaps best known for his classic 1970s TV show. Before he was in charge of *Fantasy Island*, Ricardo Montalban was on the island of Jamaica!

The Music Man (1957)

The Music Man is one of the rare shows with book, music, *and* lyrics all by the same person: Meredith Willson. On the surface, *The Music Man* appears to be an old-fashioned show with old-fashioned values, but it's actually a very forward-thinking show. Rather than celebrate so-called small-town values, the show mocks the closed-mindedness of the citizens of River City, the fictional Iowa small town where the action takes place.

In the song "Iowa Stubborn," they flat-out admit how unyielding and cold they are, and then ladies of the town appear to be inches away from banning books in "Pick a Little, Talk a Little." Basically, the entire town is the villain of the story except for the town "spinster," Marian the Librarian, originated by Broadway soprano Barbara Cook. Marian believes the people of her town need to read great literature and expand their minds. But her mother tells her, "When a woman's got a husband and you've got none . . . why should she take advice from you?" Robert Preston portrayed the con man Harold Hill and, through him, Willson shows how easy it is to con small-minded people. In the song "Trouble," Willson demonstrates brilliantly how to manipulate a mob by simply namedropping words like "scarlet women" and "shameless music."

Besides the forward-thinking values, the score itself is groundbreaking. Rap music is a musical form of vocal delivery that incorporates rhyme, rhythmic speech, and street vernacular. Was *Hamilton* the first musical to incorporate rap? No, *The Music Man* was! The entire opening number is rapped. Not one word is sung. It's all rhythmic speaking that takes place on a train and the rhythm of the speaking parallels the train starting, speeding up, traveling, and then slowing down. Groundbreaking!

Furthermore, Willson didn't want dialogue to end and then a song to begin — he wanted songs to flow naturally from dialogue. The song "Trouble" starts as if it's just another spoken line of dialogue, but it's actually the beginning of the song. It's a seamless transition from scene to song, something that had never been done before. So the next time someone mocks *The Music Man* for being an old chestnut, remind them how brilliant and cutting edge it is!

West Side Story (1957)

Another Broadway classic was birthed in 1957. *West Side Story* is based on Shakespeare's *Romeo and Juliet,* but instead of being about two feuding families, it's about two rival gangs: The Sharks, whose members are of Puerto Rican heritage, and The Jets, whose members are of Polish heritage, represent the Capulets and the Montagues. Tony (Romeo), who's a Jet, meets Maria (Juliet), whose brother is a Shark; although Maria's close friend Anita (Juliet's nurse) warns her to stay away in the song "A Boy Like That," the two are in love. The show is filled with hit after hit: "Tonight," "I Feel Pretty," "Something's Coming," and "Somewhere," which became a hit *again* almost 30 years later when Barbra Streisand recorded it for 1985's *The Broadway Album.*

West Side Story is also notable because it was the Broadway debut of Stephen Sondheim who co-wrote the lyrics with the very established Leonard Bernstein (who wrote the score). The credits list Sondheim as the sole lyricist because, the story goes, Bernstein knew that if his name were associated with both music and lyrics, Sondheim wouldn't get any attention or credit so Bernstein had his name removed. #Classy.

The book was by Arthur Laurents, and Jerome Robbins served as director and co-choreographed the show with Peter Genarro. Not since *Oklahoma!* had dance played such a huge role in the show, and dance is almost equal to *West Side Story's* book, music, and lyrics. In "The Rumble," the two gangs fight each other, ending Act One with two deaths. "The Rumble" could have been staged as a scene, but instead it's underscored with music and all the fighting is completely choreographed with dance integrated to advance the plot.

On a side note, Robbins's name is most often associated with *all* the choreography in the show, but that's because Robbins engaged Genarro as a co-choreographer only *if* Genarro agreed to relinquish the rights to all the work he created for the show! That's why the New York City Ballet will have a night of Robbins's choreography and feature "America," even though it was completely choreographed by Gennaro. The inside scoop is Robbins focused more on the choreography for The Jets like "Cool" and "The Jet Song," and Genarro did the choreography for the Shark numbers like "America" and "Mambo." But Liza Genarro, Peter's daughter, has a wonderful website where she explains that her dad had even more choreography in the show. Check out https://artsandculture.google.com/story/peter-gennaro-the-west-side-story-you-haven-t-heard-new-york-public-library-for-the-performing-arts/BAWxTxP-6nqAKQ?hl=en.

John Springer Collection/Getty Images

FIGURE 2-4:
Chita Rivera (up front) dances in *West Side Story*.

I call bull****! The role of Anita, created by Chita Rivera (see Figure 2-4), requires not only comedic *and* dramatic acting chops, but also Broadway belting, and incredibly difficult dancing *while* singing. By all accounts, Chita was brilliant as Anita. Infuriatingly, not only did Chita *not* win a Tony Award, but she wasn't even nominated. I've been traumatized by the unfairness since 1957, and I hadn't even been born!

Gypsy (1959)

Gypsy is a musical fable based on the story of Gypsy Rose Lee, the famous stripper, and many consider it to be the all-time greatest American musical. Jule Styne wrote the music, and like *West Side Story*, Sondheim wrote the lyrics (his second Broadway musical) with Laurents on book.

The story centers on Mama Rose, a frustrated wanna-be performer who's the archetype for what now is called a *stage mother*, someone who puts all of her showbiz hopes and dreams onto her child. Mama Rose is obsessed with making her young daughter, June, a star while ignoring her other daughter, Louise. In the middle of the show, June deserts her mother who then refocuses all her attention onto Louise. Louise winds up becoming world famous as Gypsy Rose Lee and no longer needs her mother's career guidance, leading Rose to sing one of the most famous 11 o'clock numbers, "Rose's Turn." (*11 o'clock numbers* are the bring-down-the-house songs that happen right near the end of the show. Chapter 3 discusses them in greater detail.) The score also has the Act One finale showstopper "Everything's Coming Up Roses," one of Broadway's most famous songs, and the overture is largely regarded as the best Broadway overture ever.

Merman originated the role of Mama Rose, and although it's considered her greatest role, she didn't win the Tony Award. That year it went to Mary Martin for *The Sound of Music,* adding fuel to the fire of their supposed feud. In truth, they were good friends and, on a side note, if you're wondering what a Tony Award goes for, Mary Martin's sold at an auction in 2015 for $35,000! I thought a nun takes a vow of poverty!

The Sound of Music (1959)

The Sound of Music represents the end of the Golden Age. Not only was it produced in 1959, which most people consider the final year of the Golden Age, but it was also the final musical written by R&H whose *Oklahoma!* started the Golden Age. The final lyrics that Hammerstein wrote were for the sweet folk tune "Edelweiss." The show is based on the Von Trapp family singers and, proving again that Broadway embraces aging much more than Hollywood, Martin was 46 when she played the young virgin nun. Besides the title song, the show has the classic, "My Favorite Things," which many consider a Christmas song for some reason. I guess because it references winter and presents?

The show is notable because not only was it considered a huge hit on Broadway, but the film version is one of the most successful movie musicals ever made, contrasted by the fact that it was critically reviled when it opened. Pauline Kael described the score being filled with "sickly, goody-goody songs" and *The New York Times* posited that it would destroy the genre of movie musicals. Spoiler alert: It didn't.

SETH SPEAKS

The Sound of Music was done as a live musical on NBC in 2014. Audra McDonald played Mother Abbess and was excited/nervous about performing the show-stopping "Climb Every Mountain." She was texting with her teenage daughter Zoe while backstage during the show. Right before "Climb Every Mountain," she told Zoe she had to go out for her big number. She finished on her sustained high A flat, ran backstage, and picked up her phone to see what Zoe thought. She saw the following text, which her daughter sent during the song: "Mom, I'm doing a wash. Where are the dryer sheets?" And that's how kids keep you humble.

Moving into a New Era — The Post Golden Years (the 1960s)

The death of Oscar Hammerstein was a symbolic end to the Golden Age. Even though scores to musicals were still being written in the style of the Golden Age, tastes were changing and Broadway was straining to keep up. Some mega-hits from the 1960s are on par with hits from the 1950s in terms of popularity, but the amount of hit shows that were produced in the 1950s was never matched again.

How the '60s changed musical theatre

The 1960s not only gave audiences the start of the careers of some brilliant theatre creators (the composing team of Kander and Ebb, Michael Bennett as choreographer, Jerry Herman as composer/lyricist, Hal Prince as director), it also gave audiences the first hit show for which Stephen Sondheim wrote *both* music and lyrics (*A Funny Thing Happened on the Way to the Forum*).

The 1960s was also the decade when shows started getting away from the romantic couple leads (Curly and Laurie, Sky and Miss Sarah, Professor Harold Hill and Marian Paroo) and began to spotlight the leading lady as the star: Dolly Levi, Sally Bowles, Mame Dennis, and, of course, Fanny Brice. The '60s is when these diva roles really began in earnest, eventually leading to Evita and Elphaba.

The shows that defined the '60s

The 1960s were a time of great change. Even though fashion and haristyles had evolved between the 1940s and 1950s, think about how the looks of the 1960s were different. That's when some *radical* changes happened! Beehives, unique eye makeup, mini-skirts, and thigh-high boots were on the women, and men suddenly had *long hair!* Fashion was changing and so was Broadway.

The music in the shows of the 1960s began to move away from the influences of tin pan alley and light classical fare toward the new style of music that was on the radio — rock 'n' roll. Though many shows didn't embrace the new musical sounds of current day pop music, that type of music certainly began to infiltrate Broadway for the first time. As a matter of fact, this era began with the first electric guitar being heard on Broadway (*Bye Bye Birdie*) and ended with Broadway's first official rock musical: *Hair*. The 1960s were also a time of expanding civil rights, which Broadway reflected. The following shows illustrate the new styles, sounds, and values of Broadway.

Bye Bye Birdie (1960)

The title role in *Bye Bye Birdie* is an Elvis Presley type named Conrad Birdie who's been drafted into the Korean War. Conrad's agent (Dick Van Dyke) and his agent's secretary (Chita Rivera) devise a publicity stunt to give Conrad "one last kiss" with a typical American teenager (Susan Watson) before he joins the army. It doesn't quite go as planned.

The show is notable because it was the first rock musical on Broadway. Yes, *Hair* is officially considered the first rock musical (refer to the later section on *Hair*), but some consider *Bye Bye Birdie* the first because it has . . . rock music! I told composer Charles Strouse it should be considered the first rock musical because of his amazing music, but he wasn't on board because he considers the songs to be spoofs of rock songs. Maybe so, but they sure sound exactly like songs Elvis Presley would have recorded. Listen to the original Broadway cast recording at www.youtube.com/watch?v=xAJDhD8-1nw&list=PLlzxFKnXc_Gw4HHHjObixs8xtaEuPmMNN.

SETH SPEAKS

Van Dyke's understudy was the fabulous Charles Nelson Riley, or as Chita calls him, "Zazu." Why? Well, the first time he went on, he forgot the lyrics to "Put on a Happy Face." Instead of "Grey skies are gonna clear up, put on a happy face," he sang, "Grey skies are gonna clear up, *doo doo do zazu zay*." Mind you, he didn't forget a random lyric from the middle of a phrase; he forgot the lyric that's the title of the song! After he recovered, the two thought it was so hilarious that from then on, she always called him Zazu!

Camelot (1960)

Camelot is on this list not because it was a long-running hit (it wasn't), but because it represented an era during the 1960s. But first, a little history. *Camelot* was a troubled show from the beginning. Lerner and Loewe knew that their next show would always be judged as inferior against their mega-hit *My Fair Lady* no matter how good it was. Besides that issue, plenty of other mishaps befell the musical, including the director having a heart attack while the show was being revised out of town. You can read about that and more in the brilliant book *The Street Where I Live* by the librettist and lyricist Alan Jay Lerner.

The show has a lovely score, including

>> The boastful "C'est Moi," sung by Lancelot, giving audiences Robert Goulet's Broadway debut

>> "The Simple Joys of Maidenhood," sung by Guinevere played by Julie Andrews, doing her second Lerner and Loewe Broadway show (and her last Broadway musical until more than 30 years later)

>> "How to Handle a Woman," sung by King Arthur and played by movie star Richard Burton and husband (twice!) to Elizabeth Taylor

In the 1960s, the title song "Camelot" became inexorably linked with the years of the Kennedy administration. Not only did the young golden couple seemed like a modern-day King Arthur and Guinevere, but they were also connected to the show because Lerner was a Harvard classmate of JFK and because it was known that handsome John and his glamorous wife Jackie listened to the album nightly.

The connection went further. Not long after her husband's assassination, Jackie referenced the lyrics to the title song: "*Don't let it be forgot. That once there was a spot. For one brief shining moment, that was known as Camelot.*" She then said in an interview with *Life* magazine, "There'll be great presidents again, but there will never be another Camelot again."

How to Succeed at Business without Really Trying (1961)

This musical has been revived on Broadway twice, most recently with Daniel Radcliffe playing the leading role of J. Pierpont Finch in 2011 (He was replaced in that same production by Darren Criss and Nick Jonas.) And before that, in the mid-1990s when Matthew Broderick took on the role of Finch and won a Tony Award for Best Actor in a Musical. Originally on Broadway (and in the film), Finch was played by Robert Morse, and the show provided a wonderfully comedic look into what New York high-powered business was like in the 1960s.

Loesser wrote a tuneful score that looked at corporate culture with songs like "The Company Way," which skewered company loyalty by implying that allegiance to big business, *no matter what*, was the most secure way to keep your job. He also penned scathing social commentary with songs like, "Happy to Keep His Dinner Warm," which illustrates how women of that time who worked in the business world would almost always have no choice but to remain as secretaries and the most they could hope for was to marry an executive and "bask in his perfectly understandable neglect."

A Funny Thing Happened on the Way to the Forum (1962)

A Funny Thing Happened on the Way to the Forum is a farce with a book by Burt Shevelove and Larry Gelbart. Most notably, it's the first Broadway musical to have both music and lyrics by Sondheim, beginning his decades-long career as what many consider Broadway's greatest composer/lyricist. The Broadway musical (and the film) starred Zero Mostel as Pseudolous, a Roman slave yearning for freedom, and Jack Gilford as his extremely nervous sidekick, Hysterium.

Interestingly, the most famous song from the show wasn't written until after previews began. The story goes that even though the musical was chock-full of jokes, the audience simply wasn't laughing. Uh-oh! What's a comedy *sans* laughs? Answer: a drama without drama. The creatives wondered, was it simply not funny? They decided they needed an outside eye so the skilled director/choreographer Jerome Robbins was brought in to add his expertise. Robbins told the creative team that the show was definitely funny, but the audience needed permission to laugh. They had to be literally told it was a comedy!

At that point, the opening number was "Love Is in the Air," which highlighted the romantic aspect of the show. But Robbins felt that romance was the wrong message to begin with. The audience needed to know that a big, fat comedy was about to happen. Sondheim took his advice at face value and wrote the song "Comedy Tonight." Suddenly, the exact same jokes that weren't landing, were now getting raucous laughter! (P.S. Robbins didn't give advice like this for free. After the show opened, he sent a letter to the producer detailing his contributions to the show and asking for more royalties than originally offered. It's called show *business* for a reason!)

As brilliant as Robbins was, he was complicit in a very dark part of history. He was called to testify before the House of Un-American Activities Committee and, instead of staying silent, he named names, meaning, he revealed artists he knew who had some kind of communist leanings. Anyone who was named was put on a blacklist and their careers stalled. One of the names Robbins named was Mostel, who was starring in *A Funny Thing . . . .* When the powers-that-be decided to bring in Robbins to help with the show, they asked Mostel if he would be okay with it. Mostel famously said, "Of course, I'll work with him! We of the left do not black-list!" He had a much more hilarious line when Robbins showed up at rehearsal. Apparently, everyone lined up and Robbins went down the line, greeting everyone. When he got to Mostel, the famous comic took one look at him and said, "Hi ya, loose lips!"

No Strings (1962)

R&H had been the composing team synonymous with the Golden Age. Hammerstein's death left composer Rodgers with no lyricist. What to do? In *No Strings*, the first musical Rodgers worked on after Hammerstein's death, he decided to take over Hammerstein's role and write both music *and* lyrics (which he also did with the songs "I Have Confidence" and "Something Good" for *The Sound of Music* film). *No Strings* was about a romance between a white man played by Rich-ard Kiley (the future *Man of La Mancha*) and a Black woman (played by Diahann Carroll, the future *Julia* on TV) living in Paris.

The show opened in 1962 (when interracial marriage was still illegal in the United States for five more years), so the casting was indeed progressive and aligned with Rodgers's liberal values. He apparently saw Carroll on *The Tonight Show* and decided he wanted her to play the leading lady in his new musical. He knew he wouldn't have to make any script changes because the leading couple's on-again, off-again romance had nothing to do with their races and, as a matter of fact, their respective races were never mentioned at all. There was just a small refer-ence at one point when Carroll's character mentions that she grew up "north of Central Park," implying a Harlem childhood.

The most well-known song from the show is "The Sweetest Sounds," which Carroll sung in a wonderful performance on *The Ed Sullivan Show*. Check it out at www.youtube.com/watch?v=9dTxv4raZd0.

The show is considered historic because it led to Carroll winning a Tony Award, the first Black woman to do so. Brava!

Oliver! (1963)

Oliver! was a harbinger of what the 1980s would bring Broadway: imported British musicals. Producer David Merrick saw *Oliver!* in London and decided to bring it to Broadway with some of its British stars in tow, notably Georgia Brown as the ill-fated Nancy, Barry Humphries (yes, Dame Edna!) as the undertaker Mr. Sower-berry, and for the Artful Dodger, future heartthrob, soon-to-be Monkee and Marcia Brady crush, Davy Jones!

The show was based on the Charles Dickens's book *Oliver Twist* with book, music, and lyrics by Lionel Bart. It wound up being a Broadway hit, a hit movie, and, just to show the fickleness of Broadway, a flop when it was revived in the 1980s. That's show biz!

The score is wonderful and the beautiful song "As Long As He Needs Me" perfectly describes an unhealthy codependent relationship, and "Consider Yourself" and "It's a Fine Life" have a raucus British music hall feel. There's also the lovely "Who Will Buy," which Barbra Streisand later recorded for her second Broadway album (*Back to Broadway* released in 1993), as well as "Where Is Love," sung by the title character of Oliver and later recorded by Broadway star Liz Callaway alongside fashion icon (and Broadway everything) Billy Porter.

She Loves Me (1963)

She Loves Me marks the first musical directed by the man who wound up winning more Tony Awards than anyone: Hal Prince. It's based on the film *The Shop around the Corner*, which was also the basis for the film *You've Got Mail* with Tom Hanks and Meg Ryan. The score is by Jerry Bock and Sheldon Harnick and includes the classic title song as well the heartbreaking "Will He Like Me?," the joyous "Tonight at Eight," and the tour-de-force "Vanilla Ice Cream."

The show is about two co-workers, Amalia and George (originally played by Barbara Cook and Daniel Massey) who hate each other. However, they each have a pen pal they're in love with whom they write to daily. The twist is, even though they hate each other in person, they don't realize they love each other as pen pals! Many consider *She Loves Me* to be a perfect jewel box of a musical, even though it didn't have an extremely long run. The good news for fans is there are three recordings because *She Loves Me* has been revived twice on Broadway. The second revival starred Laura Benanti, Zach Levi, Gavin Creel, and Jane Krakowski, and was filmed and is available online at www.BroadwayHD.com. (The site costs $11.99 per month and has some great content.)

SETH SPEAKS

In the first revival of *She Loves Me*, the wonderful Lee Wilkof (the original Seymour in *Little Shop of Horrors*) played Sipos, a shopworker, and told me he was a nervous wreck on the day *The New York Times* was coming to review the show. He was singing the opening number, and it came to the part where Arpad (played by Brad Kane, who acted and sang the title role in the film of Disney's *Aladdin*) sings, "And we get the tilt of our hats right!" and Lee is supposed to then sing, "That's right!" Well, Lee was so nervous that when it got to Kane's solo, Wilkof suddenly started singing. And not Brad's solo, "And we get the tilt of our hats right." No, Lee sang the lyrics, "And we get the clop of our clopper!" Lee emphasized to me that not only did he sing a solo that *wasn't his*, but for some reason he changed the lyrics to "And we get the clop of our clopper." Twist ending: Lee got his information wrong and *The Times* critic *wasn't* there. Final ending: His lyric mishap was so famous among the actors of the show that anytime someone did something wrong during the run of *She Loves Me*, they'd say "Boy, he really clopped his clopper!"

Fiddler on the Roof (1964)

No fancy costumes, no pretty scenery, no scantily-dressed women, no hunky men. No, this musical featured dark clothes, women with no makeup, and a stage full of poverty-stricken people. These are the reasons why *Fiddler on the Roof* was such a tremendous gamble as a Broadway show. *What audience wants to see that?*, one would think. And yet *Fiddler on The Roof* became a huge hit worldwide. The musical had heart, plenty of humor, thrilling dances by Robbins (especially the bottle dance where men balanced actual glass bottles on their heads), and an amazing score by Bock and Harnick. Most importantly, though, it dealt with the universal issue of how much should someone hold onto their traditions and values and how much should they change with the times?

As I mention in the section about *A Funny Thing Happened on the Way to the Forum* earlier in this chapter, Robbins knew the importance of opening numbers. When the show was first written, the opening number was "We've Never Missed a Sabbath Yet," where Golde and her five daughters sang about getting all the various foods ready for Sabbath. Robbins was working closely with Bock and Harnick and bookwriter Joseph Stein and kept asking what the show was about. They'd give the literal answer that it was about Tevye and his five daughters. He'd press and press them, and finally one of them said that the show was about tradition. And that revelation changed the opening from "We've Never Missed A Sabbath Yet" to the classic "Tradition."

Hello, Dolly! (1964)

Hello, Dolly! was composer/lyricist Jerry Herman's first huge hit and was based on the Thornton Wilder play *The Matchmaker*. Carol Channing (see Figure 2-5) played the title role in the original production as well as the Broadway revival in the 1970s and then again in the 1990s!

That's why Gerard Allesendrini wrote the hilarious lyrics about her in *Forbidden Broadway* parodying the song "Call on Dolly."

> Call on Carol!
>
> She's the one that producers recommend when they're producing *Hello, Dolly!*:
>
> Either Broadway or summer stock
>
> She'll play Dolly Levi from 7 to 12 o'clock!

FIGURE 2-5:
Carol Channing in
Hello, Dolly!

Those appearances made her the only person to play the same role on Broadway in three different decades. Anyone who saw her live can attest that she was always brilliant in that show, which she also toured across North America through the 1990s. She was succeeded on Broadway by a slew of incredible leading ladies, including Ann Miller, Phyllis Diller, and Ethel Merman (whom Jerry Herman had originally written the show for but who didn't want to do any more long runs).

Hello, Dolly! also starred Pearl Bailey when Merrick recast the entire show with Black performers. Even though Richard Kiley and Diahann Carroll were lovers in *No Strings*, there was still little audience acceptance of interracial couples, so Merrick thought if the main couples were going to be Black, he needed to make the entire cast Black. Thankfully, Broadway audiences became more open-minded as time progressed. Check out Pearl Bailey's wonderful performance at www.youtube.com/watch?v=zEyYx7mTEsU.

The title song of the show became a worldwide hit when Louis Armstrong recorded it. As of 2022, Armstrong is still the oldest artist to have a number one song on the top 100 (he was 62)! The film version, starring Barbra Streisand, is well-known, too — for having the unenviable reputation of being one of the films that killed Hollywood musicals. #Ouch

In 1969, the gap between old-school Broadway music and current day rock 'n' roll was wide and contributed to the lack of interest in the film. The good news is, Hollywood film musicals have since come back and the show itself is constantly produced all over the world. As a matter of fact, the 2017 revival was a huge hit and garnered Bette Midler her first Tony Award as a Lead Actress in a Musical.

A DAY IN THE LIFE WITH HELLO, DOLLY!

My friend (and Broadway star) the late, great Marcia Lewis did *Hello, Dolly!* with Ginger Rogers who rose to fame as a pinup girl during World War II. Rogers had some vocal problems during the run, and when Lewis asked if she was concerned with not singing perfectly, Rogers replied, "Marcia, I'm famous for two things . . . and I'm standing on them."

Marcia also told me one of the lessons she learned from a Dolly Levi who would stand center stage and not shift from side-to-side or make needless movements. Marcia saw how much power this star would command by firmly standing in one place as she sang. "Merman taught me to plant it!"

Cabaret (1966)

Like *Fiddler on the Roof*, *Cabaret* succeeded against all odds. A musical with Nazis? Based on a book about a gay man in Berlin? With a leading lady who has an abortion? Not surprisingly, the show was considered too dark when it began its out-of-town tryouts; in fact, many audience members walked out. But when it finally opened on Broadway, the show became a hit because of the fabulous score and script and, importantly, the guiding hand of brilliant director Hal Prince who balanced the dark and light in the show. Because of *Cabaret*, Prince won the Tony Award for directing (his first for directing). His ability to make an entertaining musical with dark material soon became one of his signatures, and he went on to direct shows like *Evita*, *Sweeney Todd*, *Kiss of the Spider Woman*, and *The Phantom of the Opera*, which all have leading characters who die or kill people.

Cabaret also solidified the career of Joel Grey, who not only won a Tony Award for playing the Emcee, but who also reprised the role in the film and won the Oscar. Winning the Oscar alongside him were the film's leading lady Liza Minelli and the film's director/choreographer Bob Fosse. *Cabaret* was also the first huge hit for the songwriting team of Kander and Ebb, who later went on to write *Chicago*, *Kiss of the Spider Woman*, and the title song from the film (and 2023 Broadway musical) *New York, New York*.

Fosse directed and choreographed the film and wanted to cast people who hadn't done the Broadway musical, so they wouldn't have any preconceived ways of playing the roles. So, instead of Grey, various people were considered for the role of the Emcee . . . including Ruth Gordon! It sounds so off-the-wall, but she kind of plays the same role in *Rosemary's Baby*, doesn't she? Just without the singing and dancing!

Grey recounts the long road to being cast in the film version in his extremely well-written autobiography *Master of Ceremonies*. Author/agent/actor Richard Seff reveals another interesting factoid in his fabulous book, *Supporting Player*. Dick (as he's known) was sort of a Zelig of Broadway, meaning he was always around during important events . . . like convincing Rex Harrison to go on for the first preview of *My Fair Lady* when Harrison was having a panic attack about not being able to sing well enough. Seff writes that one day in the 1960s, Ebb called him and asked for a five-syllable French phrase that one would use as a greeting. Seff pitched, "Je suis enchanté" and that's how that lyric got into the opening number, "Wilkommen"!

Mame (1966)

Jerry Herman's second huge hit musical was based on the book *Auntie Mame* by Patrick Dennis. This musical made the late, great Angela Lansbury a bona fide musical theatre star and marked the first of her five Tony Award wins. The show has a fantastic score and second act torch song, "If He Walked into My Life," remains a cabaret favorite while "It's Today" is one of the most joyous songs ever performed on Broadway. Herman said that song was based on an ordinary day in his childhood when he came home from school to find that his mom had set up a little party. Young Jerry asked what the occasion was, and she replied, "It's today!"

Unfortunately, just like *Hello, Dolly!*, the movie version isn't well-regarded and is also one of the films mentioned as part of the death of the Hollywood musical. One of the main problems cited is Lucille Ball playing the title role. Even though she was indeed a brilliant comedic and dramatic actress, she didn't have Lansbury's Broadway belt. Although Lansbury isn't in the film version, you can see original stars Beatrice Arthur *and* Jane Connell. Connell plays mousy Agnes Gooch who leaves Mame's employ to see the world and "live" as per Mame's advice . . . and comes back pregnant.

Arthur created the role of Vera, and she and Lansbury had a hilarious duet called "Bosum Buddies" about their frenemy-like relationship. They share this exchange at one point:

MAME: "How old are you, Vera? The truth?"

VERA: "How old do you think?"

MAME: "Oh, I'd say somewhere between 40 . . . and death."

A hilarious line written by Herman and made all the funnier by Arthur's reaction. Anyone who knows Arthur's oeuvre knows that she got some of the biggest laughs simply from her stares. There was one moment where Lansbury sang that she was planning on writing a book about "who is the bitchier bitch" and Arthur would simply deadpan stare (riding the laugh) and then say, "I concede." One night the stage manager timed how long she held the audience in her hand with that dead-pan stare — and it was 11 seconds. Try it. It's a long time! She took that glare and used it during *Maude* ("God'll get you for that, Walter . . .") and then during *Golden Girls*, especially when Rose Nyland (portrayed by Betty White) would tell a story about her hometown of St. Olaf. When you got it, glare it!

Sweet Charity (1966)

Sweet Charity is based on a film *Nights of Cabiria*, which was about ye olde trope: the hooker with a heart of gold. However, to make the show more palatable to a 1960s Broadway audience, the leading lady's profession was changed from "the oldest" into that of a taxi dancer. Back in the day, a man could go to a seedy dance hall and, for a dime, he could get a woman to dance with him. Hence the old song "Ten Cents a Dance."

The Charity of the title refers to Charity Hope Valentine who was played by Gwen Verdon. Verdon was not only the show's leading lady but also the wife and muse of the show's director/choreographer, Bob Fosse. Fosse had choreographed Verdon in *Damn Yankees, New Girl in Town, Redhead,* and, in ten years, he'd be helming her final Broadway triumph: the role of Roxie Hart in *Chicago.*

If you want to see the classic Fosse style, check out a photo of Charity's fellow taxi dancers lined up to sing "Big Spender" — sexy/blank-faced faces and a bunch of angles and turned-in legs. The show's hit songs by Cy Coleman and Dorothy Fields include not only "Big Spender," but also "If My Friends Could See Me Now" and the fabulous trio "There's Gotta Be Something Better Than This." Shirley MacLaine played Charity in a film version, and the show was revived on Broadway in 1986 (Debbie Allen) and in 2005 (Christina Applegate) *and* Off-Broadway in 2016 (Sutton Foster).

In 1986, Allen won the Tony Award for playing Charity, and Bebe Neuwirth won her first Tony Award for playing Nicki, her tough-talking, warm-hearted friend. Interestingly, Neuwirth played Nicki as well as understudying Charity. And speaking of understudies, the 2005 Broadway production starring Applegate as Charity had Charlotte d'Amboise as her understudy. Charlotte was already starring as Roxie in *Chicago*, but the producers of *Charity* were the same as the producers of *Chicago* and asked if she'd do double-duty. They simply wanted her to learn the role and be an understudy in name only because they knew Christina would never miss. Cut to: Christina broke her foot(!), and Charlotte had to leave *Chicago* and do the opening night for *Sweet Charity* on Broadway. Christina did come back, Charlotte went back to *Chicago*, but amazingly, she remained as her standby. So Charlotte played Roxie in *Chicago* and would occasionally miss a show to play Charity in *Sweet Charity*. Sometimes, she'd perform a matinée as Roxie and a night show as Charity!

Hair (1968)

The show that defined how Broadway was evolving in the 1960s was *Hair*. The plot of *Hair* is about a young man meeting a bunch of hippies and grappling with whether to go to Vietnam. Popular music and Broadway music were moving farther and farther away from each other, but *Hair* (see Figure 2-6) brought them together again. The phenomenal score of *Hair* by Galt MacDermot (music) and Gerome Ragni and James Rado (lyrics) had songs like "Donna," "Where Do I Go?" as well as the title song, which all sounded like songs that could have been performed by the Rolling Stones or the Beatles. As a matter of fact, the pop group The Fifth Dimension recorded a combo of the opening song "Aquarius" and the finale "Let the Sunshine In" that topped the pop charts . . . something that hadn't been done by a Broadway song in years.

FIGURE 2-6: The original West End production of *Hair.*

Larry Ellis/Getty Images

This musical was different because the actors sang onstage holding microphones, which changed the sound from the Ethel Merman school of Broadway belting to that classic amplified rock sound. The most notorious aspect of the show, however, was the end of Act One where the cast was nude! This was part of a trend of onstage nudity that hit its peak in the 1970s with *Oh, Calcutta*, which at one point was *the* longest running Broadway show!

Hair was groundbreaking in many ways, one of which was replacing the leading lady role of Sheila. Originally, a white actress played the role, but soon Black actress Melba Moore took over . . . and nothing was changed. As I mention when discussing *Hello, Dolly!* in that section earlier in this chapter, when Pearl Bailey took over the role of Dolly, the entire cast had to be Black. Melba is proud of the fact that she was the first Black woman to replace in a role that was originally white.

Hair was the first Broadway show I ever saw! It was still running in the 1970s when I was four, and I went with my whole family. I joke about how inappropriate it was, but the reality is, it's a great show for kids. It's almost all music (more than 30 songs) so kids don't get bored, and it features lots of people in outrageous costumes that kids can look at, even if they can't follow the plot. I love the show so much that I put together a concert version of it in 2004 on Broadway (directed/choreographed by Devanand Janki and Chris Gattelli) that was a fundraiser for The Entertainment Community Fund. It had an incredible cast that can be heard on the (Grammy-nominated) CD and includes Jennifer Hudson singing "Easy to Be Hard" in her Broadway debut. Soon after that concert, Jennifer was scheduled to audition for the film version of *Dreamgirls*. They asked her to sing a song like "And I Am Telling You" but *not* "And I Am Telling You." She chose "Easy to Be Hard"! Long story short: She got the role *and* won the Oscar. The music from *Hair* continues to be relevant; the 2009 revival won the Tony Award for Best Revival.

Promises, Promises (1968)

Promises, Promises is based on the film *The Apartment*, which is about a man named Chuck Baxter in New York City who lends his apartment to his boss, so his boss can have romantic trysts *not* with his wife. However, Chuck soon finds out his boss is having an affair with the young woman that Chuck is in love with!

Burt Bachrach and Hal David were a songwriting team with an incredible array of pop hits like, "This Guy's in Love with You" and "What the World Needs Now Is Love." Amazingly for musical theatre fans, they turned to Broadway to write a musical but, devastatingly for fans, it's the only musical they ever wrote! Even though the songwriting team churned out plenty of pop hits, only one song from the show made the charts: the lovely "I'll Never Fall in Love Again."

Promises, Promises (with a book by hit master Neil Simon) was a smash on Broadway and then in London and also cemented Jerry Orbach's status as a Broadway leading man (he had previously starred in *Carnival* and the Off-Broadway hit *The Fantasticks*). The brilliant director/choreographer Michael Bennett was only choreographing at this point (with his trusty assistant Bob Avian) and choreographed the incredible number, "Turkey Lurkey Time."

On paper, "Turkey Lurkey Time" sounds like its title: a turkey. It has bizarre lyrics like, "Tom Turkey ran away, but he just came home," and features a verse about Goosey-Poosey who "was a gad about, but she's back again." Plus the whole song has an odd syncopated sound. However, put together with Michael Bennet/Bob Avian's brilliant staging led by the incredible Donna McKechnie, and you have one of the greatest numbers ever performed on Broadway. Go to YouTube and check out the Tony Awards from 1969 to watch the brilliance (www.youtube.com/watch?v=izgG6C_J33s).

The show was revived in the 2000s with Sean Hayes demonstrating what an incredible musical theatre performer he is with Tony Award winner Kristin Chenoweth playing his love interest, Fran. (Check out Figure 2-7 for a photo of Chenoweth and Hayes bowing with Molly Shannon in *Promises, Promises*.) Because Chenoweth is such a world-renowned singer, Bacharach/David classics "I Say a Little Prayer" and "A House Is Not a Home" were added to the score to highlight her vocal chops.

FIGURE 2-7: Kristin Chenoweth, Molly Shannon, and Sean Hayes in the 2010 revival of *Promises, Promises*.

Jim Spellman/Getty Images

1776 (1969)

1776 is the story of America's Declaration of Independence. As most people are aware, it's simply not that interesting to watch a show when you know the ending. That's why book writer Peter Stone joked that everyone thought *1776* was going to be a dud. He remarked that when he told people what he was working on, they'd fall asleep between the "17" and the "76." However, writers can create brilliant works of art, no matter how difficult, if they're extremely skilled, and Stone's hilarious and moving book plus (high school history teacher) Sherman Edward's incredibly hummable score combined to make a huge hit.

The trick was, in my opinion, humanizing these historical figures whom most people only knew by name. You hear the names Benjamin Franklin and Thomas Jefferson and think of people from yesteryear who were nothing like us. People assume they spent the whole day speaking in ye olde English about philosophy and government theory. In *1776*, the opening number showed that the Continental Congress in the late 1700s was actually *just* like you and me. Instead of the curtain opening on a polite group of men discoursing on manners and higher education, a crabby John Adams is yelling about independence while a bunch of guys are complaining about sweating up a storm in a non-air-conditioned room. Half of the congress is begging someone to open a window to get some air while the other half is imploring them to keep the windows closed because there are too many flies.

The one thing they can all agree on is the fact the John Adams is "obnoxious and disliked," and they all sing "Sit Down, John!" (in thrilling harmony). John in turn responds "NEVER!" and the conflict is set. By the end of the show, you're actually wondering against your own knowledge whether or not there will ever be a Declaration of Independence!

Please Hello! The '70s and the Rise of Sondheim

The 1970s were the *Golden Age* of Stephen Sondheim musicals. Sondheim, whom many consider to be the greatest musical theatre composer/lyricist of all time, wrote five musicals during the 1970s, four of which are among his best-known and most produced works. And although *Pacific Overtures* isn't done as often as shows like *Sweeney Todd*, *Company*, *Follies*, and *A Little Night Music*, it's still considered a brilliant show. Though it's true that Sondheim continued to win Tony Awards and even the Pulitzer Prize in future decades, he never was more prolific than in the 1970s. The following sections delve deeper into Sondeim's shows and some other musical theatre hits during this decade.

Identifying the new sound of Broadway

Even though New York City was near bankruptcy in the 1970s and the theatre district was dangerous, a plethora of groundbreaking shows were still produced throughout the decade. It wasn't just Sondheim who took Broadway by storm in the 1970s. That decade also saw the ascension of the most successful (in terms of financially) composers: Andrew Lloyd Webber (naturally); the brilliant Stephen Schwartz who brought a whole new sound to musicals; and director/choreographer Michael Bennett whose career peaked and who created what would become (for many years) Broadway's longest running musical.

The shows that defined the '70s

In the 1970s new styles of music were taking center stage — much more dissonance, electronic instruments, rock 'n' roll, and even disco! Plus the overall sound was much more like pop music because of the more common use of handheld mics

(*Grease*) and, later in the decade, body mics. Here are some of the shows that defined that decade.

Applause (1970)

Applause is the musical version of the film *All about Eve*, which is about a Broadway leading lady, Margo Channing, who befriends a seemingly sweet fan who winds up being a scheming, double-crossing, she'll-do-anything-to-be-a-star *Nachtmare*. This show is historically important because it was one of the first Hollywood films turned into a musical. Of course, this became a huge trend 30 years later with numerous hit movies turned into musicals, but it was extremely rare when *Applause* came to Broadway. Musicals were either totally original stories or based on plays. *All about Eve* was a huge hit film winning numerous Academy Awards, and its leading lady was film star Bette Davis. *Applause* also had a film star in the lead: Lauren Bacall making her musical debut. It was also the Broadway musical debut of future Tony Award winner Len Cariou who played Bacall's love interest (onstage and off!). The score by Charles Strouse and Lee Adams was a great example of Broadway's changing sound; It had a classic Broadway sounding title song but within the song was electric guitar.

SETH SPEAKS

Applause also featured a young woman who represented the singers and dancers in the ensemble. The woman's character's name was Bonnie because that was the name of the performer, Bonnie Franklin. *Applause* made her a Tony Award–winning star and this brought her to the attention of Norman Lear; she told me he asked to meet with her and, after a quick chat, offered her the lead on TV's *One Day at a Time*. No audition! Sadly, she never came back to Broadway, but her TV show became a hit.

If you read the book *All about All about Eve*, you can find out that the musical couldn't legally be based solely on the film — anything in the musical had to occur in the original short story. Anything that was in the film but *not* in the short story couldn't be in the musical. For example, Margo's maid and confidante, Birdie, played by Thelma Ritter in the film, isn't mentioned in the short story. That character therefore had to be different and became Duane in the musical. Duane's character is Margo's confidante like in the film, but he's her hairdresser rather than her maid. And, in a huge step forward for representation he's gay! Yes, the 1969 production of *Coco* starring Katherine Hepburn had a gay character, but he was *very* stereotypical and not likeable. So gay Broadway aficionados herald Duane as the first gay character who's not a clichéd stereotype and/or a villain. Betty Comden and Adolph Green, who wrote the lyrics and the script, found a clever way to let the audience know about Duane; Margo asks Duane to spend a night on the town with her, but he tells her he has a date. Her reply? "Bring him along!"

I was friends with Broadway legendary musical director/conductor/arranger Donald Pippin who was hired to conduct *Applause*. When Bacall was cast, she asked him to come to a voice lesson to see if she could pull it off. She sang for him and afterward asked him to be frank. He replied. "You sound like a moose, but . . . a *musical* moose!" It was actually a compliment! He meant that the quality of her voice wasn't necessarily pleasing to the ear, but she had an innate musicality and that meant she could pull off the role. He was right. Lauren Bacall won the Tony Award for Best Actress in a Musical! And she won it again when she starred in *Woman of the Year* ten years later.

Company (1970)

Company was the beginning of the fruitful Sondheim and Prince collaboration that defined the 1970s. *Company* isn't so much a book musical as it's a series of scenes that feature 35-year-old bachelor Bobby, three of his girlfriends, and Bobby's friends who are all couples. The musical ponders whether the bad in a relationship ("Someone to sit in my chair and ruin my sleep . . . ") is worth the good ("Someone to make you come through, who'll always be there . . ."). Spoiler alert: It is. The show is a perfect example of the Sondheim sound — contemporary and sometimes dissonant melodies that feature lyrics containing brilliant internal rhymes and rapier wit as well as expressions of deep human feelings.

This musical is historically important not only because *Company* was the first of Sondheim's five 1970s musicals, but because it also was the first cast album recording session ever filmed. If you want to see the ups and downs of trying to record an entire Broadway musical score in one day, watch the documentary! Not only does it give you a great glimpse into what it was like in 1970 — positives: an incredible orchestra with an entire string section; negatives: *so* many people are smoking . . . *in* the recording studio! — but it has the drama of Elaine Stritch doing take after take of the classic, "Ladies Who Lunch." Her big song is the last one scheduled to be recorded, and her session starts around 3 a.m. After numerous tries, the session ends without a useable version. Does it finally get recorded? You can watch to see what happens (www.criterionchannel.com/original-cast-album-company).

Speaking of videos, one of my favorite songs from the show is "Another Hundred People" — the words, the music, the original performance by Pamela Myers and the brilliant Jonathan Tunick orchestration. Watch www.youtube.com/watch?v=aFaWBmVrCAM&t=604s.

Jesus Christ Superstar (1971)

This Andrew Lloyd Webber and Tim Rice musical is about the end of Jesus's life and, even though it's known as a *rock musical*, it incorporates a combination of musical styles. It's true that "Heaven on Their Minds" and the title song have a definite rock sound, but there are nods to gospel ("Simon Zealots"), the '70s singer/songwriter ("I Don't Know How to Love Him"), and, going old school, there's a vaudeville/music hall tune ("King Herod's Song"). This show was the first international hit for Webber and Rice, and it was the first musical born from a concept album. In other words, the music from the entire show was recorded and released before it was ever staged. The original concept album hit the pop charts, something very rare once the 1960s ended, and one of the songs was actually on the charts *twice!* Both Yvonne Elliman *and* Helen Reddy had hits with "I Don't Know How to Love Him." This trend of releasing a concept album continued with other shows like *Evita, Chess,* and *Jekyll and Hyde.*

In another first, this show began the *sung-through* or *through-composed* musical, which has no dialogue. Everything is sung. Tip o' the hat to the expression "everything old is new again" because the opera has always been sung through. This really wasn't a new concept, but it *was* new to musical theatre and, since then, many shows have followed suit.

Godspell (1971)

If you want to hear the new type of music that hit Broadway in the 1970s and continued to influence future musicals, then listen to the *Godspell* cast album. Composer/lyricist Stephen Schwartz told me that he was in his early 20s and wanted to write the type of music he heard on the radio. Not the rock songs by groups like the Rolling Stones or the Grateful Dead; he wanted to write in the style of singer-songwriters like Laura Nyro, Carole King, Carly Simon, and Paul Simon. He started this singer/songwriter style of Broadway music that's still popular on Broadway like *Dear Evan Hansen, Next To Normal,* or *Waitress.*

Godspell also launched the careers of many future stars:

>> The 2011 revival featured future Tony Award winner Lindsay Mendez and future *Orange Is the New Black* multi Emmy Award winner Uzo Aduba.

>> The 2000 revival featured future Broadway stars Shoshana Bean, Leslie Kritzer, Barrett Foa, and Capathia Jenkins.

>> The early 1970s Toronto production launched the careers of superstars Eugene Levy, Andrea Martin, Martin Short, Victor Garber, Gilda Radner, and music director Paul Schaffer.

Grease (1972)

The musical *Godspell* began the trend of singer-songwriter music on Broadway, but *Grease* had an even wider effect on the zeitgeist; it began the trend of

'50s nostalgia, which led to hit films like *American Graffiti* and the long-running TV show *Happy Days*.

First staged in a tiny theatre in Chicago with no seats (the audience sat on newspapers! Fire hazard?), *Grease* is now one of the most produced shows around the world, especially in high schools (even though the dubious lesson is that in order to keep a boyfriend, you have to dress in black leather and heels and act tough). The score has incredibly catchy tunes like "Summer Nights," "Greased Lightning," and "Those Magic Changes," and all its characters are identifiable to anyone who went to high school.

Grease was the longest running Broadway show until *A Chorus Line* broke the record; the film version was also so popular that it spawned a sequel, a how-it-all-began TV show, and a film soundtrack that went to number one on the charts. The film solidified the stardom of John Travolta who began his *Grease* journey as an 18-year-old on the national tour playing the role of Doody.

Grease had a plethora of young people who went on to become stars, not just Travolta. Veterans of *Grease* include Marilu Henner; Richard Gere; two-time Tony Award winner Judy Kaye; TV and film star Peter Gallagher; multiple Tony Award–winning director Jerry Zaks (who played Kenickie in the national tour); and international superstar Billy Porter who originated the role of Teen Angel in the 1994 revival. If you haven't heard him sing "Beauty School Dropout," drop everything and listen to www.youtube.com/watch?v=VAhH8VJaNUA.

Pippin (1972)

Pippin has a score by youthful wunderkind Stephen Schwartz who was still in his early 20s and riding on the success of *Godspell* when the show opened on Broadway. It starred Ben Vereen, who interestingly, auditioned for the show even though there wasn't a role for him. Turns out, Vereen was so fantastic that they created the role of the Leading Player for him, and it led to his Tony Award as Best Actor in a Musical! *Pippin* not only has an incredible score featuring songs like "Magic to Do," "Corner of the Sky," and "No Time At All," but it also has an important place in theatre history because of its TV commercial. Nowadays, it's common to see a TV commercial for a Broadway musical with moments from the show, but *Pippin* was the very first show to do it.

Here's the story: Business wasn't good for the show at first, and Fosse, the show's director/chorographer, came up with the idea of having a commercial with a filmed moment from the show. It featured a voice-over offering a "free minute of *Pippin*" as Vereen and two female dancers danced a section from the song "Glory." Near the end, the voice-over said, "You can see the other 119 minutes of *Pippin* live at the Imperial Theatre . . . without commercial interruption." It worked! The show that wasn't selling well wound up running for 1,944 performances! Check out the commercial at www.youtube.com/watch?v=D_Tj8Wi0dFs.

Chicago (1975)

Most people nowadays think of *Chicago* as a huge hit, but when I was a kid, I remember asking adults if they knew *Chicago*, and they'd sing the old Judy Garland song. The show wasn't part of pop culture the way it is today. *Chicago* is an example about how important timing is on Broadway. One can write a wonderful show, but if that show opens at the wrong time, it may not be the success it should be.

SETH SPEAKS

MAKING A SONG WORK IS ABOUT MORE THAN JUST THE SONG

The story of the creation of *Grease* is wonderfully told in the book, *Grease: Tell Me More, Tell Me More* by Tom Moore, Adrienne Barbeau, and Ken Waissman. The whole book shows the incredible skill it takes to create an original musical. Nothing is written in its final version right away. The skill is figuring what works and what doesn't and how to fix it. One of the most interesting stories in the book is about the song, "There Are Worse Things I Could Do." It's now one of the best-known songs from the show, but it was almost cut. And I mean it was *extremely close* to being cut. During previews, after the original Rizzo Adrienne Barbeau would sing/belt her heart out, the audience would barely applaud. A person who isn't familiar with creating a musical would probably think, "I guess the song isn't good." But what's fascinating about theatre is that it takes a combination of things to make something work. Maybe the lights aren't bright enough so you can't see an actor's face. Or the key isn't right, so the actor isn't singing in the best part of their voice. Or the song is featured in the wrong place in the show.

In this instance, producer Waissman writes that he saw the show while standing next to the show's music publisher, Sylvia Herscher. He told her they were probably going to cut it, even though they all loved the song. She told him the song was great and that the song itself wasn't the issue. She felt the issue was the scene leading up to it. When the gang finds out Rizzo is pregnant, they don't care. Therefore, when Rizzo sang the song, the audience didn't care either. So, the next day, the scene was rewritten so Rizzo's pals all acted concerned; there were added lines where Sonny tells Rizzo that she can always talk to him about anything, and Roger offers her money if she needs it. Suddenly, the exact same song got tons of applause and it became a hit! Here is Barbeau on the original recording sounding great: www.youtube.com/watch?v=Zd_uGbw5PHw.

As of late 2022, *The Phantom of the Opera* is the longest running musical on Broadway and *Chicago* is the longest running American musical on Broadway. (*Phantom* premiered in England and was written by Brits, whereas *Chicago* premiered on Broadway and was written by Americans.) However, the *Chicago* on Broadway is a revival that opened in 1996. The original opened in the '70s and only ran a few years. Perhaps Broadway audiences didn't want a cynical musical after having dealt with Watergate and New York City's near bankruptcy.

Even worse than a wrong theme was the competition *Chicago* had during the year it opened. Originally set to open during the 1974–75 season, the show wound up being postponed after the first day of rehearsal because Fosse, the show's director/choreographer, suffered a heart attack during the lunch break. That meant the show opened during the same season as another musical that, unfortunately for *Chicago*, became one of the hugest hits Broadway had ever seen: *A Chorus Line*.

No other musical could compete with the locomotive that was *A Chorus Line*, and *Chicago* fell by the wayside. However, timing then worked in *Chicago*'s favor. After the success of the 1992 revival of *Guys and Dolls*, Broadway audiences were hungry for another revival of a show that had a great script and score. The *Chicago* revival opened in 1996 to glowing reviews (as opposed to the mixed reviews of the original), won numerous Tony Awards, and then the 2000 film won the Oscar for Best Film, cementing *Chicago* as a worldwide hit musical.

Gwen Verdon's co-star in *Chicago* was the realization of her prediction back in the 1950s. As I mention in the section, "Shining the Spotlight on the Golden Age," earlier in this chapter, *Can-Can* launched the career of Gwen Verdon. Also in that show was an ensemble dancer who went on to become a great Broadway star: Tony Award winner Chita Rivera. Chita told me that at one point she auditioned to be Verdon's understudy in *Can-Can*. After her audition, she was summoned to Gwen's dressing room. Chita recounted that it was a *huge* deal to enter a star's dressing room. Back in the day, there was a major separation between the stars and the chorus; a dressing room visit was quite uncommon. Chita entered after knocking and Gwen told her that she watched her audition and felt Chita should *not* be an understudy . . . she should be playing roles. Chita recounted that it was the first time she really had confidence to pursue featured roles and, a few years later, she was creating the role of Anita in *West Side Story*. A little less than 25 years after that, Chita and Gwen were sharing the spotlight opposite each other in *Chicago!* The boost of confidence Gwen gave to Chita led to Gwen having a fabulous co-star all those years later! See Figure 2-8.

A Chorus Line (1975)

A Chorus Line (see Figure 2-9) was groundbreaking in so many ways that it's difficult to write a short section on it. Read the amazing book, *On the Line: The*

Creation of A Chorus Line by Robert Viagas, Baayork Lee, and Thommie Walsh for a lot more insight.

FIGURE 2-8: Chita Rivera (middle, front) reviving her role in *Chicago.*

Bruce Glikas/Getty Images

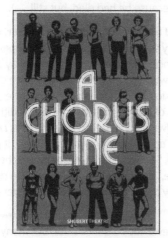

FIGURE 2-9: *A Chorus Line.*

Bridgeman Images

Here are a few highlights: So many things about *A Chorus Line* shouldn't have worked in terms of what came before, such as the following:

>> **It had very little of the glitz and glamour that many musicals are known for.** Pundits claim that audiences want to "see their money onstage." In other words, an audience doesn't want to spend money for a theatre ticket and

not see lots of expensive costumes and sets. The plot of *A Chorus Line* is an audition for a Broadway musical, the costumes were mainly dance rehearsal clothes (only in the final number did the cast wear fancy outfits), and the set was a bare stage that would *sometimes* have mirrors in the back.

So bye-bye pundits! *A Chorus Line* proves you can have a hit show with just a great script and score . . . everything else is cake. P.S. The plainness of the stage combined with the quotidian rehearsal clothes made the contrast of the "One" finale (when the cast wore golden outfits that were reflected in glittering mirrors — see Figure 2-10) that much more thrilling.

>> **It's based on interviews with dancers about their childhoods and careers.** Shows have been based on people before, but this show wasn't based on anyone famous. These were dancers who danced in the chorus, from show to show — so-called *gypsies*. While the show was being put together, many of those same dancers who had been interviewed were then cast in the show, often playing a version of themselves! That meant many of them were on Broadway, telling private moments from their lives that had been put into the script or turned into a song. Although there have been biographical musicals about famous people, the people whose life it was about didn't star in the show! Alexander Hamilton couldn't even get an audition for *Hamilton* (mainly because he had died, but still . . .).

>> **It also shouldn't have worked because of its subject matter.** One can hear the naysayers who undoubtedly squawked before the show opened, "How can you think a show about dancers auditioning for a Broadway show will be successful? Most people in the world have never taken a dance class, let alone auditioned for a Broadway musical. The show is only for a niche audience." They were wrong. The specifics of training as a dancer and auditioning for a musical resonated with a worldwide audience making *A Chorus Line* the longest running musical (until *Cats* took the crown years later). It proved that what's specific can be universal. Sheila talks about a ballet teacher who spoke rhythmically, "like a metronome," perhaps a term many people don't know, but she's also talking about how dance helped her to escape her unhappy home life.

Maybe no one in the audience ever took a dance class, but many people can relate to doing something that makes one feel good to escape pain. Furthermore, so many people related to Donna McKechnie who played Cassie Ferguson. Cassie is a dancer auditioning to be in the chorus like everyone else, but the difference is, she was on her way to becoming a star, and it didn't work out. She basically begs Zach the director for a job. Donna told me that she would receive letters from audience members all the time. Yes, dancers wrote her, but many letters were from middle-aged men who had lost their jobs and identified with the desperation of wanting to work again. The show won numerous Tony Awards and spawned companies all over the world. And, according to the book *Razzle Dazzle: The Battle for Broadway* by Michael Riedel, the success of the show helped save Broadway, which wasn't doing so well in the 1970s, and having that major tourist attraction saved New York City from bankruptcy!

FIGURE 2-10:
The cast of
A Chorus Line
singing "One."

**SETH
SPEAKS**

Kelly Bishop, who played Sheila, told me that when the show first started, each performer would have a mini-nervous breakdown when their family came. She should know — she sang about her mother finding earrings in the family car. "I knew that they weren't hers, but it wasn't something you'd want to discuss." Imagine being in the audience and hearing about the devastating time you found earrings in your husband's car in the lyrics to a song. Hopefully, the public revelation and invasion of privacy was counteracted by the thrill that her daughter won a Tony Award for singing about it!

The Wiz (1975)

The Wiz put a contemporary spin on *The Wizard of Oz* with an R&B score and an entirely Black cast. People sometimes think Andrea McArdle was the first teen to be a leading lady in a show (in *Annie*), but Stephanie Mills beat her by two years. Mills played Dorothy starting in 1975 and introduced the fabulous songs "Ease on Down the Road," "Be a Lion," and the wonderful "Home," which made it onto the pop charts. Mills soon became a bona fide pop star and landed on the charts with numerous hits including "I Never Knew Love Like This Before."

The show is historically important for many reasons, not the least of which is being a hit musical with a score written by a Black man and with direction by a Black man, still rare today. And like *Pippin*, the show wasn't doing well at first, but became a huge hit because of the commercial. (You can see it at www.youtube. com/watch?v=IIM2uYDiHEY.)!

It was also the breakout role for a man who won his first award *years* later. *The Wiz* was the first Broadway musical where André De Shields had a leading role (he played The Wiz). Remember, this was in 1975. For decades after that, he did show after show and *finally* won his first Tony Award for *Hadestown* in 2019 — when he was in his 70s (see Figure 2-11)!

FIGURE 2-11:
André de Shields poses with his Tony Award in 2019.

lev radin/Shutterstock

Annie (1977)

Making a musical about the comic strip Little Orphan Annie was Martin Charnin's idea in the early 1970s, but it took many years to finally make it to Broadway. The show has a similar conceit as *Wicked* in the sense that the audience gets the back-story of well-known characters: How did this orphan in comic strips come to live with millionaire Oliver Warbucks? *Annie* went through many concepts, including the notion of having Annie played by (an adult) Bernadette Peters. But eventually, the creators decided that kids should play kids, and 13-year-old Andrea McArdle, who happened to be the first girl to audition, wound up getting the title role (see Figure 2-12). She also became the youngest person nominated for a Tony Award in the Lead Actress in a Musical category.

The story revolves around an orphanage run by a mean lady named Miss Hannigan who hates "Little Girls" (also the name of her song). Dorothy Loudon hilariously portrayed Miss Hannigan and won a Tony Award as Best Lead Actress in a Musical. And if you really wanted to see Miss Hannigan hate children, imagine what would have happened if Andrea McArdle had won instead!

FIGURE 2-12:
Reid Shelton as Oliver Warbucks, Andrea McArdle as Annie, and Sandy.

Bettmann/Getty Images

Anyhoo, one day Miss Hannigan is approached by the secretary of millionaire Oliver Warbucks who tells Miss Hannigan that Mr. Warbucks is giving one orphan an opportunity to live in his house for a short time. Of course, it ends with Annie being adopted and, spoiler alert, Miss Hannigan going to jail!

The show provided the beautiful Broadway ballad "Maybe," the bring-down-the-house boisterous "Easy Street," and the Broadway classic "Tomorrow." Thankfully, *Annie* was nominated for Tony Awards during the years when Broadway shows performed multiple numbers. That original cast performing three songs is one of the best Tony Award performances ever. Check out www.youtube.com/watch?v=ZDSX1NAyPvE.

The show spawned numerous productions, numerous films, a live television special, and two Broadway revivals!

SETH SPEAKS

Andrea McArdle often chats about what a *Nacht mare* of a child she sometimes was in terms of pushing boundaries. For instance, in order to look like she had been living in an orphanage for years, her contract stated she couldn't go out in the sun. Well, bratty Andrea thought, "It says no sun. However, it doesn't say I can't have a tan!" She promptly got herself a self-tanner and, she admits, it was the horrible kind from the 1970s that wound up turning her skin orange. She told me that in the final scene where she's wearing the bright red curly wig, she looked like an Oompa-loompa!

Sweeney Todd (1979)

Sweeney Todd was another of the Sondheim hits from the 1970s and is the only successful horror/thriller Broadway musical. Director Hal Prince was able to establish a tone that was a combination of terrifying *and* funny. Truly brilliant. The story is based on a "Penny Dreadful" about a murderous barber. The show creators turned that character into a barber named Benjamin Barker, who's banished from London because an evil judge wants to be with his wife. Benjamin escapes years later (with the new name Sweeney Todd) and comes back with the goal of finding his wife and getting revenge. He winds up teaming up with Mrs. Lovett, who bakes "the worst pies in London." Eventually they start a business together: He kills his barbershop customers, and she bakes them into pies.

For those of you familiar with the numerous productions of this show, it seems almost mundane. But imagine what it was like getting this show on Broadway. I'm sure they heard a lot of, "Who the hell wants to see a musical about murder and cannibalism?" Turns out, a lot of people do, and it wound up winning the Tony Award for Best Musical. Furthermore, Barbra Streisand recorded both "Pretty Women" and "Not While I'm Around," which became hits from her first Broadway album.

Sweeney Todd has had three Broadway revivals, a movie, as well as numerous other productions, but the difference between *Sweeney Todd* and other Broadway musicals is that it's not just theatres doing productions. Yes, *Sweeney Todd* was considered a musical when it opened, but because there's so much singing and the singing is in a style called *legit* (in the classical style), even opera companies are doing it.

SETH SPEAKS

When *Sweeney Todd* began performances, it still wasn't common for performers to use body microphones. The story I heard is the sound person started giving some cast members body mics, and after a show one night, Prince approached him and said, "You have to turn down Len Cariou's body mic. He's louder than anyone else." The sound person replied, "Len isn't wearing a body mic." That's old-school vocal training paying off!

Evita (1979)

Like Sondheim who began and ended the 1970s with a hit, Andrew Lloyd Webber and Tim Rice also had two hits bookending the '70s. (The only difference is Sondheim had hits in between.) *Evita* tells the story of Eva Perón's rise to fame as the first lady of Argentina and ends with her death, which happened at a fairly young age. Eva or "Evita" was a polarizing figure and, in the show, she's opposed by a group of aristocrats whose power she usurped, and on the other end of the socio-economic spectrum, there's the character of Ché Guevera. Although Ché probably never met the real-life Eva, in the show he represents all of her critics and is constantly commenting and often interacting with her. Like *Jesus Christ Superstar*, *Evita* began as a concept album.

In 1978, two years after the album was released, *Evita* was *put on its feet* (meaning fully staged), became a hit on the West End and made leading lady, Elaine Paige, a star. A year later, *Evita* opened on Broadway and made Patti LuPone and Mandy Patinkin bona fide Broadway stars — and Tony Award winners. Like *Jesus Christ Superstar*, the show is sung-through, but unlike *Jesus Christ Superstar*, it has dialogue scenes set to music, which are actually my favorite parts of the show. Watch my deconstruction at www.youtube.com/watch?v=emwx1ZngNgM&t=93s.

Madonna and Antonio Banderas starred in a movie version; a revival on Broadway starred Elena Roger and Ricky Martin. It's one of *the* most difficult female roles to sing on Broadway and, in my opionion, no one has ever sung it better than Patti (see Figure 2-13). Check out www.youtube.com/watch?v=5QtZxxbStjs.

FIGURE 2-13:
Patti LuPone
as Evita.

Hulton Archive/Getty Images

Cor Blimey! The British Invasion of the 1980s

In the 1950s, the musical *The Boyfriend* was a hit in London and then came to Broadway; in the 1960s, *Oliver!* was a hit in London and was brought to Broadway by producer David Merrick. That's about it for musicals beginning in London and crossing the pond to hit the Great White Way. But, as I discuss in the previous section on the '70s, the ratio doubled from one British musical per ten to two. Well, even though *Evita* opened in 1979, it maintained a huge presence on Broadway and national tours throughout the '80s and was joined by *six* other musicals that were imported from the land of afternoon tea. These weren't just brought to Broadway to last a fortnight (a British term that I think means two weeks), these British imports all became huge hits. Here I discuss the 1980s, which was the decade of the British invasion.

From musical to MEGA-musical

I remember a comic talking about supermodels and saying basically, "Wait, I already have to compete with beautiful models. Now I have to compete with *supermodels!?*" Hilar! So, musicals have been around for decades, but the '80s British invasion consisted mostly of mega-musicals (save for *Me and My Girl*, which was more in the style of a traditional musical). *Mega* meant everything was bigger; often the concept (singing cats!), certainly the singing (*Les Misérables*, *Joseph and the Amazing Technicolor Dreamcoat*, and *The Phantom of the Opera*) and, very often, the *set!* Audiences were excited about seeing the *Phantom* chandelier fall or the *Les Misérables* turntable and especially the *Miss Saigon* helicopter. These musicals were not only mega when it came to these elements, but they also became mega long running.

Grease was the longest running musical in the early '80s with 3,388 performances, but *A Chorus Line* surpassed that and eventually closed with 6,137 performances. *Les Misérables* surpassed it with 6,680, then *Cats* with 7,485, and now *Phantom*, which opened in 1986 and will close in 2023 after more than 13,000 performances.

This phenomenon isn't just because people enjoy these shows, but because producer Cameron Mackintosh knew how to tap into the ticket-buying public and keep these shows going for years (refer to Chapter 7 where I discuss the role of the producer). They also weren't just mega-musicals, they also were mega money-makers. The prices of tickets skyrocketed during this time . . . mainly because people were willing to pay for them. They came from "across the pond" as the saying goes. The following section examines the musicals that were major players in the British invasion.

Joseph and the Amazing Technicolor Dreamcoat (1982)

Andrew Lloyd Webber and Tim Rice had two hits under their belt when they brought *Joseph and the Amazing Technicolor Dreamcoat* to Broadway. Even though it was their third Broadway musical, it's actually their first collaboration, written in the 1960s. It tells the biblical story of Joseph using a variety of song styles: country, calypso, French *chanson*, and good ol'-fashioned tuneful Broadway showtunes.

The brilliant idea to change the gender of the narrator from what it originally was, is what, in my opinion, made the show a hit. When they first wrote it, the narrator was a man, but for the Broadway production, they made the narrator a woman. And not just any woman — none other than Laurie Beechman who was one of the pioneers of high Broadway belting. When Beechman brought her signature phenomenal voice to the show, she turned what were just fun and tuneful songs into thrilling tour-de-forces because of her incredible vocal chops. Listen to that cast album start to finish, and you'll see what I mean!

If you're never heard her incredible belt, listen to this: www.youtube.com/watch?v=mYKY3s2K8PE.

Cats (1982)

Lloyd Webber continued his Broadway success with *Cats* in 1982, which became the show that beat *A Chorus Line* as the longest running musical. After seeing it, many people ask: How the *H* did it run so long? Well, it has something to do with construction. *Cats* (see Figure 2-14) isn't a revue, but it's certainly not a show with a classic Broadway throughline. It's basically various cats describing who they are and describing each other and, at the end, one of them takes a tire up to the top of the theatre, which the audience is supposed to interpret as she's going to heaven, which is called "The Heaviside Layer." Basically, *what?* Well, the lack of a clear plot paid off because one was able to see the show without understanding a word of English and still enjoy it. The show was a hit with tourists, English speaking and non, because the appeal was in the visuals (actors dressed as cats!), the singing (some fantastic Lloyd Webber songs), and the fun, joyful, athletic, and yes, cat-like dancing.

FIGURE 2-14:
The cast of *Cats*.

Betty Buckley originated the role of the glamour cat Grizabella who sang the show's well-known song, "Memory," but she told me she was nervous that her outspokenness at the audition would cost her the role. Betty had done Broadway in the early '70s but left when she got the role of Abby Bradford on TV's *Eight Is Enough*. After the show went off the air, she felt her contemporaries had all established themselves on Broadway with their signature roles while she had been in Los Angeles. Betty said she had numerous auditions for *Cats* and knew they were considering other women so she decided to advocate for herself. Right after her final callback, she went to director Trevo Nunn and said, "Listen, I know there are plenty women in this town who can sing the song as well as I can. *But* there is nobody who can sing it better. And it's my turn!" She was right — she got the gig *and* a Tony Award!

Even though Betty said there were women who could sing it as well, it's hard to imagine *anyone* singing the song anywhere close to her level of performance. Check out www.youtube.com/watch?v=t9Ru0IBs4Lo.

Starlight Express (1987)

Starlight Express is another high concept Lloyd Webber musical. This time, as opposed to actors playing animals, they play inanimate objects —specifically, the various cars of a train. The entire theatre on Broadway had tracks installed all around . . . not just on the stage . . . but above the audience as well, and the actors all wore roller skates and zipped everywhere! The show didn't have the same long-running appeal as *Cats*, but it did feature future Tony Award winner Jane Krakowski as Dinah the dining car and the original little orphan *Annie* herself, Andrea McArdle.

Andrea was in the show, much to the chagrin of her agents. They believed she shouldn't be part of an ensemble show and told her that if she took the gig, they would drop her as a client. The good news is that some show businesspeople are true to their word; Andrea joined *Starlight Express* and her agents did indeed drop her. And, speaking of dropping, lots of people dropped out of the show for various time periods because the skating was so fast and people easily got injured. Andrea told me she had a massive crash and injured her cheekbone, right before the Tony Awards. She put a ton of makeup over her bruise and the camera stayed way back during her segment. Like most young people, she didn't tell her mother she was injured, and her mom kept asking after the Tony Awards, "Why did the camera stay so far back? You're young! You have great skin!"

Les Misérables (1987)

Les Misérables was a hit show that had gravitas. Although shows like *Cats* and *Starlight Express* seemed silly entertainment vehicles, *Les Misérables* had the pedigree of beginning in London's Royal Shakespeare Company. It told the story of the classic French Victor Hugo novel of the same title. It ran for *three hours and fifteen minutes,* the longest (in terms of run time) Broadway musical!

Les Miz (see Figure 2-15) followed in the style of the popular sung-through musical, meaning it didn't have dialogue. The singing had Broadway belting but also a legit, almost operatic style, and the male lead had most of his songs in super-high and difficult-to-sing keys. All of that results in a truly enjoyable score to listen to . . . and that's probably why there are so many different recordings avail, from the original London, to Broadway, to the anniversary, to the movie version. The British invasion would have almost been all Webber if it hadn't been for *Les Misérables,* and, interestingly, *Les Misérables* might never have come to Broadway!

FIGURE 2-15:
The cast of *Les Misérables.*

Joan Marcus

When it first opened in London, it received not-good to flat-out bad reviews. Often that could close a show and certainly not make it a good candidate to transfer to Broadway. However, the show survived those reviews because the Royal Shakespeare Company produced it and scheduled a pre-planned length of time the show would run no matter what. That meant that people had a chance to see it and spread the word about how much they loved it. Because of that, it wound up becoming the longest-running musical on the West End and one of the top ten longest-running shows on Broadway . . . and a major player in the British invasion!

The Phantom of the Opera (1988)

The Phantom of the Opera is currently the longest running Broadway show. "He's there . . . the Phantom of the Opera" . . . and he has been since the show opened in 1987. Even though it has some dialogue, most of the story is told in Andrew Lloyd Webber's signature through-sung genre. The music has a light opera style, with some lush sweeping melodies as well as some more tonally modern 20th century melodies. But it also kept current (for the 1980s) in the title song with the use of electric drums!

HELLO? BON JOUR? WHAT'S HAPPENING?

Les Misérables was so successful that the show was translated into many languages. Louise Pitre (who originated the role of Donna in *Mamma Mia!* on Broadway) is Canadian and, like many Canadians, she speaks English and French. She was starring in a bilingual production of *Les Misérables* in Canada, which had the schedule of one day the entire show is in English, and the next day the show is in French, and so on.

Actors can easily zone out when they're doing the same thing over and over again, and during one performance, Louise wasn't fully concentrating. That didn't result in her forgetting the lyrics, which often happens to actors; she remembered the lyrics and sang them. However, she sang them in French. During the all-English production. The audience was like . . . huh? From then on, Louise told me, during the English show there was an enormous ENGLISH sign on both sides of the conductor that the cast could see during the show and a big, fat FRENCH sign during the French performances! *Mon dieu!*

SHE'S ALIVE! SHE'S DEAD! SHE'S . . . A BOY?

Directors John Caird and Trevo Nunn staged *Les Misérables* as an ensemble piece. When you weren't playing your leading role, you joined the ensemble as another character. For instance, during the "Lovely Ladies" sequence, two of the prostitutes are played by the same women who later play Eponine and Cosette. One of the most interesting roles to play is Fantine who begins her role at the beginning of Act One, dies (spoiler alert), but then stays offstage for the rest of the act missing many opportunities to join the chorus. *But* she then appears suddenly in Act Two dressed as a boy. Why? Well, Patti LuPone was in the original British cast, and she told me that after they staged her death scene, they asked her to stay to be in the next ensemble scene.

She explained that she was doing double-duty; rehearsing *Les Misérables* during the day and performing *The Cradle Will Rock* at night and couldn't put any stress on her already fatigued body. She had to leave to "rest her voice." Years later, she flat-out admits she was exaggerating. She just didn't want to do the chorus work! So, they continued staging Act One without her while her show was running. But then *The Cradle Will Rock* finished its run. Patti came back to rehearsal and hid in the back, so she wouldn't be put into a scene.

Cut to someone from the creative team saw her peering through the seats and called "Patti! Your show has closed! You can be in this scene." It was during Act Two when everyone was on the barricade and an annoyed Patti said, "Fine! I'll play a boy!" and that's how it came to be that Fantine dies, has an hour break until the end of Act One, and then comes back dressed as a boy to sing on the barricade!

Side note: Because Patti was onstage during the Act Two scenes on the barricade, she was part of the scene where everyone falls asleep onstage and Jean Valjean sings "Bring Him Home." She told me that hearing Colm Wilkinson sing that every night made her journey into the ensemble worth it!

Interestingly, *Phantom* proved that films don't hurt musicals. I was playing in the orchestra before the film came out and it seemed audience attendance was lagging. *The Phantom of the Opera* film then hit cinemas and audiences for the musical started filling up again. Broadway has realized that people love familiarity. Having heard of a show or seen a movie version makes people buy tickets (see *Chicago* whose film version came out in 2000). *Phantom* not only has given joy to the millions that have seen it, but also to the millions that have seen *In the Heights* and *Hamilton*. Lin-Manuel Miranda told me that the first show he really identified with was *The Phantom of the Opera*. "It knocked me out. It was about an ugly songwriter who can't get girls. That was me!" Thank you, Sir Lloyd Webber, for inspiring that aspiring genius!

SETH SPEAKS

Phantom is one of the longest running gigs I ever had, playing piano in that pit off and on for 15 years. It's also the birth of one of my signature mishaps, which you can see me reenact if you go to www.youtube.com/watch?v=VVGEMXrv_8o&t=4s.

Miss Saigon (1991)

I'm including this show in the 1980s even though it opened on Broadway in the '90s. My reasons are thus: I wanted to lump the British invasion together in one section *and* the show opened in London in 1989 so it's *technically* a 1980s show! *Miss Saigon* is a musical about a young Vietnamese girl who meets an American soldier during the war and the ups and downs (and there are a lot of downs) that happen to them and the people around them. It's also one of the shows that created the obsession with having an amazing set. It recreated the fall of Saigon and had a helicopter land onstage and take off. The show was also the first $100 ticket on Broadway because of the "best seats in the house" — not the best seats to hear the singing, but the best seats to view the helicopter. Yes. The $100 tickets weren't for the orchestra section; they were the front of the mezzanine.

The show featured Lea Salonga as young Kim, who not only became an international star but also the first Filipino Broadway star. The creative team had auditions all over the world, including in the Philippines, and she took a break from her studies to be a doctor, to audition for the leading role. The medical world lost Dr. Salonga, but Broadway gained one of the most beautiful voices to grace its stage.

The shows that defined the '80s

In addition to the British invastion, the '80s also had some good ol' homegrown musicals that included major artistic beginnings and endings: The '80s saw the beginning of the successful James Lapine/Stephen Sondheim collaboration as well as the final hit shows from three Broadway titans: Gower Champion, Michael Bennett, and Jerry Herman. Read about all of this and more in the next section.

42nd Street (1980)

The decade began with a throwback to musicals. *42nd Street* is based on the film of the same title. The plot is that ol' chestnut of an understudy becoming a star, the songs are all from yesteryear, and the dialogue is definitely old-school and pretty corny. Why was it a hit? After years of genre-breaking Sondheim and Lloyd Webber, perhaps audiences hungered to go back to old-fashioned musicals.

When *42nd Street* opened, no other show on Broadway had a big, splashy movie musical-style tap extravaganza, and audiences obviously desired those types of production numbers. However, one of the other reasons *42nd Street* became a hit was also because Merrick understood that familiarity leads to sales. If you've heard of a show, you're more likely to be comfortable buying tickets. And in Merrick's typical way, he took an unfortunate event and used it to make the show internationally famous.

On opening night, the director/choreographer Gower Champion unexpectedly passed away. Merrick made sure that *nobody* except a small circle of people knew about it. He then invited a slew of reporters to the opening that night and told them headline-making news would be announced at the end of the performance. Well, the show ended, and Merrick got onstage. He then told the audience *and the cast* that Champion had died that morning. There were screams, cries, and fainting from the cast, and the curtain came down.

That moment was on the front pages of newspapers around the world. Well, let me be specific: *42nd Street* was on the front pages of newspapers around the world. When tourists came to New York City, and not just theatre fans, everyone had heard of *42nd Street*, and a long-running show was born. You couldn't get better advertising. The show also won the Tony Award for Best Musical and the 2001 revival won the Tony Award as well!

Dreamgirls (1981)

Dreamgirls was important for so many reasons, one being every leading actor and actress is Black. It wasn't a revue; it was a current story about the American music business featuring clearly defined characters who were Black. That's still not very common on Broadway and was definitely groundbreaking in 1981. *Dreamgirls* seems to be based on the story of the pop group, the Supremes, though the creators deny it. Like the Supremes, the Dreamettes (see Figure 2-16) are an up-and-coming group of three Black women, and the pretty, thin woman with the sweeter voice (Diana Ross in the Supremes, Deena Jones in the Dreamettes, portrayed by Sheryl Lee Ralph) is moved front and center and the heavier, R&B singing woman (Florence Ballard in the Supremes, Effie White in the Dreamettes, portrayed by Jennifer Holliday) is kicked out of the group.

FIGURE 2-16: Jennifer Holliday, Sheryl Lee Ralph, and Loretta Devine in *Dreamgirls.*

The New York Public Library

The tale of these women is set in the middle of a broader story about how songs become radio hits often by paying people off, how musical tastes have changed, and how success doesn't equal happiness. This was the last musical of the brilliant Michael Bennett and a sad testament to how much theatre fans lost when he passed away from AIDS. Think of what else he could have brought to Broadway. The Tony Award performance is perpetually in everybody's top 10 best Tony Award performance list. When you watch it (www.youtube.com/watch?v=K5QR_EBKWpg&t=8s), note that Holliday gave that soul-wrenching, incredibly sung, brilliantly acted performance at only *21 years old!*

SETH SPEAKS

I've always been obsessed with the musical, and in 2001, I put together a one-night concert on Broadway to raise money for the Entertainment Community Fund starring Audra McDonald, Heather Headley, Lillias White, Tamara Tunie, Norm Lewis, and Billy Porter. We're very proud that we raised a million dollars for the fun! It was an incredible cast, and I filmed every rehearsal. Here's an incredible behind-the-scenes glimpse at those Broadway stars throughout the process (www.youtube.com/watch?v=z434H6tVYRs&t=786s).

La Cage Aux Folles (1983)

One of the unlikeliest hits of the 1980s was *La Cage Aux Folles*. Yes, there had been gay characters in previous musicals, but they were always side characters. The two leading men in *La Cage Aux Folles* were gay. *And* they were a couple — a long-lasting couple. In the 1980s, long before marriage equality, gay men were still perceived to be promiscuous with multiple sex partners, so showing two middle-aged men who had many of the same issues their married straight audiences had — aging, trying to keep the marriage fresh, and annoying children — was revolutionary. The fact that this older gay couple was shown being in love and not as a joke was indeed groundbreaking. One of the hit songs from the show is called "Song on the Sand," which is about the time they first fell in love — yes, a love song between two men.

The musical was based on the French film of the same name, which was then remade into *The Birdcage* with Nathan Lane and Robin Williams. *La Cage Aux Folles* merged Golden Age vet Arthur Larents who directed, 1960s *wunderkind* Jerry Herman who wrote the music and lyrics, and the new kid on the block, Harvey Fierstein who was in his 20s.

The show was also momentous because HIV/AIDS cases started to rise when the show opened and, instead of sympathy toward the ill and dying, there was extreme judgment from many toward the gay community for spreading the disease due to their so-called lifestyle. Perhaps some anti-gay people came to the show and afterward started to see gay people as humans with feelings and not promiscuous sex machines who deserved what they got.

Sunday in the Park with George (1984)

Sunday in the Park with George started a new Sondheim collaboration that led to three hit shows. After *Merrily We Roll Along* closed abruptly (despite its brilliant score), Sondheim and longtime creative partner Hal Prince stopped working together. Young James Lapine became Sondheim's collaborator (see Figure 2-17), and not just as director like Prince, but as a book writer as well. You *must* read Lapine's book, *Putting It Together*, about the making of this musical. It's fascinating to see how a single image (a postcard with the George Seurat "Grand Jatte" painting) can lead to an entire musical.

This musical made Bernadette Peters known as a premier Sondheim interpreter and has one of the most stunning Act One finales, called "Sunday," ever written *and* staged. The theme of the show is about the focus and determination it takes to create art and balancing that with human connection. Right after Sondheim passed away in 2021, members of the Broadway community sang "Sunday" as a celebration/farewell. You can see it at www.youtube.com/watch?v=fr99DVmFt2c. One word: Stunning.

The Mystery of Edwin Drood (1985)

The Mystery of Edwin Drood (see Figure 2-18) is performed in the style of British music hall shows from the 1900s and takes place in London — a perfect show to exemplify the British invasion of the 1980s. And yet . . . it was entirely written by an American. #TwistEnding. All right, all right . . . he was *born* in the U.K, so he's British-American, but he moved to New York City when he was 6 so he's *mostly* American. Rupert Holmes (who became internationally famous for writing and singing "The Piña Colada Song") wrote the book/music/lyrics and orchestrated the show as well. The British creative connection of *The Mystery of Edwin Drood* is that it's based on a book by Charles Dickens he was writing when he unexpectedly died. Not only did he never finish it, but he also never revealed the mystery of who indeed killed Edwin Drood!

Holmes devised the ingenious idea that, because Dickens never revealed who the killer was, the audience would *vote* on the killer. The character chosen would step forward and sing a song specifically tailored to that character describing why and how the killing happened. It certainly kept the show fresh, not only for audience members if they came more than once, but also for the cast because there were never eight shows in a row that were the same.

FIGURE 2-18:
*The Mystery of
Edwin Drood.*

Bridgeman Images

REMEMBER

The style was based on British music hall shows and as was the style, the leading man was played by a belting woman, the brilliant Betty Buckley. You can read about that type of casting in one of my favorite books: *Tipping the Velvet* by Sarah Waters (Riverhead Books). Back to belting Betty — belt she did! The show continued the trend of high belting on Broadway (first begun by Barbra Streisand in *Funny Girl*) but took it to the next level by containing the first belted and sustained E note on Broadway. It's an Olympic feat! Here's my deconstruction of that brilliance: www.youtube.com/watch?v=rnpEYAhTGFg.

Into the Woods (1987)

Into the Woods was the second Sondheim/Lapine collaboration and was a definite hit but had the bad luck of opening the same year as *The Phantom of the Opera*, which won the Tony Award for Best Musical. However, the show has so far been revived twice on Broadway (and once in Central Park) *and* was made into a fabulous film directed by Rob Marshall with none other than Hollywood legend Meryl Streep playing the role of the Witch, the role originated on Broadway by Bernadette Peters (see Figure 2-19).

Into the Woods takes classic fairy tale characters (Cinderella, Rapunzel, Little Red Riding Hood, The Wolf, a Witch, Jack and the Beanstalk, the Giant, Prince Charming, and so on) and puts them all together in one story. Instead of being a broad children's theatre-type show, the action is played realistically as if these characters are just like you and me. The themes in the show are incredibly adult and include the pain of having to let a child grow up as well as fidelity in a long-term relationship. The show's most famous songs are probably "No One Is Alone" and "Children Will Listen." But my personal favorite is "Your Fault" because it reveals amazing insight into people who are constantly trying to find a link to someone, *anyone*, other than themselves who can be blamed (a.k.a. an issue in therapy I have to always address).

FIGURE 2-19: Songwriter and lyricist Stephen Sondheim rehearses with Bernadette Peters for *Into the Woods.*

Oliver Morris/Getty Images

SETH SPEAKS

WHEN COULD IT EVER BE THIS GOOD?

I love insight into how actors get roles as well as their process during rehearsals to create classic characters. This is from my interview with Chip Zien who played the Baker in *Into the Woods.* Zien was in Los Angeles doing TV work, and Ira Weitzman (the fabulous producer) called to tell him he was being considered for the role of the Baker but added that if anyone called and asked him to audition, he should say no! Weitzman felt the creative team didn't know what they wanted, and if Zien came in, they would find a reason why he wasn't right. If he *didn't* come in, they would just offer it to him. Well, Zien was asked to come in and audition, and he said he wasn't able to make it. Cut to: They offered him the role! Weitzman knew what he was talking about.

Zien still remembers Sondheim coming into a rehearsal room at La Jolla Playhouse and performing new music for them. He said it was so moving when he saw Sondheim sit at the piano, get out his sheet music, lay it out neatly, and then sing, "No One Is Alone." He recalls Paul Gemignani, the music director who's a big, imposing presence, with tears streaming down his cheeks. And Zien remembers that when the show was rehearsing in New York, Sondheim presented the song "No More." Zien couldn't believe that Sondheim was writing songs based on how Chip played the character, what his range was, and so on, and that *he* was actually going to be able to sing that brilliance onstage!

(continued)

(continued)

Zien's fondest memory is about when they filmed *Into the Woods* for PBS. (You can watch it at www.youtube.com/watch?v=kqCsQCsinK4.) The audience was filled with Sondheim fanatics who loved the show. Zien went back to his dressing room after the curtain call and noticed that it was dark even though he had left the light on. He opened the door and saw someone sitting there. Zien turned on the light, and Sondheim looked up at him with tears in his eyes and said, "When could it ever be this good?" How sweet is that? Isn't it nice to know that it's not just the audience that's moved by a genius's work, but the genius himself can be moved by the piece, the performances, and the love from the audience, too.

Jerome Robbins' Broadway (1989)

This production was an '80s musical about the past of Broadway. Since 1944, Jerome Robbins had directed and choreographed many of the biggest hits of Broadway, and this show was a kind of documentary that featured a narrator/host (Jason Alexander) sharing fun insights into the songs and dances that the cast of more than 50 people performed!

REMEMBER

Robbins truly did direct and/or choregraph some of the biggest hits of Broadway: *On the Town, West Side Story, The King and I, A Funny Thing Happened on the Way to the Forum, Peter Pan, Fiddler on the Roof, Gypsy,* and so many more! During a decade where many signs were pointing toward British musicals ruling Broadway, it was a big boost to old-fashioned American musicals to celebrate how fantastic they are!

I wish a documentary had been created about the making of this show because it sounds so incredible. Back in the day, shows weren't filmed, so Robbins had to recreate his original staging using dance notation that had been written down from each show (probably by the show's dance captain — for more on dance captains, see Chapter 10). And here's the part I really want to see in a documentary: Because not everything was written down, Robbins had many original cast members come during the rehearsal process so they could wrack their brains together trying to remember how they did the numbers on Broadway all those years ago.

Jerome Robbins' Broadway won many Tony Awards, including one for Alexander who, just a few years later, created his brilliant George Costanza on *Seinfeld*.

City of Angels (1989)

Cy Coleman had lots of hits on Broadway, his last big one being *City of Angels*. Although Coleman had been composing musicals for Broadway since the 1960s, his lyricist for this show was first-timer David Zippel, who then went on to write lyrics to films like *Hercules* and *Mulan* and, with Andrew Lloyd Webber, the recent

Bad Cinderella. P.S. It's always nice when an old timer gives somebody new a chance! And it's even nicer when the somebody new does an amazing job!

City of Angels is about an author and the gumshoe character he created. The show was double-plotted, and the audience watches the story the author is writing as well as the author's real life. To help tell the difference between the two plotlines, everything happening in the author's life is in color and everything in the gum-shoe story (costumes, lighting, and so on) is in black and white as if the audience were watching film noir.

Interestingly, the end of the song that Randy Graff and Kay McClelland perform has a Coleman jazz scale that would be typical for a sax, but not for someone to sing. Yet the two women did it eight times a week, and they said it was often a nightmare. Because not only is it really hard to sing each fast-moving note correctly, but the black and white/color opposition placed them on opposite sides of the stage, so they had difficulty hearing each other to match pitch and rhythm. They told me that, amazingly, on the night of the Tonys, they nailed it! #Phew (Check out www.youtube.com/watch?v=1BZ0nhYkFL8.)

City of Angels is one of the few original hit American musicals of the decade yet, as of 2022, it hasn't been revived on Broadway. It was revived in London, but sadly, closed in previews due to Covid and never reopened. Bring it back ASAP!

525,6000 minutes of the 1990s

The 1990s continued the slow climb of Broadway back to the money-making center of New York it was in the 1950s and is again today. With long-running hits like *A Chorus Line*, *Cats*, *Phantom*, and *Les Misérables*, international audiences were discovering Broadway again. Sadly, many of the new shows from the '90s didn't have the luster that previous Broadway did, but these new shows were surrounded by two other types of shows that were planting their feet on the Great White Way.

Revivals and Disney shows started to hit their heyday in the '90s. Even though Broadway had seen revivals in the past, they weren't common. As a matter of fact, I once told Tommy Tune that seeing the revival of *The Pajama Game* (starring Barbara McNair, Cab Callaway, and Hal Linden) in the 1970s when I was a little boy is what got me hooked on Broadway. He told me he remembered that he and his Broadway buddies were confused when the show was announced. *The Pajama Game*, he thought? *But that show already played Broadway.* He said his circle of friends all said, "Broadway creates new things . . . and then those shows go to the regions. The shows don't come *back* to Broadway!"

That's how it had been since the start of Broadway, but in terms of the new stuff Broadway was churning out, people weren't buying. Most new shows were opening to not-glowing reviews and very few shows in the '90s are considered classics. And producers felt people wanted to see classics. If the current crop of Broadway writers couldn't create them, then classics could be brought back to a hungry audience. And those producers were right; some of the biggest hits of the '90s were from yesteryear — as Christine Pedi sang as Liza Minelli in the hilarious *Forbidden Broadway* (to the tune of "Everything Old Is New Again"). *Everything old is still old again!*

The shows that defined the '90s

Even though the 1990s started the trend of revivals as well as the rise of Disney musicals, a bunch of musicals weren't part of those trends. In this next section, I focus on three movie-to-musicals, the beginning of the Broadway career of songwriting team "Ahrens and Flaherty," and a musical that became a worldwide sensation on par with *Hamilton*.

Once on This Island (1990)

Once on This Island was the first hit for the songwriting team of Lynn Ahrens and Stephen Flaherty as well as the first hit for former dancer Graciela Daniele as a director/choreographer. Before the show, Daniele was mainly known for dancing in many Broadway shows and creating the character Hunyak in *Chicago* ("Not guilty"). In a time when audiences were obsessed with sets, *Once on This Island* bucked the trend by being staged on a simple set designed to look like a tropical island with a cast of barefoot islanders. It told the story of a girl in love with a boy and the issues with her color and class that divided them.

SETH SPEAKS

Lynn and Stephen approached the author of the book for the rights for *Once on This Island* and had to present the material to her for final approval. Lynn's description of that experience is hilarious because first they had to disguise how they were going to end the show. Lynn says the book concludes with something like "And then a large storm engulfs the island and Ti Moune's dead body is put on the side of the road for the garbage collectors." Stephen then added, "The End." What a fun musical!

Lynn wrote an outline for approval and mysteriously ended it with "And at the end of the play, the gods bless Ti Moune" — in other words, she kept it vague. They invited the author to Stephen's apartment and presented four songs to her. Lynn remembers that after the songs were sung there was an extremly long silence. Finally, after the tortuous nothingness filled the air, the author intoned, incredibly slowly, "Well . . . that . . . was . . . wonderful." Why make the wait so terrifying? P.S. Back to the ending of the piece (spoiler alert), if you don't know, after Ti Moune's love marries another girl, she dies and one of the gods transforms her into a tree. I bought my sister Nancy tickets to see the show (20 years ago), and she was traumatized by the ending. P.S.S. She is still mad at me that I didn't "warn her." To this day, whenever I take her to a show she'll glare before the show begins and ask, "Does anyone turn into a tree?"

Tommy (1993)

The Who's *Tommy* was not only a big Broadway hit, but also one of the only pure rock musicals to play Broadway in the '90s. It has a score by a band that's known for being rock icons — not pop icons like Bachrach and David — but rock icons! Director Des McAnuff and choreographer Wayne Cilento ingeniously staged the Broadway show with high energy dancing, video screens, and flying. With broad appeal, attracting Broadway audiences, movie fans, and The Who fans, it also gave Broadway debuts to a bunch of wonderful performers including the hilarious Sherie Rene Scott, the velvet-voiced Norm Lewis, future Tony Award winner Alice Ripley, and future two-time Tony Award winner Michael Cerveris!

Kiss of the Spider Woman (1993)

Right across the street from *Tommy* was its arch-nemesis, *Kiss of the Spider Woman*. I don't literally mean they hated each other, but it was very much old school versus new school. *Kiss of the Spider Woman* had director Hal Prince doing a dark musical about a corrupt government, similar to the subject matter of *Cabaret,* which he directed in the '60s. Triple threat Chita Rivera, who began her ascension to stardom during Broadway's Golden Age, played the Spider Woman. Kander and Ebb who began working together in the early '60s composed the music.

The new-school rock *Tommy* was pitted against the old-school *Kiss of the Spider Woman* at the Tony Awards . . . and *Spider Woman* won! The rivalry worked out perfectly in terms of keeping the shows running because the rock music–loving audiences flocking to *Tommy* wouldn't care (or even know) if the show won a Tony Award, and the theatre-loving audiences flocking to *Spider Woman* were extra encouraged to buy tickets because of the Tony Award. Rivera was playing an incredibly sexy woman while in her 60s (talk about still got it!) and won her second Tony Award!

Sunset Boulevard (1994)

After *The Phantom of the Opera,* Andrew Lloyd Webber never created another long-running international hit. That's not to say *Sunset Boulevard* didn't have a healthy Broadway run and play all over the world, but it didn't achieve the beloved embrace from the public that most of his previous shows did.

Based on the Billy Wilder film, *Sunset Boulevard* has a juicy role for its leading lady with bring-down-the-house songs and a mad scene to play as well. Many luminaries have played the role of Norma Desmond, including Patti LuPone and other Broadway/West End stars like Betty Buckley and Elaine Paige, and a combo of singers, TV, and film stars like Diahann Carroll, Rita Moreno, Petula Clark, and, of course, Glenn Close who won a Tony Award for her portrayal of Norma Desmond.

SETH SPEAKS

I saw Betty Buckley star as Norma Desmond on Broadway, and she was brilliant. I love hearing stories about things going wrong and quick-thinking performers. Here's one Sunset-related Betty told me about an incident that happened in the scene where Norma calls Joe Gillis's girlfriend Betty Schaefer to tell her that Joe is now living in Norma's mansion. Joe Gillis comes storming in during the call, grabs the phone, tells Betty Schaefer the address of Norma's mansion and hangs up. The rest of the play hinges on him having given the address or else Betty Schaefer wouldn't know where to find him. Well, at one performance, John stormed in, grabbed the phone from Norma . . . and promptly hung it up! The phone hanging up was the cue for the orchestra to play crazy music as she and Joe struggle, but Betty realized that "Betty Schaefer" didn't know the address, and it would make no sense for her to suddenly show up. It's not like Silent Screen Star Norma Desmond is listed in the phone book. Well, while the orchestra was playing the crazy music, Betty Buckley ran back to the phone, dialed it, and said, "Someone wants to speak to you!" and handed the phone back to John. John didn't know what he was supposed to do . . . and then suddenly realized his mistake and yelled the address into the phone. Betty was proud of saving the plot, but then after the show, she was surprised that the stage manager tried to bust her for changing the blocking! Ugh! Why didn't anyone appreciate her quick thinking? Happy ending: As she left the theatre, a British girl who had seen the show many times approached her. She smiled at Betty and said, "Thank you for saving the plot." Brava!

Victor/Victoria (1995)

Victor/Victoria should have been the triumphant return of Julie Andrews to Broadway after around 30 years away. Well, she did return, but it wasn't completely triumphant. *Victor/Victoria*, based on the film of the same name that also starred Andrews, was of the many new shows to open in the 1990s to not-stellar reviews.

The nadir of the experience was when the show garnered only one Tony Award nomination. Just one! *Victor/Victoria* had glamorous costumes, huge production numbers choreographed by future Hollywood darling Rob Marshall, a giant luxurious set, fantastic performances by stars Michael Nouri, Tony Roberts, and Rachel York, and a hilarious book by Blake Edward. And I mean *hilarious*. By 1995, I had played a fair amount of Broadway shows, and I can't think of one that got the amount of laughs *Victor/Victoria* did. It's one thing to have a competitive year for nominations, but it clearly seemed like a snub.

To add to the obviousness of a snub, the Tony Awards Committee decided to nominate *Chronicle of a Death Foretold* for Best Musical. I played in the orchestra for *Chronicle of a Death Foretold,* and it was a super creative show. But it was a limited run and had been closed for months by the time the nominations came out. It seemed like the committee wanted to have a fourth show to nominate and tried as hard as it could to *not* be *Victor/Victoria.* When Andrews got the one nomination, she called a press conference and *gave it back.* She said she was rescinding the nomination because the rest of the people who worked on the show were "egregiously overlooked." Brava, Julie!

Besides that drama, it was indeed a momentous show because Andrews was back on Broadway and it continued the trend of films being turned into musicals. The whole show was filmed, so take a gander when you get a chance https://www.filmedlivemusicals.com/victorvictoria.html. So many fantastic moments!

Rent (1996)

The most famous song from *Rent* is "Seasons of Love," and interestingly it was also the first song the cast learned in rehearsal. I find it fascinating that when the cast assembled in that small downtown theatre, making a salary that required most of them to keep their day jobs, they had no idea that the song they learned on that first day of rehearsal would become the center of a show that would become a worldwide sensation.

Rent (see Figure 2-20) was *the* show that defined the '90s. It's considered a rock musical and was marketed for people who "hate musicals," but that really was just a marketing tool. Yes, it features rock music, but its structure is old-school Broadway, so it's actually for people who *love* Broadway. As many people know, the night before the first public performance of *Rent,* its creator, Jonathan Larsen, unexpectedly died. That tragedy definitely gave the show publicity, but the fantasticness of his writing gave it longevity.

Rent is groundbreaking in so many ways, mainly in its unabashed look at HIV/AIDS and the fact that the show has characters of all different races, both gay *and* straight with HIV plus drag queens, bisexuals, lesbians, yuppies, and the list goes on. Suffice it to say, it's the real world onstage. The show first played Off-Broadway in a tiny theatre and then transferred to Broadway and won award after award, including the Tony Award for Musical and the Pulitzer. Amazingly, it was the Broadway debut of so many future stars: Adam Pascal, Idina Menzel, Taye Diggs, Jesse L. Martin, and Daphne Rubin-Vega!

FIGURE 2-20:
The original cast of *Rent* celebrates the show's tenth anniversary in 2006.

Ragtime (1998)

Ragtime is based on the book by E. L. Doctorow and is about white people, Black people, and Jewish immigrants living at the turn of the 20th century. It takes an unflinching look at the racism prevalent in America, but it's also a show about love, forgiveness, and hope. The stunning score is by Flaherty and Ahrens and is in the style of turn-of-the-century Americana . . . most notably Scott Joplin.

Sadly, it opened the same year as two huge Broadway hits: the revival of *Cabaret* and *The Lion King.* Those other shows won most of the Tony Awards, and *Ragtime* didn't last as long on Broadway as it should have, in my opinion, but the majority of the people who saw it, loved it. The opening number is one of the greatest in terms of the writing and the brilliant staging by Graciela Daniele. Check out www. youtube.com/watch?v=l7wP55Dqlbg.

Revivals — Everything old is still old again

The trend of bringing revivals to Broadway increased exponentially in the '90s. As a matter of fact, the Tony Awards used to have a category for Best Revival, and plays and musicals were combined. But bringing musicals back to Broadway became so popular in the 1990s that the Tonys created an entire new category of Best Revival of a Musical. You can read here how the trend began.

Guys and Dolls

This musical started it all. After Broadway audiences were inundated with British hits in the '80s, the 1992 revival of *Guys and Dolls* reminded people that Americans created musical theatre. Audiences came in droves to see the fabulous script and hear the wonderful songs. The opening night was such an event that it was on the front page of the *New York Times* — not the front page of the Arts Section, I must add, the actual A-1 front page! It ran for years and Faith Prince was awarded a much-deserved Tony for her universally lauded performance of Miss Adelaide. This show proved to producers that taking a classic and bringing it back can pay off all the way to the bank.

Grease!!!

Grease was the longest running Broadway show at one point, and a little more than ten years after it closed, it came back. But this time it was expanded (an entire ensemble was added) and what was down and dirty about the original was now bright and neon. Most importantly, this production is notable because it started the Weissler casting trick. *Grease* opened with movie star (who then became a huge talk show star) Rosie O'Donnell playing Rizzo. After she left the show, the Weisslers replaced her first with TV star Maureen McCormick (Marcia Brady) and then model-turned-film star Brooke Shields. Then they changed it up and instead of making Rizzo the role that had a huge star, they found roles that huge stars could play and made the other roles just regular Broadway folks. And instead of long runs, they contracted most of the stars for around three months.

SETH SPEAKS

WHO'S CALLING, PLEASE?

Audra McDonald (who won her second Tony Award for *Ragtime*) played the role of Sarah, the young woman who's in so much pain about a broken relationship that she buries her baby in the ground. Not to worry, the baby lives, but — spoiler alert — Sarah doesn't. At the end of Act One, Sarah is killed because she raises her hand at a vice-presidential rally and, because her hand is Black, someone yells she has a gun. Her body is carried offstage and then wheeled back on in a coffin while the cast sings a song of sadness and hope. That part is devastating.

This part is hilarious: When Audra would quickly get in her coffin, she wouldn't know but often the people who weren't in the Act One finale would put their beepers (this was the '90s) into the coffin. Unaware, she'd lay on top of the beepers and, during the song, they would call the numbers from the backstage payphone. That meant Audra would have to struggle to lie still and look dead while constant beepers were relentlessly going off underneath her! A prank that perhaps can no longer be played today because of the advent of cellphones. Although after reading this, my editor advised me that the gag *can* continue into the 2020s if the cellphones are on vibrate. Problem solved!

I played piano for *Grease!!!* for years, and we were *constantly* in rehearsal because new stars always had to learn their roles. I'm writing these names in off the top of my head. I did the show with famous Teen Angels like Al Jarreau and Jennifer Holliday, famous Vince Fontaine's like Joe Piscopo, Donny Most, Davy Jones, famous Patti Simcoxes like gymnast Dominique Dawes, and famous Rizzos like Joely Fisher, Tracy Nelson, Linda Blair, Jasmine Guy, Sheena Easton, Debbie Boone, and *so many more!* The Weisslers have since applied this technique many times, most notably to the next revival I mention.

Chicago

As I discuss in the section, "Chicago (1975)" earlier in this chapter, *Chicago* had a serviceable run in the 1970s, but the show was competing at the Tony Awards with the sensation that was *A Chorus Line* and audiences weren't into the comedic but dark look at America's obsession with celebrity and how easily the justice system can be manipulated. But, boy, were they ready for it 20 years later! After the revival opened in 1996, *Chicago* was (finally) considered one of the great American Broadway musicals and, a few years later, the film version won the Oscar. It's notable because it's the first Encores transfer.

Chicago was staged as a concert at Encores and kept most of the elements when it transferred to Broadway, including the cast being all in black costumes and relatively contemporary outfits, even though the show is set in the 1920s. They also sit on the side on the stage when they're not performing, and the band is onstage as well. This pared-down version really connected with audiences and, at this point, the show has been running more than 25 years! And, like *Phantom*, having a movie version has only helped ticket sales. Yay *Chicago!* Finally getting its due!

How to Succeed in Business without Really Trying

How to Succeed was a huge hit when it opened in the 1960s and a huge hit again in the 1990s. Interestingly, when it first hit Broadway, it was a contemporary look at Madison Avenue; when it returned, it went from an up-to-the-minute current exposé to a look back at what Madison Avenue was like 30 years before. The 1990s version made a star out of Matthew Broderick. Oh, yes, he was already a Broadway and film star, but this made him a musical theatre star. He won the Tony Award for Best Actor in a Musical for his portrayal of J. Pierpont Finch.

How To Succeed . . . is also notable because it was one of only a small number of musicals to have won the Pulitzer Prize for Drama. The 1995 revival is on my list of the top ten Tony Award performances. The music director Ted Sperling worked with Lillias White, who played the uptight secretary Miss Jones who then breaks out of her shell to belt up a storm. Together they created a raise-the-rafters arrangement that highlights Lillias as being one of the best Broadway singers ever. Check out my take at www.youtube.com/watch?v=L98nsYY0eKg&t=649s.

In 1994, way before she played Karen in *Will & Grace*, Megan Mullally made her Broadway debut in *Grease*. I was a sub pianist in the orchestra, or as she jokingly tells people, "I think Seth was . . . a janitorial assistant?" Anyhoo, Megan had done demo tapes and developmental readings of a musical called *Busker Alley*, which starred Tommy Tune. When the show finally had auditions and cast the out-of-town tryout that was headed to Broadway, Megan didn't get the role. She was, of course, devastated. But our mutual friend Paul Castree (who was playing Eugene in *Grease*) told her she was perfect for the role of Rosemary in the upcoming revival of *How To Succeed* (see Figure 2-21). She auditioned and got the part (Thank you, Paul)! The point of this story is: If she hadn't been replaced in *Busker Alley*, she never would have auditioned for *How To Succeed*. And if she *had* been cast in *Busker Alley*, she would have been out-of-work a few months later. Why? The show closed out of town and never made it to Broadway!

FIGURE 2-21: Megan Mullally, Victoria Clark, and Matthew Broderick in the 1995 revival of *How to Succeed in Business without Really Trying.*

Joan Marcus

On a fun note, the replacement for Mullally was Broderick's then girlfriend (now wife) Sarah Jessica Parker! They played opposite each other near the end of his run (this was before *Sex and the City*, but well after she played Annie in the 1970s). A more fun note: A number in Act Two led by White never failed to bring down the house. Not surprisingly, it was featured when the show was nominated for a Tony Award (www.youtube.com/watch?v=DHkaPSdB9w0&t=286s).

Cabaret

Perhaps the biggest hit revival of the '90s was *Cabaret*. Whereas the previous shows all kept pretty much to the original versions in many ways, *Cabaret* had lots of differences from the original 1960s run. Not only was the tone darker with much more blatant sexuality onstage, but the script and score were also changed.

New songs were added to the movie version in the early 70s. This revival took those new songs ("Maybe This Time," "Mein Herr," and "Money Money") along with another Kander and Ebb song, "I Don't Care Much," which was most notable for being recorded by Barbra Streisand, and added them to the show.

This revival was such a hit, that a revival of this revival, again starring Alan Cumming, came back to Broadway in 2014 and ran for a year! In fact, *Cabaret* has been revived three times on Broadway and, as of this writing, has a hugely successful revival running in London.

SETH SPEAKS

I was talking to Alan (see Figure 2-22), who won the Tony Award for playing the Emcee in the 1998 revival, and he told me that while he was running on for an entrance one night, he banged his head on a light. He wound up getting a concussion and had to leave the performance midway through. However, on his way out of the theatre to go to the ER, he grabbed wet wipes and frantically began scrubbing his butt cheek. Why? He was nervous the doctor might be Jewish and freak out seeing a giant Swastika on his behind!

FIGURE 2-22:
Alan Cumming and the cast of *Cabaret* performing at the 1998 Tony Awards.

Jeff Christensen/RETIRED/Getty Images

The King and I

This R&H classic came back in the mid-1990s and audiences flocked. Although this show had the same luxe look, full orchestra, and stunning dancing of the original, this production added a lot more sexuality between the two lead characters: Donna Murphy played Mrs. Anna and Lou Diamond Phillips played the King. Perhaps the Off-Broadway revue *Forbidden Broadway* described it best when they changed the title of the song "Shall We Dance" to "Shall We Boink." Anyhoo, Murphy won her second Tony Award for Best Actress in a Musical for this part, and Faith Prince went against her sassy, belty sidekick career track to take over the role to much acclaim.

"WE KISS IN A SHADOW," WE AUDITION UNDER A PSEUDONYM

This is perhaps my favorite audience story. José Llana was a 19-year-old student in conservatory as a voice major when he heard about the Broadway revival of *The King and I*. He wanted to audition, but he didn't have an agent or his Equity card. He decided to wait outside the audition room to see if they would eventually allow non-union actors to audition, which sometimes happened.

Well, after a while, the audition monitor came out to call the name of the next Equity actor who had signed up to audition, but when they repeated the name, no one appeared. José seized his chance. He raised his hand and walked into the room as if he were the person just called! He simply wanted a chance to sing and figured this was a way for the casting people to hear him and for him to experience what it was like to audition for a Broadway show. José sang his song and, lo and behold, they told him they would like him to come to a callback! Uh-oh.

He knew that if they turned over the resume the monitor had put on the table to see the photo, they'd see it wasn't him. Or when they called the number on the photo to set up the time of the call back, the actor would tell them he never auditioned. José knew he'd done something wrong, but he was so young and innocent he actually thought it was a *crime!*. He was panicking that they were going to call the police. He did what anyone would do: He started to cry. End of story: They loved that he came to the audition and didn't care about his trickery! They called him back time after time . . . and he wound up making his Broadway debut! No jail time . . . yet. Here he is telling it in his own words and singing his big song with me on piano: www.youtube.com/watch?v=2k119UbBn2w&t=13s!

Disney is here to stay

Disney always had hit films throughout the 20th century, but by the mid-1980s they had cornered a market that many thought was dead: the movie musical. A prejudice developed in the late '60s against movie musicals because seeing people sing and dance "for no reason" was mocked for being unrealistic, but it soon became apparent that the general public was willing to buy it if the people (and objects and animals) were animated. Disney started with *The Little Mermaid*, which was soon followed by *Beauty and the Beast, Aladdin, Pocahontas, The Lion King, The Hunchback of Notre Dame*, and they keep coming. The two shows that made Disney a major player on Broadway were *Beauty and the Beast* and *The Lion King*.

These films had great stories and wonderful songs. It should have been easy to make them work on Broadway, right? Well, it's true the script and scores would be solid, but the main problem was, how do you take an animated film and make it live onstage? How do you create live special effects for something that was drawn? And how do you make animals out of people? How do you make a beast from a regular man? How about a hyena? Or a meerkat? Prosthetics? Should you use a mask? How do you make a chest of drawers — or a teapot or a carpet — walk around? How do you show a stampede? End of story: Disney hired the right people who figured it out!

Beauty and the Beast (1994)

Beauty and the Beast (see Figure 2-23) was Disney's first Broadway musical and a huge hit. It retained all the fabulous songs from the film, and composer Alan Menken (now joined by Tim Rice because his original writing partner, Howard Ashman, tragically died from AIDS) wrote new ones like "Home" for Belle and an 11 o'clock number for the Beast called "If I Can't Have Her." Why the new songs? Because animated musicals have around ten songs. Broadway musicals have a lot more than that, so whenever these cartoon-to-Broadway shows are produced, they have to add songs to make a complete musical.

FIGURE 2-23:
The big "Be Our Guest" number in *Beauty and the Beast.*

Joan Marcus

SETH SPEAKS

From what I've heard from the cast, the most important issues centered around how to make the actors look like the characters in the film, *yet* not take away their humanity. Terrence Mann, the original Beast, remembers doing the out-of-town tryout in Texas. He had incredible prosthetics that made him look exactly like the film beast. He told me they performed the final dress rehearsal and immediately afterward one of the powers-that-be came backstage and started taking off his facial prosthetics! Why? Because they were blocking almost every aspect of his face. If the audience couldn't see his facial expressions, they had no way to connect with him. Finally, after much experimentation, they figured out how to make the Beast look beastly but still human . . . and they solved other seemingly impossible aspects like making Chip look like an actual chip from a cup and, instead of red and orange cellophane coming out of Lumiére's hands to represent fire, there was actual fire! I myself don't know how it was done. When any actor would be cast in the show, they had to sign something saying that when anyone asks you how something is done, you have to respond, "Disney magic." Annoyingly, people still adhere to the contract. Every time I ask for any secrets to be revealed to me, I get the answer, "Disney magic." My response is, "*The show closed more than ten years ago! The statute of limitations has passed!*"

The Lion King (1997)

The most successful Disney Broadway musical so far is *The Lion King*. Not only did it win the Tony Award for Best Musical, but it also began its run in 1997 and, as of this writing, it's still going strong. Although *Beauty and the Beast* satisfyingly rec-reated fantastical moments featured in the film like dancing utensils and the Beast transforming back into a human, *The Lion King* created every aspect of the film in a supremely creative and breathtaking way.

Director Julie Taymor created stunning elements: costumes (see Figure 2-24) that the actors control with the animal head above their own but with the actors' heads in full view of the audience; birds attached to sticks that the actors twirl in the air to make it look as if the audience is in an African aviary; and a stampede that is pure theatre magic. The songs by Sir Elton John and Sir Tim Rice are from the movie, and like *Beauty and the Beast*, additional songs were added to enlarge the score (like "Shadowland" and "He Lives in You"). The show has had lots of future Broadway luminaries such as Heather Headley, the original Nala, and Christopher Jackson who originated the role of George Washington in *Hamilton*.

FIGURE 2-24: Christopher Jackson in his costume for *The Lion King*.

Printed with permission from Christopher Jackson

Aida (2000)

Aida is important to mention not because it was a hit (although it was successful), but because it wasn't a *big enough* hit. It was the first musical Disney produced that was original, meaning it wasn't based on one of their already successful films. Apparently, that's an experiment that won't happen again. *Aida* was loosely based on the opera of the same name and the plot centered on Aida who was kidnapped with her people by Radames, played by Adam Pascal. Although Radames is betrothed to the shallow Amneris, played by Sherie Rene Scott, he and Aida fall in love. It's one of the few Broadway musicals with a tragic (albeit romantic) ending.

Even though the show ran for years and garnered a Tony Award for leading lady Heather Headley, the powers that be decided that *Aida* would be their last musical not based on Disney property. It should be noted that, as of this writing, original cast member Schele Williams who played Nehebka, will direct an all-new production slated for Broadway. So, Disney may not be doing any other original shows again, but they will do *this* original show again!

Looking Closer at Musical Theatre in the 21st Century

Broadway is located in Times Square, an area that became relatively unsafe in the 1960s and remained so for decades. However, in the mid 1990s, Disney bought up lots of the Times Square area and the neighborhood that was teeming with sex shops and possible muggings, became a bright, shiny playland with multiplexes (*not* showing triple X films), lots of chain restaurants, and even a Toys R Us with a big Ferris wheel.

Basically, corporate America took over Times Square — and some of Broadway as well. As the costs of mounting a production on Broadway rose, the sole producer like David Merrick or Hal Prince morphed into multiple producers and corporate financing. Bottom line? Broadway was costing a lot more (for various reasons) and a corporate mind-set of only doing shows that had the most chance to be financially successful was the zeitgeist.

By the 2000s, so much money was riding on each new Broadway show, that producers became increasingly concerned about whether a show would be a hit. Not a *hit* in terms of running a long time or getting great reviews. A *hit* in terms of returning its investment and then turning a profit.

REMEMBER

Broadway got increasingly nervous about doing art for art's sake and began to take fewer risks. Although there wasn't an official Broadway producers' meeting to decide that theory, it seemed like many Broadway producers agreed that the best way to assure a hit was to turn a Hollywood blockbuster into a musical. That theory wasn't based on facts *at all* (many film-to-musicals haven't been successful), but for some reason, the film-to-musical genre began its ascension in the 2000s and has continued to this day. These three reasons are the basis for the theory:

>> **Nowadays, even a niche musical costs a lot of money to produce.** In other words, if your show is probably only going to run for a short time, it's possible to recoup the investment only if the investment is small. But it costs a *lot* to produce even a small show these days so producers often feel they need to focus on shows that (they think) will run for years and years and therefore have a better chance at paying back their investment and turning a profit. Many think film-to-musicals are the way to go.

>> **The general public likes things they're already familiar with and is averse to trying new things.** That's why producers feel the people will be more comfortable seeing a musical version of their favorite film rather than a show they know nothing about.

This theory also pertains to the rise of the *jukebox musical,* which is the genre of show with music that already exists, be it from a certain time period or a specific artist or group. Why hope the general public will see a new show and like the music enough to leave humming the score? If the audience *goes in* humming the score, there's less risk. They already like it!

>> **The rise of both the film-to-musical and the jukebox musical have something to do with AIDS.** How? Well, the creative community lost an immeasurable number of artists to AIDS. Artists who would have come into their prime in the 2000s and would have been creating new stories and songs for Broadway died at an extraordinary rate in the 1980s and 1990s (until medicines finally were created that made HIV/AIDS much more manageable). If no one is creating new stories and songs, producers turned to stories and songs that already existed.

Here I examine some hits of the two genres that dominated the 2000s.

The film turned musical

This genre wasn't invented in the 21st century. In the '60s, the film *Lily* became *Carousel,* and in 1970 the film *All about Eve* became *Applause.* But this is when this genre took off. Instead of one film-to-musical every few years, there are usually now few every year.

The Full Monty (2000)

The Full Monty was based on the film of the same name and is notable because it was the first Broadway hit for composer/lyricist David Yazbeck, who went on to write many shows including the Tony Award–winning *The Band's Visit*. This musical seemed on the fast track to win multiple Tony Awards but ri-i-i-i-ight before the Tony Award cutoff deadline, another show opened: *The Producers!* Yep, *The Full Monty* didn't achieve their Tony sweep because the first mega-hit of the 2000s was suddenly its competition.

That wasn't the end of the trouble for *The Full Monty:* Its national tour was slated to tour for a full year . . . but right when it began, the 9/11 terror attacks occurred, which caused ticket sales to nosedive, closing the tour within weeks. Regardless, the Broadway musical ran for years and was responsible for starting the stardom of Broadway leading man and future Hollywood star Patrick Wilson.

The Producers (2001)

The Producers was the first mega-hit of the 2000s. Mel Brooks took his beloved film and found a team of creative people to help turn it into a musical. And for anyone who thinks they're too old to do something they yearn to do, he did it all in his 70s!

The show teamed up Nathan Lane and Matthew Broderick as the two leads, and the public loved them so much that after they left the show (see Figure 2-25), they came back to the show a few years later *and* they teamed up again for the revival of *The Odd Couple*. The show won 12 Tony Awards, more than any other musical ever, and added much needed laughter to New York City after the horror of 9/11.

FIGURE 2-25:
Nathan Lane (left with flowers) and Matthew Broderick (right with flowers) bow at their last performance.

Getty Images Entertainment/Getty Images

Thoroughly Modern Millie (2002)

This show is unique because it's a rare hybrid; *Thoroughly Modern Millie* was a film that used mostly songs already in existence from the 1920s plus a fabulous original title song. When the show came to Broadway, the creative team kept those classic '20s songs (as well as the title song, which was written for the film), and composer Jeanine Tesori wrote additional songs with lyricist Dick Scanlon. So the score is half jukebox musical and half original. Not common at all! Actually, I can't think of another one like that! It's also noteworthy for being the first Tesori musical on Broadway, leading to hits like *Fun Home* and *Kimberly Akimbo*. Arguably, the most notable element to the production is that it made a star out of Sutton Foster. She was the understudy for the leading lady, and when the show was about to begin previews, they gave the role to her. Chapter 9 covers understudies in more detail.

SETH SPEAKS

I met Sutton when we did *Grease!!!* together when she was about 20 years old. I loved her high belt, and when I heard she was auditioning for Millie, I told my old friend Dick Scanlon to cast her. She didn't get it at first . . . but she then took over the role and won the Tony Award for Best Actress in a Musical. I was thrilled, *but* I told her that I wanted her to belt higher in her next show! I knew she had amazing high notes, and I felt she was playing it a little too safe in Millie because she was nervous about hurting her voice. I understood. She was a first time Broadway leading lady and had the pressure of carrying the show and therefore couldn't really afford to miss a show. Regardless, her next show was *Little Women* and, during rehearsals, she left me this message:

> "Seth, it's Sutton. I'm rehearing my new show *Little Women* and just went over my song called 'Astonishing.' I am belting an E flat!"
>
> Then she paused and finally added, "I'm back. I'm back!"

BRAVA!

Hairspray (2002)

Hairspray not only won many Tony Awards (including Best Musical), but it's also notable for being the first musical from the songwriting team of Marc Shaiman and Scott Wittman who went on to write many more Broadway shows as well as the score to TV's *Smash* and Hollywood's *Mary Poppins Returns*. Some boundaries it broke seem quaint now, but nonetheless deserve great praise:

» The show featured a leading lady, portrayed by Marissa Jaret Winokur, who didn't fit the typical look of an ingenue. And she wasn't there just to make jokes or be the butt of jokes; she was the romantic desire of the hot male lead. And Marissa won the Tony Award!

>> Equally groundbreaking, her mom was played by an out gay actor dressed in drag, portrayed by the legendary Harvey Fierstein (see Figure 2-26) who also won a Tony Award for the role. He wasn't playing a man dressed as a woman like in *La Cage* or *Chicago*; he was playing a woman. That had never been done before on Broadway (but it was soon followed by Miss Trunchbull in *Matilda*).

FIGURE 2-26: Harvey Fierstein and Marissa Jaret Winokur in *Hairspray*.

Bruce Glikas/Getty Images

Not to be too dishy, but many of the shows on Broadway starting in the 2000s that were known as musical comedies had scores that were pleasant and enjoyable but didn't have genuine Broadway showstoppers. The *Hairspray* score, however, is full of incredible song after incredible song — tuneful and catchy and chock-full of clever and hilarious lyrics. No wonder it was then made into a film *and* a live TV version!

Wicked (2003)

Wicked is one of the shows that could eventually move *Phantom* off its perch as longest running musical. Although it's now an international sensation, it certainly didn't garner rave reviews — again proving that good reviews can be helpful, but marketing and word-of-mouth really can make a show a hit. *Wicked* tells the behind-the-scenes story of Glinda the Good Witch and Elphaba the Wicked Witch of the West, but nothing is as it seems in *The Wizard of Oz*.

Turns out, Elphaba isn't so wicked, and Glinda is actually a "mean girl." In another case of my old axiom of, *Awards shows don't really make sense because how is* anything *best*, Stephen Schwartz yet again didn't win the Tony Award. I love the score to *Avenue Q*, which won (refer to the later section, "Avenue Q (2003)" for more details about *Avenue Q)*, but I'm talking about the fact that Schwartz has written so many stunning scores for Broadway and has *never* won a Tony Award!

The reason so many people have a deep love for *Wicked* is because they're fans of the film *The Wizard of Oz*. Interestingly, the show couldn't get the rights to anything *solely* from the film. Anything Oz-like mentioned in *Wicked* has to also be in the book *The Wizard of Oz*. If it's only mentioned in the movie, it ain't in the show. That's why when Toto is mentioned by Glinda, she asks, "What's your dog's name? Dodo?" And when Nessa Rose (the future Wicked Witch of the East) gets the emerald slippers, they're referred to as "jeweled shoes." I wish I had been at those creative meetings! "How about green shiny shoes? Or emerald sketchers? Or verdant clodhoppers?"

Spamalot (2005)

Spamalot by John Du Prez and Eric Idle is noteworthy because it made the (what is considered by many) bold choice of *not* using the title of the film on which it's based. Marketing teams and producers seem to think it's vital for a film being made into a musical to have the same title. However, they decided *not* to call it *Monty Python and The Holy Grail: The Musical* and instead decided to simply call it *Spamalot*. The title didn't make a difference; the show was a hit, disproving the experts who insist that name recognition is vital.

This musical had comedy superstars like David Hyde Pierce, Hank Azaria (making his Broadway musical debut), Tim Curry, and "newcomer" Sara Ramirez, although she was hardly a newcomer. She had been doing Broadway musicals since the '90s when she graduated Juilliard, but none had run very long — *The Capeman*, *Fascinating Rhythm*, *A Class Act* — all shows with short runs. As a matter of fact, I saw her walking down 46th Street and she told me she was moving away from show biz. She lived in a small apartment with a bathroom down the hall and didn't want to struggle for her art anymore. I was traumatized because I knew how talented she was and I didn't want her to give up theatre. Well, the next thing I knew, she was The Lady of The Lake in *Spamalot*, won the Tony Award for Featured Actress in a Musical, and then spent the next seven years starring on *Grey's Anatomy*. I'm glad she gave it one last chance!

Legally Blonde (2007)

Legally Blonde with a score by married couple Lawrence O'Keefe and Nell Benjamin is based on the film of the same title and featured Laura Bell Bundy as Elle Woods. The show is historically noteworthy because it's the first Broadway musical to replace a lead via a reality show! When Tony-nominated star Bundy decided she was leaving, an MTV show went on the air to find the next leading lady. It started with an open call, and 12 women made it to the finals. Each week these women learned scenes, songs, and dances from the show, and at the end of each episode, one woman was sent home.

What's fantastic is the actual casting director, book writer, and director/choreographer from *Legally Blonde* were there each week auditioning (and rejecting) the potential stars. The show wasn't entirely realistic because a lot of young women who wanted the role didn't want to be on a reality show, so it wasn't a true look at actresses who would normally be auditioning to replace a lead in a Broadway show. But the feedback the women received from these Broadway luminaries each week was indeed real so it's a good show to watch if you're thinking of pursuing theatre. The most fun thing for me was . . . I was on it! I was the vocal coach who worked with the women each week, and it was a great gig! Most amazingly, MTV then asked me to do a deconstruction of each episode every week. I had an even better time doing that! Watch www.youtube.com/watch?v=s6A0EjRBpIk.

The full show is one of the few Broadway shows that was filmed in front of a live audience, so you can watch it www.youtube.com/watch?v=47D8ZJUMI8k.

Coolest of all, Lin-Manuel Miranda was a fan and did his own parody version of the reality show. His show was about replacing Eliseo Roman, the Piragua Guy from *In the Heights* and was called *Legally Brown*. Again, I was thrilled to be asked to do it. Most hilariously are the diverse crew of actors auditioning: folks like Matt Morrison, Norm Lewis, Cheyenne Jackson, and Allison Janney! You can watch it at www.youtube.com/playlist?list=PL62C312E819EEB478.

Xanadu (2007)

The films-turned-musicals of huge Hollywood hits haven't necessarily had big Broadway success. See *Rocky*, *Ghost*, *Big*, *Nine To Five*, and so on. The musicals based on films that *have* been successful seem mostly to be based on independent or cult classics like *The Producers*, *The Full Monty*, *Hairspray*, *Once*, *The Band's Visit*, and *Waitress*. What makes *Xanadu* an incredible triumph is that it wasn't based on a big Hollywood hit or a beloved cult classic. It was based on a *bomb!* Usually, film-to-musicals are sold to investors with the pitch that "Everybody loves this film! Everybody's going to want to see the musical version!" They couldn't haul out that line with this turkey.

Douglas Carter Beane was able to take the essence of the film's plot (a daughter of Zeus comes to earth to be a muse for an artist) and write hilarious dialogue that skewers the film with love yet gives the show heart. And the center of it all are those incredible songs by Electric Light Orchestra. *Xanadu* is actually a perfect segue to the later section, "The jukebox hits of the 2000s," because it was a film-to-musical *and* a jukebox musical.

Billy Elliot (2008)

Billy Elliot continued Sir Elton John's love affair with Broadway that began with *The Lion King*. What made this show so special is that the leading man was a boy and not just a boy who could sing charmingly and act with confidence (like the majority of role requirements for children on Broadway). No, the title character had to be able to dance. And not just have an innate ability to dance; he had to be able to perform with high-level ballet technique.

What seemed an impossible task wasn't so hard after all. Turns out, the world has a lot of talented people, and boys were found from everywhere on earth who were talented enough to be cast; the Broadway musical and its multiple productions around the world were hits.

Speaking of many talented boys, *Billy Elliot* is also notable because the title role is split between three boys. According to UK child labor laws, a child can't do all eight shows a week. When *Billy Elliot* opened in London, three different boys played a few performances each week. The Broadway production kept that same system in place, even though the United States doesn't have that law. If a kid wants to sing and dance nonstop, let 'em! Regardless, three different boys originated the role on Broadway. That equation brings the stress of who does opening night and who does the album.

The album issue was resolved when it was decided there wouldn't be a Broadway cast album. That's a typical West End move. Often, a show from the West End comes to Broadway and producers think, "Why make another cast album when we already have one? Let's save money!" It's a cost-saving gesture, and it's prevented Broadway fans from hearing Judy Kaye's Tony Award–winning high notes in *The Phantom of the Opera*, Louise Pitre's sass in *Mamma Mia!*, Liz Callaway's claret tones as Ellen in *Miss Saigon*, and Orfeh's showstopping singing in *Saturday Night Fever*.

Back to all three boys: When Tony Award time came around, *all three* were nominated as Best Actor in a Musical . . . and all three won! So far that's been the only time three people won *one* award!

The jukebox hits of the 2000s

The three hits mentioned here are the three main styles of jukebox musicals that became staples on the Broadway scene since the year 2000.

Mamma Mia! (2001)

Probably the jukebox show all aspire to be (in terms of longevity and money) is *Mamma Mia!* (see Figure 2-27). This type of jukebox musical is the one where an original story is made up around a music group's songs — in this case, ABBA.

FIGURE 2-27:
Karen Mason, Louise Pitre, and Judy Kaye in *Mamma Mia!*

Joan Marcus

I love the cleverness of the title because of the double meaning: It's a famous ABBA tune *and* the show is about a mom. Daughter Sophie doesn't know who her dad is so she invites three possible fathers whose names she discovers in her mom's 20-year-old diary. *Mamma Mia!* ran in Europe for a long time as well as on Broadway. A popular film version followed *and* a sequel (not common for film musicals) and a *second* sequel (unheard of for film musicals!). The only thing holding back a fourth film: How are there *possibly* any more ABBA songs to put in a film?

Movin' Out (2002)

Movin' Out is the style of jukebox musicals that is a revue of an artist's songs — in this case, Billy Joel.

Twyla Tharp is a titan of the dance world, and she brought her brilliant choreography to Broadway with an all Billy Joel show. The dancers loosely represented various people mentioned in his songs (Brenda and Eddie, and James, Judy, and Tony) and a sort of plot moved the show along. Turns out audiences love Billy Joel music and whether or not they followed the plot didn't matter because his music combined with stunning dancing was a winning combination. *Movin' Out* garnered great reviews, had a healthy Broadway run, and gave birth to multiple productions. Instead of the ensemble of dancers having to also sing (like in *Dancin'*) the entire cast of dancers only had to dance. And, holy cow, did they dance up a storm! This is because all the Billy Joel songs were sung by one singer/pianist, originally played by Michael Cavanaugh. This allowed Tharp to cast the ensemble based solely on their dance ability and not whether or not they could belt "Scenes from an Italian Restaurant."

Jersey Boys (2005)

Jersey Boys is the style of jukebox musicals that uses the songs of an artist or group and tells the story of that artist's (or group's) rise to fame (and sometimes fall) — in this case, The Four Seasons.

Jersey Boys is important not just because it was a huge hit, but because it again shows that the powers-that-be don't necessarily know everything despite their know-it-all attitude. By 2006, a string of Broadway jukebox musicals had opened on Broadway and not done well. When the *Jersey Boys* team tried to raise money to come to Broadway, they were mostly told that nobody wanted to see jukebox musicals anymore. Because those previous jukebox musicals had failed, the *Jersey Boys* creators were told *all* jukebox musicals would fail.

The team faced rejection after rejection, but finally found people who believed in the show and, boy, did the investment pay off! *Jersey Boys* ran for years, played all over the world, had *two* movie versions, and won the Tony Award for Best Musical! Take that, people who make big pronouncements about what people do or don't want to see!

Daniel Reichard told me he was obsessed with playing Jean-Michel in the revival of *La Cage Aux Folles*. He had lots of auditions and really hoped he'd get the role, but he didn't. He was devastated and felt he had no choice but to take the other gig he was offered — not only a jukebox musical (he wasn't a fan of the genre) but a musical decidedly *not* on Broadway. As a matter of fact, it was on the other side of the country. Turns out, the musical he didn't want to do was *Jersey Boys,* which had its first incarnation in La Jolla, California. Reichard flew across the country, created the role of Bob Gaudio, and then took it to Broadway where he played it for years. Meanwhile, the *La Cage Aux Folles* he was so desperate to be in lasted just six months! #BeCarefulWhatYouWishFor

Musicals not based on a film or full of songs from a jukebox

Although the 21st century saw the rise of the jukebox musical and the film-to-musical, Broadway still had original musicals. And some of them were truly groundbreaking! Not only puppets as stars as well as bipolar disorder being examined within a musical, but the first great work of today's most successful Broadway creator: Lin-Manuel Miranda (see Figure 2-28).

Avenue Q (2003)

Avenue Q (see Figure 2-29) was probably the biggest surprise hit of the decade . . . as well as the most unique! It was a surprise because it was a show that seemed more suited to Off-Broadway; not only did it have a small cast, but also the majority of the cast performed with puppets.

FIGURE 2-28: Lin Manuel Miranda.

Theo Wargo/WireImage/Getty Images

FIGURE 2-29: The cast of *Avenue Q*.

Frank Micelotta/Getty Images

I find the origin story of *Avenue Q* so interesting: The creators wanted to write an adult version of a show like *Sesame Street*. Instead of lessons about life for children, it was lessons about life for adults — some of it quite X-rated! And, like *Sesame Street*, it would be a TV show starring a mix of humans and puppets with occasional songs. After writing a version of the show, they decided to do a presentation for various producers to show the material that would be in the TV show. On a TV show, in order for puppets to move around, the puppeteers have to be hidden under and around the set. The creators didn't want to spend money building a set because they wanted to highlight the material, so they did the show with puppeteers exposed. Yes, the puppets "sang" and "acted," but the audience saw the people manipulating them.

After the presentation, various people who attended suggested to the creators that instead of *Avenue Q* being a TV show, it should be turned into a theatrical show. The audience really loved being able to see the puppeteers in action. Why not do a live show with the puppeteers being in full view? Well, the advice was taken and the stage show opened at the Off-Broadway Vineyard Theatre to rave reviews and then transferred to Broadway where it wound up winning the Tony Award for Best Musical over the multimillion-dollar *Wicked*. It's a great lesson about how you never know where inspiration will come from; because the creators decided to save money on building sets for the presentation, they wound up creating a type of show that had never been done before!

Spring Awakening (2006)

Spring Awakening (see Figure 2-30) continued the tradition of *Avenue Q* in the sense that it was a relatively small cast Off-Broadway show that transferred to Broadway and won the Tony Award for Best Musical. Based on an 1891 German play, the theme, which is about adults not being comfortable guiding teenagers in their emerging sexuality, is still true today. The 2006 show was filled with mainly young people, all of whom were unknown at the time. Since then, many have become stars! Jonathan Groff, Lea Michele, Skylar Astin, Lilli Cooper, and John Gallagher Jr. all had prominent roles and one of the understudies was the fabulous Krysta Rodriguez.

FIGURE 2-30:
The cast of *Spring Awakening.*

Bryan Bedder/Getty Images

The show borrowed from *Grease* and *Hair* in that all the solos were sung into hand-held microphones, and the production also started a new trend: wearing a version of period clothes *yet* singing in a modern-day style. Old combined with new. Sound familiar? Take a look at the costumes versus the style of music in *Hamilton*. Old combined with new! *Werk!*

In the Heights (2008)

In the Heights is not only a fantastic show (I saw it ten times), but it's also historic because it was the first musical with a score by global superstar Lin-Manuel Miranda. I remember seeing an early workshop and thinking, "Where did they get such an amazing leading man?" I had *no idea* he also wrote the score!

It's also historic because it was one of the first Broadway musicals with a mostly Latinx cast to win a Tony Award. Sadly, it never achieved the world-wide obsession of *Hamilton*, but holy cow, it deserves it. The musical is about the relationships of various people who live in one area of Washington Heights and features incredible songs, a beautiful moving (and funny) story, brilliant performances by an ensemble cast of actors, and thrilling choreography by Andy Blankenbuehler. I could go on and on, and you can see some of my obsession here: www.youtube.com/watch?v=x3ffCP9hkyo.

Let me write what I always tell *Hamilton* fans: I feel you aren't allowed to be obsessed with *Hamilton* until you have memorized *In the Heights*. *It's so good!* Watch the film to see what the hoopla is all about!

Next to Normal (2009)

Next to Normal not only won numerous Tony Awards (including one for leading lady Alice Ripley as well as Best Musical), but it also won the Pulitzer Prize. Yes, it's momentous for those reasons but also important as a counter argument to those who write off musical theatre as silly and trifling. *Next to Normal* is anything but silly and trifling. The show's subject matter is mental illness, and I can't over-state the effect the show had on the audience.

I've spoken to so many people involved with the show who told me that time and again audience members would reach out and thank them for telling their story. Whether they themselves had mental illness or whether a family member did, seeing the story onstage was emotionally wrought but also healing. This show opened late in the 2000s and was the bridge to the next ten years of shows where musicals taking on serious issues became the norm.

"A Whole New World" — 2010s

"A Whole New World" is a song from *Aladdin*, and the title refers to Aladdin showing Jasmine all the things she's never seen. (Side note: The original refrain was "The World at Your Feet," but Howard Ashman realized sustaining a note on the word "feet" wasn't a recipe for a hit song.) I use that song title as a way to describe the 2010s because Broadway was dealing with issues that Broadway musical audiences had never seen dealt with in such a deep way. Mental illness, domestic violence, the skewering of religion, closeted sexuality leading to suicide, and sexual abuse were all subjects featured in hit Broadway musicals of the 2010s.

Some of these subjects had been explored in musicals before (for example, *Carousel* had domestic violence and *West Side Story* had sexual abuse) but never so completely. And, furthermore, some of these subjects had *never* been in a Broadway musical. The skewering of religion? Well, Maria did indeed leave the convent, but I'm pretty sure she and the Von Trapps never pranced around singing "F you, God"! (*Maybe* during early previews, but surely R&H cut it while the show was still out of town.)

The 2010s will no doubt always be remembered as the decade that birthed the biggest hit Broadway had ever known: *Hamilton*. And "hit" encompasses the big three: Reviews, audience response, and money. Nothing in all the years of Broadway has ever compared to *Hamilton*. That not only has to do with how great the show is, but also what was happening in the world at the same time. I'll get to it in due time. As Aaron Burr sings, *"Wait for it!"*

Not Hamilton — Other musical greats of the 2010s

The 2010s proved Broadway could have a musical that tackles major societal issues and still be entertaining. The other trend of the 2010s: the Off-Broadway to on Broadway transfer. *Hamilton* began Off-Broadway, transferred to Broadway, and won the Tony Award for Best Musical. Many shows of the 2010s took that same path, which was quite different from the Golden Age when shows would tour from town to town and then open on Broadway. Those out-of-town tryouts were a wonderful way to gauge the reactions of audiences around the country, but touring a show began to be expensive for various reasons.

Not only did many award-winning shows in the 2010s begin Off-Broadway, they also weren't giant Broadway shows filled with large casts and large sets being shoved into small Off-Broadway houses waiting to fill a giant Broadway stage. They were intimate affairs that Broadway (and the Tony Awards) welcomed.

I discuss in the following sections how smaller shows were very much in vogue during the 2010s.

The Book of Mormon (2011)

Everyone expected a musical spearheaded by the creators of *South Park* to break boundaries and be funny, but I don't think many people expected it to have so much heart and raise such deep philosophical questions. *The Book of Mormon* musical (see Figure 2-31) is historic because it dares to take on not only a specific religion and the hypocrisy the creators see in that specific religion, but also questions the validity of all religions.

FIGURE 2-31: Andrew Rannells (center) and the cast of *The Book of Mormon*.

Joan Marcus

The leading man Elder Price (originally played brilliantly by Andrew Rannells) is a devout Mormon, who sings "a Mormon just believes." But the more he's forced to question his beliefs, especially because of the working relationship he's forced to have with his mission partner played by the wonderful Josh Gad, the more he rejects them. And by the end, he comes to an understanding about what he sees as the purpose of religion: not something completely true, not something you're not allowed to question, not something that is without hypocrisy, but something that can provide comfort.

The show is so extremely funny and shocking that the journey of the characters is perhaps overlooked, but note that it took incredible skill to write (and direct) a show like this. And, like many shows that don't fit a mold, when the show was first being presented in readings, the people involved were told that it would never be a success. It was way too dirty/anti-religious/over-the-top/and so on to be a commercial run. The creators stuck to their vision, and the show won the Tony

Award for Best Musical and has played successfully around the world. Brava on sticking to your vision!

SETH SPEAKS

Rory O'Malley was hired to be in the ensemble of *The Book of Mormon* and as the show continued to do readings and workshops, he kept being given lines and eventually . . . a song. By the time the show opened on Broadway, he had an actual role. And when the Tony Awards nominations were announced, he was nominated for Best Featured Actor! He began in the ensemble and eventually had a Tony-nominated role. It was both shocking and thrilling for him, but even more shocking to his mother who still lived in the Midwest and couldn't believe her son was doing so well. This was the conversation Rory told me he had with his mom on the phone on the day of the Tony Award nominations. Mind you, her attitude wasn't undermining; it was in awe.

RORY: Mom! I just got nominated for a Tony Award!

RORY'S MOM: Are you sure!?

RORY: Yes! Matthew Broderick just announced it.

RORY'S MOM: (nervously) Well, somebody better double check!

Yes, Rory's mom, it was true, and your son will now always be known as Tony Award–nominated actor, Rory O'Malley!

Beautiful: The Carole King Musical (2014)

Beautiful: The Carole King Musical is a combo platter of trends:

>> It's a jukebox musical, a genre that really hit its stride in the 2000s. The show celebrated Carole King and featured many of her hits.

>> It deals with mental illness, a subject matter first addressed comprehensibly in *Next to Normal* (refer to the section, "Next to Normal (2009)" earlier in this chapter). The musical shows King's marriage to Gerry Goffin, which was marred by his struggles with mental illness, which was exacerbated by his use of hallucinogenic drugs.

Interestingly, even though the show is *Beautiful: The Carole King Musical*, a lot of focus is on her best friends, songwriting team Cynthia Weil and Barry Mann, and a number of their songs are featured as well. *Beautiful* is an important show because Jessie Mueller (who played Carole) won the Tony Award that year for Best Actress in a Musical, and it moved her into the echelon of Broadway star (her next Broadway shows were leading roles in *Waitress* and *Carousel*).

SETH SPEAKS

Anika Larsen, who played Cynthia Weil, is a close friend and told my family this story during our 2013 New Year's Eve Party. During rehearsals for *Beautiful*, she had stomach pains for a while and finally, after feeling a lump(!) decided to go the hospital. But, being a cheapskate actor, she didn't want to spend money on a cab so she *walked*. The hospital was only about eight blocks from her house, but when she got there, she was exhausted and in a lot of pain. Because she wasn't bleeding or missing a limb, the admitting nurse made her wait a long time to see a doctor. And that's when Anika fainted.

Suddenly, she was on a gurney with a mask over her face. They gave her something disgusting to drink so they could do a test and discovered she had been born with a twisted colon (who ever heard of that?). Her colon was completely blocked, and the doctor told her that if she had waited five more hours, she would have died! She's so thankful she walked there because that's what made her faint and get seen right away. The doctor scheduled immediate surgery to remove part of her colon, and everyone in her family managed to show up right before she went in. Anika wrote me this email detailing what happened next, and I love the way she writes:

> When they were wheeling me off into the operating room, my mom and sisters were there, and my dad had just arrived in time to wave goodbye, and he and my mom and I are all crying, and my dad puts his arm around my mom and I haven't seen that in 20 years, and I think, "Stop crying. Say something funny. You may not come out the other side on this one, Larsen, what are your last words gonna have been?" And I said, "Hey, guys, when this is over, I'll have a semi-colon." Not bad under pressure (and morphine). And that is why I will now be signing my name, An;ka.

Because she told her cast that story, the stage manager had the nameplate for her dressing room at *Beautiful* altered (as shown).

Published with permission by An;ka Larsen

Once (2012)

Even though this musical didn't follow the 2010s trend of exploring mental illness or social justice, it was part of the trend that began in the 2000s: the movie-to-musical and it exemplified my theory that the less well-known films wind up becoming hit musicals. It also followed the other trend of having the actors double as the musicians, which began its ascension with the 1998 *Cabaret* revival when the ensemble covered most of the orchestral parts and continued with the revivals of *Company* and *Sweeney Todd*.

What's also noteworthy about *Once* is that the story isn't a will-they-won't-they romantic relationship between the leading man and leading woman. The show is about the two of them learning from each other in a nonromantic way and moving on to other people. It again proves that Broadway musicals come in many sizes. Broadway has giant, lush shows like *The Phantom of the Opera* that win the Tony Award for Best Musical as well as small, intimate shows like *Once* that win the same award.

SETH SPEAKS

Because the actors provided the band for *Once*, they remained onstage for much of the show, even when they weren't in the scenes. That's a nice idea in terms of having a community always onstage to provide a backdrop, but sometimes watching the same thing eight times a week without zoning out — or falling asleep — isn't easy. My friend Anne Nathan who played the mom in *Once*, struggled . . . and finally succombed. Yep, while she was onstage she literally fell asleep. Perhaps no one would have noticed her nodding off if it weren't for the instrument she played. If she had a flute in her hand, maybe it would have quietly hit the floor when her head lolled to the side. Instead, she was holding an *accordion!* She told me it squeezed together forming a cacophonous chord when she entered dreamland, and *everyone* in the theatre heard it! Talk about busted!

Kinky Boots (2013)

Kinky Boots is on trend for the 2010s because it deals with the social justice issues of queerphobia. And it's momentous because it *finally* made Billy Porter (see Figure 2-32) a legitimate Broadway star, leading to him eventually becoming an international star. The fact that Porter didn't get to originate a leading role until he was in his 40s shows how difficult it is to be a star on Broadway if you don't fit the mold. Billy is Black and gay, and there weren't/aren't many Broadway star vehicles for Black men who appear gay. Although he did appear on Broadway in a few musicals, nothing showcased all his brilliant talents — that is until *Kinky Boots*.

SETH SPEAKS

I met him in summer stock when he was 19, and I had just graduated from college. I kept saying to anyone who would listen that he needed someone to write him his *Funny Girl*, a show that would let him do all the incredible things he could do. He started auditioning for shows in the 1980s and didn't get to originate this leading role until *Kinky Boots!* To have world-class talents like he has and basically have to beg to be on Broadway (read his incredible autobiography, *Unprotected*) proves that, even though Broadway is ahead of the curve in terms of nontraditional casting compared to TV and film, it hasn't moved fast enough and still has a long way to go. Regardless, the show won the Tony Award for Best Musical and Porter won the Tony for Best Actor in a Musical. *And* the album won the Grammy and therefore Billy won the Grammy. And around five years later, Billy won the Emmy Award for *Pose*, so all he's missing for his EGOT is the O!

FIGURE 2-32:
Billy Porter in
Kinky Boots.

**SETH
SPEAKS**

I've memorized so many of the amazing phrases Billy has thrown my way and I must share some. At one point, I was calling him to be on my SiriusXM radio show, and he wasn't responding. I didn't realize he had taken off a week from the show and was out of town. Regardless, I tried him again, and he answered and simply said, "The word is 'vacation' and I'm on it!"

Another time, pre-*Kinky Boots*, I called him to do my radio show. He was starring in a New York City revival of the play *Angels in America* in a dramatic role. I told him that after the interview, I wanted him to sing a song. He responded, referencing his nonsinging role in *Angels in America*, "Girl, I'm an actress now!" Hi-larious!

Fun Home (2015)

A musical that tells you right at the beginning that the leading lady's father is going to die by suicide isn't your typical show.

And *Fun Home* had *a lot* of other aspects that made it atypical; not only was the leading lady a lesbian, not common at all on Broadway, but the entire show is based on a graphic memoir (the memoir's full title is *Fun Home: A Family Tragicomic* by Alison Bechdel). Although Broadway musicals have been based on plays, films, TV shows, comic strips, and documentaries (see Chapter 11), *Fun Home* is the first to be based on a graphic memoir. As atypical as it is, *Fun Home* is on trend with the 2010s because it's about social issues like internalized homophobia and the mental health issues that can arise in a closeted person and the person's immediate family.

The main message is to be yourself, which is the message of many shows of the 2010s (including another Jeanine Tesori show *Shrek*), and the point is proven by the fact that tragedy happens because Alison's father denies who he really is. This was yet another small Off-Broadway show that transferred to Broadway and won the Tony Award for Best Musical, proving once again that Broadway musicals come in all shapes, sizes, and styles.

SETH SPEAKS

When *Fun Home* was first presented, it was at The Public Theater with the audience facing the stage, like the majority of theatres. When it went to Broadway, it moved to the Circle in the Square Theatre. Judy Kuhn, who played the mom, was at lunch with a friend and told her that the show would be at Circle in the Square. Her friend made her stand and turn completely around. Judy obliged and after her friend observed her, she told her not to worry . . . it would be fine. Judy didn't know what she meant until her friend explained that Circle in the Square was in the round, which meant that the audience would be seeing her from every angle. The friend wanted to make sure Judy's butt looked good when being viewed head on and told Judy she had nothing to worry about. That's what friends are for?

Waitress (2016)

The trend of film-to-musical that began in earnest in the 2000s continued with *Waitress* and, again, this successful musical was based on a small film and not a Hollywood blockbuster. *Waitress* (see Figure 2-33) is notable not only because it was a big success of the decade, but also because composer/lyricist Sara Bareilles wound up taking over the leading lady role, thereby being one of the few creators to star in their own show. Yes, Comden and Green did it in the '40s in *On the Town*, but it hadn't been done that much since. (Most notable, Sting took on a role for a limited time in his musical *The Last Ship*, Peter Allen starred in *Legs Diamond*, John Cameron Mitchell starred in *Hedwig and the Angry Inch*, and of course, Lin Manuel-Miranda has starred in two of his musicals.)

Waitress is on trend with the decade's themes because it deals with domestic violence as well as the moral issues of cheating. The breakout song from the show is "She Used to Be Mine," which is quite impressive. Why? Because it was the *very first song* Bareilles wrote for *Waitress*. Seriously! She was approached about writing the score and said, "Sure! I'll give it a try," and her version of "giving it a try" became the song most associated with the show!

FIGURE 2-33:
The waitresses in *Waitress*.

Joan Marcus

SETH SPEAKS

Jessie Mueller told me during one of our concerts that while she would sing "What Baking Can Do," the staging of the number had her literally working with sugar, butter, and flour, the ingredients often mentioned throughout the show. Every time she'd finish that number, she'd feel congested, have a tickle in her throat, and needed to cough. What was the culprit? After trial and error, she realized it was gluten! Throwing that dough in the air released particles of flour, and she realized she was having an allergic reaction to gluten. After that revelation, the Broadway production and all subsequent productions around the world changed to gluten-free flour! It made the song sniffle-free but probably didn't create a very delicious pie. (My kid is allergic to gluten, so we've suffered through many gluten-free birthday cakes. Basically, take a piece of something that tastes like paper and then put icing on it. There. Now you know what a gluten-free birthday cake tastes like. Enjoy?)

Dear Evan Hansen (2016)

Dear Evan Hansen with a score by Benj Pasek and Justin Paul is yet another musical from the 2010s that dealt with mental health; it's also another small Off-Broadway show that transferred to Broadway and won the Tony Award for Best Musical. However, unlike many musicals of the decade, it's a completely original story. The character Evan Hansen has extreme anxiety and, through a series of misunderstandings, he pretends to have been friends with a young man from his high school who died by suicide. Because of social media, the story of Evan and his "friend" Connor starts trending and Evan becomes a hero, even though he's being lauded for something he never did. *Dear Evan Hansen* explores how much responsibility people bear for their behavior, how much mental illness can be "blamed" for bad behavior, and how damaging social media can be when something goes viral — all themes that haven't been explored very often, or at all, in a Broadway musical.

The show cemented Ben Platt (see Figure 2-34) as a huge star based on his acting chops and stunning voice. It also cemented the songwriting team of Pasek and Paul as major players in the Broadway scene. Although *Dear Evan Hansen* takes place now (it opened in 2016 and is still considered a contemporary piece), I'm always interested in when a show becomes a period piece. I do wonder if the social media will change so much in the future that either the social media aspect of *Dear Evan Hansen* will have to change or if it will become a show that mentions in the Playbill that it takes place in 2016. By the time you read this book, it may have happened.

FIGURE 2-34:
Ben Platt,
the original *Dear Evan Hansen*.

Jagged Little Pill (2019)

Alanis Morisette took the radio by storm in the 1990s, singing about her past relationships and her spirituality ("Thank you, India!"). Those hit songs were put into a musical called *Jagged Little Pill* that wasn't a bio musical about Alanis's rise to stardom (like *Jersey Boys*). Instead, the songs were used to tell a new story with themes on trend with the 2010s: What can happen when you suppress sexual abuse as well as gender identity, sexual identity, and mental health.

Judging the success of this show in terms of longevity is difficult because it was a victim of Covid (refer to the section, "Covid Hits: The Great Shutdown of 2020," later in this chapter), but it still garnered plenty of Tony nominations and a Tony Award for Lauren Patton for Best Featured Actress in a Musical who brought down the house with her rendition of "You Oughta Know."

Moulin Rouge (2019)

Moulin Rouge is on trend with movies being turned into musicals and, as opposed to some movies that seemed difficult to musicalize (like *Rocky* or *Carrie*), *Moulin Rouge* seemed one of the most logical choices because the original movie *was* a musical! One of the reasons it breaks the mold of other jukebox musicals is that most have music from one artist/group or one particular time period. *Moulin Rouge* has music from the 1970s all the way to right around the time when the show opened.

Out of all jukebox musicals up to that date, it definitely has *the* most contemporary songs, featuring such artists as Lady Gaga and Sia. And, yes, I basically only know Broadway music, but I actually know who those current artists are (tip o' the hat to the fact that I have a daughter who came of age in the 2010s). *Moulin Rouge* was the last Best Musical Tony Award winner of the 2010s, even though it won the award in 2021. (It opened in 2019, but the Tony Awards didn't happen in 2020 due to Covid.) Leading man Aaron Tveit won the Tony Award for Best Actor. It's also notable because it *finally* got Danny Burstein his first Tony Award after he'd been nominated *seven* times! #NotSinceSusanLucci

Hamilton (2015)

The biggest hit musical of the 2010s was *Hamilton*. The biggest hit musical *ever* is also *Hamilton*. Nothing has achieved the worldwide acclaim of *Hamilton*, and nothing has the money-making potential of *Hamilton*.

SETH SPEAKS

TONY RANDALL REACTS

Danny Burstein made his Broadway debut with the National Actors Theatre founded by (*Odd Couple* star) Tony Randall. During rehearsals, Danny told Tony that he wanted to teach one day.

Tony looked at him and asked, "What would you say is the most important thing to teach someone about acting?"

Danny confidently answered, "Reacting."

"Ah . . . it's *listening*," Tony said.

Danny explained that listening is actually part of reacting.

"Don't contradict me you a**hole!" Tony said. (FYI, he didn't say this angrily, it was said with Tony's signature dry line reading.) "It takes ten years to learn how to listen correctly."

I remember hearing that story from Danny and thinking "Uh-oh. I better start learning how to listen." That was more than 15 years ago, and I still haven't started. Can't we just say the most important thing about acting is mugging? *That* I've perfected.

Here are a few factors that made Hamilton a hit (see Figure 2-35):

>> **No star power needed:** The show doesn't rely on a name star, meaning it doesn't have to have a Hugh Jackman or Audra McDonald to attract an audience. Even when it first opened, megastar Lin-Manuel Miranda took off performances every week with his wonderful cover Javier Muñoz filling in, and every performance still sold out.

>> **A simple set:** Hamilton doesn't need an expensive *Les Miz* turntable or *Phantom* expensive falling chandelier. It's all performed on a set that doesn't have frills, which keeps down bottom line costs.

>> **Social media:** Back when behemoths like *Cats*, *Les Miz*, and *Phantom* opened, Facebook, Twitter, and other social media didn't exist. Social media enabled praise about the show to spread throughout the world making it *the* hottest ticket around. As soon as the show was announced in a city, pre-sales went through the roof because *everyone* had heard of it.

A combination of all these things (along with critical nods, audience word-of-mouth raves, and relentless awards) has made this show the biggest money-maker of all time.

FIGURE 2-35:
The cast of
Hamilton.

Theo Wargo/Getty Images

Before you start resenting Miranda for having such a money-making hit, consider the fact that he didn't make a musical about a famous film or book. Meaning, he didn't take a property that he knew was already popular and therefore assume a musical version would be popular as well.

He made a musical about someone *he* found interesting — and not a sexy, modern-day star but a historical figure from the 1700s. Do you think making a musical about a historical figure is what someone does when they want to rake in the cash? No. Miranda did it because reading about Hamilton sparked creativity. And because his (and his team's) creativity was brilliant, the final result was beloved. And that final result isn't only beloved but it's also groundbreaking; the music is *the* most contemporary music that has been on Broadway since *Hair*, and it's the biggest hit show to feature a largely non-white cast.

So many talented actors who would have never had a chance to play a lead character in a musical now have a chance to be in a hit musical because of *Hamilton*. If Renée Elise Goldsberry, Chris Jackson, and Phillipa Soo were 30 years older with the same talent, what shows would have made them stars in the 1970s and '80s? It took a show like *Hamilton* to give them a chance to show the world the talent they have. I hope that has opened people's eyes to diverse casting, so people with enormous talent aren't begging for a gig (refer to the section, "Kinky Boots (2013)" earlier in this chapter about Billy Porter and the first 25 years of his career). Miranda and his team have changed Broadway permanently for the better.

While doing my radio show one day, I was thinking of *Hamilton* and got an idea. I texted Lin and told him I decided he needed to write a version of *Hamilton* that wasn't about Alexander Hamilton but was instead about *Margaret* Hamilton (the Wicked Witch of the West). Within *minutes* he sent me back amazing lyrics. Note the original lyrics are "Alexander Hamilton . . . we are waiting in the wings for you." Remember the scene in *The Wizard of Oz* with the flying monkeys? He wrote me:

"Margaret Freakin' Hamilton

We are monkeys wearing wings for you."

And that's why he's basically won every award ever.

Covid Hits: The Great Shutdown of 2020

Covid-19 started spearing around the world in early 2020. By March, someone in Westchester, New York, was diagnosed with Covid and then an usher in a Broadway theatre; by Thursday March 13, all Broadway shows were shut down. *Just for a few weeks*, they said.

At that point, cast members of various Broadway shows had Covid (especially those in *Moulin Rouge*), but all thankfully survived. But soon, Broadway star Nick Cordero (*Bullets over Broadway, Waitress*) was infected and got sicker and sicker. He lapsed into a coma, lost his leg, and then died. The Broadway community rallied throughout his illness and realized how terrifying and deadly Covid was. Tony Award–winning playwright Terrence McNally was another early victim of the disease as well as the hilarious composer/lyricist Adam Schlesinger (*Cry Baby*). It was a scary time in the world and especially New York City.

When the shutdown happened, my husband James and I realized that the Actors Fund (now the Entertainment Community Fund) would be inundated with requests for financial assistance. Most people connected to show business live check to check, even when working on Broadway. On March 13, 2020, those checks all stopped abruptly. And not just people working on Broadway. Wedding singers, ballet teachers, people who cater on movie sets, ushers, makeup artists, and so on were affected. How would people pay rent? Pay for medicine? Groceries? We knew they would turn to the Actors Fund. So James and I started a livestream called *Stars in the House* (the name was courtesy of Brian Stokes Mitchell) featuring interviews and performances with stars from Broadway, film, and TV. We started the show on Monday March 16, 2020 with the schedule of two shows a day at 2 p.m. and 8 p.m.

We wound up connecting with Dr. Jonathan LaPook, who is the chief medical correspondent from CBS. He joined us almost every show to keep us updated on the latest Covid developments — from masks, to vaccines, to boosters. We often had reunions of TV shows like *ER, Frasier, Little House on the Prairie,* and *Grey's Anatomy,* but the bulk of our guests were from Broadway. Almost every Broadway star made an appearance, and we had gatherings of contemporary casts like *Jagged Little Pill, Wicked, Dear Evan Hansen,* and more, and original cast members from classics like *A Chorus Line, Cats, Les Miz,* and *Ragtime.* We heard from our audiences around the world that the twice-daily livestream helped them feel connected when we were all isolating and, in turn, our loyal audiences donated to the Entertainment Community Fund while watching us live or catching the shows later on our website StarsInTheHouse.com or YouTube channel www.youtube.com/@StarsIn TheHouse. Plus we were able to pay for our small staff with the help of the Berlanti Family Foundation and StreamYard, so *all* of the money being donated could go directly to the Fund. By June of 2022, we had raised $1.1 million dollars and, though not as often, we're *still* doing the livestream!

We're very happy to have raised that much, but that amount was just a fraction of what the Actors Fund/Entertainment Community Fund gave to the entertainment community during this time. Since the 1980s, HIV/AIDS greatly affected the entertainment community because so many artists died in the prime of their careers or before they even had a chance to reach their prime and those who have AIDS/HIV have to often grapple with setbacks due to their health. Thankfully, Covid wasn't as deadly, but it hurt so many people financially because show business shut down for such a long period of time. And not just financially; actors get their health insurance based on how many weeks they worked. That meant a *great* percentage of people lost their health insurance because the work stopped. To be clear — they lost their health insurance during a pandemic.

The Entertainment Community Fund stepped in and helped people get the health coverage they needed. Suffice it to say, nothing had ever shut down the arts for such a length of time and the fund's chairman of the board, Brian Stokes Mitchell, thinks it will take a full five years for the entertainment community to fully recover. Thankfully, the Entertainment Community Fund will be there helping the whole time.

Defying Covid — 2021 to Now

Covid doesn't seem to be going anywhere. Through trial and error, Broadway has figured out a way to reopen and keep casts and crews (relatively) safe. When shows came back, audiences were told they had to be masked. Many people thought that people would rather stay home than sitting through shows wearing a mask the entire time. They were wrong! Audiences came back to Broadway, and watching a show in a mask was much better than no show at all. It reminded me of when smoking was banned in New York City restaurants, and restaurant owners complained vociferously that people would stop eating out and ruin the restaurant business. People continued to eat out without smoking indoors, and audiences continued to go to the theatre *with* masks on the whole time.

Sadly, though, as I write this in late 2022, Broadway is still paying the price. Many Broadway musicals experience *Covid closings,* meaning shows had so many cast members sick with Covid, they couldn't sustain performances and had to close. *Jagged Little Pill* and *Waitress* are just two that come to mind. And *Mrs. Doubtfire,* which started previews right before the shutdown, came back when Broadway reopened, shut down for a few performances because so many cast members got sick right after opening, started performances again, shut down a few weeks later because of Omicron, came back *again* in the spring, but didn't gain enough momentum and quickly closed after only getting one Tony nomination.

However, just when it looked like another complete shutdown was coming, swings and understudies showed everyone the heroes they've always been and kept Broadway open. Some went on for roles they weren't prepared to do and some played multiple roles in the same show. Certain shows took a break during the winter months, and others closed prematurely, but the horrific period proved that Broadway may go away for a short time . . . or even a long time . . . but it will *never* go away forever!

Recovering from the shutdown of 2020 is taking a long time, and Covid is still around and hurting the entertainment community. However, like "The Farmer and the Cowman," Broadway and Covid have learned how to live "Side-by-Side (by Sondheim)." Now go out and buy a ticket to a show!

IN THIS CHAPTER

» **Introducing the characters, setting up the conflict**

» **Taking a breather from the drama**

» **Seeing how the story shakes out**

Chapter 3

Finally . . . the Anatomy of a Musical

When I was at Oberlin Conservatory (which counts Broadway royalty Julie Taymor, Judy Kuhn, and John Kander as alumni), I studied classical piano. We had to learn fairly strict forms like the sonata, minuet, and rondo form (side note: I don't remember *any* of them. Let's just say I wasn't asked to write *Classical Music For Dummies*). I'm bringing that up because, unlike classical music, there's no set structure for a musical. The musical form is constantly evolving. But almost every musical has at least one of the following scenes or songs . . . and many musicals have almost all of them!

Act One — Telling the First Part of the Story

Act One consists of a bunch of scenes and songs (sometimes only songs like in-through composed musicals such as *Jesus Chris Superstar*) and usually ends on an unresolved conflict. I will, however, say that not all musicals have two acts. Some have just one act (like *A Chorus Line*), and a few have three acts (like *The Most Happy Fella*). But the majority do indeed have two acts.

I was going to write that the one constant is Act One always begins at the beginning . . . until I remembered musicals like *The Last Five Years* and *Merrily We Roll Along* where Act One starts at the *end* of the story and then works backward. So, again, this ain't the strict format of classical music!

These sections break down the different parts of a musical that happen during Act One.

The overture — Y'all! The show's starting!

The overture is like almost everything I'm going to mention in this chapter —a common part of the musical format, but not a constant part. It was most common in musicals pre-1970 where 99 percent of musicals had overtures, but nowadays it is mostly uncommon.

REMEMBER

The *overture* starts the musical theatre process. It reminds me of those articles for insomniacs that tell you to prepare your body for bedtime before you actually go to bed. You know — lower the lights, play soft music, and so on. What is the exact purpose of the overture? The overture does the following:

>> **It informs the audience that they're about to see a musical.** Having the lights dim and then listening to the overture is a transition from the outside world to the world of sitting in a theatre and soon watching people onstage make believe.

>> **It introduces various musical themes that the audience will hear that night.** During the overture, usually around four songs from the show are highlighted in instrumental versions sandwiched between an ear-catching beginning moment and exciting ending. The reason that those four songs are introduced is because the more you hear a song, the more you can remember it. When the song is sung later in the show, you'll probably enjoy it more because the melody is now familiar to you.

Also, if you remember a tune (and hopefully like it), the intention is that you leave the theatre doing that old chestnut: humming a tune. And not only humming a tune but seeking it out. Yes, every composer hopes that you go out and buy the show album or the individual song recording. And that was even more so in the Golden Age (see Chapter 2 for more information).

>> **It originally lured the audience to buy records.** Hearing the melodies numerous times led to people seeking them out. When musicals first began, and for years after, the pop music charts consisted of songs from musicals. Every show aspired to have at least one song popular enough to be recorded by a famous recording artist. The overture is not only the transition from the outside world to the theatre world but also is part of the grand scheme to induce the audience to buy records, which helped make the show more popular.

THE BEST MUSICAL THEATRE OVERTURES

Musical theatre fans love to debate which Broadway overture is the best. Although there's no official final consensus, here are five that many mention:

- *Gypsy:* It begins with the famous and grand "I Had a Dream!" motif played by the trumpets, segues to the boisterous "Everything's Coming Up Roses," gives the audience the lilting "Small World," and then moves to the raunchy and rousing stripper triplets from "Rose's Turn" with the first trumpet player going wild on high notes. Many Broadway fans love this overture because it sounds like pure Broadway.

- *Funny Girl:* The first main song in this overture is the joyous "I'm the Greatest Star," which then segues into one of the most gorgeous ballads ever written for Broadway — "People." Soon, there's an extremely exciting, repeated phrase of fast eight notes played by the xylophone and then the violins, and it soon becomes the frenetic accompaniment for "Don't Rain on My Parade." This overture is often tied with *Gypsy* as the number one overture, which is not surprising because Jule Styne composed both of them.

- *Candide:* This overture is often played by symphonic orchestras because, even though *Candide* is a Broadway musical, it sounds less Broadway and more 20th century neo-classical. Not surprisingly, Leonard Bernstein who brilliantly straddled the world of classical music and Broadway wrote it. Seeing this overture played live is thrilling because the violins have some virtuosic lines that are fun to watch. I especially love it because all of the sudden rhythmic and dynamic changes give the whole overture a wonderful comedic flair.

- *On the Twentieth Century:* Cy Coleman first became well known as a jazz musician, but he could compose in any style: old-school Broadway (*Wildcat*), country flair (*The Will Rogers Follies*), big band noir (*City of Angels*), and . . . operetta! Yes, *On the Twentieth Century* tips its hat to operetta. The overture transports you back in time to luxury train travel with its lush orchestration. To really bring in the main character of the musical, which is the railroad that connects Chicago to New York, the overture incorporates the bells and steam sounds of a train. As a matter of fact, the whole overture is like a train ride — it starts slow and then gets to full speed at the end complete with clanging train bells!

- *Merrily We Roll Along:* The *Merrily We Roll Along* overture begins with a fast-paced back-and-forth between wind/brass and percussion/drums. The show takes place in New York City, which is immediately what you feel; you're trying to balance your career, your friendships, and your love life while dodging taxis zooming up Amsterdam Avenue. The beautiful ballad "Good Thing Going" is sandwiched between brass and woodwinds battling it out for the most exciting 16th note phrases. And tip o' the hat to Sondheim's first musical, there are some super high notes for the trumpets that all scream BROADWAY!

The opening number — Introducing the show's theme

The *opening number* is just another way to say the first song in the show. There's no set formula for what the opening number is; however, it usually puts the audience into the world of the musical. For example, in *Cabaret*, you're an audience member at the Kit Kat Club. In *Ragtime*, you're introduced to various characters from the story and find out the attitudes of early 1900s America. In *Wicked*, you discover the wicked witch is dead *and* the audience sees a flashback to her birth.

REMEMBER

The theme of the entire show often is introduced in the opening number . . . but, interestingly, experts have said it shouldn't be written until the rest of the show is finished. Of course, the opening number is often written first, but by the time the show is finished, the first song is often significantly revised or completely replaced. That's because it's often not until the show is finally finished that the full theme of the show is clear to the creative team (refer to Chapter 8 for who is part of the creative team).

Director/choreographer Jerome Robbins was called in to fix *A Funny Thing Happened on the Way to the Forum*. The show was being performed in out-of-town tryouts, but the audience wasn't laughing. He told composer/lyricist Stephen Sondheim it wasn't because of anything in the main show; it was because of the opening. At that point, the opening number was "Love Is in the Air." It was charming and told the audience what the title suggests; love is all around and people are partaking. But Robbins said the opening number needed to tell the audience they were about to see a comedy. And not just a comedy, a *broad* comedy. Sondheim wrote "Comedy Tonight," and suddenly the jokes in the show that weren't previously getting laughs were bringing down the house.

SETH SPEAKS

When I interviewed the late great Marvin Hamlisch, he told me that the original opening number to *A Chorus Line* was called "Resumé." Not until the show was fully written did the creative team realize the show's theme was the desperation of performers trying to get their next job. The opening number needed to reflect the fact that all the dancers on that stage wanted/needed a job, so they changed "Resumé" to the plea: "I Hope I Get It."

"I want" song — Stating the quest

Closely following the opening number is often the "*I want*" *song*, which tells the audience what the main character, or multiple characters, is/are seeking. The characters involved in this song are unsatisfied with their current life and are looking for something that will satisfy them. This *want* propels the action for the rest of the show.

Classic *"I want"* songs are

>> "Corner of the Sky" from *Pippin* where Pippin sings of wanting to find his purpose ("I've got to be where my spirit can run free...")

>> "Part of Your World" from *The Little Mermaid* where Ariel sings about her wish to be on land ("Wish I could be part of your world...")

>> "Maybe" from *Annie* when Annie sings about her hope to meet her lost parents ("So maybe now it's time and maybe when I wake. They'll be there calling me 'baby.' Maybe...")

REMEMBER

Often the character gets what they want, but the results aren't exactly what they thought. For instance, Pippin is convinced by the leading player that his purpose is to die by suicide and be special, but he decides his purpose is to be ordinary. Ariel sells her voice to finally be on land . . . but she doesn't realize that, without her voice, it's a horrific experience. And Annie thinks that her only chance of a family is with her parents . . . but when she finds out they've passed away, she finds a new family with Daddy Warbucks!

"I am" song — Revealing a character's traits

The main character gets the "I want" song. However, the audience often finds out about the other characters in a show with an *"I am"* song. This song tells the audience the main trait of that character and often informs the characters' actions for the rest of the show.

Here are some examples of *"I am"* songs:

>> Lancelot in *Camelot* tells the audience that he's the bravest and most noble night with "C'est Moi."

>> Mama Morton in *Chicago* informs the audience that she'll do anyone a favor . . . if they pay up in "When You're Good to Mama."

>> In "I Can't Say No" from *Oklahoma!* Ado Annie admits she loves to have fun with men even though she knows she shouldn't.

Of course, sometimes the character who's sure of what they are finds out they're *not* what they thought they were. Lola in *Damn Yankees* sings "Whatever Lola wants . . . Lola gets!" But by the end of the show, she doesn't get what she intended (Joe's heart and soul). And the aforementioned Lancelot sings in "C'est Moi" how the ways of the flesh have no allure for him, but by the end of *Camelot* he finds out they sure do when he starts an affair with Guinevere.

"In one" song — Obscuring the activity behind the drop

Another type of song you may see in a musical is a song that was originally done "in one." The very front section of the stage is called *one* and that's where these songs were written to take place — literally, "in one."

"In one" songs are mainly from the Golden Age because of old-school set design. In film, scenes can take place in many different locales without any pause in the action, but in theatre, different locations are represented by different sets, and some sets were behemoths that took time to set up. Before there was automation, crews had to move the last set offstage and the new set onstage, and songs would cover the length of time it took for those set changes.

Even though these types of songs can move the story along, their main purpose was to cover the move of the scenery. In order for the audience not to have to watch a bunch of backstage folks push set pieces on and off and/or see giant set pieces descend from above, there'd be a painted drop brought in that would obscure everything happening behind it, and these songs would happen in front of the drop while the set behind them was changing.

Examples of an *"in one"* song include the following:

>> In "Little Lamb" from *Gypsy* Louise sings in her bed while the set behind the drop is changing to a vaudeville theatre for "Dainty June and Her Farmboys."

>> Fanny Brice's Mom and Fanny's close friend Eddie in *Funny Girl* sing "Who Taught Her Everything She Knows." While they sing of teaching Fanny all of her skills, the set behind the drop is changing to the Ziegfeld Follies so Fanny can star in "His Love Makes Me Beautiful."

There's no longer a need for these types of songs because scene changes can now happen seamlessly thanks to the advances of automation. But if that need hadn't existed, fabulous songs like "You Gotta Have Heart" from *Damn Yankees* and the title song from *Guys and Dolls* would never have been written!

Scene change music — Covering a small set change

Related to songs "in one" is scene change music. Musicals used this type of music for the shorter set change. If a few chairs had to go off stage at the end of a scene and a park bench and a hot dog stand had to come on for the next scene, a show would often have a blackout while the orchestra played some scene change music.

Musicals during the Golden Age often used scene change music. Today however, the goal is to make everything seamless and not have blackouts for set changes. But if you're seeing an old-school show and the scene change music begins, this is an ideal time to whip out your program to see how many more songs there are before you can take a much-needed bathroom break.

Dance break — Give them a chance in their wooly jazz pants!

When you're listening to a cast album and you hear the singing stop and the orchestra take over, you're probably listening to a dance break. Yes, some songs feature performers singing and dancing at the same time, but the heavy-duty dancing happens during a dance break. This is a way to make dancing the entire focus; plus, it's difficult to do exerting dance steps while singing full out!

Dance breaks more often happen in group numbers, like The *Pajama Game*'s "Once A Year Day," "Dancing through Life" from *Wicked*, and "We're in the Money" from *42nd Street*, but they also happen during small group or solo numbers. For example, in *West Side Story*'s "America," Anita and her Shark girls have light dancing throughout their singing segments; at the end of every chorus, there's a long dance break where they really break out the kicks, turns, and all-around amazing dancing. Same thing with "The Music and the Mirror" from *A Chorus Line*. Cassie has some poses/moves while she's singing, but two extended dance breaks in the song allow her to go to town . . . ending in relentless double pirouettes!

REMEMBER

These examples of dance breaks really highlight the fact that Broadway performers are often athletes. To be able to dance up a storm and *then* sing up a storm takes such training. Think about how out of breath you are after doing 30 minutes of cardio. Then try to sing a big Broadway song. That's what Chita Rivera and Donna McKechnie had to do eight times a week. After each dance break, they'd come back singing without the huffing and puffing most people would be doing. #AddDanceBreakstotheOlympics

SETH SPEAKS

Marissa Jaret Winokur, who had to do a lot of dancing and singing at the same time in *Hairspray*, told me she prepared for the role by jogging on a treadmill while singing the score! That way she got used to being able to belt *while* out of breath. It worked, and she has the Tony Award to prove it!

Underscoring — Adding emotion to a scene

The orchestra plays this music while scenes are happening, as opposed to scene change music that happens between scenes. Although underscoring is much more common in films, it happens during musicals and, like in films, it helps an audience know the emotion of a moment. Something lush can make a love scene more romantic; something bouncy and peppy can add humor to a comedic scene.

Underscoring is almost never featured on cast albums unless the scenes themselves are recorded, too. If you're curious to hear scene music from a show, get a complete cast recording. Usually, albums are just the songs, but complete cast recordings have underscored dialogue like *South Pacific* with Paige O'Hara and Justino Díaz or *Guys And Dolls* with Gregg Edelman, Kim Criswell, Tim Flavin, and Emily Loesser. (Yes! The composer Frank's daughter!)

Uptempos and ballads — Expressing emotions on both ends of the spectrum

These terms "uptempos" and "ballads" pertain to the tempo of a song (fast is *uptempo* and slow is *ballad*). During a Broadway rehearsal, people don't normally say "Let's run the ballad!" or "Let's work on the uptempo!" However, the terms are used at auditions because performers are often asked to bring an uptempo and a ballad to show how they'd perform the two types of songs. The theory at auditions is that uptempos are usually positive songs and ballads are usually sad songs, and a performer can show their acting range by singing both types of songs.

Ballads often convey negative emotions like romantic pain ("So in Love" from *Kiss Me, Kate*), regret ("She Used to Be Mine" from *Waitress*), loneliness/simmering anger ("Lonely Room" from *Oklahoma!*), mourning ("It's Quiet Uptown" from *Hamilton*), or anything else that's on the sad spectrum. On the flip side, musicals have sometimes used the dramatic nature of a ballad for comedic purposes, like when Sara Ramirez's character wasn't seen for a large portion of *Spamalot* and finally came onstage singing the ballad "Whatever Happened to My Part?" (called "Diva's Lament").

SETH SPEAKS

"Whatever Happened to My Part" is similar to "Dance Ten: Looks Three" from *A Chorus Line*. Why? Because the repeated phrase in "Diva's Lament" is "Whatever happened to my part?" and repeated phrases are often the titles of songs. But if the audience flipped through their Playbill and saw that song title coming up, they'd know what the joke was before Sara sang it. So the title is "Diva's Lament" in order not to ruin the laugh. The same with "Dance: Ten, Looks: Three." The repeated phrase (NSFW!) is "Tits and ass." That actually *was* the title of the song when the show first began performances at the Public Theater, but the audience wasn't laughing as hard as they should when the lyric was first sung because they were expecting it. So, the title was changed to "Dance: Ten, Looks: Three" which made "tits and ass" a surprise, getting a huge laugh.

SNAP, SNAP! PICK IT UP

SETH
SPEAKS

Sometimes a pianist at an audition does play an uptempo too slowly and either the singer is stuck singing the song too slowly or the singer can try to speed up the tempo by singing faster to see if the pianist picks up on the hint. Or Kelli O'Hara style, the singer can take things into their own hands. Or should I say their own fingers? Kelli told me that when she was first starting out and not familiar with the legends of Broadway, she went to an audition but discovered the pianist was at lunch. She had a limited window and had to audition then or not at all. A few people in the audition room were involved with the production, and one of the men volunteered to play the piano.

When he began her uptempo, he played too slowly so she snapped her fingers in his direction to get him to move it. It was a little pushy on her part, but she was desperate to impress the people auditioning her and the pianist was bringing her down. Little did she know, one of the people she needed to impress was her fill-in pianist: *Marvin Hamlisch*! She didn't realize the composer of the musical himself was the one who volunteered to play for her! Luckily, he thought it was hilarious and not only did she get the role in *Sweet Smell of Success*, but she also ended up years later concertizing with him around the country, and he'd always tell the audience the story of when she snapped at him.

Uptempos are often songs conveying positive emotions ("Put on a Happy Face" from *Bye Bye Birdie* or "Gimme Gimme" from *Thoroughly Modern Millie*), but they can also be songs of bitterness ("Leave You" from *Follies*), comedic mental deterioration ("Breaking Down" from *Falsettos*), frustration ("Show Me" from *My Fair Lady*), or any other emotion. The one constant is that the tempo isn't slow.

Duets, trios, quartets . . . Not a solo, not a group number

These types of songs feature more than one person. The most common of these combinations in musical theatre is a *duet*, where two people sing together. Often, they sing of being in love with each other ("You Are Love" from *Show Boat* or "All the Wasted Time" from *Parade*), but they can also be used to convey other feelings — like a discontented marriage ("Every Day a Little Death" from *A Little Night Music*), pondering the meaning of existence ("Why Am I Me?" from *Shenandoah*), feeling too old to get married ("I'm Past My Prime" from *Li'l Abner*), romantic competition ("Mine" from *On the Twentieth Century)*, or anything else.

Trios are songs featuring three people, and these songs rely less on the theme of love than duets. Certainly, I can't think of any song where all three are equally in love with each other. Broadway hasn't graduated to a happy throuple yet. However, sometimes two of the people are in love and one is left out ("A Heart Full of Love" from *Les Miz*), or sometimes three people sing about their dissatisfaction with dating the same person ("You Could Drive a Person Crazy" from *Company*). And sometimes one person is commenting to the audience about the actions of the other two who are falling in love ("Been a Long Day" from *How to Succeed in Business without Really Trying*).

Quartets are . . . wait for it . . . songs with four people singing together. You guessed it! Yes, love is sometimes the theme, like the two happy couples in "You're Gonna Love Tomorrow/Love Will See Us Through" from *Follies*, or, like the other groupings, a quartet can be about anything: four men singing about their enjoyment of watching various women pass by ("Standing on the Corner" from *The Most Happy Fella*), four kids doing a school assignment ("The Book Report" from *You're A Good Man, Charlie Brown*), or four people declaring that they don't want their art to be ordinary ("Nine People's Favorite Thing" from *[title of show]*). The only constant is having four people singing.

After quartets there are *quintets* (with five people), the most famous being the "Tonight Quintet" from *West Side Story*, and *sextets* (with six people, also known as anything from the musical *Six*). After you get more than six people, the song is usually called a group number.

Group numbers — Mixing up the singing with most of the cast

There's no definition for how many people are in a group number. For this book's purposes, I go with more than six. Often, the entire cast or almost the entire cast of the show is singing. Group numbers can be placed anywhere in a show — opening, closing, and everywhere in between. They can start with just one soloist and then expand to many people singing together, like "Before the Parade Passes By" from *Hello, Dolly!* They can have multiple soloists and groups of people singing throughout like "96,000" from *In the Heights*. Or they can be an entire group singing the entire time like "The Ascot Gavotte" from *My Fair Lady*.

Finale of Act One — Ending on a high note!

Almost every musical that has multiple acts ends Act One with a song. The majority end with a group number that has a big finish like "One Day More" from *Les Misérables* or "Go, Go, Go Joseph" from *Joseph and the Amazing Technicolor Dreamcoat*. *Wicked* ends Act One with "Defying Gravity," which is basically a duet that brings in the entire ensemble for the final moments, so the act ends with everyone singing a big chord together. A few shows end Act One with a solo song like "There's a Fine, Fine Line" from *Avenue Q*, "The Story Goes On" from *Baby*, or "Don't Rain on My Parade" from *Funny Girl*, but they aren't as common (though those songs are fantastic!).

A finale should make the audience want more. They often advance the plot and leave the audience with a question: Effie from *Dreamgirls* is kicked out of her singing group . . .what will happen to her? There's a beautiful wedding, but the Cossacks attack. Will the Jews be able to stay in *Fiddler on the Roof*'s "Anatevka"? The chandelier just almost killed Christine and Raoul in *The Phantom of the Opera*. Can their love survive? There's an entire second act to see, and the finale needs to make the audience want to come back and find out what happens.

Intermission! Time to Stand Up and Stretch (or Go to the Restroom)

The majority of musicals have two acts. Though this seems completely normal to musical theatre aficionados, it's a very theatrical contrivance.

When you go to a cinema to see a film and the lights come up, that's the universal signal that the film is over. House lights coming on in a theatre after Act One is the universal signal that you have a short break until the second act begins. That short break is called the *intermission*. And if you're across the pond, the Brits call it the *interval*.

I've heard from various people who have taken newcomers to the theatre and been asked "Is that it? Is it over?" when the house lights come on. Of course not! There are so many questions to be answered in Act Two! Before the audience gets those answers, though, they have a break that lasts around 10 to 15 minutes. The audience can stay in their seats and flip through the Playbill, get in the line for the bathroom, go into the lobby and get a snack/drink, or step outside for some fresh air (or the opposite of fresh air: a smoke). Make sure you take your ticket with you! Many theatres check your stub to allow you back in.

Intermission is also the time when the audience gets to talk to each other about what they just saw and that's why during previews or out-of-town tryouts (when the show is still making changes), many a creative team person will stand around trying to pick up what the buzz is. If they hear lots of "I got bored during the leading man's big ballad," you can bet there're going to be changes made (see Chapter 4).

The intermission is also a break for most people who work on the show. The cast members often have a costume/wig change but can then visit with each other, and the orchestra members, who've been in the pit for the whole first act, can make a much-needed bathroom break. The crew, however, is often at work because the top of Act Two can sometimes have a completely different set than the end of Act One.

Act Two — Answering the Burning Questions

After intermission comes Act Two. There's not much of a difference in structure between Act One and Act Two except that by the end of Act Two all the unanswered questions from Act One will be answered, such as:

» Will the two couples finally get together? (*Oklahoma!, Guys and Dolls,* and countless other musicals)

» Will the pajama factory get their raise? (*The Pajama Game*)

» Will Jenna stay in her bad marriage or leave it? Will she end up with her married gynecologist? And will she win the pie baking contest? (*My Fair Lady.* Just kidding! *Waitress*)

The one show that has a *huge* difference between Act One and Act Two is *Song and Dance*. The entire first act is just songs with no dialogue. The entire second act is all dance . . . hence the title *Song and Dance*.

These sections examine the different parts of Act Two so you know what to expect as you settle back into your seat after intermission.

Entr'acte — Welcome back to the world of make believe

The *entr'acte* is, like the overture, a medley of themes from the musical that the orchestra plays. It's essentially a palate cleanser like the overture, helping transition everyone from the intermission back to the show. It's also an aural cue for those still in the bathroom line to run back to their seats and hopefully hold it in for the remainder of the show!

Reprise — Repeating a song for a new reason

When a song (or segment of a song) is performed again, it's called a *reprise*. The reprise is usually shorter and sometimes the lyrics are changed. *Note:* A reprise doesn't always happen in Act Two. They can happen in Act One as well. They just have to happen after the initial song is sung.

TIP

A note for how to pronounce reprise: I was always pronouncing it wrong until I heard the lyric in *A Day in Hollywood/A Night in the Ukraine* that rhymed Grauman's Chin*ese* with repr*ise*. That's how I remember it's not pronounced re–*prize*. Thank you, Jerry Herman!

REMEMBER

Reprises happen in musicals for a few reasons:

>> Sometimes the character is reiterating their intention from the first time they sang the song (Rose singing the "Some People" reprise in *Gypsy*).

>> Sometimes the same lyric is sung with a different meaning because circumstances have changed (Angel and Collins sing "I'll Cover You" as a happy love song in Act One of *Rent* and, in Act Two, Collins sings it as a mournful farewell at Angel's funeral).

>> Sometimes the song is sung by another character so it takes on a new meaning (In Act One of *Funny Girl*, Fanny is going to follow her heart and leave her job to be with Nick Arnstein. She sings "Don't Rain on My Parade" to show her singlemindedness. In Act Two, Nick Arnstein is giving up on living a clean life and decides to do something illegal. He also sings of his singlemindedness with "Don't Rain on My Parade").

REMEMBER

One of the reasons for a reprise is the same as the overture: to reiterate a tune so the audience will hopefully leave the theatre humming it.

11 o'clock number — Preparing to wrap things up

Near the end of Act Two, there's often a big number that can be a solo or a group number, but it's big in terms of emotion and/or furthering of the plot. It's also big in terms of enjoyment. An *11 o'clock number* has to be a crowd pleaser.

Why are they called 11 o'clock numbers, you ask? Well, back in the Golden Age, Broadway shows began at 8:30 p.m. and ran until around 11:15. These big numbers aren't the final songs in a show — they happen *before* the final song, around

15 minutes before the end of the show . . . which was around 11 p.m. Hence the name "11 o'clock number."

They can be emotional bring-down-the-house solos like "Home" from *The Wiz*, where Dorothy sings of her yearning for home and how Oz taught her to love; joyous song and dance numbers like "I'm a Brass Band" from *Sweet Charity*, where Charity is overjoyed to finally have somebody love her; songs of self-questioning and regret like "If He Walked into My Life" from *Mame*, where Mame wonders if her "live and let live" attitude was the wrong way to raise her nephew; or comedic tour-de-forces like "Betrayed" from *The Producers* where Max hilariously goes through every plot point of the entire show.

Side note: Nowadays, many Broadway shows start at 7 p.m. The term "9:30 number" still hasn't taken off.

Finale of Act Two— Wrapping it up

Like the finale of Act One, the finale of Act Two is the last song of the act. However, unlike the finale of Act One, which raises questions, this song is often the final resolution to any lingering questions raised in the show.

Sometimes the finale is a brand-new song like "We're Getting a New Deal for Christmas" from *Annie* where everyone celebrates FDR's New Deal, which they hope will end The Great Depression. And the audience knows where Sandy the dog is . . . (spoiler alert!) he's been delivered to Annie in a gift box. Or sometimes it's a reprise of a song like in *Guys and Dolls* where the title song is sung again, but this time the audience sees both couples in their wedding finery.

Back in the Golden Age, the entire cast was usually in the finale and the number would end in a big pose: arms up, smiles forward, women perched on the edge of men's shoulders.

SETH SPEAKS

Chita Rivera told me that it was a huge transitional moment in musical theatre when Gower Champion staged the ending of *Bye Bye Birdie*. Instead of the entire cast being onstage, it was just Chita and Dick Van Dyke. *And* instead of ending facing the audience and ending in a pose with the entire cast, they turned *away* from the audience, held hands, and walked upstage. No big finish . . . just a romantic walk. That had never been done before!

Forty years later, a very similar ending was used in *The Producers* when Matthew Broderick and Nathan Lane sang the final number and then walked upstage to their destiny as famous producers. Not a romantic couple, but business partners and friends forever.

However, the majority of finales still do include the entire cast and end with everyone singing a huge chord and hitting a final pose. *And Juliet* opened on Broadway in late 2022 and the finale has most of the cast singing together and ends with them in a line holding one arm up. Everything old is new again!

Bows — Accepting the audience's adoration

The *bows* are when the cast comes out after the finale, no longer in character, and receives appreciation from the theatre patrons by bowing as the audience applauds. The order of bows usually begins with the ensemble bowing first, then the bigger roles bowing, and it leads up to the final bow being taken by whomever is considered to be the star of the show. (Refer to Chapter 9 for more about bows.)

The megamix — Singing and dancing along

The *megamix* began with the show *Joseph and the Amazing Technicolor Dreamcoat* back in the '80s and has gotten more and more popular. It's like a mini-overture — but instead of the orchestra playing all the themes, the cast sings them.

Megamixes are very common in jukebox musicals where a medley of back-to-back pop songs can get the audience riled up and dancing before they exit the theatre. During the show proper, audiences have to stay in their seat, but everyone usually stands during a megamix and lets the music take over their body. There's clapping, swaying, and literal dancing in the aisles. It all adds up to the audience leaving the theatre filled with endorphins — probably more likely to recommend the show to someone rather than if they left the show directly after the bows.

One of the smart things *Mamma Mia!* did was to have a medley of ABBA hits the audience had heard throughout the night . . . but they also added one hit song that wasn't in the show. Yes, the megamix included "Dancing Queen" and "Mamma Mia," which were both featured in the show, but it also had "Waterloo" (which is *not* in either act) as a surprise treat.

Exit music — So long, farewell

The exit music is like a mini-overture. The orchestra plays a short medley of tunes that happens as the cast leaves the stage post-bows (usually while waving goodbye). It also plays while the audience leaves the theatre. The exit music doesn't last until the last audience member leaves because that would be at least a 15-minute song, but it covers the beginning of the grand exit. After the exit music ends, the show is officially over. And like the end of the exit music, this chapter is officially over!

Chapter 4

Oklahoma, Chicago, Avenue Q: Where Musical Theatre Takes Place

People tend to associate musical theatre mostly with Broadway in New York City. But that's just the flashy tip of an enormous iceberg. In major cities across the country and around the world, you can find musicals just like those on Broadway but with their own flavor, or as the kids say, flava. This chapter examines where musical theatre takes place outside New York City so, wherever you are, you don't feel theatre deprived. Musical theatre is an American art form but a global phenomenon. If you want to find a musical, do as the Schuyler sisters suggest; "Look around! Look around!"

You may be doing your best Schuyler sister imitation right now and looking around (and if you don't know what I'm talking about, listen to the *Hamilton* cast recording), but all you see is your dog sleeping on your bed (which is what I'm looking at). However, if you turn your head in the *other* direction, you may see your laptop and, as the pandemic taught most people, all you have to do is push a few buttons and *voila!* . . . you're watching a streaming musical! And, after you're done watching that, you can leave your abode and go see a brand-new musical that's being created just around the block or a national tour of a smash blockbuster that's visiting your local theatre.

The good news is musical theatre is everywhere, no matter where you are. This chapter explores where you can find one. From schools to places of worship to community theatres to regional theatre to black boxes to backyards to amphitheaters, you don't have to look far to experience live musical theatre!

Identifying the World Capitals of Theatre

Over time, certain cities worldwide have emerged as *theatre capitals*, places where productions and performances are concentrated and frequent in number. They're often destinations to see the best theatre on the planet. This section discusses the different locations known for musical theatre throughout the world.

Broadway in New York City

Times Square (see Figure 4-1), 42nd Street, "The Great White Way," Broadway. Many names describe what's considered by many to be the musical theatre capital of the world. Nestled in the heart of New York City, it's a place of hope, struggle, and (sometimes) triumph. P.S. I'm applying a *very* generous use of the word sometimes.

Often a musical can open to glowing reviews, last for years and still not make back its initial investment. But, despite those odds, opening a musical in a Broadway theatre is the ultimate dream of every musical theatre writer. And being in a Broadway audience is the place where every theatre lover longs to be.

Here I dive deeper into the numbers — of Broadway theatres, of how many seats a theatre needs to have, of new productions each year, and of yearly patrons.

The number of Broadway theatres

Broadway, also referred to as the Theatre District, refers to an area in the midtown Manhattan area of New York City between 40th and 57th Streets and between 6th and 8th Avenues. This range contains 40 commercial theatres. One theatre (The Vivian Beaumont Theatre Complex) is located on West 65th Street a part of the Lincoln Center Theatre, which brings the grand total of Broadway theatres to 41.

Luis Dalvan/Pexels

The 41 Broadway theatres represent the world's most prestigious and important venues for producing musicals. If you see a Broadway show, you should expect to see shows with significant budgets, top-notch talent, and the result of hard work that's been in process for (in most cases) at least several years. Any of the 41 theatres you visit has so much musical theatre history within its four walls. One of my favorite things to read in a *Playbill* is the "At This Theater" page where you can find a list of all the previous productions held at venue. I love sitting in the audience at, say, the Winter Garden and seeing the current *Back to the Future* and also knowing that someone sat right where I am and saw Betty Buckley in *Cats* or Barbra Streisand in *Funny Girl* or Chita Rivera in *West Side Story*.

The number of seats a theatre must have

To be considered a Broadway theatre, a venue must have a minimum of 500 seats. Anything fewer than that number of seats qualifies as either an Off-Broadway or Off-Off Broadway theatre.

Broadway theatres are all *commercial*, or *for-profit* venues, meaning their primary goal is to make money. Producers hope to get long-lasting productions into these spaces to generate revenue for their investors and the theatre owners.

Many other theatres in New York City and elsewhere, however, are *noncommercial* or *nonprofit* theatres. Any revenue they take in goes back to keeping the theatre and the organization running. A famous example is the Public Theatre, founded by director and producer Joseph Papp in 1954. The Public has been responsible for some of the most successful and groundbreaking musicals in history: *Hair*, *A Chorus Line*, and *Hamilton*.

The number of new shows

On average, 40 shows open on Broadway yearly, with approximately 15 being musicals. Some of these musicals last for months and some have been there for years. The longest running musical currently on Broadway is the revival of *Chicago*, which opened in 1996. *Chicago* also happens to be the longest running American musical ever. (As of this writing, the longest running Broadway musical ever is *The Phantom Of the Opera*, which opened nine years before *Chicago*).

The number of patrons

In total, 15 million patrons regularly attend a show on Broadway each year. In 2019, these patrons helped Broadway producers make just less than $1.8 billion in gross revenue. Undoubtedly, the commercial Broadway theatre is one of the most important drivers of the economy for New York City. #Respect

WANDERING OFF-BROADWAY

What makes a theatre Off-Broadway, you ask? Certainly not the fact that the address isn't on Broadway proper. Truth be told, the majority of Broadway theatres aren't actually on the street called Broadway. Most Broadway theatres are actually *off* Broadway, meaning you walk down Broadway and then turn onto a cross street like West 44th or West 45th street to get to the theatre.

An Off-Broadway theatre is considered Off-Broadway if it seats 100 to 499 patrons. (Off-Off-Broadway houses seat less than 100.) Having a small seating capacity doesn't mean small in terms of success. Many hit Broadway musicals started Off-Broadway at theatres like the Lucille Lortel, the New York Theatre Workshop, or Playwrights Horizons. Shows like *Spring Awakening, Once, Sunday in the Park with George, Hedwig and the Angry Inch,* and *Falsettos* all began Off-Broadway and then became huge hits on Broadway. And other musicals like *Forever Plaid, Nunsense,* and *Jacques Brel Is Alive and Well and Living in Paris* stayed Off-Broadway with fantastically long (and financially rewarding) runs. One Off-Broadway show called *The Fantasticks* didn't play Broadway, but that didn't stop it from becoming *the* longest-running musical in history with more than 17,000 performances.

Other musical theatre institutions exist alongside On and Off or Off-Off Broadway. The most successful these days is The Encores! series, which was established to perform concert-style renditions of older and often more obscure musicals. And like Off-Broadway, some shows presented in these stripped-down versions have been so well-received that instead of just running for the scheduled two weeks, they've transferred to Broadway for successful runs like the 1996 revival of *Chicago* and the 2022 revival of *Into The Woods*.

Elsewhere in the United States

Musical theatre is performed in every state in the union, but a few cities are known to have top-notch productions. I'm not referring to the Broadway national tours that come through, I mean the fantastic productions featuring city natives. Those cities include the following:

>> **Chicago:** Chicago has a plethora of high-quality musicals. Not only does it have nearby Northwestern University, which churns out future Broadway stars, but it has plenty of theatres doing limited runs of musicals. They also have their own version of a Tony Award called the Joseph Jefferson Award, or the "Jeff," which is coveted by actors everywhere.

>> **Washington D.C.:** Washington also has plenty of wonderful theatres (including the Signature Theatre, which is technically in Virginia, but people consider a D.C. theatre). Probably the most well-known D.C. theatre is The Kennedy Center, which houses national tours, but also puts on its own productions as well. The theatre produces a wonderful Sondheim series that had a plethora of Sondheim musicals like *Sunday in the Park with George* starring Raúl Esparza and Melissa Errico and *Passion* with Michael Cerveris and Judy Kuhn. More recently the theatre produced a critically lauded *Guys and Dolls* starring Jessie Mueller and James Monroe Iglehart.

>> **Boston:** Bean Town has always had a rich, theatrical history because it usually served as a stop when Broadway shows toured before they opened on Broadway. Broadway creative teams used these pre-Broadway tryouts to make changes, and Boston was especially important because theatre critic Elliot Norton would offer constructive criticism. He served as a critic for 48 years until he retired in 1982. Now an award is named after him for the best of Boston theatre — the Norton Medal. New musicals still stop there before their first bow on Broadway, but you can find plenty of Boston theatre that's not on its way to Broadway.

    And I must also give a plug for nearby Provincetown where I host and music direct concerts with amazing Broadway stars like Audra McDonald, Gavin Creel, and Sutton Foster.

>> **Los Angeles:** Although some people dish Los Angeles for being culturally dead, plenty of wonderful musicals are performed there, especially at the Hollywood Bowl which has seen outdoor productions of *A Chorus Line*, *Hairspray*, and *Les Misérables*.

The West End in London

Rivaling Broadway in terms of being a center of musical theatre is the *West End* in London. However, unlike Broadway, the exact boundaries of the West End are open to debate. As the name implies, the area is to the west of the central part of London and is north of the River Thames that flows through the city.

London is one of the most storied cities in history for theatre and music. Opera and operetta have been part of its cultural attractions over the past centuries so it's no surprise that it became the capital of commercial musical theatre across the pond.

Here I look closer at the West End theatres and what they produce.

A closer look at the West End theatres

Not all the theatres in London are concentrated in the West End, but the West End does have the greatest concentration. Today, the West End has 38 theatres in total, with the oldest venue being the Theatre Royal, Drury Lane (see Figure 4-2), which originally opened in 1663. To compare: The oldest Broadway theatre is the Lyceum, which opened in 1903, so London wins in terms of history. All the hit Rodgers and Hammerstein shows from the United States would open in London at the Drury Lane and that theatre also saw the London debuts of *A Chorus Line, The Producers, Sweeney Todd,* as well a ten-year run of *Miss Saigon*.

FIGURE 4-2:
The Theatre Royal, Drury Lane — the West End's oldest theatre.

Grant Rooney Premium/Alamy

Many of the venues in the West End are in historical buildings that are hundreds of years old, which can mean lovely architecture but occasionally cramped legroom.

If you're seeing a show in London and you're on the stiff side and/or you're a tall drink of water, try to pick a show that's not super-lengthy or at least has an intermission so you can stretch. West End theatres regularly undergo renovation, however, to improve their audience capacity and backstage capabilities so you may luck out and be in a theatre that has ample space for those Tommy Tune legs of yours!

What the West End produces

The West End regularly produces musicals that have either already been seen on Broadway or new ones that are hoping to transfer to New York. A musical that plays in London and New York will look the same in both cities, however, producing musicals on the West End is significantly less expensive than on Broadway because unions aren't as strong in London as they are on Broadway.

The lower production costs in London benefit producers as well as the audience because ticket prices are definitely cheaper than on Broadway, but it does *not* benefit the people working in theatre. For instance, the minimum salary for a Broadway performer negotiated by the union is almost double that of a West End actor — and London isn't a cheap city to live in. Producers like Cameron Mackintosh also own their own theatres in the West End, enabling them to maximize their profits because they don't have to pay rent.

The West End has had lots of long-running hits, and many, like *Cats*, *Evita*, and *The Phantom of the Opera*, also played on Broadway to mega-success. But interestingly, some shows that were major hits on the West End didn't find success on Broadway and vice versa. *Groundhog Day* won the Olivier Award for Best Musical in London but didn't last long on Broadway, and *The Drowsy Chaperone* (which I *loved* when it was on Broadway), hardly made an impression on the West End. There's no exact formula for why certain shows are hits in their respective cities; if you figure it out, contact me ASAP!

In 2022, the longest-running musical in the West End was *Les Misérables*, which opened in 1985. One West End show, however, outranks any other in the world, but it's not a musical: *The Mousetrap* by Agatha Christie opened in 1952 and is still going strong.

Europe

The continent of Europe is so wide, as Liza Minelli sang in the film version of *Cabaret*. Not only up and down, but side to side. The same goes for the scope of musical theatre in Europe. Strong bonds connect musical theatre in Europe and North America. Most musicals that become hits on Broadway and the West End are then staged throughout Europe. Many are international tours, which are a wonderful exchange between nations, cultures, and peoples.

You may be wondering, *won't the shows I attend in Europe be performed in the local language? How will I understand what is going on?* Never fear! Many theatres that attract international audiences have shows performed in English *or* they offer *supertitles* projected above the stage or on the back of seats.

Before you go see a show in Europe, always do your research! You need to know:

>> What shows are playing and where.

>> When the shows are playing (summer seasons are different from the rest of the year).

>> How and where you can safely purchase tickets. Recognized travel sites and guides can help you avoid falling prey to tourist scams.

>> How much of the local currency you'll need.

TIP

You can likely catch an international tour of a Broadway musical if you're traveling, but why experience something you can always get at home? Seek and explore something new! Make sure, however, to learn beforehand what customs and behaviors are expected of audience members. Cultural competence is always essential! For instance, standing ovations have become the norm on Broadway, but they're much less common outside of the United States. If you jump to your feet after a show in Europe, you may be the only one standing . . . except the ushers.

Here I take a jaunt through some European cities that are known for their love of musical theatre. I highlight just a few cities, but other capital cities — like Rome, Madrid, Stockholm, and Amsterdam — also have many musical delights to absorb.

Paris, France

The city of Paris is a short trip from London, and it has an equally important place in theatre and music history. Plenty of songs and musicals have been written about the city, its architecture, its people . . . and its inherent magic! Today, Paris has nearly 150 theatres, and thousands of people attend them daily for spoken drama, musicals, and everything else you can think of!

Even though there's always been a rivalry between Paris and London, the longest running show on the West End actually got its start in France. Yes, *Les Misérables* has music by French natives Claude-Michel Schonberg and lyrics by Alain Boublil — and the original lyrics are completely in French. When the show was brought to London, the Royal Shakespeare Company expanded and staged it with Herbert Kretzmer writing the English lyrics.

As I discuss in the section, "Preparing for a Broadway run — Out-of-town tryouts," later in this chapter, new musicals sometimes do a tour before they come to Broadway to make changes before officially opening. The usual cities for these pre-Broadway tours are Seattle, Chicago, and Boston. Well, another city that's a lot farther away is none other than Paris, France! Yes, Broadway hits *On the Town* and *An American in Paris* were first performed at the Theatre du Chatelet. The City of Lights is becoming the city of out-of-town tryouts!

Berlin, Germany

Just over the eastern border of France, Germany has more theatres per capita than most nations, thanks to generous funding from government sources. The capital of Berlin has been a thriving theatrical hub for more than a century, and no matter what type of musical is your taste, Berlin probably has it! You can find highly experimental new musical theatre works in black box spaces, staples of Broadway's Golden Age at major opera houses, and, of course, cheeky cabarets starring modern-day Sally Bowles!

SETH SPEAKS

I toured Germany with *A Chorus Line*, and the German people love musicals . . . perhaps just as much as sauerkraut. Seriously. It was served with everything. I was so excited when I found an Italian restaurant in Frankfurt so I could escape the German cabbage obsession for one meal. I ordered good old-fashioned spaghetti with tomato sauce and was thrilled to be in a sauerkraut-free zone. Well, as soon as it was served, I dug in and discovered the spaghetti was sitting on a bed of . . . sauerkraut. OMG!

Vienna, Austria

South of Germany is the country of Austria, famous as the home of the Von Trapp family in *The Sound of Music*. The capital city Vienna has a rich tradition of opera and operetta. You can still find these traditional shows playing alongside new works and established hits.

One of my favorite American singers, Drew Sarich, moved to Europe and is constantly starring in shows in Vienna. He's played the lead in Vienna's productions of *Jesus Christ Superstar*, *Jekyll and Hyde*, and the Phantom in *Love Never Dies*, the sequel to *The Phantom of the Opera*. If you're in Vienna and see that he's starring in a show, get tickets as soon as possible! And look him up on YouTube.

Asia

The countries of Asia and the Pacific boast theatrical traditions — many with the essential components of music and dance — that are hundreds and thousands of years old. You can see traditional Asian shows in any Asian country you visit, but a few countries within Asia love Broadway and the West End and have a plethora of opportunities to see classic and contemporary musicals.

Japan

The theatre of Japan relies heavily on an interplay of music, movement, and dance so it's no surprise that its citizens also love Western musical theatre. Not only can you see hit shows like *Wicked* and *Les Misérables* in Japan, but you can also attend concerts with giant orchestras featuring American Broadway stars. Check your local listings when you arrive in your city and see the musical theatre offerings that are available. And, if you see a Broadway/West End musical in Japan, know that it will probably be performed in Japanese. Have some fun and avoid reading the English subtitles. It's fun to see how much of the story you can understand just from the acting choices.

China

China isn't known for creating musical theatre, but the Chinese are known for their traditional opera. Though the name is the same, Chinese opera is different than European opera. Not only does Chinese opera have stylized singing with pitch wavers, crooning, and droning, it also has the traditional extreme makeup that contrasts with the simple sets. Instead of a full orchestra of Western instruments, Chinese opera uses only traditional percussion instruments.

Although an original musical from China has yet to come to Broadway or the West End, Western musical theatre started to be performed in China in the 1980s. Since then, many famous titles have been performed in the country. So much so that since 1991, China has built 25 theatres to accommodate their new love of musicals.

Singapore

The island city-state of Singapore is a world travel destination. Musical theatre here has a truly international flavor, with many companies and tours performing in more than a dozen major venues. The expansive Esplanade Theatre on the Bay complex, completed in 2002, is just one of many venues dedicated to performing arts. Feel free to see your share of musicals when you visit but remember that Singapore has a lot of strict laws.

South Korea

Seoul, the capital of South Korea, has a vibrant theatrical scene with almost 400 theatres and upward of 16 million admissions per year. Even though tours and licensed international productions account for the majority of performances, musicals created by Korean artists are slowly growing in number, thanks to international exchanges of artists, technologies, and ideas.

South America

Those visiting South America will be happy to know that musical theatre is performed in many different South American countries. If you're visiting through that continent, you can see productions of Broadway and West End musicals in Argentina, Brazil, Columbia, and *mas país* (yes, I took three years of Spanish in high school).

SETH SPEAKS

I'm personally very happy that parts of South America have embraced musical theatre because that love contributed to one of my favorite musicals. Back in the 2008, I saw [*title of show*] ten times because I think that show is brilliant. I happen to know that the composer (and co-star) Jeff Bowen and one of the female leads Heidi Blickenstaff met doing *Tommy . . .* in Brazil! So, if Brazil hadn't embraced musical theatre, one of my all-time favorite shows might never have been created!

Africa

The center for musical theatre in Africa is in South Africa. You can see classic Broadway and West End shows as well as see original musicals if you visit Cape Town. As a matter of fact, two original musicals created in South Africa became international hits!

>> *Kat and the Kings* began in South Africa and transferred to the West End. It not only won the Olivier Award in London for Best Musical but the *entire* cast also won the Olivier for Best Actor!

>> *Sarafina!* moved all the way to Broadway in the late '80s. *Sarafina!* was nominated for four Tony Awards.

Australia

You can find plenty of musical theatre Down Under. The capital of Sydney continues to be a world hub of cultural activity. Many around the world will recognize the famous "shells" of the Sydney Opera House, but opera is just part of the vibrant musical theatre culture of the city. Australia has given the world Australian native and Broadway and West End star Hugh Jackman and, in return, Broadway and the West End have given Australia plenty of musicals that play all over the continent.

You can find musical theatre all over the country including:

>> **Sydney:** The Capitol Theatre and the Sydney Lyric Theatre provide international works, and you can also find plenty of home-grown hits to experience.

» **Adelaide:** The Adelaide Cabaret Festival in South Australia has featured lots of Broadway stars in concert like Kristin Chenoweth, Emily Skinner, Bernadette Peters, and Mandy Patinkin.

» **Melbourne:** Melbourne also has its share of musical theatre (see Figure 4-3), but beware: It's not pronounced "Mel-born" as I thought while I was there on tour with Megan Mullally. You're supposed to pronounce it "Mel-bin." Don't be Aussie shamed as I was!

FIGURE 4-3:
A production of
Chicago in
Melbourne.

Sam Tabone/Getty Images

Introducing the Pros in Your Hometown

You may not be able to travel to New York or London or any of the other fabulous locations in the previous section to see a live musical. Although there's nothing like seeing a live show in a world-renown theatre capital, you can see live musicals right where you live — from out-of-town previews to touring productions, to dinner theatres to summer stock, from . . . you get my point. Keep reading for details.

Preparing for a Broadway run — Out-of-town tryouts

A Broadway musical needs more than just a smile and a pair of tap shoes to be a hit. Having time to test and try out a show in front of a paying audience is a crucial phase of a production's development.

Historically, producers and creators wrote and rehearsed a show in New York City. However, before they ever performed before a paying New York audience, they'd take the show out of town for *out-of-town tryout performances*.

The highs of out-of-town tryouts

Out-of-town tryouts can be an exciting time in a musical's development. Getting out of the high-stakes environment of New York City can lessen the stress on creators and performers while giving them time to fix issues with the show. A show can get into excellent shape while in the rehearsal studio, but it can't be molded into its final version until it's been performed in front of an audience.

Knowing what moments gets laughs, what gets applause, what's confusing, what's moving, what's boring, and so forth is what a live audience tells a creative team. They take in the information they're receiving from the audience and use these days, weeks, and months out of town to perfect the show. That often includes rewriting scenes and adding or removing songs. These constant changes mean that audiences at out-of-town tryouts can see a different show from evening to evening. The changes may be incremental during this process, but after amassing these out-of-town fixes, a show can look completely different from its first out-of-town preview to when it finally debuts on Broadway.

Sometimes even a show's name can change out of town. When Rodgers and Hammerstein took their musical version of the play *Green Grow the Lilacs* to the Schubert Theatre in 1943, it was entitled *Away We Go!* Only after a certain song was added did the show gain its immortal title, *Oklahoma!*.

The lowest of the low times

Often, however, the process of fixing a show out of town is *not* pleasant. There's the famous saying that if Hitler were alive today, his punishment should be doing an out-of-town tryout with a show that's in trouble! Why? Well, it's not just changing scenes and songs. Sometimes the producer, director, and writer can write out roles in a show, and/or replace members of the cast and creative team. The list of actors (as well as directors, choreographers, and any other cast members and creative team members) fired out of town and then replaced is lengthy.

One of the most tumultuous out-of-town tryouts was for *The Baker's Wife*, which featured a score by the brilliant Stephen Schwartz. By the end of the out-of-town tryout, the powers that be wound up firing the leading lady, the leading man, *and* the director. When the out-of-town tour went to D.C.'s Kennedy Center, which was its last stop before Broadway, it set the record for The Kennedy Center's smallest audience attendance. Yay? Heartbreakingly for everyone involved, even after the relentless changes to that musical, producer David Merrick felt it still wasn't up to snuff and decided to close it before it opened on Broadway! All that drama and no opening night on Broadway.

SETH SPEAKS

Yes, the stress level while making changes is super high. As a matter of fact, while *Promises, Promises* was in Boston, lyricist Hal David wound up getting so sick that he entered the hospital with pneumonia. But his experience led to a charming lyric; after his release, the creatives realized the audience wanted to see the two romantic leads connect in Act Two so Hal and Burt Bachrach wrote the song "I'll Never Fall in Love Again." With a tip of the hat to his recent illness, Hal added the lyric: "What do you get when you kiss a guy? You get enough germs to catch pneumonia. After you do, he'll never phone ya . . . "

The highs and lows are worth it

With the right creative team and producer, the stress on the road can pay off and wonderful changes are made that turn shows into hits. As I mention in Chapter 11, *Hello, Dolly!* added "Before the Parade Passes By" during its out-of-town tryout because audiences weren't responding to the original ending of Act One that focused on the character of Horace Vandergelder.

Another example of a great out-of-town change is from the musical *Mean Girls*. After it played D.C., the creative team realized the audience loved the character of Damien and wanted more of him in Act Two. This prompted the song writing team to add the fabulous song "Stop" that featured actor Grey Hanson singing up a storm *and* tap dancing.

REMEMBER

WHERE YOU CAN CATCH AN OUT-OF-TOWN PREVIEW

In the early 20th century, cities like New Haven, Boston, and Philadelphia were regular stops for out-of-town previews. For various reasons, those cities aren't common stops anymore for future Broadway shows (except for Boston). Today out-of-town previews can be found in most of the major regional theatre cities in the United States, including Chicago, San Francisco, Washington, D.C., and Seattle.

Being an audience during an out-of-town tryout makes you part of the creative process. The writers and director notice what the audience responds (and doesn't respond) to and they make changes based on your reactions. So, if you have an opportunity to see a show before it comes to Broadway, buy a ticket and be proud that you've contributed to the creation of a new Broadway show. Maybe one day you can tell people "I was at (fill in the blank) before it became the hardest ticket to get on Broadway!"

Taking a show on the road — Touring productions

Usually after a Broadway show has closed, and sometimes while it's still thriving on Broadway, producers send the show across the country or the world in a *touring production*. These tours (sometimes several of the same show are out on the road simultaneously) offer a chance to keep the show's brand and popularity alive and make some money for the investors, creative team, and so on. Sometimes, however, the reverse happens and a production that hasn't played Broadway yet and is not necessarily even slated for Broadway tours as a way to test out potential success on Broadway. For instance, the very British *Six* hit the road before it announced it was coming to Broadway.

Musical theatre tours sometimes feature members of the original cast. I always recommend seeing these tours if possible because those cast members were there when the show was being created and have a special connection to the show. Sometimes a tour doesn't have original cast members, but it will have a recognizable star name to boost ticket sales. For instance, Adam Pascal toured with *Pretty Woman*, Ralph Macchio was Finch in *How to Succeed*, Marie Osmond was Maria Von Trapp in *The Sound of Music* tour, and Betty Buckley led the *Hello, Dolly!* national tour.

If the show became extremely famous on Broadway — like *Hamilton* or *The Phantom Of the Opera* — it doesn't need a star name to be a successful tour. Additionally, a national tour set isn't exactly the same as the Broadway set because it has to be transported to each city and set up at different theatres so modifications have to be made. For instance, when I saw *Legally Blonde* on tour, the sorority girls were all jumping excitedly on the stage during the opening number instead of on the second floor of their sorority house.

First national tours usually visit big cities and stay for at least a week. As the tour continues and the cities become smaller, the stays become shorter. The cast usually flies from city to city on the initial tours. After those larger markets are exhausted, a new tour often goes out where the cast travels by bus on the so-called "bus and truck" tours, named because the cast goes in a bus and the set goes in a truck. Sometimes, however, a show is such a big hit that instead of visiting a city, producers will open a production in a city as an open-ended run. Shows like *Phantom*, *Wicked*, and *Hamilton* all ran for long periods of time in cities outside of New York City.

EQUITY VERSUS NON-EQUITY TOURS

When discussing the Broadway and West End in the section, "Identifying the World Capitals of Theatre," earlier in this chapter, I mention the union. Equity is the Actors and Stage Managers Union for Broadway and the West End, and it exists so actors aren't at the mercy of people in power, which was the case before the union was established.

Being in an Equity show means rules have to be followed that protect performers and stage managers from being exploited. If someone feels that they are being treated unfairly, they can turn to Equity for help. All musicals on Broadway are under Equity contracts.

Tours, however, can be described as "direct from Broadway," with ticket prices the same as a tour that's filled with Broadway actors, yet the tour may be non-Equity and *not* be direct from Broadway at all. Non-union tours are done as a cost-saving device for producers, which unfortunately may come at a cost for the people involved with the show. In a non-Equity show, the performers and stage managers on the tour have none of the guaranteed protection of the union.

Those protections cover the following:

- Rehearsals can run for hours and hours with no breaks. Equity mandates breaks for actors during rehearsals.

- There can be more than eight performances per week affecting the health of the actors. Equity limits how many performances can happen per week.

- There might be makeshift dressing rooms that don't have ample room for the amount of actors hired. Equity investigates dressing rooms in theatres before they're approved for Equity actors.

- There might not be enough bathrooms for everyone backstage. Equity requires a certain amount of bathrooms to which actors have access.

- There are no contributions made for health insurance or pension. Equity mandates that producers make contributions each paycheck that go toward the actors' health insurance *and* their pension.

If you want to buy a ticket to a tour, remember the campaign from Equity to "Ask if it's Equity." Find out if the show you want to see is Equity and then decide whether you want to buy a ticket. If the show is non-Equity, ask why. That's to make producers and presenters aware that the public does care about truth in advertising ("Direct from Broadway" ain't true) and that theatre lovers want their beloved actors and stage managers to have all the protections their union provides. if you buy a ticket for a non-union tour, you may possibly see a wonderful production with wonderful performers, but you can't be certain of how the cast and stage managers are being treated because of the lack of oversight.

Providing professional talent to locals — Regional theatre

Many people tend to think of Broadway as the be-all and end-all of musical theatre in the United States. Although it's certainly important, by no means is it everything! From coast to coast, major American cities have plenty of robust theatre companies producing musicals as good as those in New York City.

The Little Theatre Movement (see the nearby sidebar) strives to provide performances to local theatre audiences across the country without concerns about making a profit. As a result, many regional theatres (but not all) follow nonprofit models today. That doesn't mean people work for free, but salaries are lower than in commercial theatre often with *subscriptions* offered to audiences (pay one price to see all the productions that season). Because of this movement, the rise of the great American playwright happened. Regional theatres didn't face the pressure of making money, so they could create different types of shows.

Over the following decades, financial support from major foundations like the Ford Foundation, and organizations like the National Endowment for the Arts enabled regional theatre companies to grow in size and scope and become major forces in American theatre. Some examples include the Guthrie Theatre in Minneapolis, the Goodman Theatre in Chicago, and La Jolla Playhouse in San Diego.

INTRODUCING THE LITTLE THEATRE MOVEMENT — GET RID OF PROFIT

At the start of the last century, cinema began to replace live theatre. Cities and towns across the country began to have movie houses with packed audiences as opposed to theatres with packed audiences. Why? Ye olde dolla dolla bill, y'all. A ticket to a movie cost much less than a ticket to the theatre. Theatre lovers and theatre makers feared that live theatre would go the way of the dinosaur. Thus was born the Little Theatre Movement, which strove to keep theatre alive across the country, despite Hollywood's growing grip on entertainment.

But how could theatre producers/owners still make a profit? After all, the money the public had been spending on theatre was now going toward new-fangled talking pictures. And another concern was variety — the shows that the general public wanted to see were melodramas and comedies. How could any type of new show be developed when the only way to guarantee profitable ticket sales was to keep churning out melodramas and comedies? Idea: Get rid of the profit!

Many large- and small-scale regional theatres initially intended to produce classical plays and contemporary works that didn't have commercial prospects on Broadway. In recent decades, more have expanded their seasons to include revivals of classical musicals and new works.

Rather than undertake a conventional out-of-town tryout, many producers and creative teams now partner with a regional theatre to develop and premiere a new musical before eventually taking the work to Broadway. The Old Globe in San Diego is a prime example. The hit musicals *Into the Woods*, *The Full Monty*, and *A Gentleman's Guide to Love and Murder* started there.

You can sometimes see big-name stars from Broadway and Hollywood starring in regional theatre musicals. Look at the star-studded cast that did *Follies* at the regional Papermill Playhouse: Ann Miller, Donna McKechnie, Phyllis Newman, Tony Roberts, *and* Kaye Ballard were all singing and dancing on that regional stage. And just because you don't recognize any of the names on the marquee doesn't mean you should walk past the theatre. Each city has their local stars who may be as brilliant as your favorite Broadway star, but they've chosen to stay in their town for various reasons.

"We Open in Venice" (California) — Summer stock

You may notice that plenty of theatres advertise special seasons of productions only during the summer months. These organizations are part of the long tradition of *summer stock* theatres.

Traditionally, summer stock productions featured rotating productions of established or recent theatre works with stock scenery, hence the name. Casts consisted of young professionals and local actors as well as big name stars who did the summer circuit around the United States. TV stars would have the summer off and scratch their theatre itch, and it also provided (and still provides) future Broadway performers a chance to learn the ropes and have a great time!

Summer stock productions often took place in multipurpose venues or outdoor theatres or tents to take advantage of the summer weather. Often performances happened in converted barns, as famously depicted in the MGM movie *Summer Stock*.

SETH SPEAKS

When I did my first summer stock, called the Surflight Theatre on Long Beach Island, we were in a converted garage with a tin roof. When it rained, it was *impossible* to hear the show because the rain on the tin sounded like 1,000 people tap dancing. The most incredible part was the schedule — 12 shows in 12 weeks.

Seriously! We started the first week in June rehearsing *Promises, Promises* and began performances the second week. While we did *Promises, Promises* at night, we rehearsed *Applause* during the day. The next week, we performed *Applause* at night and rehearsed *Grease* during the day — for 12 weeks! And after the performances began, we never had a night off! It was grueling but so much fun! And what an amazing way to get to know all those musicals in a short period of time. If you're a performer and have a chance to do summer stock, I highly recommend it!

Today, you can still find plenty of summer stocks around the country, at least one located in every state. Some have been around for decades and decades like the Cape Playhouse on Cape Cod, Theatre-By-The-Sea in Rhode Island, the Music Circus in Sacramento, and more. Go visit and stay for a few days. Many of them are located in summer tourist destinations so you can see a fabulous musical while on vacation. Some summer stock theatres bring in a new cast for each show, and some (like Surflight Theatre did when I was there) have a cast of actors that take on a new role for each musical performed.

Many of these theatres aren't large and have a "let's put on a show" atmosphere, which adds to the charm, but some major ones are *huge* and have been around for decades. For example, the St. Louis Municipal Opera Theatre (nicknamed "The Muny") presents epic-scale musical performances in a vast outdoor amphitheater that seats 11,000 people! These huge theatres often bring in Broadway stars to perform because the runs are usually short (like two to three weeks), allowing a busy star to take a break in their schedule and play a role they've always wanted.

SETH SPEAKS

DE PLANE, DE PLANE

My favorite summer stock story is about the outdoor Starlight Bowl in San Diego's Balboa Park. It was constructed before San Diego had an airport and, when the airport was constructed, the theatre was in the *direct path* of landing planes. Those planes would drown out any and all noise as they landed, including the orchestra and singing. A system was devised that was used for years — someone would sit on top of the theatre and watch the sky. The pit also had a huge traffic light facing the stage. If no planes were coming, the light was green.

When the lookout saw a plane in the distance, they'd contact the stage manager who would change the light to yellow. When the plane was extremely close and the sound would soon drown out the actors, the light was changed to red and *all* action/music/singing/movement would halt while the plane roared toward a landing. As soon as the plane was out of earshot, the show would resume *exactly* where it left off . . . often in the middle of a song. #CompletelyTrue!

Combining a show and food — Dinner theatre

Dinner theatre can take many forms depending on the location. Some dinner theatres offer food and drink through their exclusive restaurants as part of a complete experience. Others adopt a nightclub or Vegas-style arrangement with special tables or booths for diners and separate seats for those just wanting to see the performances.

Dinner theatres had their heyday in the 1970s and 1980s. Much like summer stock theatres, audiences at dinner theatres in that era could regularly see actors from television in various roles. Many dinner theatres were set up as franchises in major American cities, suburbs, and vacation spots. Some still operate, like the long-running Beef & Boards Dinner Theatre in Indianapolis where I recently saw *Mary Poppins* starring my pal Cara Serber. I say *brava* to the production, and the food was delish — what a combo! I was able to love her performance and gain five to seven pounds, which I'm hoping I burned off from applauding. That's cardio, isn't it?

THE HARD KNOCKS I LEARNED DURING SUMMER STOCK

SETH SPEAKS

My professional debut at a dinner theatre — at the lavish Northstage Dinner Theatre on Long Island — taught me that show business is a business. I was cast at the age of 12 in a production of *Oliver!* that starred Shani Wallis who played Nancy in the film version. I told you stars did dinner theatre! *I loved it*! It was a top-notch production with the same set design used on Broadway, the same choreography (the director/choreographer, Tom Panko, assisted the film version) and, as previously mentioned, the same star from the film! I had my own solo in "Who Will Buy," I got paid (!), and, best of all, I got to leave school early on Wednesdays because we had matinées!

However, right before the *New York Times* came to review the show, I was cut from the finale of Act One. No reason was given. One day we were doing a brush-up rehearsal (Chapter 12 discusses what happens during a brush-up rehearsal) of the number I had been performing every night during previews. Suddenly I was told, very matter-of-factly, that I was no longer in it. Wowza. Did that hurt! I assumed then I was cut because I was overweight (I still don't know the reason!) and, holy cow, I was devastated. Talk about cry me a river. I was *sobbing* — out of earshot; after all, there's no crying in rehearsals.

If you're wondering whether or not you want your child to do professional theatre, I don't *not* recommend it. I really loved 90 percent of it, but your kid has to be strong and have confidence. As a performer, you're there to serve the piece and your feelings really aren't really considered. #CautionaryTale

Mixing thrills with song — Theme parks

Theme parks are a huge part of the vacation landscape that some families traditionally enjoy from late spring to early fall across the country. They are very prominent in the Midwest with famous locations like Six Flags in St. Louis, Great America in Chicago, King's Island in Cincinnati, Cedar Point in Sandusky, Ohio, Hershey Park in, you guessed it, Hershey, Pennsylvania, and, of course, the behemoth: the Disney theme parks.

Most theme parks specialize in roller coasters, themed areas (Harry Potter or Epcot or The Simpsons), and areas that have water features and rides. Many also employ musical theatre performers, designers, choreographers, and directors for the various shows, parades, and other entertainments they offer their patrons.

Most of these productions are built like variety shows, talent shows, or elaborate spectacles like Las Vegas. Theme parks like Six Flags and Walt Disney World draw on their company's roster of movie characters for inspiration.

Few of these musical theatre creations are ever serious in tone, meaning you won't see *Spring Awakening* next to the log ride. Instead, they feature a series of song selections or group numbers spliced together with a thin plot — or often no plot at all.

Musical theatre shows at theme parks can vary from year to year, with musical genres ranging from dance-heavy selections to Motown-meets-Broadway to country-inspired routines in more rustic settings. These examples show just how wide the possibilities of musical theatre are across the entertainment landscape of the United States!

SETH SPEAKS

So many Broadway performers come from theme parks: Paul Castree (ten Broadway shows), Kristin Chenoweth (Tony winner), Wayne Brady (*Kinky Boots*), Stephanie J. Block (Tony winner), and many, many more got their start in theme parks. Tony Award winner Betty Buckley was doing multiple shows every day in Texas theme parks before she ever hit Broadway. Once she said in a concert we did together: "You haven't truly paid your dues until you've learned to belt a song outdoors and, as you're singing swallow a bug . . . and continue singing!"

"Sit Down, You're Rocking the Boat" — Cruise ships

Cruise ships have always had live variety shows, often with at least one Broadway-themed night, but nowadays they have actual musicals being performed at sea. They're *truncated* (shortened) Broadway musicals, because people on a cruise ship don't want to sit for two and half hours seeing a full musical. Why? People, that chocolate fountain is not going to eat itself. But cruisers still enjoy plot along with their songs hence recent shows on cruise ships have included *Hairspray*, *Six*, and *Mamma Mia!*

Many Broadway stars have gotten their starts on cruise ships including Norm Lewis (*The Phantom of the Opera*) and Jennifer Hudson (Oscar winner). And a certain author I know (me!) has his own Broadway-themed cruises! I started Seth's Big Fat Broadway Cruise where I sail around the world every few months and bring three Broadway stars with me. Join me for the belting, the Broadway and the buffet.

BRINGING MUSICAL THEATRE TO THE BIG SCREEN —HOLLYWOOD

Hollywood (alongside Broadway) is a major focal point of entertainment. Although cinema and live theatre operate by different rules and expectations, they have had a symbiotic relationship for more than a hundred years and it's gotten even stronger in the last two decades.

With the advent of synchronized sound in film, musicals became very attractive and lucrative projects for Hollywood studios, producers, and artists. Many movie musicals were adapted from popular Broadway works (think *West Side Story, Fiddler on the Roof, My Fair Lady,* and so many more), but plenty of movie musicals were original works such as *Holiday Inn, Mary Poppins,* and probably the most popular movie musical of all time, *The Wizard of Oz.*

During the 1970s, movie musicals fell out of favor. However, in the 1980s, Disney changed that with enormous success with the animated musicals *Aladdin, The Little Mermaid,* and *Beauty and the Beast.* In 2000, Rob Marshall directed and choreographed the Oscar-winning *Chicago* starring Renée Zellweger and Catherine Zeta-Jones. Musicals could win an Oscar (which translates to money)! Soon movie musicals were back like it was the 1950s.

Before *Chicago,* Hollywood had gone decades without making any Broadway musicals into films; however, since *Chicago* movie versions have been made of *Nine, Into the Woods, 13, Sweeney Todd, Rent, The Prom, In the Heights, Dear Evan Hansen, Matilda,* and more. And now, a new house on the block is bringing Broadway to the masses: the filmed live Broadway performance. To me, that's thrilling because the actual Broadway show with the original staging and the Broadway cast is filmed. Since then shows like *Memphis, Come from Away, She Loves Me,* and that behemoth called *Hamilton* have been filmed. I hope this trend continues so people who never can make it to New York can see hit Broadway musicals as they look onstage.

Meeting the Thespians
in Your Neighborhood

Fans of musical theatre don't just love musicals as a whole, they love Broadway and West End stars! Just go onto any theatre message board like AllThatChat.com or BroadwayWorld.com, and you'll see post after post about why so-and-so is the best Mama Rose *ever* or why so-and-so must have a musical written for them as soon as possible!

Broadway stars of the past like Ethel Merman, Mary Martin, and Leslie Uggams and today's stars like Audra McDonald, Bernadette Peters, Nathan Lane, Sutton Foster, and Lin-Manuel Miranda may command attention, box office success, and relentless posts from fan sites, but they aren't the only performers out there. Plenty of tremendously talented musical theatre performers don't star in musicals on Broadway, but they do star in musicals elsewhere. You can find them in your own neighborhood. The next section gives you some help in finding them.

Shining the spotlight on local performers — Community theatre

Community theatres exist out of a desire to perform without commercial pressures and allow local folks to engage and express their creativity.

Community theatres operate year-round or only during the summer when people have more time to participate. And, because the participants aren't full-time actors, rehearsals are usually at night and on weekends so everyone can keep their regular jobs. (Figure 4-4 shows an example of the Booth Tarkington Civic Theatre, a community theatre in Indianapolis.) Community theatres sometimes have use of the local theatre for their performance, but sometimes other types of venues serve as their playing space: from houses of worship to high school auditoriums to town squares and parks to backyards.

As a matter of fact, when Patti LuPone was growing up on Long Island, she played the role of Louise in her neighborhood's community theatre production of *Gypsy*. She was a member of the Patio Players, so named because the shows were literally performed on a patio — specifically her friend Cathy Sheldon's patio. These shows consisted of young people; however, most community theatres use people of all ages. It truly is *community* theatre!

FIGURE 4-4:
A production of
*Matilda, The
Musical* at Booth
Tarkington
Civic Theatre.

**SETH
SPEAKS**

My co-host on SiriusXM Christine Pedi got her start playing leads in Westchester community theatre, trotting the boards as Evita in *Evita* and Fanny Brice in *Funny Girl*. Her co-star also happened to be her dentist, Dr. Shlotman, but you may not have known that looking in the program because his stage name was Jeff Scott.

Creative teams, performers, and crew members in community theatre give of their own time and energies, often without compensation. The sheer joy of the experience is their reward. And because young people can participate, many actors who go on to professional careers get their first start in community theatre.

Training tomorrow's Broadway stars — University productions

Several outstanding musical theatre schools exist across the country, offering unique training programs for any aspect of theatre a young artist wants to pursue. University settings allow students to hone their talents and give theatre lovers a chance to enjoy high-quality shows at affordable prices.

Today, more than 150 universities and colleges across the United States offer degree programs in musical theatre. Even those without formal musical theatre training units often produce musicals during their yearly production season.

University productions adapt professional models to educational settings. Their seasons span the academic year (that is, fall and spring semesters) and vary in scope based on the institution's size, the available budgetary resources, and the skills exhibited by the students within the program.

Most programs rely on musicals to be the largest revenue-producing events of their production seasons, mostly due to the universal reach and interest associated with musicals across the country. Plenty of up-and-coming talent grows out of these programs. For instance, if you were near Carnegie Mellon University in the '80s, you could have seen *A Chorus Line* with the role of Richie played by future Tony Award winner Billy Porter. If you were in Illinois a few years before that, you could have gone to Northwestern and seen *West Side Story* with Anita played by a future Emmy Award winner Megan Mullally!

GETTING INTO A MUSICAL THEATRE PROGRAM IS RIGOROUS

Being admitted to competitive training programs in musical theatre has become a big business akin to recruiting for major sports. High school students regularly audition for upward of 20 to 25 schools to get into at least one program. Students who can afford it employ private coaches who help them gain skills and access to some of the more prominent programs in the country. This financial reality has elevated the importance of accessibility to an even greater degree across the country.

Still, the choice can be daunting with several factors students must consider when deciding what school to choose, such as:

- **Location (urban versus rural universities):** I know that when you're a young person in school, you often crave the fun of a big city. However, I went to Oberlin College, which is in a *little* town in the middle of Ohio. I'm so happy that we had basically nothing to do in terms of bars and clubs because it meant I really got to know my fellow students (game nights!) and created friendships that have lasted to this day.

- **Specialized conservatories versus liberal arts institutions:** Oberlin is a conservatory, but I'm so glad it was attached to the college because it allowed me to meet other people who had interests outside of the arts, *and* it allowed me the opportunity to take different types of classes. I'm not saying not to go to a conservatory because those training programs can be fantastic but try to get as much education in other areas as you can!

- **Schools that emphasize just acting versus musical theatre schools that emphasize all aspects of performing:** Musical theatre requires acting skill. Furthermore, most musical theatre conservatory students have to study all different types of plays and playwrights — Shakespeare, American contemporary, American classic, French farce, Greek, and so on. Why not study all of that *and* singing and dancing at the same time? If there's any possibility you're going to pursue musical theatre, get that training at the same time you're getting acting training!

(continued)

(continued)

- **Opportunities:** Some theatre schools provide few opportunities for students, meaning the first year they're only allowed to do crew work, the second-year ensemble work, the third-year secondary leads, and the fourth year possibly feature roles. Find a school that allows you various performance opportunities from the beginning. I'm not saying you should be playing leads your first year, but you should have chances for scene study classes, cabarets, full musicals, student musicals, black box festivals, and so on.

- **Cost:** It's your money and your time, so get the most out of those four years. Theatre schools can be extremely expensive. Apply for scholarships, even if it's not a "top tier" school. You don't want to graduate and have to take a full-time job outside the theatre that doesn't allow you the opportunity to perform just so you can pay back your college loans!

   My advice: Go to theatre message boards like AllThatChat.com or Broadway World.com and ask other people for the inside scoop on any school you consider. The people who have been there know best and can tell you what's great and what's not so great.

Teaching students the ways of theatre — K-12 school productions

Many performers and audience members get their love of musical theatre from productions put on at their local schools. Theatre at public and private K–12 institutions can be the gateway to lifetimes of interest and passion in musicals and much more.

I don't mean just being in the shows, I also mean seeing the shows as an audience member. I've been seeing Broadway shows since I was 4, but I was even more mesmerized when I went to the local junior high or high school to watch their musical productions. Seeing kids *like me* putting on a show made me *so* look forward to getting older so I could do theatre at school!

Certain K-12 schools can offer students even more specialized training in the performing arts. You can often find immersive schools of the arts in most major cities. The most famous example is Fiorello H. LaGuardia High School, which was the setting for the movie musical and television series *Fame*. P.S. If you've never seen the movie, do so as soon as you can. It holds up and accurately shows training for the arts and the hopes that sustain you as well as the horrible realities that sometimes destroy your hopes.

TIP

If your local school doesn't offer a musical theatre program, go to SchoolTheatre. org run by the Educational Theatre Association and investigate their JumpStart Theatre Program. This fully funded program helps schools put on their very first musicals by providing all the material, training, and budget that they need to put on a show.

Showcasing outside-the-mainstream productions — Fringe events

Fringe theatre encompasses events and styles of performance that operate outside of mainstream models. They offer adventurous productions with adventurous subject matter in adventurous locations. Fringe theatre embraces the unconventional and unexpected, so never expect the expected.

The phrase "fringe festival" may sound familiar. These events gather selected fringe-style performances in a particular location during a specific period of time. Some, like the famous Edinburgh Fringe Festival, started as a response to major international summer festivals. Today, you can find dozens of fringe festivals across the world. As off-the-grid as the name implies, these productions can wind up becoming commercial successes. The international hit show *Six* began at the Edinburgh Fringe Festival and the multi-Tony Award winning *Urinetown* got its start at the New York International Fringe Festival. Take a trip to a fringe festival and, no matter what, you'll see something memorable!

Chapter **5**

Experiencing the Magic of Musical Theatre

Being a *patron* (also known as an audience member) of musical theatre isn't just a matter of showing up. Attending the theatre involves customs and more, and the more you understand them, the more fruitful and positive your theatre-going experience will be.

You may be wondering:

» How do I get tickets?

» Must I mortgage my house to pay for a ticket?

» What are the best seats?

» What should I wear?

» How will I best experience the work on stage as a member of the audience?

Let me answers these questions (and more!) for you and soon, you can answer those questions for other live theatre newbies.

Naturally, your experience will vary based on where you go to the theatre. After all, seeing a show on Broadway certainly isn't the same as seeing a dinner theatre show in Tennessee, a collegiate production in Indiana, or a touring musical on the

West Coast. Nevertheless, there are many important "ground rules," so to speak, for you to know. Here I begin by using the Broadway experience as a reference point as you embark on the magical journey of attending the theatre.

Overture — What Happens before the Curtain Rises

Going to the theatre doesn't involve *just* going to the theatre. It should be a whole experience that includes before *and* after the actual show. Transportation, food, drinks, (and even getting autographs) are all part of attending live theatre, all which I discuss here.

"This Is All Very New to Me"

When I was a kid, my parents or older sisters would buy the cast albums of current shows. Yes, I said albums. Back in the '70s, there were no CDs, and certainly no laptops, smartphones, tablets, and so on, and the words "downloading" or "streaming" weren't in the zeitgeist — nor did I know what the word zeitgeist meant. I'd listen to the albums over and over and memorize them. Then I'd beg my parents to buy tickets to the show.

Hearing the songs I knew so well performed live in front of me was thrilling. *And* it was so much fun to see the staging of each song. Yes, I knew the lyrics backward and forward, but I had no idea what it would actually look like when those lyrics were sung. However, as I got older, I began to see shows I knew nothing about, which was also super fun. Hearing a score for the first time *live*, and, if I liked it, going out and buying the album to listen obsessively to the songs I loved. My point is, you can either listen to a show before you see it *or* see it without knowing any of the music. Both have advantages!

"Far from the Home I Love"

Getting to the theatre is an important part of the experience. Transportation needs can vary by situation. The people who experience Broadway either are residents of New York City and its surrounding boroughs or visitors from other parts of the country and the world.

REMEMBER

Those traveling within the city or from the surrounding boroughs usually take public transportation to reach their theatre destination(s). You can find many cost-effective options available via subway or bus, but make sure you research your route beforehand to plan for construction and other issues and leave plenty of time so you aren't late. And don't assume riding in a cab/ride share is the fastest way. I have experience taking a cab from the Upper West Side during bad traffic and arriving too late to see the show! I wasn't that upset about missing the show because I knew I could get tickets again. It was the relentless "I *knew* we were leaving too late" comments from my mother that still ring in my ear and make me ever-aware to hop on a subway when running late. If you decide to use your own car, just know that parking can be expensive, and if you want to park on the street, I wish you good luck! I advise parking somewhere on the cheap side — not in the theatre district — and then taking public transportation.

TIP

If you must bring your own vehicle (or a rental) into the city, try to locate a parking garage close to the venue for your show *without* it being within the Theatre District proper. Doing so will help make your exit easier after the performance.

Also, if you plan to go out for drinks or food after the show, make sure the location where you park allows vehicles to be there late. After all, the last thing you want is to arrive at your garage at 1 a.m. and find it closed! I remember doing a benefit concert with Vanessa Williams and after the after-show celebration, she couldn't get her car! If a former Miss America can't get a parking garage to open after closing, there's not much hope for us common mortals.

Finally, no matter how you travel, ensure that you budget enough time to arrive at the theatre on time, if not early. Nothing is more stressful than sprinting across city traffic to make your performance! Just ask my blood pressure after I took that cab with my mom.

"Food, Glorious Food"

You can enjoy a pre-show dinner or drinks in areas surrounding the theatre before your show starts. Helpful hint: Make a reservation (especially if you have a larger party) ahead of time because restaurants fill up quickly.

In New York City, theatre fans love to visit a few specific restaurants, and you can often see Broadway stars there as well! "Restaurant Row" on 46th Street between 8th and 9th Avenues in the Theatre District has two dining establishments where you'll see some of your fellow theatre fans and perhaps a Tony winner or two. One is Orso and the other is Joe Allen. Both are delicious, and if you visit Joe Allen, you'll see its famous adornment of Broadway show posters. The concept of having show posters is famous, but the shows themselves aren't famous to most people. Joe Allen displays posters only from shows that are considered "flops."

Of course, one person's flop is another person's cult favorite, but the requirement to get on the wall is a show that played very few performances. Eyeing your show on the wall can sting for some people, but others see it as a badge of courage. Priscilla Lopez and I did an act together, and she talked about *Breakfast at Tiffany's* being her first show poster at Joe Allen's. Another theatre favorite is Sardi's on 44th Street between 7th and 8th Avenues. If eating in a restaurant with working actors is something you definitely want to experience, then go out for a meal *between shows,* meaning between a matinée and a night show on a Wednesday or Saturday.

And go to 9th Avenue in the West 40s. Lots of performers don't want to head home after a matinée and will head over there to hang out with their friends.

Like on a safari, you can use visual clues to know for sure whether you're seeing a working actor. Back in the '80s, they'd be wearing a show jacket, which were all the rage. The jacket had the name of the show you were in — a perfect way to keep warm *and* brag. Nowadays, you can easily recognize the women because almost every female on Broadway is wigged. After you do your *wig prep* (putting your hair under a wig cap), you don't want to do it again for the night show. Furthermore, eye makeup and lashes are an ordeal many don't want to repeat. Look for females in full over-the-top eye makeup/lashes who are wearing a baseball cap or some kind of hat to cover their wig cap!

Make sure you give yourself time to eat and drink and arrive at the theatre without being rushed. Also, don't overindulge beforehand, because doing so can impede your enjoyment of the performance — and the audience around you. In many theatres, if you leave your seat to use the restroom, you can't reenter the theatre until intermission. And I know this is dark information but I've been in the orchestra pit during a show when audience members have had heart attacks. Sometimes it's because they've eaten up a storm at dinner and then exerted themselves climbing the stairs to the balcony. So eat lightly and stay alive!

"Put on Your Sunday Clothes"

It seems that dressing for the theatre has gone the way of dressing for an airplane ride. Back in the day, people were in the most fabulous "see and be seen" outfits to attend an Ethel Merman vehicle or take a flight to L.A. Nowadays it's anything goes outfit-wise for a flight or a show. It certainly feels great to dress up to see a show and makes the experience more special and celebratory . . . but just remember theatre temperatures vary. You may be cold or hot, so layers are helpful. And what looks fabulous doesn't always *feel* fabulous when sitting for a few hours. Feel free to dress up but perhaps not in your favorite corset. Wearing comfortable and casual clothing is certainly allowable and acceptable.

When selecting clothes for Broadway productions, remember the following:

>> **Wear clothing that works for whatever pre-show or post-show activities you have planned.** Going to the theatre is an event that will often be part of a more significant, more expansive evening or day. For example, if you plan on walking through Central Park after your show, plan accordingly. Yes, there is a coat/bag check at the theatre but arrive early enough to use them. It drives me crazy OCD-wise when someone has a coat on the back of their seat, and I can feel it on my knees or my arm!

>> **Wear sensible shoes.** Stairs are often something you may need to negotiate in the theatre, which can and should affect your footwear choices — particularly if you're seated in the balcony.

>> **Avoid wearing large hats.** Many times, people are seated directly behind you, which may make large hats problematic for your fellow audience members. Quite frankly, a hat that isn't completely flush with your head doesn't really have a place in the theatre unless you're in the back row. Just say no to Elaine Stritch's question from *Company* ("Does anyone . . . still wear . . . a hat?")

>> **Make smart jewelry decisions.** If you wear jewelry, make sure that it's not loud or distracting to you, fellow audience members, or worse, performers. When you see *Meet Me in St. Louis,* "clang, clang, clang" should go the trolley . . . not your chunky necklace. And, before you ask, "Why is he mentioning a movie musical?" I'll tell you that it was also a Broadway musical in the late 1980s. And future Tony Award winner Rachel Bay Jones was just 19 years old and in the ensemble.

>> **Be aware of smells.** Yes, I love my cologne, but just know many people *hate* the smell of perfume/cologne. I'm not saying *don't* apply anything but keep it so it's only noticed if someone is nuzzling your neck. However, if you make the bold choice of wearing a tank top or something else on the more upper-body-revealing side, slather on the deodorant. And save the crystal for your yoga group because I have to experience it every working!

"Days and Days"

Broadway no longer has a set schedule. And shows can change their schedules every few months, so make sure you check your ticket for curtain time.

When I began working on Broadway, productions typically happened Tuesday through Sunday with 2 p.m. matinées on Wednesday and Saturday and night curtains at 8 p.m. Monday was the day off. Then *everything* changed.

When I did *Grease!!!*, there was a time period where we had an 8 p.m. Thursday and Friday show, a 2 p.m. and 8 p.m. Saturday show, a 1 p.m. and 5:30 p.m. Sunday show, an 8 p.m. Monday and Tuesday show, and Wednesday was our day off! The late '90s revival of *You're a Good Man, Charlie Brown* had one weekend day with *three* performances!

TIP

If you arrive late for a show, you don't always get to rush to your seat muttering "Sorry." There are certain shows that won't allow you in until a certain point in Act One. So, *know your curtain time!*

Understanding the Inside of a Theatre —Stage and Seating

The following sections can help you understand where you want to sit. It's all about how the seats are laid out, as well as the type of stage as well as personal preference. Read on!

Considering the type of stage

The *house* is the part of the theatre where the audience sits, as distinct from the *stage*, which is where the performers are.

SETH SPEAKS

The audience sometimes isn't just sitting in the house, they're also on stage. A few shows in the early 2000s had onstage seating: *Xanadu* and *Spring Awakening*. And *Natasha, Pierre and the Great Comet of 1820* not only had onstage seating, but you were at a table . . . and served some delicious pierogies to get you in the mood for a musical that took place in Russia!

No two theatres are exactly alike, but you can count on some similarities. Most Broadway venues are *proscenium* stages (see Figure 5-1), meaning the house is separate from the stage where the actors perform. The stage functions almost like a picture frame with an invisible wall.

Sometimes theatres are built or configured according to other designs. With *thrust stages* (see Figure 5-2), the audience surrounds the stage on three sides. The stage is thus thrust into the middle of the seats.

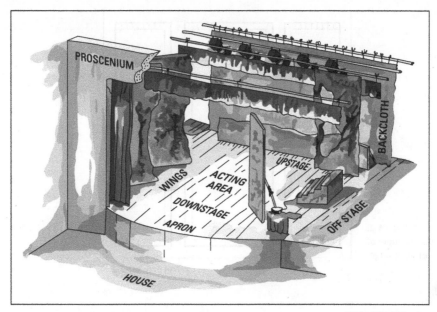

FIGURE 5-1:
An example of
a proscenium
stage.

© John Wiley & Sons, Inc.

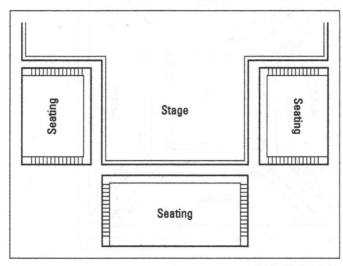

FIGURE 5-2:
An example of a
thrust stage.

© John Wiley & Sons, Inc.

An *alley stage* (refer to Figure 5-3) means the audience sits on opposite sides of the stage area, which runs down the middle, like an alley.

Sometimes, the audience surrounds the stage on all sides! This layout is called *in the round* (refer to Figure 5-4) because everywhere the performers look around, they see the audience.

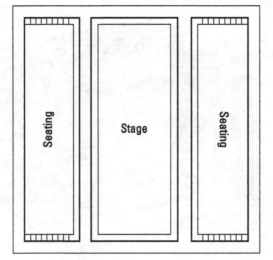

FIGURE 5-3:
An example of
an alley stage.

© John Wiley & Sons, Inc.

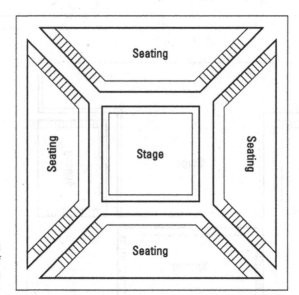

FIGURE 5-4:
An example of
a theatre in
the round.

© John Wiley & Sons, Inc.

SETH SPEAKS

When Tony Award–winning *Fun Home* transferred from The Public Theatre to Broadway's Circle in the Square Theatre, Judy Kuhn went to lunch with her friend and was telling her about the transfer. Immediately, her friend asked Judy to stand and turn around. Judy was confused but obliged. Her friend nodded and told her "You'll be fine!" Judy realized that her friend was preparing her for an audience on all sides of her . . . and, because Judy would be seen from the back, she wanted to make sure Judy's butt looked good. Thankfully, her friend approved!

IS THERE A MUSICIAN IN THE HOUSE?

The most common type of stage for musicals was and still is the proscenium. It became the most common because it allows room in front for an orchestra pit. The pit has that name because it's on a level below the stage. The musicians take the stairs down from stage level to enter the pit. The conductor is also in the pit but is usually standing on a platform so the performers on stage (as well as the musicians) can see the conductor at work.

Back in the Golden Age, the pit had no covering because the sound of the orchestra came up from the pit and filled the theatre. Nowadays, everything is done through an electric sound system, so although the proscenium is still common, the pit has changed. Sometimes it's completely covered (because the instruments are mic'd so there's no need for an open top) and sometimes there's no pit at all. The musicians can be anywhere in the theatre. During the Golden Age, you could walk to the front of the theatre and look over the pit and see a bunch of musicians in black outfits staring up at you. Nowadays, you can't do that at every musical, but rest assured that every musical has live musicians playing. They just sometimes do it in a tucked-away place!

Identifying the best seats in the house

Getting the best seats in the house for any musical theatre event is a thrilling experience. But where exactly are the best seats? The following sections break down the different seating options in a proscenium-style theatre. Figure 5-5 shows an illustration of these seating options.

Sitting in the orchestra (No, not next to the violinists)

When going to the theatre, specifically a proscenium-style theatre, the best seats are often called *orchestra seats*. Of course, they aren't in the orchestra pit itself, but they're closest to where the orchestra pit is, hence the name orchestra seats. *Note:* I don't know if that's the actual reason for the name, but it makes sense so I'm committing to it.

REMEMBER

That's not to see that every seat in the orchestra section is the best. Being all the way on the right or left can cut off your view of the opposite side of the stage making you constantly whisper to your seatmate, "Wait, who's talking right now? I can't see!" And being in the very first few rows can mean that you have to have your head tilted at an angle that might necessitate a deep tissue massage the next day.

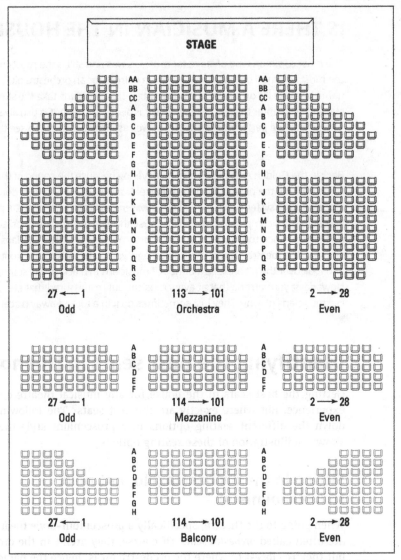

FIGURE 5-5:
The seating
options in
a house.

© *John Wiley & Sons, Inc.*

TIP

For maximum comfort/best viewing, most people prefer orchestra seats from around the fifth to the 15th row — and the more toward the center, the better. And, if you want to be super comfortable, an aisle seat allows you your own private arm rest and the opportunity to stretch those gams!

No matter how amazing your seat is, the seats themselves seem to be getting narrower. (I'm not saying that (necessarily) because middle-age spread has begun.) It's often because some theatres have been "updating" their seats. Updating doesn't mean making them more comfortable; it often means cramming more seats in the theatre. Why? Money! The more seats there are, the more tickets can be sold and the more money a theatre can make.

REMEMBER

Because orchestra seats are usually the best seats, you can probably guess that they're also the most expensive seats in the house. Also, very popular shows cost more money. In 2022, shows like *The Music Man* and *Hamilton* had an average ticket cost of more than $225 per ticket, with orchestra seats being closer to $350.

Cue the "in my day" speech. Seriously. I remember my mom getting my tickets to *Chicago* with Chita Rivera and Gwen Verdon. I was a kid and was excited she was spending 9 whole dollars on a ticket! Ticket prices have *not* matched inflation. They have far exceeded it. Plenty of articles have been written about why the cost has gone up so much, and all I will say is it's not because of musicians. The good news: You can get low-cost tickets if you know where to find them. (I offer some suggestions in the section, "Getting Tickets to the Hottest Show in Town," later in this chapter.)

Getting a bird's-eye view of the stage from the mezzanine

Most Broadway theatres have a second level above the orchestra, referred to as the *mezzanine*. These seats are *often* cheaper than the best orchestra seats, and many people prefer them to orchestra seats because they're higher up and give a more expansive view of the entire performance. Also, because of how the second level of the theatre is constructed, these seats are often closer to the stage than those seats in the back of the orchestra.

THE PROS AND CONS OF BOX SEATS

If you've been to the theatre before, you may have noticed those obvious private seating areas along the side walls of the auditorium or maybe on a special balcony level. Those areas are called *boxes,* and the seats within them are called *box seats.*

People tend to think of box seats at the theatre as super exclusive, which was indeed true back in the day. The historical purpose of box seats was for the rich and powerful to see and for them to be seen, sometimes even more than the event people were attending.

Today, box seats may still seem to exude power and privilege, but on a practical level, they usually aren't constructed at the best angle to experience a performance compared to orchestra seats. Basically, one half of the stage is blocked so you miss a lot of the action, but at least your amazing outfit gets to be admired, right?

Sitting in the balcony

The most affordable choice for seats is also the most isolated. The *balcony* offers theatregoers a personal but distant opportunity to be "in the room where it happens." Balcony seats are by far the cheapest option available to patrons.

In the balcony, you're often far away from the stage. Patrons often bring binoculars to help them see. If you choose, bring a small and lightweight pair.

Don't let the distance discourage you. These seats attract some of the most interesting patrons. You could find yourself with students attending their first Broadway show, with local theatre lovers enjoying their favorite show for the umpteenth time, or with a touring company specializing in a New York City experience.

REMEMBER

Balcony seats have some very real and practical benefits:

>> **They offer a clear view of the entire stage.** Balconies also offer a bird's-eye view of the stage, the orchestra pit, and backstage.

>> **You may have room to stretch out.** That's particularly true if your show isn't the most popular in New York City or it's a Tuesday or Wednesday night where the house may not be full.

>> **You get a behind-the-scenes understanding of how the magic of Broadway works.** You can often see performers waiting offstage to enter or the mechanics of certain special stage effects. P.S. Some people are fascinated by what happens behind the scenes, but others may find it distracting.

SRO! STANDING ROOM ONLY

SRO in an old-school term that stands for Standing Room Only. Shows were Standing Room Only when every seat in a theatre was sold so the only available way of seeing the show was to stand. Nowadays, a show doesn't have to be completely sold out for standing room tickets to be available. so ask the box office if you're interested. P.S. Standing room is a misnomer because it's not an actually separate room. It's a standing area and it's located behind the last row of the orchestra.

Tickets to standing room are cheaper than orchestra seats and the worst thing about it is the possibility of varicose veins from standing for around two and a half hours. But if you're willing to risk that, it ain't bad. It seems like it would be a free for all, with everyone jockeying for space, but you get an actual area assigned with your ticket. And there's a velvet topped wall in front of you so you can lean comfortably during the show. From personal experience, I've seen quite a few shows in standing room and greatly enjoyed them!

However, remember balcony seats are often the most uncomfortable and narrow seats you'll find in any theatre.

Getting Tickets to the Hottest Show in Town

"I wanna see (fill-in-the-blank) but I know it's sold out for years so I guess I can't go until I'm old! WAH". Fear not my theatre-going friend, you have many ways to snag those coveted tickets, all which I discuss here.

Planning in advance: At the theatre's website or box office

If your number one priority is seeing your favorite show, in the best seats, at a specific time, with no hassle, then the best option is to plan ahead. That means buying your tickets months in advance and planning to pay significant, although not astronomical, prices.

The good news is that popular musicals release tickets six to eight months in advance. That allows patrons to plan an entire Broadway trip (like booking plane tickets, securing vacation time, and getting hotel rooms) and experiences (like seeing other tourist attractions) well beforehand.

You can purchase tickets through the production's website directly or by visiting the theatre box office. Buying directly from the box office is ideal because it allows you to make sure you're paying the actual ticket price listed versus a higher price through processing fees or additional charges from a ticketing agency. And if you don't live in New York City, surely you know *someone* who does, right? Ask them to go to the box office for you and snag those tickets!

Taking a chance: At a TKTS booth

Sometimes you can't purchase tickets in advance. If you're not set on a specific show, a wonderful and definitely cheaper option is to visit a TKTS ticket booth.

REMEMBER

TKTS ticketing booths sell *day of* tickets anywhere from 25 to 50 percent off the regular ticket price. That adds up to substantial savings for you and potentially fuller audiences for struggling or less popular shows. A show's producer(s) makes these tickets available to TKTS because the show isn't sold out. On the other hand, shows that do sell out often aren't available on TKTS. You can count on popular shows being available, but not the most hot ones.

TKTS has four locations in New York City, with the most well-known being in Times Square (see Figure 5-6); London has one in Leicester Square for West End shows. These booths traditionally open four to six hours before shows begin and are run by the Theatre Development Fund in New York City and The Society of London Theatre in the West End.

FIGURE 5-6:
The TKTS location in Times Square.

saaton/Shutterstock

TIP

If you live near New York City or visit regularly, then the Theatre Development Fund (TDF) is fabulous to join. If you're eligible, it's only $40 a year, and you get lots and lots of tickets to Broadway, Off-Broadway, and Off-Off Broadway shows offered at discounted prices. Check out www.tdf.org. And if you're going to be spending time in the U.K., check out https://solt.co.uk/ to buy Theatre Tokens, which can be used to get tickets to more than 260 venues in the U.K. — they have no expiration date!

I have so many fond memories of going into New York City with my dad on the weekends and lining up on 47th Street. One of us would run ahead and see what shows were on the board. If there was one we really wanted to see, we'd be thrilled but so anxious waiting in that long line because the available tickets for the show we wanted to see could be gone by the time we finally got to the booth. Therefore, then, as well as now, it's always important to have a second choice.

Nowadays, you can download the TKTS app, which is extremely helpful, especially on the days leading up to your theatre adventure. Why? Because you can check every day to see the shows that are available so you can get a sense in advance of what you want to see. And, you can see if your favorite show is listed every day and, if not, what day is the most likely for your show to be available. Getting discounted tickets to the most popular shows on the weekend is more difficult. Weekday nights are a better time to visit TKTS.

Playing the lottery and winning big

Another option is to explore whether or not your favorite show has any lottery options. *Lottery sales* on the day of a show can include tickets sold in the front two rows of a theatre, reduced-price tickets for students with a valid student ID, or cancellation lines for those who purchased seats but unexpectedly have to cancel. Whereas TKTS is the place to get tickets to shows that don't sell out, lotteries are the best bet for shows that almost always sell out.

Go to the show's website to find out what their lottery process is before you trudge to the theatre. Lotteries began during *Rent* and the sight of people camped out hours before the show added to the show's reputation as a mega-hit. And during *Hamilton*'s lottery, Lin-Manuel Miranda and other cast members would often put on a live show on the sidewalk to entertain those waiting to see if they'd win. Search for those shows on YouTube — they're so fun.

You don't have to be special to win the lottery. It's a number's game, so if you have time on your hands, enter lotteries often. The more you do it, the more chance you have of winning those coveted tickets. And just because you won this week doesn't mean they won't let you enter next week. If you're obsessed with a show, lotteries are a great way to see your obsession multiple times without declaring bankruptcy.

GET YOUR TICKETS TODAY

A relatively new and wonderful way to tickets is through TodayTix.com, which offers nicely priced tickets for same day, same week, or advance sales of Broadway shows (and many other events). They also have same day lotteries *and* rush seats available. To enter, you usually just have to post something on social media announcing that you've entered the lottery. TodayTix has expanded from New York City to around the world so download the app onto your phone for when you're travelling and want to know what performances are happening in the city you're visiting.

Buying from a reseller: When ya just gotta see it

Sometimes, you find yourself with little to no options other than getting out your credit card and paying whatever it takes. When you find yourself in that situation, going through a ticket broker or reseller is your only avenue.

REMEMBER

One of the risks associated with this option is the possibility of using a reseller who sells you fake tickets or tickets at exorbitant prices (such unsavory types were previously known as *scalpers)*. Just like with sporting events, make sure you realize that any tickets you acquire that aren't from the theatre or an approved vendor can be a dicey proposition. That's why you should carefully vet any ticket agency you eventually use.

Going through a reseller or secondary ticketing agency includes paying extremely high ticket prices, but it also helps ensure that you can get what you pay for: the best tickets, on the best day, in the best location. Before you buy these tickets, feel free to vet whether they're legitimate by posting on a theatre message board. They are full of major theatre fans who can tell you if you're being scammed. I recommend AllThatChat.com for quick responses from knowledgeable theatre folk.

A friend of a friend: Grabbing house seats

The business of show business is often about *who* you know. Knowing a show's producer or investor, a cast member, a crew member, someone from the creative team, or an orchestra musician can allow you to ask for the opportunity to buy house seats from the theatre.

REMEMBER

House seats are typically the *best* seats and are reserved for those individuals who are somehow connected to the show or a true VIP. Chances are if you see a movie star, a politician, or a famous singer at a Broadway musical, they're sitting in house seats.

Although not always possible, house seats offer a way to work the system and get your tickets for face value versus paying an exorbitant amount of money to see your favorite musical in the middle of New York City.

SEE A SHOW AND SUPPORT THE ENTERTAINMENT COMMUNITY FUND

The Entertainment Community Fund, which was originally called The Actors Fund for around 100 years, changed its name so their mission was clear that they help *everyone* in the entertainment field — actors, musicians, opera singers, stage managers, agents, camera operators, agents, craft services, publicists, makeup artists, hair people, ushers, you get the picture.

In the 1980s, they needed money to assist everyone who needed help. The late, great Hal Prince (who won more Tony Awards than anyone) had just directed *The Phantom Of the Opera,* and getting tickets to it was impossible. Because he was the director, he had access to house seats. He offered to give those house seats to the Actors Fund who then resold them to raise money. This started a bigger tradition — which is the ninth show of the week. Almost every Broadway show does a ninth performance once or twice a year.

The actors and the orchestra don't get paid for the ninth show, and the rest of the ticket price goes to the Entertainment Community Fund. Go to the website (www. entertainmentcommunity.org) and see if a show is coming up. If it's a play or musical you want to see, buy a ticket. The cost of the ticket is the same with all the proceeds going to this charity. Even better, you get to see a special performance because the audience is often filled with Broadway stars! And the cast is so excited to perform for their friends that it's usually an amazing performance.

Knowing What to Expect When You Arrive at the Theatre

You have your ticket in hand, and you're ready to embark on your theatrical experience. So, what can you expect when you arrive at the theatre? Although each theatre in New York is different, some universals are always in play regardless of the show or venue you attend, and I examine them here.

Getting in the door

Most theatres allow the audience into the physical space around 30 minutes before the performance begins. In most theatres, audience members go through a security checkpoint where bags are checked as they enter the theatre. This is also where any mask mandates in place are enforced.

On Broadway especially, expect long lines as you enter the venue. Most of these theatres don't have tremendously large lobby spaces. Also, many venues in the Theatre District are close to one another, and lines can overlap; sometimes there's a line for ticket holders, a line for people waiting to buy tickets, and a line for people waiting for cancellations, so make sure you're in the right line!

Ticketing 101

Although physical tickets are still standard and regularly used, *electronic tickets* (or e-tickets) are becoming increasingly popular and an easy way to ensure you don't misplace your physical ticket.

Most tickets list where your seat is by an abbreviation:

>> ORCH (Orchestra)

>> MEZZ (Mezzanine)

>> BALC (Balcony)

Tickets also list the row number and seat number.

E-tickets are sent directly to your email address or downloaded from a link you receive from the ticketing agency you worked with to buy the seats. Members of the theatre staff (sometimes called *house staff*) will scan either a barcode or QR code (whichever is on your ticket) to admit you.

Make sure you have your ticket handy (either the paper copy or on your phone). Holding up the line while searching your email can lead to delays and other patrons getting frustrated. Do your part to keep the lines moving and organized. I like to take a photo of my e-ticket so it's easier for me to find than searching my email and downloading it again.

Heading to the restroom

After you get in the door, I highly recommend that you go to the bathroom immediately! One of the most frustrating aspects of theatregoing in New York City is that theatres have very small and cramped restroom facilities often because of a lack of physical space in older historic venues and a lack of infrastructure to ensure a suitable number of facilities. Going to the bathroom as soon as you arrive at the theatre and before you take your seat can also help prevent you from waiting in long lines at intermission.

Checking out the lobby and the merch

New York City offers some of the best theatre architecture in the world. Some may be confining, but many are beautiful in design details and craftsmanship. Some, like the New Amsterdam Theatre, have storied places in theatre history reaching back more than a hundred years and have been restored to something approaching their original glories.

Despite cramped lobby spaces, you'll always find an area where merchandise is sold, including traditional items like shirts, hats, magnets, souvenir programs, and posters, plus old-school items like CDs of cast recordings (for those who still use a CD player) and show-specific memorabilia like Aladdin's lamp from *Aladdin*, a Simba stuffed animal from *The Lion King*, or a blood-soaked handkerchief from *Moulin Rouge*. Don't worry! It's not real blood! One of the really fun things to buy is a souvenir program. They're larger than the show's Playbill and have *lots* more photos and information about the show.

If you want something to eat or drink, head to the bar before you take your seat. You'll find traditional candy, bottled water or sodas in commemorative glasses, and show-themed alcoholic drinks. Whether the We Drink Pink cocktail inspired by *Mean Girls* or the Ozmopolitan at *Wicked*, Broadway theatres have made sure you have many opportunities to spend your money and remember your experience. Many theatre bars serve drinks with lids so you can take your drink to your seat.

REMEMBER

Theatre bars aren't cheap. If you do partake, remember to tip the bartender. And keep the sipping and chomping sounds to a minimum during the show!

Going into the theatre proper

When I was the vocal coach on the *Legally Blonde* reality show, I told the ladies auditioning that stage managers often say, "If you're early, you're on time. If you're on time, you're late." P.S. I may have said that axiom, but I've basically never followed it. Ask my Broadway stage manager who had to write me up to Equity for being late to *half hour* (the call time; see Chapter 13) — multiple times. My excuse: Adult ADHD. They're response: <Yawn>.

Well, you should probably apply that saying to audience member as well. The earlier you get there means that more time you'll have for the bathroom, refreshments, flipping through the Playbill, getting comfortable, and you hopefully won't have to climb over other audience members to get to your seats.

REMEMBER

Where you're sitting may mean ascending stairs to upper floors of the theatre. Be advised that Broadway elevators are limited in size and, when available, will have a long wait, so if you're physically able, take the stairs.

When you enter the auditorium proper, several ushers can help you find your seat and answer any other questions you might have. They can also help solve problems if you have any question about seats and seat numbers.

After the usher shows you to your seat, they'll give you a *Playbill,* which serves as a program for the show. In addition to a cast list, you can also find cast and creative team biographies, song lists, synopses of the show, details on the history of the theatrical venue, and cover stories about what's happening on Broadway.

Playbills also serve as a great piece of memorabilia to commemorate your Broadway experience. I always advise to save your Playbills. It's always fun to look at them years later and see who in the cast has now become a huge star . . . like the people in *The Scarlet Pimpernel* in the 1990s with chorus member Sutton Foster. And don't forget, a *Playbill* is free! That's opposed to the West End in London where you have to *pay* for a program. Hmph. No wonder the United States fought for independence.

TIP

If you have young kids or need added height to see the stage, ask the usher for a booster seat. They're available and can help assure that everyone at the theatre can view the stage unencumbered.

Remembering important do's and don'ts

As the curtain rises, remember these helpful do's and don'ts of the theatre . . . the italics are specific reminders for me.

» **Do:** Focus attentively on the performers. *You don't need to crane your neck constantly to see if anyone recognizes you.*

» **Don't:** Talk during the performance. *Even when you want to tell James something you think is hilarious/insightful. You know he'll stare straight ahead and refuse to engage because he's told you repeatedly that your version of whispering is somehow louder than your speaking voice.*

» **Do:** Applaud loudly after musical numbers, when stars may enter the stage for the first time, and when the performance is finished. *You don't have to add a YAS QWEEN unless necessary.*

» **Don't:** Chew candy, ice, or mints loudly during the performance. *Remember the time you were munching popcorn loudly during the film Precious? You don't ever want to be that mortified again.*

» **Do:** Turn off your cellphones before the curtain goes up. *Turn them on during intermission and post a photo of yourself at the theatre only if the lighting is flattering.*

» **Don't:** Check your phone, text, or call anyone during the performance. *Again, during intermission . . . anything goes!*

» **Do:** Unwrap any gum or hard candy before the show begins — *unless you're Sally (Rudetsky). She can take an entire act to slowly/loudly unwrap one piece of gum.*

» **Don't:** Video or audio record any aspect of the performance. Taking photos during the performance is also a no-no. *If you're ever tempted to do so, just remember that the universe spared you anyone videotaping your performance in The Riz when you were wearing your Act Unitard and, by accident, your dance belt was on backward.*

2

The People Who Make Musical Theatre Happen

Look behind the curtain to see who creates the musical, including the librettist, composer, and lyricist.

Identify the VIPs who cast the musical and make the most important decisions, including the producer, director, and choreographer.

Find out more about the creative people who design the world the musical is set in, including the costume, set, lighting, sound, and hair designers.

Introduce the cast of characters, both onstage and in the pit, who bring the musical alive.

Gain a clearer understanding of all the backstage professionals who run each production and handle everything from costume changes to props.

Chapter 6

Making the Musical — The Creators

Musical theatre has been called *the* most collaborative art form because so many people need to work together to make a musical. I'm talking about choreographers, stage managers, lighting designers, costumers, musicians, makeup artists, orchestrators, dressers, sound designers, and, as Yul Brenner intoned as the King of Siam for thousands of performances, *et cetera, et cetera, et cetera* . . . . But as important as all these aspects are, three elements are at the core of each musical: the music, the lyrics, and the book (also known as *the script,* also called the *libretto*).

"What about *Swan Lake?*" you ask, "That show didn't have *any* lyrics, but it was still considered a musical at the Tony Awards!" Check out Chapter 1 where I mention *that very show,* but I admit that, yes, some musicals don't have books or lyrics. The majority of musicals have music, lyrics, and a book. So, can you and I just agree majority rules and focus on those three elements?

I'm assuming your silence means you agree.

Thank you.

In this chapter, I examine those three job titles and what each is responsible for: the composer, the lyricist, and the librettist. P.S. Just because I'm listing them separately doesn't mean every musical has three different people creating those three elements. Many musicals have a different person in charge of the music, lyrics, and book (*Gypsy*, for example, has music by Jule Styne, lyrics by Stephen Sondheim, and a book by Arthur Laurents). Some have just one person who does both the music *and* lyrics whereas another writes the book (*Wicked* has music *and* lyrics by Stephen Schwartz and a book by Winnie Holzman.) And one person does *all three* in some musicals (such as Meredith Willson, who wrote the book, music, and lyrics to *The Music Man. Yas*, overachiever!). And there are many other permutations. Regardless of how many people are involved, here I examine what the composer, lyricist, and librettist do.

"Mr. Cellophane" — the Librettist

I start with the person who's often ignored — the librettist.

The librettist — The script writer

After a great musical, you hear people in the lobby talking excitedly about the lyrics and the music, the acting and the singing and, often since the 1980s, the set. But I've yet to hear people leaving the theatre saying, "What a libretto!" First of all, most people don't call it a libretto; they call it a book or a script. But also, people just don't seem to talk very much about the libretto. That doesn't mean audiences don't appreciate a great libretto and laud the writers.

However, for some reason, audiences usually only give kudos to the libretto for writers of plays without music. Broadway *playwrights* often have name recognition ("It's a Neil Simon play! It's going to be hilarious!" Or "Get ready to be devastated by some Tennessee Williams!") Even though a libretto for a musical is basically the same thing as a play, the people who write the libretto aren't often known by name.

Test question: Don't you love the musical *Cabaret*? Mmm . . . that fantastic Kander and Ebb score! The creepy Emcee, the unaware Sally Bowles, that brilliant original Hal Prince direction and Sam Mendes/Robby Marshall's reinvention for the revival? The singing! The dancing! Right!? It's a fantastic musical.

Okay then . . . who wrote the libretto?

Silence.

Joe Masteroff!

Full disclosure: I love *Cabaret*, too, but (no joke) I went online to confirm that Masteroff indeed wrote it.

Why do most people who love *Cabaret* know Kander and Ebb, Hal Prince, Sam Mendes/Robby Marshall, and probably Joel Grey, Alan Cumming, Natasha Richardson, Liza Minelli, and Bob Fosse, but they don't know who wrote that actual script? Musical theatre fans seem to focus on the direction/choreography, the stars, and the songs. Yet, without a great script, the production would just be a concert of great music performances with no emotion attached to it. That's what the script does. Those songs and performances take on a whole new meaning when they're within the context of a script.

I've noticed that when a Broadway musical is a hit, the positive focus is usually on the actors and the score. But when a Broadway musical isn't successful, the same people who ignore the books of hit musicals, turn around and blame the book for the show failing. The book of a good musical is invisible to many people.

Regarding Broadway, many people seem to think the book should serve the show and not stand out. That isn't to say the show can't be filled with hilarious or dramatic scenes, but all those scenes are lead-ins to the songs. Basically the songs are the stars. One of the greatest book writers on Broadway was Arthur Laurents, who wrote the brilliant librettos to *West Side Story* and *Gypsy*, and he was a master of minimal writing.

SETH SPEAKS

I spoke to one of Laurents's students Winnie Holzman (who later created the TV show *Freaks and Geeks* and wrote the libretto to *Wicked*) who said that Laurents felt strongly about "judicious editing." He worked hard with his students to have dialogue get across what needed to be said in the fewest words possible. Laurents would sit with students and show them where they had extraneous words and help them find what words they could cut without losing the meaning. And in case you think the skill of being a good librettist is just being curt and dry, you should know that another skill he felt was super important was to go for "emotional glitz." He told his students that the "special effect" they should have in their shows shouldn't be something with the set or with the lighting, but instead with emotion. You can totally see that in all of his writing. Think of the pain the audience feels when Mama Rose discovers Dainty June has run off with Tulsa, or when Maria points her gun and asks how many bullets are left? A musical's music and lyrics evoke so many emotions and so should a libretto. But Laurents felt it should be done in as few words as possible!

On a side note, although the playwrights who write Broadway plays are lauded, the scriptwriters of *Hollywood films* are often ignored. In Hollywood, the *director* gets the name recognition. ("It's a Spielberg movie! It has amazing special effects!" Or "Wow! Ang Lee keeps stretching his boundaries as an artiste!") Why can't all the creative people get equal lauding?

Identifying the best-ist librettist(s)

The lack of name recognition/praise/acknowledgment seems to be *de rigeur* when it comes to being a musical librettist. I hope to change that by naming some fantastic Broadway librettists!

Oscar Hammerstein II

The grandfather of the modern libretto, Hammerstein was an equally brilliant librettist as he was a lyricist. The book *Something Wonderful* details the work he had to do on a show like *South Pacific* — taking various James Michener stories and putting them together into one cohesive plot for *South Pacific.* Brilliant!

Notable shows include *Showboat, Oklahoma!, South Pacific, The King and I,* and *The Sound of Music.*

Arthur Laurents

See the preceding section for his theories about how succinct a libretto needs to be. Besides his fantastic Broadway librettos, he wrote the hit play *The Time of the Cuckoo* and the brilliant films *The Way We Were* and *The Turning Point.* Notable Broadway musicals include *Gypsy* and *West Side Story.*

Neil Simon

Probably the most successful comedic playwright, Simon was also librettist for musicals. But his special skill earned him the nickname of "Doc" Simon. Yes, he was a show doctor meaning he was often called in *to doctor* or fix a musical that was in trouble. His most famous doctoring was for *A Chorus Line,* which went on to become (for a lengthy period of time) the longest running show on Broadway!

His classic line:

> LARRY (the assistant choreographer): Zach, can the kids take a break?

> SHEILA (the more knowing dancer): And smoke? Can the adults smoke?

Notable scripts include *Sweet Charity, Promises, Promises,* and *They're Playing Our Song.*

Joe Masteroff

Joining fellow luminaries like Laurents and Irving Berlin, Masteroff lived well into his 90s! His first big musical (*She Loves Me*) was adapted from a film and has been revived twice on Broadway; his second was adapted from stories and has been revived three times on Broadway as well as made into an Oscar-winning film! I'm talking about his notable shows: *She Loves Me* and *Cabaret*.

Peter Stone

I will always remember Peter Stone's hilarious comment about writing the libretto to 1776, the musical about the signing of the Declaration of Independence. He claimed that most people thought the idea was so boring that when he answered the question, "What are you working on?" the person he was responding to would fall asleep between the "17" and the "76"!

Notable shows include 1776, *My One And Only Titanic*, *The Will Rogers Follies*, and *Curtains*.

Tom Meehan

Tom Meehan is a wonderful writer who wrote two of his biggest hit shows after the age of 70! That's encouraging, isn't it? Notable shows include *Annie*, *The Producers*, and *Hairspray*.

SETH SPEAKS

When *Annie* began first performances out-of-town, the creative team realized they had the wrong Annie — Kristen Vigard — who had a quality and voice that were both angelic but wrong for the character of Annie. As Andrea McArdle explains, "They had cast Oliver, but they needed the Artful Dodger." The creative team moved Andrea (who was playing "the toughest Orphan") to the title role, and Kristen wound up becoming a standby for Annie. Imagine what it feels like being fired when you're an adult. Now imagine what it's like as a kid. I'm sure it was horrible for her, even though she stayed with the show. The next musical that creative team worked on was *I Remember Mama*. During previews, they realized the show wasn't working, and they had to get rid of some characters. One of the characters had to go, the one being played by Vigard! Meehan told me he vowed not to "devastate that little girl again," so he spent all night writing. The next day, instead of being fired, she was given an entirely new character that Meehan had created for her so she could stay in the show! #BeKind

James Lapine

James Lapine is one of the few librettists who's also a director for his own work. Although he has teamed up with various composers and composer/lyricists, his most successful collaborations to date are with William Finn and Sondheim. You can read about how the Pulitzer- (and Tony Award) winning musical *Sunday in the Park* was created with Sondheim in Lapine's fabulous book, *Putting It Together*.

Notable shows include *Falsettos, Sunday in the Park with George, Into the Woods,* and *Passion.*

Marsha Norman

Marsha Norman is a novelist, a Pulitzer Prize–winning playwright, a lyricist, and one of the few female librettists on Broadway. She collaborated with Jule Styne on his final Broadway musical and Lucy Simon on her first! Notable shows include *The Secret Garden, The Color Purple,* and *The Bridges of Madison County.*

Terrence McNally

An extremely successful playwright, Terrence McNally was beloved by his Broadway brethren. His plays, like the farce *The Ritz* (which took place in a gay bathhouse) or *Love! Valor! Compassion!* (which took place at a vacation house being used by eight gay men) were groundbreaking because almost all of them had gay characters in main roles. He turned to musicals late in his career and had great success. He teamed up with various collaborators, but he must have loved Kander and Ebb because he did three musicals with them!

Notable shows include *Kiss of the Spider Woman, Ragtime,* and *The Full Monty.*

Joseph Stein

Joseph Stein was a librettist who had *huge* stars in his shows: Zero Mostel, Anthony Quinn, Patti LuPone, Jackie Gleason, and so many more. He wrote one of the longest running musicals (*Fiddler on the Roof*) and one that closed out of town before it got to Broadway (*The Baker's Wife*). He epitomized the ups and downs of show business!

Notable shows include *Plain and Fancy, Take Me Along, Fiddler on the Roof,* and *Zorba.*

Harvey Fierstein

Harvey won Tony Awards for acting *and* writing the play *Torch Song Trilogy,* all before he was 30 years old. He then wrote the book for his first musical, *La Cage Aux Folles* and won the Tony Award for that as well. He's one of the few librettists to keep up an acting career while writing librettos. Fierstein won the Tony Award for Best Actor in a Musical for *Hairspray* 20 years after his first Tony Award, and he's still churning out new musicals!

Notable shows include *La Cage Aux Folles, Newsies,* and *Kinky Boots.*

Michael R. Jackson

The youngest person on this list, Jackson's career is just beginning. His first musical — *A Strange Loop* — won the Pulitzer Prize *and* the Tony Award for Best Musical. What's next?

"I Feel a Song Coming On" — The Composer

The *composer* writes the music for the musical.

Well, my work here is done.

Now you can move on or get more details if you're interested! I call the composer "the magician" because, to me, there's nothing more magical about creating a musical than writing the score. And I mean magical because, like a magician, the composer makes something appear out of nothing. And what they create can be beautiful, or scary, or romantic, or thrilling, or make you want to dance, or make you want to cry, or make you feel every feeling there is. *How do they do it!?* I truly don't know. That's why I think of them as magicians.

If you get a chance, look at a piano keyboard. You'll start to see a pattern of white and black keys that repeats. The pattern is the 12 *tones*, the notes that all Western composers use and the only notes that every Broadway composer has used. Yet from those 12 tones, *an entire score is written!* A lyricist has the entire English dictionary (as well as dictionaries in other languages when they want to add a fancy foreign word or phrase). A composer just has these 12 tones. They put those 12 tones together to form chord changes and then put a string of notes on top that forms a melody. Eventually, it's a song with a beginning, middle, and end.

Some of these songs are songs people remember for the rest of their lives . . . yet they began with nothing! Think about it: Jule Styne sat at a piano, fiddled around with the twelve tones, and created the melody and chord changes of "People." That song didn't exist, and then it did. To me, that's *magic!*

Although many musicals have lyrics written by two people (the most famous team being Betty Comden and Adolph Green), original scores on Broadway are always written by one person except for these exceptions:

>> **Jukebox musicals:** Jukebox musicals often have multiple composers, especially the ones that focus on songs from a certain decade (like *Rock*

of Ages) or certain decades *(Moulin Rouge)*. Those shows have multiple composers because the score isn't about the songs of one person (like *Movin' Out,* which is all Billy Joel).

» **Musicals that originally intended to have one composer:** Sometimes a composer has no choice but to accept outside help. That happens when a show hasn't yet opened, and a producer or director decides to bring in another composer to assist. Refer to the nearby sidebar for a rare example where this happened.

Some shows have rumors about who wrote what ("So-and-so didn't really write fill-in-the-blank!"), but here are two shows I know where more than one composer created the music:

- *A Day in Hollywood/A Night in the Ukraine:* This is one of my absolute favorite shows, and most of the fantastic score has music by Frank Lazarus with lyrics by Dick Vosburgh.

  However, those two were first-time Broadway songwriters, and when the show was being put together, director/choreographer Tommy Tune wanted more songs. Maybe he wasn't sure if they could churn out new songs quickly or maybe he wanted a little different flavor, but whatever the reason, he turned to someone he knew who had a proven track record of fabulous songs: Jerry Herman. Tune had a relationship with Herman from years before because Tune played Ambrose in the film version of *Hello, Dolly!.* So, although many of the songs in *A Day in Hollywood/A Night in the Ukraine* are indeed by Lazarus/Vosburgh, four (including the opening number) have music and lyrics by Herman. Here's my deconstruction of one of my faves: www.youtube.com/watch?v=qPOU5o_dOMA&t=5s.

- *Grand Hotel:* Interestingly, the other show that comes to mind with a new composer coming in is *another* Tune musical. The original composer/lyricist team was Robert Forrest and George Wright (who were also a real-life couple and had a huge hit with *Kismet*). Tune wanted new songs, so he brought in another composer/lyricist he knew well — this time Maury Yeston. Tune had directed/choreographed *Nine* (Yeston had composed the music and lyrics) a few years earlier, and he asked Yeston to write some new songs for *Grand Hotel* while it was out of town. See the nearby sidebar.

HOW A MUSIC ROYALTY NEGOTIATION ERASED A GREAT PERFORMANCE

Figuring out how to divide music royalties between the different writers of *Grand Hotel* sadly took a long time and that process delayed the album from being produced. I say "sadly" because the negotiations weren't settled for a few years. During that time leading man David Carroll got sicker and sicker with AIDS. On the first day of recording the album, he showed up to the recording studio even though he was sick. Before he could record anything, he passed away. His death was just one of many AIDS losses the Broadway community has endured.

The wonderful Brent Barrett took his place on the recording. The theatre community not only mourned David, but they also mourned the fact that his stunning performance originating that role wasn't preserved. Thankfully, the album producer took a recording of David's big song that he had sung at an AIDS benefit (just with a piano accompaniment) and put that on the album, so there's a permanent record of how amazing he was. Here's my deconstruction of his brilliant performance of that Maury Yeston song: www.youtube.com/watch?v=GmW5ShDCh3M.

"Words! Words! Words!" — The Lyricist

The bon vivant! The wordsmith! The person with the catchy turn of a phrase! That's the kind of person you (or at least *I*) love to hang out with at a party. They always make me laugh, keep me interested, inspire me. On the flip side, they can make me feel insecure about my own intelligence and hate myself. But regardless, *that's* the kind of person who becomes a successful lyricist. Here I examine what a lyricist does and provide some examples of great lyrics.

Focusing on what a lyricist does

The *lyricist* writes the lyrics (the words) to the songs. To answer that age old question: Which comes first, the music or the lyrics? *There is no one answer.* Sometimes the lyrics come first, sometimes the music is written first, and sometimes both are written at the same time (either with two people working together at the piano or a composer/lyricist figuring both out at the same time). Sometimes the song's *hook* (the main musical phrase that's repeated) is written along with the lyric that sums up the song (think "Tradition!" from *Fiddler on the Roof*) and *then* the composer writes the rest of the music and gives it to the lyricist to add lyrics, or the lyricist finishes the rest of the song. There are *so many* permutations.

Whatever way the music is written, the lyricist adds the words. And not just any words: These words have a job to do. If you listen to the radio, pop songs are 99 percent about love: Being in love, unrequited love, desperate for any love, devastation that love is gone, and of course, many songs are just about lust. You don't hear many songs about a successful lyricist being interviewed and expressing frustration with his composing partner who's more interested in money than art. But Broadway had a song like that! It's called "Franklin Shepard, Inc." from *Merrily We Roll Along* (www.youtube.com/watch?v=_LWLDJgwMG8).

My point is that a musical theatre lyricist has to have way more skill than a pop song lyricist because theatre songs must (usually) move the plot forward. Theatre songs have to be like a scene. The lyricist not only has to express a thought, a feeling, a story, and so forth, succinctly, *but it has to rhyme.* (Many new pop-type lyricists for theatre seem to think it's edgy not to rhyme words. It *is* edgy, if edgy means lazy and lacking skill. #IWentThere) The skill set that being a lyricist requires is so difficult to acquire and to hone!

Giving characters the words to sing and express their feelings

A common question about musicals has an old chestnut for an answer, but it's true: Why do people sing in a musical? The answer usually given is: When someone's feelings are so strong that they can no longer speak, they have to sing.

And that means, they have to sing *lyrics* that express those strong feelings.

Here are just some types of lyrics that are written for Broadway songs:

>> **Lyrics describing a character's emotional state:**

- **Love:** "A Wonderful Guy" (*South Pacific*)

- **Hate:** "I Hate Men" (*Kiss Me, Kate*)

- **Competitiveness:** "Mine" (*On the Twentieth Century*)

- **Insecurity:** "I'm a Part of That" (*The Last Five Years*)

- **Joy:** "On a Wonderful Day Like Today" (*The Roar of the Greasepaint, The Smell of the Crowd*)

- **Anxiety:** "I'm Calm" (*A Funny Thing Happened on the Way to the Forum*)

- **Excitement:** "Tonight at 8" (*She Loves Me*)

- **Conceit:** "The Lees of Old Virginia" (*1776*)

- **Pushing down devastation with false positiveness:** "Everything's Coming Up Roses" (*Gypsy*)

» **Lyrics about leaving a job:** "I'm Going Back" (*Bells Are Ringing*)

» **Lyrics about leaving a husband:** "Meadowlark" (*The Baker's Wife*)

» **Lyrics about the creation of art:**
  - "The Spark of Creation" (*Children of Eden*)
  - "Move On" (*Sunday in the Park with George*)

» **Lyrics celebrating a holiday:**
  - "Once a Year Day" (*The Pajama Game*)
  - "One Short Day" (*Wicked*)

» **Lyrics giving hope:**
  - "You Will Be Found" (*Dear Evan Hansen*)
  - "If You Believe" (*The Wiz*)

» **Lyrics telling a story:**
  - **About a summer fling:** "Summer Nights" (*Grease*)
  - **About a soldier dying on the battlefield:** "Mama Look Sharp" (*1776*)

» **Lyrics about a desperate lesbian looking for a girlfriend:** "Old Fashioned Love Story" (*The Wild Party*)

» **Lyrics about a man fired passive-aggressively who vows to come back and destroy everyone, including sleeping with one of his co-worker's wives:** "Grand Knowing You" (*She Loves Me*)

» **Lyrics while having phone sex:** "A Call from the Vatican" (*Nine*)

As you can see, Broadway lyricists have to be a lot more specific than "Ah . . . love to love ya, baby!"

Recognizing the Very Best

This list isn't comprehensive in terms of composers, lyricists, composing teams, *and/or* the shows and songs they're known for. There are so many people I don't mention simply because they didn't have tons of hits but investigate the creators and cast albums of *Snoopy* (Larry Grossman/Hal Hackaday), *The Best Little*

Whorehouse in Texas (Carol Hall), *Runaways* (Liz Swados), *The Wiz* (Charlie Smalls), and any cast album you can get your hands on. This list can get you started!

Composer/lyricist teams

These are the composing teams who have written a myriad of successful musicals. Their names go together like bread and butter . . . or, if you're on a low-carb diet, lettuce and butter.

Richard Rodgers and Oscar Hammerstein II

Showboat is considered the grandfather of the modern-day musical and Oscar Hammerstein II wrote the lyrics with Jerome Kern on music. Then, in the 1940s, he teamed up with Richard Rodgers and created *Oklahoma!*, what is considered by everyone as the first musical of the Golden Age of musical theatre. Together these titans were at the center of the birth of modern musicals and Hammerstein's death represented the end of the Golden Age.

Notable shows (besides *Oklahoma!*) include *Flower Drum Song, The King and I, South Pacific*, and *Carousel*.

Notable songs include anthems like "Climb Ev'ry Mountain" and "You'll Never Walk Alone," love duets like "People Will Say We're in Love" and "Only Make Believe," fabulous group songs like "Do Re Mi," and the title song from *Oklahoma!*

Interesting facts: Hammerstein's final show was *The Sound of Music* and the last song he wrote was "Edelweiss." After Hammerstein's death, Rodgers teamed up with Hammerstein's protégé Stephen Sondheim for *Do I Hear a Waltz?* and actually wrote his own lyrics for the movie version of *The Sound of Music*, with one of my favorite songs "I Have Confidence."

His family line continued the tradition: His daughter Mary wrote the fabulous *Once Upon a Mattress* and grandson Adam Guettel won the Tony Award for best score for *The Light in the Piazza*.

Jule Styne (teamed with various lyricists)

Jule Styne kept composing until right before he passed away in 1994 with 1993's *The Red Shoes*. Notable shows include *Gentlemen Prefer Blondes, Gypsy*, and *Funny Girl*.

For notable songs, he cornered the early market on fabulous Broadway bring-down-the-house diva songs like "Everything's Coming Up Roses" and "Don't Rain on My Parade," and is also known for "Diamonds Are a Girl's Best Friend" and "People."

Barbra Streisand loves to fiddle around with melodies. Many of the melodies that fans know from her famous songs aren't what were originally written —she changed them! Marvin Hamlisch did some vocal arrangements on *Funny Girl* and came backstage one night to figure out how to fix "Sadie Sadie," which was having problems. He told me this was the conversation:

MARVIN: Hi, Barbra! Some of the new melodies you're adding to "Sadie, Sadie" are clashing with the vocal arrangements I wrote.

BARBRA (in a nice, but direct manner): Marvin, are people coming to the show to hear me? Or your vocal arrangements?

MARVIN (Realized she was correct and silently closed her dressing room door)

Andrew Lloyd Webber, Tim Rice, and Elton John

No, they aren't a throuple, but it's easier to team them together because they're connected.

Lloyd Webber and Rice began their string of hits at an incredibly young age (I'm talking early 20s!). After their partnership ended, Rice first teamed up with Benny Anderson and Björn Ulvaeus from ABBA and wrote *Chess*, which was a hit in London (but not on Broadway). And then Rice teamed with Elton John who was a huge pop superstar who turned his eye toward theatre. They wrote the smash hit film *The Lion King*, which then became a Tony Award–winning Broadway show. They also wrote *Aida* together, which wasn't as successful but is slated for a revival on Broadway in 2023.

Lloyd Webber had various writing partners after Rice and also parlayed his composing prowess into producing as well. His musical, *The Phantom Of The Opera*, for which he also adapted the story, is the longest running musical on Broadway.

Here are their notable shows:

>> **Lloyd Webber/Rice:** *Joseph and the Amazing Technicolor Dreamcoat, Jesus Christ Superstar,* and *Evita*

>> **Lloyd Webber with other lyricists:** *Cats, The Phantom of the Opera,* and *Sunset Boulevard*

>> **Tim Rice with Elton John:** *The Lion King and Aida*

Here are their notable songs:

>> **Lloyd Webber and Tim Rice:** "Don't Cry for Me Argentina" and "I Don't Know How to Love Him"

Interesting fact: Lloyd Webber is one of the key people who brought high belting to Broadway. In the 1960s, women belters usually hit B flats in their songs and their top notes were belted Cs. However, when *Evita* came to Broadway in 1979, Patti LuPone had to belt a G! Listen to "A New Argentina." That's *five steps* above what was considered a high belt note in the 1960s. I myself love high belting and thank Lloyd Webber, as do all the doctors who've made a bundle treating vocal damage! (Before I get angry emails: Yes, it's possible to belt high notes and be vocally healthy!)

Alan Menken and Howard Ashman

Alan Menken and the late, great Howard Ashman hit it big with their long-running Off-Broadway hit *Little Shop of Horrors*, which then became a hit film. They continued their success with animated musical films like *The Little Mermaid* and *Beauty and the Beast*. After Ashman's early death due to AIDS, Menken teamed with other lyricists and continued his success with *Sister Act* and *Newsies*.

Their notable shows include *Little Shop of Horrors*, *The Little Mermaid*, *Aladdin*, and *Beauty and the Beast*. Notable songs include "Suddenly Seymour," "Part of Your World," "A Whole New World," "Beauty and the Beast" title song, and "Friend Like Me."

Interesting facts: Menken and Ashman both wanted Angela Lansbury to play Mrs. Potts and sing the title song in the film version of *Beauty and the Beast*. They were excited when they wrote it and sent it to her to see if she'd agree to do it. Turns out, she passed! Lansbury claimed it really wasn't her style. *What?* It was *so* her style, but she was adamant. They couldn't figure out why she wasn't interested until they realized they had indeed sent her the title song, but it wasn't the version for the character of Mrs. Potts. It was the pop version meant to be sent to Celine Dion and Peabo Bryson! Let's be real: Lansbury was *not* known for her fierce riffs so she was like "CUT!" When they sent her the proper version, she agreed and, another interesting fact, the version you hear in the film was her *only* take! She recorded it once, and everyone agreed it was *perfect! #OneTakeLansbury*

Marc Shaiman and Scott Wittman

Marc Shaiman and Scott Wittman are the only composing team who had a hit show while they were a romantic couple, and they continue to write hit shows after they've ended their romantic relationship. It shows how strong the connection between them is!

The producer Margo Lion asked Shaiman (who had worked as a music director/arranger/composer for Hollywood films and Bette Midler and who had co-written those amazing Billy Crystal Oscar–opening numbers) to write the music. He asked if she minded if he could co-write the lyrics with Wittman. She was wary; what if there was a couple spat and they didn't want to work together?

They wrote three songs and submitted them for approval, and the songs were so fabulous that they were hired! *And* all three songs stayed in the show! "Good Morning Baltimore," "Welcome to the 60s," and "Big Blonde and Beautiful" were the start to *Hairspray*.

Known for hummable melodies and clever/hilarious lyrics, they've been churning out shows ever since. And even though their romantic relationship ended, they're still a first-class composing team and their 2022 musical *Some Like It Hot* got critical raves!

Notable shows include *Hairspray, Martin Short's Fame Becomes Me, and Some Like It Hot.* Their memorable songs include "You Can't Stop the Beat," "Without Love," and "Fly, Fly Away."

SETH SPEAKS

I'm constantly telling people there needs to be a new category at the Tony Awards. Think about it: What are musicals known for? Their songs. And yet there is no Best Song category, but the Oscars have a Best Song category. Let's start a campaign! I bring this up because I first thought of the idea when I first heard the score of Marc and Scott's *Catch Me If You Can.* I was so blown away by the song "Fly, Fly Away" and the stunning performance by Kerry Butler. I'd tell people that if there had been a Best Song Category at that year's Tony Awards, I bet this would have won. Listen to how great it is — www.youtube.com/watch?v=3xoXD83pe5w.

THIS OL' THING?

SETH SPEAKS

When Alan Menken and Howard Ashman were writing "Be Our Guest" for *Beauty and the Beast,* they talked about the style of the song and how it would be mapped out. Alan told Howard he would whip up a dummy version of the song so Howard could start attaching lyrics. A *dummy version* has the style and feel of the song, and the right number of notes for the melody, but it's done quickly just to give a lyricist something to work with.

After Howard attached lyrics, Alan would then take time and *really* write a proper melody and the right chord changes. Howard finished the lyrics and before Alan could change it up, Howard told Alan he loved the quick version and not to change a note! So the melody and chord changes of "Be Our Guest" that everyone knows and loves was whipped up by Alan in minutes!

Composers with various partners

These composers "played the field" — not (necessarily) in their romantic life . . . I'm referring to the fact that they had various writing partners.

Cy Coleman

Cy Coleman hit it big with pop tunes like "Witchcraft" and "The Best Is Yet to Come." He started writing musicals in 1960 with *Wildcat!* and wound up having a string of hits. Notable shows include *Sweet Charity*, *City of Angels*, and *Will Rogers Follies* and *On the Twentieth Century*.

Memorable songs include "Big Spender," "If My Friends Could See Me Now," "You're Nothing Without Me," and "Hey There, Good Times."

Interesting fact: His first Broadway score was also Lucille Ball's first (and only) musical! *Wildcat* opened in 1960 and, though not a critical hit, was an audience favorite.

SETH SPEAKS

Dancer Valerie Harper (later TV's Rhoda) was in the ensemble, and she told me that the musical had a dog in it. Not surprisingly, during one of the performances, that dog came onstage and "did his business." Valerie remembers that everyone was about to go onstage to do a dance number . . . and they were wearing white, which led to panic in the wings. What to do? Lucy to the rescue. She went onstage, literally cleaned it up, *and* added her own signature sass. She turned to the audience after her poop scooping and lamented, "Oh, boy. I should have read my contract more carefully!"

Tom Kitt

Tom Kitt has teamed with Brian Yorkey, Amanda Green, Lin-Manuel Miranda, Michael Korie, and Cameron Crowe. He's also done many productions as an amazing music arranger. Oh, and he won a Pulitzer (for *Next to Normal* with Yorkey)!

Notable shows include *Next to Normal* and *Almost Famous*. Notable songs include "I Miss the Mountains" and "I'm Alive."

Robert Lopez (with Jeff Marx, Matt Stone and Trey Parker, and Kristen Anderson-Lopez)

Robert Lopez, or Bobby as he's known, is the youngest person to become an EGOT (winning the Emmy, Grammy, Oscar, and Tony). Wow! He first won the Tony Award for Best Score along with his songwriting partner Jeff Marx on their first Broadway show, *Avenue Q*. Lopez then co-wrote the score to *The Book of Mormon*

(Tony Award again for Best Score) with the *South Park* creators as his collaborators but, a la *The Wizard Of Oz*, he finally realized the best collaborator was right there the whole time . . . his wife! Yes! He and Kristen Anderson-Lopez hit it big with *Frozen*, and they've been a songwriting team ever since! Talk about bringing your work home with you. I guess when one of them starts an argument in the apartment, the other tells them to "Let It Go." #I'mHereAllWeek

Notable shows include *Avenue Q*, *The Book of Mormon*, and *Frozen*. Notable songs include "There's a Fine Fine Line," "I Believe," and "Let It Go."

Charles Strouse (with Lee Adams, Martin Charnin, Betty Comden and Adolph Green, and Stephen Schwartz)

Charles Strouse had success with many different collaborators, but the most success he had was with Martin Charnin; together they wrote the score to *Annie*. Side note: Even though his show *Rags* closed the weekend it opened, it was arguably his best score! Make sure you listen: www.youtube.com/watch?v=c_-jNTA5pw4.

Notable shows include *Bye Bye Birdie*, *Applause*, and *Annie*. Notable songs include "A Lot of Livin' to Do," "Put on a Happy Face," and "Tomorrow."

Jeanine Tesori (with Dick Scanlon, Lisa Kron, Brian Crawley, David Lindsay-Abaire)

Jeanine Tesori has teamed up various lyricists to great success. She's one of the few female composers who has had *multiple* hit shows, and she's still writing new ones! Her first splash in New York was the Off-Broadway musical *Violet*, which then came to Broadway almost 20 years later starring Sutton Foster. Tesori has composed in various styles from old-timey Broadway in *Thoroughly Modern Millie* to minimalistic modern in *Fun Home*. I think of her as a "hometown gal makes good" because she began playing in the pit like I did!

Notable shows include *Fun Home*, *Kimberly Akimbo*, and *Thoroughly Modern Millie*. Notable songs include "Gimme Gimme," "Ring of Keys," and "Better."

Stephen Flaherty and Lynn Ahrens

Stephen Flaherty is the composer, and Lynn Ahrens is the lyricist; together they've had multiple hit shows starting in the 1990s. FYI: Ahrens also writes music *and* sings! If you grew up in the '70s, you'd recognize Lynn's singing voice because she wrote *and* sang the Schoolhouse Rock "Interplanet Janet" and "The Preamble!" ("We the people . . . in order to form a more perfect union . . .")

Notable shows include *Once on This Island, Ragtime, Anastasia,* and *Seussical.* Notable songs include "Mama Will Provide," "Wheels of a Dream," "Ragtime," and "Journey to the Past."

Interesting fact: Flaherty grew up in Pittsburgh and wrote the score for his first musical when he was still in high school. Each scene was set in a different Pittsburgh neighborhood, and each neighborhood had its own style of song — rock 'n' roll, country and western, a big Broadway-style showstopper, and so on. He differentiated the styles by using a different colored pen for each song. His piano teacher — who also coached him on composing — pointedly asked, "Do you think Sondheim uses different colored pens?" I don't think Stephen ever asked Sondheim that specific question, so it remains unanswered. Flaherty, however, set the stage for his career with those colored pens because his scores have continued to cover a myriad of styles! *Once on This Island* and *Anastasia* sound completely different from one another, and neither of them sound similar to *Ragtime.* He jokingly calls himself a "musical Meryl Streep." Basically, he changes styles as often as she changes accents.

Alan Jay Lerner and Frederick Loewe

Alan Jay Lerner and Frederick Loewe will always be known for writing *My Fair Lady,* which is considered by many to be the perfect musical. Sadly, their success from *My Fair Lady* put a lot of pressure on them to write another hit, and their next show *Camelot* was fraught with problems (including the director Moss Hart having a heart attack while the show was still out of town). Unfortunately, their partnership didn't survive. Loewe retired, but Lerner (who also wrote the librettos) stayed in showbiz and teamed up with various composers, including Burton Lane — they wrote *On a Clear Day You Can See Forever* (which has a fantastic movie version with Barbra Streisand). You can read about the making of the Lerner and Loewe shows in Lerner's excellent book, *The Street Where I Live: A Memoir* (W&W Norton & Company).

Notable shows include *Brigadoon, My Fair Lady, Camelot,* and *Gigi.* Notable songs include "I Could Have Danced All Night," "On the Street Where You Live," "Camelot," and "C'est Moi!"

John Kander and Fred Ebb

John Kander and Fred Ebb first teamed up in the early 1960s and wound up becoming one of the longest-lasting Broadway song writing teams in history. They had shows opening on Broadway in the '60s, '70s, '80s, '90s, and then even *after* Ebb passed away in 2004. It's true! Their musical *The Visit* finally made it to Broadway in 2015 and garnered multiple Tony nominations! As of the writing of this book, Kander is *still* writing music for musicals, and *New York, New York* is opening on Broadway in 2023 (with additional lyrics by Lin-Manuel Miranda!).

Notable shows include *Cabaret*, *Chicago*, and *Kiss of the Spider Woman*. Notable songs include "All That Jazz," "Cabaret," "Maybe This Time," and "New York, New York."

Benj Pasek and Justin Paul

Benj Pasek and Justin Paul, known as Pasek and Paul, are just beginning their careers but have achieved so much in their young lives! Tonys and Oscars and Grammys, oh my!

Notable shows include *Dear Evan Hansen*, *A Christmas Story*, and *Dogfight*. Notable songs include "Waving Through a Window" and "You Will Be Found."

SETH SPEAKS

BROADWAY VETS SUPPORT UP-AND-COMERS

After Pasek and Paul won their Tony Award for *Dear Evan Hansen*, I heard from Jeff Marx, the brilliant composer/lyricist (who wrote *Avenue Q* with Bobby Lopez):

"I met them both when they were freshmen in college. Benj emailed me, saying he was in the same college acting program I had attended, and asked if he could be my assistant for the summer. I said sure — he worked for me that summer, and we became great friends. He never played his songs until the end of the summer because he was afraid I wouldn't like them. They were fantastic, and I told him he and his writing partner could really have shows on Broadway. He didn't believe it yet (they were only 21 years old!), but I did.

At the end of the next school year, he wanted to come back out to New York City and I encouraged him to bring Justin, so they could write songs all summer, get better at it, and start writing a show. Justin said he couldn't come to New York City because his deal with his parents was that they would pay for college, but during the summers he had to work. I asked him how much he would realistically earn, and he said ideally probably $7,000. I told him I would give him $7,000 so he could come work in New York for the summer, but he didn't feel right about accepting such a gift. I said, "Okay, we'll call it a loan. And just to make it interesting — and give you a deadline — let's say you'll pay me back only if you have a show open on Broadway before you're 30. Otherwise, you'll just keep the money."

(continued)

(continued)

He accepted the loan, and they continued writing. Seven years later, their show *A Christmas Story* opened on Broadway and, on opening night, he gave me a check for $7,000. They beat the deadline by three years — they were only 27 years old.

Love, Jeff

Isn't that fantastic? Let it be known that established Broadway supports Broadway newcomers. Why not apply it to your life, and see who you can encourage in your own field? (Chad, did I put this story in another section? Can't remember!)

Richard Rodgers and Lorenz Hart

Before Richard Rodgers teamed up with Oscar Hammerstein, Rodgers teamed up with the prolific Lorenz Hart. Sadly, Hart had much internal conflict about being gay, which contributed to his alcoholism, which then contributed to his early death at age 48. But, even with all of his personal problems, Hart was a pioneer of the modern musical and helped create classic shows. Irving Berlin called him the "first of the sophisticated word writers."

Notable shows include *Babes in Arms, Pal Joey,* and *On Your Toes.* Notable songs include "Bewitched, Bothered, and Bewildered," "There's a Small Hotel," "Where or When," and "The Lady Is a Tramp."

Alain Boublil and Claude-Michel Schonberg

A French songwriting team, their show *Les Misérables* remains the longest running musical on the West End. (Sorry, Lord Lloyd Webber. *Les Miz* opened the year before *Phantom!*) Mention must be made of the brilliant lyricist Herbert Kretzmer who translated the French lyrics into the brilliant English ones that audiences know!

Notable shows include *Les Misérables* and *Miss Saigon.* Notable songs include "Bring Him Home," "I Dreamed a Dream," "Why God Why," and "On My Own."

Richard Maltby Jr. and David Shire

Though they wrote with others and though the Broadway shows they wrote as a team weren't super successful, they have an incredible canon of songs, the most famous being from their Off-Broadway musicals. And it must be noted that even their Broadway show *Baby* didn't have a very long run, it's one of the best Broadway scores out there!

Notable shows include *Baby, Closer Than Ever,* and *Starting Here! Starting Now!* Notable songs include "Starting Here! Starting Now," "The Story Goes On," and "Life Story."

Henry Krieger and Tom Eyen

Like Howard Ashman, Tom Eyen passed away from AIDS, so audiences will never know what other shows Krieger/Eyen would have created had Eyen lived. But what a legacy he left! *Dreamgirls* remains one of the most brilliant shows ever to be on Broadway. After Eyen's death, Krieger teamed up with Bill Russell (lyrics and libretto) to create *Side Show* that gave audiences one of the top 20 Tony Award performances (in my opinion!)

Notable shows: *Dreamgirls, The Tap Dance Kid,* and *Side Show* (with Bill Russell). Notable songs include "And I Am Telling You" and "I Am Changing."

Fun fact: *Dreamgirls* was originally written with the role of Effie White being played by Nell Carter (who had won the Tony Award for Best Actress in a Musical for *Ain't Misbehavin'*). After Carter did a workshop of the show, she wound up getting cast in the sitcom *Gimme a Break.* At first, the powers-that-be decided to postpone *Dreamgirls* until she was available, but Eyen knew she was going to be a huge star and the show would run on TV for *years.* He told everyone they would need a new Effie, which led to the role going to future Tony Award winner Jennifer Holliday!

Dorothy Fields, lyricist and librettist

Known mainly as a lyricist, she was a co-librettist on the hit shows *Redhead* and, most notably, *Annie, Get Your Gun.* As a person who got this particular book assignment months ago and is constantly being distracted while writing it, I'm incredibly jealous she was known to work from 8:30 a.m. to 4 p.m. Yes, that's a regular workday for many people, but it's *really* hard to do when you're at home and not in an office and your phone keeps dinging because someone commented on the Andrea McArdle video you just posted. She's so *lucky* she didn't have Facebook! Dorothy is one of the few women in a creative team capacity to make a huge mark on Broadway in the Golden Age.

Notable shows include *Annie, Get Your Gun; Redhead; Sweet Charity;* and *Seesaw.* Notable songs include "If My Friends Could See Me Now," "It's Not Where You Start, It's Where You Finish," and "Hey, Big Spender."

Betty Comden and Adolph Green, lyricists and librettists

They could go from heartbreaking songs like "Some Other Time" to heartfelt ones like "Make Someone Happy" to *hilarious* tunes like "100 Easy Ways To Lose a Man." Known for their fantastic lyrics and librettos, their special skill was their amazing sense of humor. Even though this book is about musical theatre, check out their film *Singing in the Rain* for which they wrote the book. So warm and *so* funny!

Notable shows include *On the Town, Wonderful Town, Applause,* and *The Will Rogers Follies.* Notable songs include those mentioned plus "Lucky To Be Me," "Ohio," and "Applause."

The composer/lyricist

Imagine having the magical skill and the incredible intelligence to write music. That's what these brilliant composer/lyricists have. All praise these geniuses who have given so many hit songs!

Irving Berlin

Irving Berlin wrote *so many* recognizable American classics that composer Douglas Moore joked that you couldn't have a holiday without his permission! That, of course, referred to the 4th of July ("God Bless America"), Easter ("Easter Parade"), and Christmas ("White Christmas").

Notable shows include *Annie, Get Your Gun* and *Call Me Madam.* Notable songs include "They Say It's Wonderful," "Anything You Can Do," "You're Just in Love," and his final song, the fabulous "Old Fashioned Wedding."

Cole Porter

A bon vivant who had it all: looks, wealth, and an abundance of talent. He wrote so many American classic songs *and* hit Broadway shows. Sadly, he was injured in 1937 while horseback riding and spent his remaining years in constant pain (until he had his leg amputated, but then he stopped writing and lived in seclusion). Porter was known for his incredibly clever and often risqué lyrics.

And I mean risqué! The following lyrics may not sound like going too far, but they're from the 1930s! The leading lady is talking about being undressed as well as the smart set attending nudist parties!

If driving fast cars you like,

If low bars you like,

If old hymns you like,

If bare limbs you like,

If Mae West you like,

Or me undressed you like,

Why, nobody will oppose.

When ev'ry night the set that's smart is in —

Intruding in nudist parties

In studios.

Anything goes.

Notable shows include *Anything Goes, Kiss Me, Kate,* and *Can-Can.* Notable songs include "I Get a Kick out of You," "Anything Goes (title song)," "So in Love," and "I Love Paris."

Sara Bareilles

As of this writing, Sara Bareilles has only one musical; *Waitress.* But the fact that it was her first musical as composer/lyricist and it became a hit on Broadway *and* on the West End shows the incredible promise she has for her next show! And not only is she extremely gifted at writing both music and lyrics, but she's a fantastic performer as well, taking over the leading role in *Waitress* on Broadway and in London.

Her notable show is *Waitress.* Notable songs include "She Used to Be Mine," "What Baking Can Do," and "A Soft Place to Land."

Lin-Manuel Miranda

Miranda came to Broadway starring in the musical *In the Heights* for which he wrote both music and lyrics. The show was groundbreaking for many reasons, which I discuss in Chapter 2. His follow-up show, *Hamilton,* was monumental (I also discuss it in Chapter 2.) He's now probably the most famous name associated with Broadway musicals, and theatre fans all breathlessly await his next project!

Notable shows include *In The Heights* and *Hamilton.* Notable songs include "Breathe," "Paciencia y Fé," "Wait for it," "The Schuyler Sisters," and "My Shot."

Andrew Lippa

I must say that not only is Andrew Lippa a great composer/lyricist, but he's also a fantastic singer. Listen to him play the title role in his opera, *I Am Harvey Milk.* Interestingly, his Broadway show *The Addams Family* didn't get great reviews and very few Tony nominations, but it's now among *the most produced shows in the world!* Lippa is reading those original not-glowing reviews all the way to the bank!

Notable shows include *The Wild Party, The Addams Family,* and *You're A Good Man, Charlie Brown.* Notable songs include "Life of the Party," "Pulled," and "My New Philosophy."

Michael John-LaChiusa

Michael John-LaChiusa is mainly known for his very cutting-edge Off-Broadway musicals. His second Broadway show, however, has a very unique story attached; LaChiusa came across the poem "The Wild Party" and thought it would make a great musical. He wrote the music and lyrics, and the musical came to Broadway in 2000 with an amazing cast featuring Toni Collette, Eartha Kitt, Mandy Patinkin, and Norm Lewis. In a bizarre confluence of events, there was *another* musical version of *The Wild Party* that opened Off-Broadway during the *exact same season.* Think about it: The poem *The Wild Party* isn't particularly famous. It's not as if there were two musical versions of a well-known entity like *Romeo and Juliet.* No, there were two musical versions of an obscure poem that opened at the same time! The Off-Broadway *Wild Party* was by Andrew Lippa and also had an amazing cast: Julia Murney, Brian d'Arcy James, and Taye Diggs. Sadly, instead of seeing each show as individual fabulousness, the two musicals were endlessly compared to one another, and neither could withstand to the barrage of criticism and comparisons. Both of their runs were way too short. But get each album! *So great!*

Notable shows include *Hello, Again,* and *The Wild Party.* Notable songs include "See What I Wanna See" and "Tom."

Jason Robert Brown

Jason Robert Brown usually writes his own lyrics but has teamed up with Amanda Green a few times to great success. Out of all current Broadway composers, he probably has the most songs written for Broadway and Off-Broadway shows that are then performed in piano bars and cabarets. Basically, if you walk into a piano bar anywhere in the country, you're bound to hear one of his songs.

Notable shows include *The Last Five Years* (Off Broadway), *Songs for a New World* (Off Broadway), *Parade,* and *Mr. Saturday Night.* Notable songs include "Stars and the Moon," "Moving Too Fast," and "All the Wasted Time."

Frank Loesser

I'm constantly reading that one should sleep seven to nine hours a night, but poor Frank Loesser rarely slept more than four hours in a row! Holy bags-under-your-eyes! Regardless, with that little amount of sleep, he still had the mental focus to write brilliant shows and is also well-known for the song he wrote to perform with his wife at parties. That little ditty wound up winning an Academy Award. I'm talkin' "Baby, It's Cold Outside."

Notable shows include *The Most Happy Fella, How to Succeed in Business without Really Trying*, and *Guys and Dolls*. Notable songs include "I've Never Been in Love Before," "I Believe in You," and "Adelaide's Lament."

Jerry Herman

Jerry Herman not only wrote stunning melodies and fantastic lyrics, but he also knew how to create joy with his music. Just listen to any of his scores, and you hear the joy bubbling through. He had two smash hits open within two years of each other: *Hello, Dolly!* opened in 1964 and *Mame* opened in 1966. He said he would often see Act One of *Hello, Dolly!* and then stroll down the street and see Act Two of *Mame*. Speaking of *Mame*, I defy you to find a song more joyous than "It's Today!"

Notable shows include *Hello, Dolly! Mame*, and *La Cage Aux Folles*. Notable songs include "Hello, Dolly," "If He Walked Into My Life," "Before the Parade Passes By," "It Only Takes a Moment," and "I Am What I Am."

Meredith Willson

One of the rare creative triple threats, Meredith Willson wrote the music, lyrics, and libretto to his smash hit *The Music Man*. Willson was not only a fantastic writer, but he also was the musical theatre version of what they call on *Project Runway* as "fashion forward." His writing on *The Music Man* had a brand-new way of starting songs. Instead of the dialogue ending and the song beginning, there was a blurred line between when the dialogue ended and the songs began. That was his goal, according to his brilliant book, *But He Doesn't Know The Territory* (University of Minnesota Press), which is all about the writing of *The Music Man*. Just listen to the beginning of "76 Trombones." "May I have your attention please, your attention please . . . " It sounds like dialogue, but it's actually the beginning of the song!

Notable shows include *The Music Man* and *The Unsinkable Molly Brown*. Notable songs include "76 Trombones," "Goodnight My Someone," and "Til There Was You."

Stephen Sondheim

Considered the master by many, Stephen Sondheim was what most Broadway writers aspire to be: someone who always pushed harmonic boundaries and penned lyrics so insightful and clever that it's *shocking* they also rhyme!

Backstory: His parents happened to have a summer house near the original master of musical theatre, Oscar Hammerstein, and Hammerstein became his mentor and surrogate father. You can read about his mastery in any of several books, but suffice it to say, in the annals of musical theatre, no one is more revered than Sondheim.

Notable shows include *A Funny Thing Happened on the Way to the Forum*, *Company*, *A Little Night Music*, *Sweeney Todd*, *Sunday in the Park With George*, and *Into the Woods*.

Notable songs include "Send in the Clowns" (his only worldwide hit), "Being Alive," "Losing My Mind," "Broadway Baby," and "Children Will Listen."

IN THIS CHAPTER. . .

» **Introducing the casting director**

» **Meeting the directors**

» **Dancing with the choreographers**

» **Eyeing the producers**

» **Understanding who the music team is**

Chapter 7

Creating the Big Picture — "The Room Where It Happens"

When an actor auditions for musicals, they usually have a final callback where they have to sing for a bunch of folks sitting *behind the table*. Who are the group of people in that powerful position — the people who sit there with their diet sodas and half-eaten sandwiches deciding the fate of the actors who, in essence, are singing the lyrics from *A Chorus Line*, "I Really Need This Job!"? The composer, lyricist, and librettist (see Chapter 6), to name just three. After all, they wrote the show, so they should have a decision in who gets to say their words and sing their songs.

But who else is part of the final decision? Usually, the choreographer (*Can they dance it?*) and the music director (*Can they sing it?*). And the person who oversees everything just mentioned — the director — makes the final, *final* decision. Although, someone *is* above the director, the person who controls the purse strings of the production — *the producer*. If the director is new or doesn't have that much power yet, then the ultimate decision maker is the producer.

The jobs of these various people don't end with the audition; often that's just the beginning of what they do for a musical. I explain all of this in this chapter. But first, I discuss who brings the actors in to audition in the first place!

Finding the Talent — The Casting Director

The *casting director* reads the script of the musical they've been hired to cast and consults with the creative team to get a sense of what's needed. Then they bring to the creative team the actors they think are right for the show, which saves the creative team lots of time. Instead of sitting through days and days of auditions with actors who may not be right for the show, the creative team see only the people who have a good chance of being cast. Of course, there stories have many exceptions to the rule (see the nearby sidebar).

REMEMBER

How does the casting director find these performers that (hopefully) eventually get cast on Broadway? By doing a combination of the following:

>> They put out the word to agents with a *breakdown, which* is a list of characters that the show is casting. The agents then submit clients whom they think meet the description of what's needed. The casting office looks through these submissions and brings in just the people whom they think are right for the show. If they're certain the performer is suited for the show, they'll bring the performer directly to the director and/or choreographer to audition. However, if they want to make sure the person is right, they'll first bring that actor in just for the casting director or associate and, if they pass muster, *then* they'll go to the next level of audition.

>> When they're casting a Broadway show, they're not just considering the actors who are submitted through agents. After all, not every performer has representation. When the casting office is hired for a particular show, the casting director looks through the offices' files for people they've seen throughout the years and then they compile a list they think will make the director happy. Casting offices have files on people they've cast in other shows, people they've never cast but whose work they know of, people who have come into audition and are talented but were wrong for what they were auditioning for . . . basically, a casting person's job is to have information on everyone and anyone who performs.

Casting people are continually replenishing their files. How? They sit through general auditions with people they've never seen before so they can start files on them. And these auditions often feature people they *have* seen before but who haven't gone to the next level of audition. These performers come back hoping a different song or improved dance skill or better outfit will make the casting people see them in a different light.

SETH SPEAKS

You may ask: Why use a casting director if the creative team ultimately makes the final decision? Consider this example. I wrote the musical *Disaster!* with my friend Jack Plotnick; when we went to Broadway, the casting process for the leading roles was basically me texting my friends and asking if they wanted to do a new Broadway show and that's how those roles were cast (Adam Pascal, Kerry Butler, Max Crumm, Lacretta Nicole, Jennifer Simard, Rachel York, Keven Chamberlin, and Faith Prince).

But we needed an ensemble who could sing, dance, act (and do great comedy), *and* understudy all the leads. I didn't know a lot of the new young people who were starting out on Broadway, and the Tara Rubin Casting Office brought in some amazing people for us to consider. I'm grateful to them because that's how we cast most of our ensemble. Almost all of those performers were unknown to me, and they were so talented! My point is, I don't know how I would have found them if Tara Rubin hadn't listened to what we were looking for, scanned her enormous list of talented folks, and brought in enough people so we had choices but weren't overwhelmed.

CASTING EXCEPTION-TO-THE-RULE STORY

The casting office is usually the gatekeeper of not only who can audition but who can audition for which part. The casting director knows the show and understands the creative team's vision, and they don't want to waste time bringing in the wrong people. However, they're human and can make mistakes. Terrence Mann wanted to be considered for the role of Javert in *Les Misérables*. However, he had just originated the role of Rum Tug Tugger, the super-sexy rock 'n' roll cat, in *Cats*. When you think Javert, you don't think young and you don't think rock 'n' roll.

The casting office wanted him to audition for Enjolras, the student revolutionary leader. He wanted to be seen for Javert, but they said no. It was Enjolras or *rien*. So, Terry (as he's known) told me he went to his Enjolras audition *but* treated it as if he were auditioning for Javert! He dressed all in black and slicked his hair back. Then he sang the dark song "Amsterdam" by Jacques Brel. The writers were sitting in front of him while he was singing, and he literally saw them look at each other and one of them mouth "Enjolras?". Then he saw them shake their heads, and the other one mouth "Javert!" and they both nodded. Suffice it to say, he got the role!

Leading the Creative Vision — The Director

The director is in charge of the creative vision of the show and has final say on the casting. Of course, exceptions to that rule usually revolve around star vehicles. A *star vehicle* is a show where the producer(s) hope that tickets will be sold because of who's starring in it, and the star or stars are often chosen beforehand. For instance, in *The Music Man* revival of 2022, noted Jerry Zaks was brought on to direct after Hugh Jackman and Sutton Foster were already cast.

Here I discuss in more detail what the director does to bring the show to the stage.

Collaborating with everyone

As I mention in Chapter 6, musical theatre is considered the most collaborative of the arts, and the director is a perfect example. The director's job is to collaborate with almost everyone involved with the show, including these people.

REMEMBER

The director is the *third eye*, the person who didn't create the book/music/lyrics and can therefore impartially see what needs to be changed. Yes, sometimes the director is *also* a creator — for example, Martin Charnin wrote the lyrics to *Annie* and James Lapine wrote the libretto to *Into The Woods* and his other Sondheim shows — but I'm writing in broad strokes so, as they say on Twitter, "don't @ me"!

Librettist/composer/lyricist

The director gives notes on the script and the score. Even though the final word on the script and the score is contractually decided by the writers themselves, meaning they don't have to change anything they don't want to change, the hope is that it never comes to a "read my contract!" type of brouhaha.

REMEMBER

If the director feels the show needs to cut a scene or it needs a different finale or a funnier joke, the creators should oblige and collaborate because, again, the director is in charge of everything creative in the show.

SETH SPEAKS

The wonderful Off-Broadway musical called *Zanna, Don't!* is about a high school in an opposite world: Being gay is the norm and being straight means being ostracized. The show originally began with the story unfolding around a couple who comes out as straight. But the director, Devanand Janki, felt that the story started too soon and the audience had to first be brought into this reverse-o world. He explained that to the writer, Tim Acito, and an opening number was then written that established the place and introduced the characters before the story started.

In other words, the director doesn't create what needs to be added/changed, the director tells the creator what needs to be added/changed and, hopefully, it works. Here's the song: www.youtube.com/watch?v=qpN8msJ7C1Q&list=PLBC003 5ACA4787579.

Set and lighting designer

The director works closely with the set and lighting designers because they have a crucial role in the look of the show. Lighting can be changed and adjusted through-out the tech period, but the set design is extremely important to have (mostly) finalized *before* rehearsals begin so the actors know what they're performing on (a platform, a staircase, a turntable, where are the doors? and so on). The director collaborates extremely closely with the set designer and includes their vision in the final product. For instance, Hal Prince enjoyed "theatre magic" meaning he relished the audience using their imagination and supplying visuals that aren't there.

The director approves all props as well . . . or lack of props. For a wonderful example of a director's vision of sparseness in set design *and* sparseness in props, watch the Tony Award performance from *Grand Hotel* (www.youtube.com/watch?v=JoB0CSsrrCo). Notice how the bar is just a wooden pole across the front of the stage and both Brent Barrett and Michael Jeter are miming bottles and glasses. No props are used at all! Tommy Tune was the brilliant director/choreographer of this show. (P.S. On a side note, this is also one of the most thrill-ing numbers ever performed on the Tony Awards).

Choreographer and fight director

The director stages the scenes (tells the actors where to move) and approves *everything* else on the stage. That means the choreographed dances, the fight scenes staged by a fight director, or any specialty moments like the trapeze/tumbling/circus acts in the revival of *Pippin* or the elaborate cheerleading seg-ments in *Bring It On*. The director approves everything, even if the director doesn't actually create that movement.

Costume, wig, and other designers

The director also approves all the other creatives' and designers' work. The designers' work — costume sketches, wig designs, and so forth — is brought to the director in advance and approved before they're fully realized. That's just the first step because as soon as these designs are actually seen off the page and in 3-D, they're often changed again.

KEEP IT MOVING!

The director is also in charge of something that seems intangible but can be managed — the pacing of a show. The *pacing* is how fast or slow a show moves. Pacing is more than just the tempo of how the dialogue flows; it's also about how long/short pauses are held, the speed of songs, and where laughs and applause should happen.

Chita Rivera told me about the big Act One final number she had in *Kiss of the Spider Woman* called "Gimme Love." The song happens because one of the main characters is describing a movie musical number he loves and the number comes to life onstage, featuring Chita. After many verses and a long dance break, the number abruptly stops. Chita would freeze in a pose, and dialogue would begin in the depressing jail cell where the two main characters live. The director Hal Prince didn't want the number to have an ending because he wanted the harshness of reality to suddenly interrupt the lush, colorful number. But Chita felt the audience wanted the number to have an ending so they could applaud. Forget it. Hal was adamant — no ending.

Chita realized it wasn't the ending the number needed, and she felt the audience wanted the release of applauding. So, she came up with a plan: Right before the switch back to reality, she was inside a giant birdcage (for real), and as it spun in a circle, she would climb inside it so she kept facing straight out. She told the male dancers who were spinning the cage to go *as fast as they could*. The faster they spun it, the more she frantically climbed inside and kept herself facing straight out to the audience. It was so incredible to watch that the audience would . . . *applaud!* And then harsh reality would set in. Yes! Chita found a way to get the audience the release of applause *without* having to officially end the number. Win-win!

One of the most devastating changes happened during *Seussical*. The costume designer drew what the costumes would look like, and the director approved them all. After the costume designer had them made (or *built* as it's often called), it was time for the *costume parade*. In a show with lots of costumes, the actors put on their various costumes and model them onstage to see if anything needs to change. Well, apparently *everything* needed to change. After the actors showed the director (and producer) the costumes for Act One, the costume designer was fired! That meant everything had to be built again from scratch. *But* the show was about to begin previews in a few days. The creative team needed to see the script/songs in front of an audience to see what worked and what didn't and it would have delayed any changes being made to the show if they cancelled any out-of-town performances. The cast shared with me that they were therefore told to go to the mall and buy some clothes to wear(!) as a temporary fix until they had their actual costumes. That means the early performances of *Seussical* featured costumes by . . . The Gap!

Figuring out what a show needs and making it happen

The director doesn't have the skill sets of everyone involved in creating the show, but their job is to tell the people with the skill sets what works and what doesn't. For example, Lin-Manuel Miranda told me that when he was working on *In the Heights*, the top of Act Two had a love song for Nina (Mandy Gonzalez) and Benny (Chris Jackson). Lin knew the song he wrote (a kind of '80s power love song) *wasn't* working.

His director Tommy Kail suggested that the song could come from a Spanish lesson. The character of Nina spoke Spanish and perhaps she could teach her non-Spanish–speaking boyfriend some phrases that led into a love song. That idea became "Sunrise," in which Nina is teaching Benny some basic Spanish words ("store" and "corner") and soon they become "heat," "last night," and "hold me." It works so beautifully in the show and demonstrates what a director does, which is figure out what a show needs and guide the creative team (or actors) to fill that need. He basically told Lin, "We both know the song you wrote isn't working. I myself can't write a new song, but here's an idea that I think could work."

"Dancing through Life" — Choreographers

Choreographers are in charge of all the dancing on stage. But that's not completely accurate because what's *dancing*? Does it have to be a fancy technical step, or can it be just a sway? Basically, that answer varies from show to show. Choreographers not only make up the dances for the big dance numbers, but they also often choreograph the numbers you don't even realize have choreography. Yes, when a 25-person ensemble is tap dancing up a storm, you know that's the work of the choreographer. But what about when it's just one person singing a song? Surely, the choreographer doesn't do anything with those types of songs, right? There are no high kicks or backflips. Well, yes and no.

Sometimes when a character sings a song, the director (not the choreographer) does the staging — that is, tells the actors to begin the song sitting, for example, stand up when they get to the second chorus, and then stay center stage until the song's end. But after that number is put together, the choreographer might see it and notice the four beats of music before the final note. And the song is about deciding to travel far away, so the choreographer tells the actor to take three steps forward during that musical moment and then point forward on the final beat. When the actor takes those steps, it not only syncs exactly with the music, which is enjoyable to an audience, but it also impacts the audience emotionally because it's as if the actor is saying, "I am dead serious about this!" And then that final point implies that actor is going to travel *far* away. That doesn't look like dancing (because it's literally just walking and pointing), but it was indeed choreographed and those final moves made the ending of the song more impactful to the audience.

Because the choreographer is in charge of any movement that happens while music is playing (see Figure 7-1), the best choreographers can work with all types of performers. Yes, they should know how to make amazing dances with skilled and trained dancers, but not everyone in a musical is a trained dancer. Someone who's known for making untrained dancers look fabulous is Pat Birch. She finds out what moves you do comfortably and then works those moves into the show. She was the original choreographer of *Grease* (and did the film as well). That cast had no legit dancers, but the numbers were so fantastic! There's a video online with the original staging of "Summer Nights," and you can see how everyone's dancing, but it's steps most anyone can do . . . and look fabulous doing! Check it out for yourself: www.youtube.com/watch?v=1nEdpAcFKFk.

FIGURE 7-1:
The choreography in *Hamilton*.

CBS Photo Archive/Getty Images

The choreographer is "behind the table" at auditions because they want to know the dance skill level of everyone in the show. The music director, choreographer, and director all hash out whom they want to cast — which may mean making sacrifices. For example, someone who doesn't tap as well may be cast because the music director really needs one solid soprano. Someone who's not the best singer might get in the show because they have a special dance skill (backflips?) that's imperative to a scene. And someone else who isn't the best singer/dancer but is still skilled might be cast because they can look various ages and the director knows they can understudy lots of roles.

Handling the Money and So Much More — Producers

The word *producer* now means different things compared to when Broadway first began. I explain how the definition has changed, but first let me tell you the reason: Broadway has gotten *very* expensive. Putting up a show now takes a huge amount of money. (Just to be clear, that's not because of paying the musicians, a frustrating myth that's been bandied about to justify the reduction of the Broadway orchestra.) Before I go on, you may think, "It's always been expensive to put on a musical." And you're not wrong, but nowhere near how expensive it is today.

These sections identify what producers involved in putting on a Broadway show do to make sure the show goes on and how the budget has changed since the Golden Age.

Money Makes the World Go Round

In 1971 *Follies* was considered the most expensive musical ever put on Broadway. The cost was $700,000. But in 2022, $700,000 is around $5.5 million, an amount that wouldn't get *any* musical on Broadway today. *Wicked* cost $14 million, and that was in 2003! So the theory that musicals have always been expensive is true, but the costs have gone up an *extraordinary* amount. If you want to know why costs have skyrocketed, there are *lots* of articles you search online. My point in bringing up costs is to illustrate why the term "producer" has changed meaning.

Broadway musicals once had just one producer per musical. Back in the day, one producer could easily raise enough money to mount a production. Now it takes multiple producers to raise those millions and millions of dollars. *And* here's the part that's changed: If an investor gives a large amount, they receive the perk of being called a producer of the show. Being a *producer* is a much more impressive title than just being an *investor*. And the best perk: If you're a producer and your show wins a Tony Award, you get to go onstage! Now you know why mobs of people flood the stage when the Best Musical is announced on the Tonys. The people on that stage are all considered producers.

Some in the Broadway community frown on this change because they feel the term "producer" has lost its meaning. Yes, the producer raised the money back in the day, but being a producer also meant being the head of *everything*. That's still the case with *lead producers* on Broadway, but the term producer is now clouded by producers who are actually just investors. A lead producer, however, is in charge of everything. The buck literally stops with them. To be clear, the producer can't make the songwriters change a song or insist the librettist change a scene or demand the director change their direction, but the producer can say, "I don't like this so I'm closing the show." In other words, they *can* make those changes via a threat. But hopefully, collaboration is still in vogue and changes are made throughout mutual give and take.

Crafting the idea and assembling the players

The producer (especially in the old days) often comes up with the idea for the show and puts together the creative team. Yes, directors are in charge of everything creatively, but the producer is often a kind of puppet master above them.

THE ABOMINABLE SHOWMAN

You can get your way via other methods besides threats if you're diabolical like producer David Merrick, known as the Abominable Showman. He was a brilliant producer in terms of assembling fantastic artistic teams and knowing how to keep a show running, but he definitely played dirty. He produced the musical *The Baker's Wife*, and he hated the song "Meadowlark," which Patti LuPone sang. The song is about a beautiful bird who was blind and suddenly gets her vision restored from a beautiful prince. Instead of going away with the prince, the meadowlark stays with the old man who loves her. But because she doesn't go with her new love, she dies. The song symbolizes what's happening to Patti's character: Does she stay with her old baker husband (and symbolically die) or the new sexy man who wants to whisk her away (and have her vision)?

Patti agreed the song didn't work perfectly in the show, but not because it wasn't a great song. She felt one of the reasons was because she sang it on the upstairs part of the set, and being that far away prevented the audience from connecting with her. Regardless, Merrick wanted it *cut.* The creative team refused to get rid of it, and Merrick notoriously said, "I'll get rid of that song if I have to poison the birdseed myself." He came up with an idea on how to get it out of the show one night; he snuck into the orchestra pit and *stole the music!* Yes! He went to every music stand and took the sheet music to "Meadowlark," so no one could play it. In those days, music was hand printed, so there wasn't a backup copy stored in a computer that could be printed for the show and, indeed, the song was cut!

Ingenious? Evil? You decide!

Here's a great example of how it happens, from idea to production, featuring Hal Prince, considered one of the greatest Broadway producers ever. This is about the first show he co-produced, in the 1950s. Before Prince was a multi-Tony award winning producer and director, he was stage-managing for theatre director/ producer George Abbott.

Bobby Griffith, who also worked with Abbott, called Prince because he saw a review of a book called, *Seven and a Half Cents.* He told Prince he thought it could be a musical. A producer often comes up with an idea from scratch or sees a book, a film, or a movie and thinks it can be a musical. (Chapter 11 discusses the different-ent materials that are used to create musicals.) So, after Griffith called, Prince read the review *and* the book and then called the rights holder — all before lunch! Prince told the rights holder that he and Griffith wanted to produce it as a musical on Broadway. The guy wanted to know why he should give the rights to two young producers who never produced a Broadway musical before. Prince told him because he could get *the* George Abbott to direct. Well, even though another big producer was interested, the guy gave Prince the rights to what would become *The Pajama Game.*

Prince had no way of knowing if Abbott would direct, but he talked big and hoped for the best! Prince approached Abbott who said yes, but he qualified it. He told Prince and Griffith they had to be in charge of getting a composer, lyricist, set person, lighting designer, and so on. Producers often take care of these details. Prince and Griffith approached Frank Loesser to write the score (great choice!), but Loesser said no. However, he recommended a young composing team: Richard Adler and Jerry Ross. They had the hit song "Rags to Riches" on the radio, and Loesser thought they could do a whole musical.

Prince then asked Jerome Robbins to choreograph, but Robbins told them he wanted to start directing (this was before *West Side Story*) and would only do it if he could co-direct with Abbott. They knew Abbott wouldn't go for it and soon their friend Joan McCraken recommended her husband, an up-and-coming cho-reographer: Bob Fosse (yes, that Bob Fosse!). Abbott asked what had happened to Robbins, and Prince told him to forget about it. Abbott pressed and finally Prince told him that Robbins wanted to co-direct. Surprisingly, Abbott said yes! He told Prince, "Give it to him. Everyone will know who really directed it!"

If you wonder why Prince was so important to musical theatre, he was responsible for getting Robbins to direct his first musical and Fosse to choreograph his first Broadway show!

Not every producer comes up with the idea. Sometimes it happens one of these ways:

>> The creative team approaches a producer with a product and asks if the producer can shepherd it to Broadway.

>> A producer will see a show that's running Off-Broadway or out of town and decide to bring it to Broadway.

>> A producer is invited to a reading or a workshop to see if they'll take on the project.

That's what happened with Broadway producers Kevin McCollum and Jeffrey Seller. They were invited to a reading of a new musical by a composer/lyricist who never had a show on Broadway. They thought the show was messy, but it had one particular song they thought was fantastic. That song convinced them to approach the writer of the show and ask him if they could take it to the next level. I'm being mysterious because I enjoy the reveal: The writer they approached was Jonathan Larson, the show was *Rent*, and the song that convinced them was "Light My Candle."

Making the plan to get on Broadway

After a producer has decided to produce a show for Broadway, they have a lot to do to get it there . . . and keep it there! Chapter 11 discusses these details, which include such producorial aspects as conducting readings and workshops, taking the show out of town (or not!), finding a Broadway theatre to open a Broadway show, and deciding when to close a Broadway show. All of these are jobs of a Broadway producer.

"The Music of the Night" — The Music Team

Most musicals have a vocal arranger who creates all the vocal harmonies in the show, a dance arranger who arranges the music for the dance segments, and an orchestrator who takes the songs the composer writes and divides the accompaniment between various instruments. But the person above them is the *music director*. The music director is present at all final casting calls. *Note:* Music direction was the field I was in for years when I came to New York City.

The music director is in charge of *all* the music in the show. They're not in charge of writing the music (that's the composer), but the music director is in charge of interpreting the music. They do that by rehearsing with the actors (and orchestra) and giving advice regarding how to perform the song.

SETH
SPEAKS

In *Sunset Boulevard*, Norma Desmond ends her first big song with the lyrics, "With one look I'll be me!" If I ever music directed the show, I would tell my leading lady to do the phrasing without a breath before the final note because that's something I heard the original star, Patti LuPone, do when I was playing a concert with her in London. I flipped out because I had always heard it sung with a breath: "With one look . . . I'll be . . . (breath) ME!" But once I heard Patti sing it without a breath, I vowed I would always music direct it that way. An actor has many different options about how to sing things, and it's up to the music director to choose one and explain why it works. To me, the long line of "I'll beeeee meeeee" is thrilling to an audience. Someone actually filmed the performance when I did that song with Patti! Check it out at www.youtube.com/watch?v=t3P9GORfSgM.

Music directors also work with composers on shaping songs. One of the most famous MDs (as they're called in Broadway parlance) is Paul Gemignani. In *Dreamgirls*, at the end of Act One, a song called "It's All Over" is a fight between six people. It's basically the same two chord changes with lots of different and fabulous melodies above those chord changes. The melodies are so thrilling, but again, it's really just two chord changes. *And* the song goes on for around four minutes. Paul was working with the great composer Henry Krieger and suggested that the song modulate, meaning change keys around every 32 bars. By making the keys get progressively higher and higher, it kept the excitement and intensity of the song amping up. That's what a music director does; they don't write the music, but they help interpret it in the best way possible. Listen at www.youtube.com/watch?v=1c5YmV4GNEw.

Music directors are also often the conductors of the show, and conductors are vital in contributing to the energy of the show. When you're onstage and you look down to see a conductor completely present and involved with the music, it keeps you engaged as an actor.

SETH
SPEAKS

Sometimes being present and involved can lead to an accident! Chita Rivera told me that Leonard Bernstein would sometimes conduct *West Side Story* and, when he did, he would stand on a box to make him taller. During one performance of "The Tonight Quintet," he was getting *really* into it . . . and suddenly disappeared! She found out he was stomping along with that amazing *West Side Story* rhythm and stomped so hard he crashed right through his box!

IN THIS CHAPTER

» **Focusing on costume designers**

» **Recognizing what set designers do**

» **Lighting the stage with lighting designers**

» **Making sound happen with sound designers**

» **Understanding what hair and wig designers do**

Chapter **8**

Delivering the Details — The Creatives

When a show is being created, just a skeleton crew of people work on it. During the initial readings, usually only the people who wrote it, a stage manager, and the performers are involved. *Sometimes* a director is there to add insight and, if the composer doesn't teach the music, a music director is used. As the show gets closer and closer to Broadway and the readings/workshops get more elaborate, more people are brought on; eventually there's a choreographer, a music director/vocal arranger, and even sometimes an orchestrator if there's a small band to add some sass to the workshop. But a certain group of people aren't brought on until the show really goes into production. These people bring the show to a whole new level.

Yes, the score is amazing, but it sounds even more incredible when you can really hear the trumpets blaring out high notes during the dance break. Yes, that actor did an amazing dramatic exit during the workshop, but now it's so much more moving because as they exit sternly through two giant doors, you're able to see devastation on their face as the set completely turns around and reveals the actor on the opposite side of the doors. Yes, the ensemble nailed the big last chord on the Act One finale, but it's so much more exciting when they cut off *right* on the blackout!

You get my point. This chapter is about the people who add all the finishing touches that are often called *production values*. Working closely with the director, these folks create the elements that make seeing a live musical a unique experience. After these elements are perfected and teched (see Chapter 11), various crew members mentioned in Chapter 10 take over the day-to-day aspects of keeping them implemented properly in the show. But first these designs have to be created. Welcome to the world of the design team!

Who Are You Wearing? — Costume Designers

Out of all aspects of the design team, costuming is probably the easiest for the audience to notice. When you see *The Phantom of the Opera*, you're aware of the over-the-top/bizarre outfits in the song "Masquerade." When you see *Moulin Rouge*, you can't help noticing the sexy hot lewks in the opening song. When you see *Evita*, you think "Whoa! That white dress is beautiful, but what if she spills coffee on it? *That* would make Argentina cry for her." That's just me?

On the flip side, when you see a show that takes place today, you may think, "Oh, those actors are just wearing clothes from their closet." Let it be known — that isn't true! The *costume designer* creates and/or culls every article of clothing onstage. And the director has to approve it all. That's because costumes are vitally important to a musical.

As a matter of fact, I know many actors who go to auditions wearing an outfit that replicates a costume. They're not wearing an actual costume, but they make sure their clothes represent the role they're auditioning for because costumes help tell the story. When the audience sees what someone is wearing, they make judgments about who that character is. So instead of exposition in a script, sometimes a character just needs to enter in a costume, and the audience knows what that character is like. For example, in *Mamma Mia!* leading lady Donna was costumed in overalls and part of the costume design was one strap being undone (see Figure 8-1). This tiny element of the loose strap indicated to the audience that she was overworked and didn't have time to focus on her appearance. But it also added an element of sex appeal, so the audience was excited when three eligible bachelors came to her Greek Island.

Here I delve deeper into the world of costume designing and explain what costume designers do and point out some examples of great costume designing on Broadway.

FIGURE 8-1:
Donna's costume in *Mamma Mia!* shows the audience who she is.

Joan Marcus

Recognizing what costume designers do

The costume designer consults with the director as well as the set and lighting designer before they start sketching. Everyone needs to be on the same page in terms of things like the time period and the style and look of the show. One of the main considerations before anything is decided is, of course, the budget. A big musical might spend up to $500,000 for costumes, which may seem like a lot of money, but think about a musical with a big cast with lots of costume changes. Not only do all of those costumes have to be created, but all of the show's understudies need costumes as well! After the budget is set for the costumes, the costume designer decides how that money should be spent for all the show's costumes. For instance, the show might have a moment where a character has to look amazing (think any show that ends with a wedding, like *Guys and Dolls*), which means not as much money is spent on some of the other costumes.

REMEMBER

Here are other decisions — just a smattering, mind you — that the costume designer makes:

>> If this is a period piece, what clothes are needed to indicate the right time frame? Is it literal? Or is it the essence of the time period, sassed up . . . like *Hamilton*?

>> Is there a dance section featuring everyday people? If so, the clothes have to look like regular clothes, but they also have to be sturdy enough to take the wear and tear of flying around the stage eight times a week.

>> Is there a change of time? Say the leading lady exits a scene and almost reenters for the next scene that takes place the next day. The designer has to figure out a way for her to change her look within seconds so she's wearing a completely different outfit at the start of the next scene.

The costume designer can shift the budget around in many ways. If the show takes place in a school, for example, perhaps make it the type of school with a daily uniform so the cast can wear the same costume in every scene and leave more money for the really important costumes.

REMEMBER

Before the costume designer sends their designs to a costume shop to start *building* the costumes, everyone's measurements are taken. And I mean *every* measurement — not just what you look at when you buy a shirt or a pair of jeans at the mall. Every single body measurement, including neck, head (for hats), and shoe size, is necessary. And sometimes it's more than just, "I wear a size 9 shoe." Some costumers don't just buy retail shoes; they have custom shoes built — especially for dance shows where a shoe should look like it's being worn by a businessman, but suddenly that Florsheim-esque shoe has to grand jeté, so it can't have a typical hard sole. It needs to point, flex, and stretch! Custom shoes are expensive, averaging $1,000 a pair, but having a shoe built for dancing can mean the difference between a great show eight times a week, or a heel falling off and injuring a dancer.

Costume designers also have to sometimes design costumes that are rigged for quick changes. Yes, it looks like a button-down shirt and pants, but the actor wearing it has to leave the stage and come back in a completely different look 20 seconds later. So, the buttons aren't actually closing the shirt. They're just permanently in a buttoned position; a Velcro strip is underneath the buttons, so actors can take it off in seconds. And the pants aren't closed with a fly and a buckle, they're specially rigged so someone backstage can pull them and just rip them off the actor. It's actually a little like being a stripper!

After the costumes are approved, they're sent to one of the costume shops in New York where they're built by that shop's team of tailors, dressmakers, fabric painters and dyers, cobblers, beaders, embroiderers, pleaters, glove makers, and milliners.

Identifying memorable costume moments in Broadway history

Costumes very much enhance the musical experience for audience, and this list shows just how integral costuming is to Broadway shows:

>> **Applause for the costumes:** You'd think only songs would get applause in musicals, but costumes often do! Especially the quick changes. A classic quick change happened in *Dreamgirls*. In Act One, the musical group "The Dreams"

are performing a song called "Heavy." An onstage curtain comes down in front of them, there's an announcement welcoming The Dreams to a brand-new city, and 10 seconds later the curtain goes up and all three women are in a *completely* new outfit. APPLAUSE! This moment was well known because it was also one of the earliest quick changes; nowadays quick changes have become more and more elaborate, but *Dreamgirls* opened in 1981 and many audience members hadn't seen anything like it before. Brava to costume designer Theoni Aldredge!

>> **Onstage quick changes:** Although quick changes often happen backstage with a team of dressers, nowadays, there are ways to do quick changes *onstage,* in view of the audience. Costumes can be rigged in a way that when a certain part is pulled, a new costume immediately appears.

Explaining it in words isn't easy, so check out the Tony Award performance of *Cinderella*. Victoria Clark begins the scene as the town crazy lady dressed in rags, but she then pulls something on her costume and is suddenly revealed to be Cinderella's Fairy Godmother, wearing a stunning dress. The change happened in front of the audience in seconds. So exciting! Check out www. youtube.com/watch?v=1e5LA4AmYfw.

>> **Famous costumes:** The fact that Broadway fans can recognize a character from a Broadway show just from their costume demonstrates how important costumes are. Here are some examples of costumes that anyone could wear and a musical theatre fan would immediately know who the character is.

- The purple Anita dress Chita wore for *West Side Story*

- The white shirt, black tie, and black pants worn by Elder Price (and all the Elders!) from The *Book of Mormon*

- The red *Hello, Dolly!* dress in the title song worn by Dolly Levi.

- Nellie Forbush's sailor suit when she sings "Honey Bun" in *South Pacific*

- Beetlejuice's striped shirt and pants in *Beetlejuice*

- The gold tuxedos and gold hats worn in the *A Chorus Line* finale

- Annie's red dress that looks just like the outfit she wears in the comic strip

- Evan Hansen's striped polo shirt and arm cast (of course) in *Dear Evan Hansen*

Who knows what signature costumes will be created in the next Broadway season?

Making the Physical Scenery — Set Designers

The set designer designs the scenery for musicals. That involves the backdrops, the structures on the stage, and the scenic elements that "fly" up and down as well as those that come on from the wings. Like costumes, sets help tell the story. For instance, the set shows an audience that the actors are standing in a forest instead of an actor standing on a bare stage and saying, "Well, here we are in the forest!"

And like costumes, Broadway sets have also received theatre-wide applause and can be recognized out of the context of the show. The most well-known are from three big British imports: The chandelier falling in *Phantom*, the turntable turning in *Les Misérables*, and the helicopter landing in *Miss Saigon* are probably the most famous. These types of sets could never have happened when Broadway first began.

These next sections show how set designers create artificial environments onstage and how sets have evolved over the years.

Eyeing the different types — From painted backdrops to mechanized sets

When theatre first began in ancient days, sets mainly showed various locations with basic painted backdrops. And I mean basic! It wasn't until the Italian Renaissance that paintings began to use perspective to show depth and different elevations. Sets became a little more like what audiences know during the Baroque period because large pieces could move on and offstage using ropes and pulleys . . . and something decidedly old school: chariots!

For the first few decades of Broadway musicals, sets were still backdrops that were painted to look like wherever that scene took place and large pieces manually pulled on and offstage. But then technology began to improve and sets became more and more elaborate starting in the 1970s. Here are a couple notable ones:

>> In 1975 Chita Rivera rose from a fabulous *Chicago* elevator in the middle of the stage right before she entered for "All That Jazz."

>> 1977's *Annie* had conveyor belts going across the stage. In the number "NYC," ensemble members were frozen in positions of classic things New Yorkers do (like a paperboy holding that day's newspaper), and they would be placed on a conveyor belt that moved across the stage.

In the 1980s, *Les Misérables* had a turntable in the middle of the stage that was a signature part of experiencing the show. Not a turntable on which to play an album, but rather a turntable large enough for lots of actors to stand. It wasn't just cool to watch, it was functional in keeping the show moving; it could turn when a scene was over and reveal different actors who'd then begin the next scene. This way the audience didn't have to wait for a scene change. The scenes could flow seamlessly. And in a show that's three hours and 15 minutes, every second counts! P.S. Previous productions had turntables (1964's *Oliver* had a set on a turntable), but those turntables were manually turned by the crew.

SETH SPEAKS

By the 1980s, many sets became mechanized. That made a lot more things possible, but also more prone to electronic error. Errors can be frustrating but can also answer the prayer of a cast! Judy Kuhn told me that on the night *Les Miz* opened in D.C., everyone went out to celebrate. The next day was a matinée, and everyone was *exhausted* from staying up so late. It would have been so nice to have the afternoon off. Well, the show started . . . and the signature turntable malfunctioned and was only able to turn at one speed: *maximum velocity*. People were actually falling left and right . . . so the show had to be cancelled. The audience was sad, but the cast got to sleep off whatever they had done the night before! Yay for mechanical error!

Spotting what set designers do

One of the main things to consider when creating a set, like with costume design, is the budget. An average Broadway musical set is around $800,000 and upwards. The most economical set is the kind that doesn't move, like in *In the Heights*. That set frame stays where it is for the whole show. Yes, various set pieces are moved in and out, but the largest pieces stay put. That type of set is different from a set like *Wicked* (see Figure 8-2), which has set pieces moving in from the sides as well as from the *flies* (the area above the stage) for the entire show. A set that moves nonstop is much more expensive.

Like all the design teams do, the set designer meets with the director (and costume and lighting designer) to choose the type of set that will be used: Will it be realistic? Like the giant mansion for *Sunset Boulevard*, which descended from the top of the stage. Or will it be more impressionistic? Like in *Grand Hotel* where, instead of the stage having rooms flying in and out and being filled with all the accoutrements of a luxurious hotel, the stage basically remained bare, and the audience simply imagined the grandeur.

Or . . . will it be both? Realistic *and* impressionistic? In *Titanic*, there's a moment when the ship is sinking and the entire stage tilts to one side. And when tilted, it made a grand piano slide all the way across the stage and smash into an actor, killing the character! It was both thrilling and terrifying to witness. Yet, in the opening number, things weren't realistic like that at all. The whole cast sings of how beautiful the Titanic is, but they're simply pointing toward the audience, so the beautiful ship they're singing about is never actually seen. Sidenote: The song is called "Ship of Dreams," but in the *Forbidden Broadway* parody, because of the cast pointing into the abyss, it was retitled "Ship of Air."

FIGURE 8-2:
The set of *Wicked* before showtime.

REMEMBER

Whatever the set will be, it isn't available for the cast to traipse on when rehearsals begin. You may wonder how rehearsals can begin with no set. Well, one of the coolest things about the first day of a Broadway show rehearsal is seeing the *model* of the set. The set designer creates a scale model so everyone can understand what the set will eventually look like, and the cast gathers around to see all the different looks. Seeing a model with all the elements of the set helps everyone rehearse with a vision of where they are. Also, the floor in the rehearsal studio has tape on it so the performers can get used to the dimensions of the space they'll have onstage. So, even though the rehearsal studio is just one floor, they rehearse as if the set is there. In other words, they act as though they're running up a flight of stairs, even though it's a flat floor.

A few weeks before rehearsals begin, the real set begins the process of being built, outside of New York City. Here's the process in a nutshell:

1. **The set designer designs the set, and the director approves it.**

2. **The designs are sent to a scenic design shop where, with the supervision of the head carpenter and the head painter, the sets are built.**

   These scenic design warehouses have carpenters, ironworkers, motion control experts, engineers, and electricians all working together to bring the designer's vision to life. One of the most famous is Hudson Scenic Studio (set builders of The *Lion King, Hamilton,* and *Aladdin*), located in Yonkers. Follow them on Instagram (@HudsonScenic) to see photos of fabulous sets in various stages of creation!

3. **After the completion of the entire set, those pieces are brought to the theatre for what's called the *load in*.**

   All the pieces are carried into the theatre and assembled by the various carpenters, electricians, crew members, and so on, supervised by the set designer and technical director.

4. **The crew, tech director, set designer, and stage management team do dry tech rehearsals without the cast.**

   Dry tech rehearsals are when all the set professionals make sure all the elements of the set work.

5. **The cast comes in to start tech rehearsals on the stage, so they can get used to how to get around the set, and the stage managers and crew members can get used to moving all the pieces at the proper time.**

REMEMBER

The next time you see a Broadway musical, think about the set beginning as a sketch, then becoming a scale model, and finally transforming into whatever you see in front of you.

SETH SPEAKS

PLEASE HOLD! — WHEN THE SET MALFUNCTIONS

Here's a classic musical theatre moment: the chandelier falling at the end of *The Phantom of the Opera's* Act One. Normally, Christine and her beau Raul are onstage singing their love song "All I Ask of You"; soon the Phantom appears above, getting angrier and angrier, and when he yells "GO!" the chandelier crashes to the stage (accompanied by a scary violin scale) and Christine, who is the target, runs off in terror. Well, Ramin Karimloo told me about his first time playing the Phantom in London. At first the show was going great. Finally, he was in the *angel* (a set piece that rises) for the final Act One song right before the chandelier falls. However, his foot got caught in the angel as it was rising! He almost had a huge injury but, thankfully, he was able to pull his foot out. However, his foot messed up the mechanical sensors and the mechanism thought his foot was *still* in the way of the chandelier trajectory. Therefore, in order to protect him, the chandelier safety lock was engaged. So, when he yelled "GO!", the chandelier didn't crash to the stage. Nor did it fall to the stage slowly. Nor did it move. *At all*. The chandelier simply stayed above the audience in the same place it had been for the whole show.

(continued)

(continued)

The conductor's cue was "GO" so as soon as Ramin yelled it, the scary violin scale was played and, of course, the other staging remained the same. In other words, there was music indicating something falling *and* Christine, as usual, ran off in fright. But . . . ran off in fright from what? Literally nothing.

I'm sure no one noticed. After all, when people think of Phantom, they don't think of the chandelier crashing to the stage, right? Right? #Refund.

Illuminating the Stage — What Lighting Designers Do

A lighting designer creates how light is used in the show. The most basic way lighting works in a musical is helping the audience see what's happening on stage. An audience can't appreciate someone's acting unless they can see their face, an audience can't marvel at the magic of a set unless they see that turntable turning, and they can't gasp at on onstage quick-change if the lights are too dim as it happens. Lights can also create a look the set designer wants, like in Figure 8-3.

FIGURE 8-3: A spotlight shines to give the texture of a rusted old painted metal wall.

ShutterStockStudio/Shutterstock

Lighting does so much more:

>> **Lighting can evoke the right mood and emotionally move the audience.** The song "Light Sings" from *The Me Nobody Knows* is titled very accurately. Just the way singing can move you emotionally, lighting can have the same effect.

One major aspect that lighting designers are always thinking of is the mood of this particular scene. They always consider how lighting can help the audience feel whatever the actors or the song or the choreography is conveying. For example, imagine a romantic scene between two actors. When they start to kiss, how would you feel if they were illuminated in overhead, fluorescent lighting? Probably like these two people are in a cold, uncomfortable relationship. Now imagine if they started kissing with low lights, shadows on the wall, and the look of candles flickering. Hubba hubba! Sign me up! The lighting changed the audience's reaction to that exact same moment.

Now, consider two young college students walking hand-in-hand across the stage. They're surrounded in darkness except for one spotlight, trained directly on them as they walk. Hm. That isn't very evocative of anything specific, is it? They could be in a hallway, in a tunnel, or in an office building. How much sweeter would it be if they were encased in a pink hue with falling leaves everywhere? Ah! They must be in a park in the fall — perfect for two people falling in love. But there are no leaves on the stage. How? That's because lighting designers can achieve that effect with a gobo. A *gobo* is a sheet with a design cut into it that's inserted on a frame at the front of the light. The light filters through the design, so the stage suddenly looks like leaves are falling. Young love is in the air!

>> **Lighting can enhance the drama.** Most people know that bright lights are great for comedy, but lighting can also enhance drama in a simple but extremely effective way. For example, imagine a character standing center stage in silence. They're grappling with a devastating realization . . . perhaps they grasp they've made a hurtful mistake, and they're wracked with guilt. If they stood and felt that emotion and then turned and walked offstage, their exit would probably dilute the emotion the audience feels watching them grapple with their pain.

But if they stood there, feeling their feelings, and the lights slowly dimmed to a blackout, the audience would not only feel their feelings, but also the implication from that slow blackout that the character is going to feel that horrible guilt for the rest of their lives. That scene couldn't have been as effective during the initial readings when there wasn't a way to dim the lights on the actor's face. The lighting added the extra emotional impact.

>> **Lighting also tells an audience where to look and where *not* to look.** In *Dreamgirls,* Effie, originally played by Jennifer Holliday who won the Tony Award, has some emotional problems and is fired from the singing group. In Act Two, she tries to make a comeback and auditions to get a gig as a club singer. Effie sings the song "I Am Changing" in a nightclub that's empty except for the nightclub manager, who's sitting at one of the tables. As the song progresses, the lights start to focus more and more on Effie and soon, just her face is illuminated.

Finally, she gets to the *modulation* (the key change), and when she sings the phrase, "I am changing" up a half step, the lights fill the whole stage. What's amazing is, without having the nightclub manager say, "You got the job!" the audience is now witnessing Effie in performance. How? Because when the lights come up, the formerly empty nightclub is now filled with patrons and Effie is in a fabulous *different* outfit! Yes, by having the lights dim and focus just on her face, actors were able to enter the stage in the darkness without the audience noticing, and Effie was able to do an onstage quick change while singing. Lighting makes magic happen!

LIGHTS SHOW THE *ACTUAL* FULL MONTY!

SETH SPEAKS

Lighting is now very advanced with lighting cues programmed into a computer. However, the more things become mechanized, the more chances for electronic errors. And that's where the unintentional comedy comes in!

If you saw the show *The Full Monty*, you know that the entire musical ends with the cast being fully nude. However, the audience never actually saw the men's family jewels because of a lighting effect. Right when the men do their final reveal, super-bright lights would shoot out from behind them so the audience was basically temporarily blinded. And, like I said, these cues were programmed into a computer.

The original cast told me that one night the finale was going on as usual, but the men soon realized the light cues were off. They didn't know if the cues were ahead or behind, but they knew they weren't the cues they were used to. Suddenly, they all realized the cues were ahead. Uh-oh, they all thought at the same time. Why Uh-oh? Because they knew that the final cue of the song was the big light from behind them, which covered their nudity and, right after that, there was the curtain call. So . . . if the cues were ahead by one cue, that would mean the blinding light would come right *before* they were totally nude. Therefore, when they dropped their underwear, the lights would be the next cue: the curtain call. What was the look for the curtain call? *Full Stage Lights!* That meant the nude scene would have the most revealing lights of the night.

All the guys made eye contact with each other, wondering what to do . . . and silently decided to finish the number as choreographed. They knew they would really be literally revealing everything to the whole audience. Star Patrick Wilson told me that right before he took it all off, he happened to lock eyes with someone in the audience. Mortifyingly, it was a teen-aged girl! He said that when the final reveal came, she looked horrified, and he ran the gamut from trying to convey sympathy with his eyes Norma Desmond-style, to complete annoyance that the girl had been brought to the show in the first place! End of story: That night *The Full Monty* really meant The Full Monty!

"The Sweetest Sounds" — Sound Designers

When musicals began on Broadway, theatres had to have good acoustics. That meant the sound was reliant on the structure of the theatre including aspects like where the orchestra pit was and the type of material on the floor and ceilings. The performers not only had to project enough to be heard in all the dialogue scenes, but they also had to be heard over the orchestra. By the 1950s, floor mics were starting to be placed at the front of the stage and overhead mics hung over the stage, and they were able to electronically amplify voices in a general way. Then came the body microphone.

The first body mics I know were worn by Anna Maria Alberghetti in *Carnival* in 1961 and Barbra Streisand in *Funny Girl* in 1964. A mic worn on their body allowed their voices to be amplified no matter where they were onstage. Still, body mics weren't widely used until almost two decades later. As a matter of fact, Andrea McArdle, who starred in *Annie* in 1977, told me that the song "Maybe" was staged with her sitting in front of a floor mic so her voice would be more amplified (even though, P.S. she hardly needed it. She had a *huge* voice even at the age of 13!).

In the late '60s, rock musicals became more common and singers had to be heard over electronic instruments, so characters in musicals like *Hair* and *Grease* held actual microphones during their songs, like in a rock concert. By the late 1970s, more and more leads in musicals started wearing body mics and by the mid-1980s, entire casts wore body mics. I'm mentioning the progression of microphones because it all has to do with the job of the sound designer, which rose in importance as sound become less acoustic and more electronic.

Comprehending what sound designers do

The sound designer must not only be in charge of making sure each actor's spoken lines are heard, but they're also in charge of the music being balanced perfectly. That means that the singers have to be heard above the orchestra, but there's so much more to sound design than just that. For instance, starting in the 1980s, orchestra pits got smaller to allow more seating in theatres. So, instead of an entire orchestra sitting in the orchestra pit (with an open top that allowed the music to flow acoustically into the theatre), sometimes orchestras are seated onstage or, like the *Cats* orchestra, completely offstage. Even more common these days, the orchestra is split up with some musicians sitting in different areas. I've seen shows where half an orchestra is seated stage right and half is seated stage left. Regardless, the sound designer has to make sure they're heard in proper balance throughout the theatre.

When I played keyboard for *The Producers* on Broadway, I was surrounded by a wonderful orchestra of winds, string, and brass instruments, but the percussionist and harp player were actually on a different floor of the theatre. The sound designer had to "mix" the sound, so it was as if we were all together. I actually should clarify: The sound designer figures out the settings of the sound levels as well as where the speakers in the audience should be placed. Everything is perfected during tech rehearsal and previews. Then the sound designer goes off to work on another show. The *sound board operator* then mixes the show every night from the back of the audience. Chapter 10 discusses this more.

You may be asking why not have the same sound design for every Broadway show? Well, not only do Broadway shows have different cast sizes and different bands/orchestra sizes and placements, but Broadway musicals all have different types of music. Thus a show like *South Pacific* needs to have a sound design that makes everything sound relatively *acoustic*, meaning not electronically amplified, even though there definitely is electronic amplification. Whereas a show like *Ain't Too Proud* needs to sound like the bass-thumping, microphone-hugging concert of The Temptations!

Making sound board magic

When I've played in the orchestras of certain Broadway shows, I consider the sound designer similar to the conductor of the orchestra. I remember one moment I had to play during a song in *The Producers*. It was a little piano riff that I could barely hear as I played it because so many instruments were next to me, playing at the same time. I happened to watch the show one night from the audience when another piano player was playing, and that little piano riff that I couldn't hear actually was a major solo! The sound designer designed it so the sound board operator would turn up the mic of the keyboard at just the right moment.

In a regular symphonic orchestra, the conductor will indicate the moments that certain instruments should play out and that instrument and the rest of the orchestra adjust their volumes accordingly, but a sound person can make that happen at their sound console. The sound designer is vitally important because you can't have a musical without music, and the sound designer is the person who makes the audience hear that music.

This is a story about a leading lady with an incredible belt who was starring a Broadway show. During intermission one night, she saw the sound board operator backstage. She told him that she was belting her face off during the Act One finale but couldn't hear herself onstage. This was making her belt louder and louder, and she was nervous she was going to hurt her voice. The sound board operator explained that her body mic was on a *leveler*, which meant that no matter how loud she sang, it stayed at the same volume level. Sort of how my piano in *The Producers* was adjusted without me knowing. Instead of her balancing herself, the sound person was controlling how much of her voice was being heard.

The leading lady asked why her voice was being leveled, and he said it was to balance her with the ensemble. Hmph. As singers know, singing louder and louder every night isn't good for your voice, so she wanted to say, "Please don't ruin my voice by putting a leveler on me. I can adjust my own singing!." But that didn't happen. In frustration she yelled something along the lines of, "You're leveling me so I balance with the ensemble? I don't give a F*** about the ensemble!" Well, like I said, in the 1980s, body mics had become common. And even though her body mic was off in the audience, it was *on* backstage, and that comment was broadcast to all the ensemble dressing rooms! Hoo boy. Let's just say there were a cold few days backstage after those choice words. #Chilly

Coifing the Do — Hair Designers

If you watch Broadway show performances on an old TV show like *The Ed Sullivan Show,* you'll see that cast is in costume but most are sporting their natural hair. Wigs were used infrequently and only for moments when regular hair just wouldn't work — like when sexy Lola in *Damn Yankees* is shown as a horrific witch-like figure. However, wigs became more and more common on Broadway in the 1980s, and now almost every woman (and some men) on Broadway is wigged. Two of the main reasons that Broadway performers now wear wigs is so an actor doesn't have to have the same haircut/color as their character *and* to protect the actor's natural hair.

The following sections focus on what hair designers do and why wearing wigs onstage has become more common.

Knowing what hair designers do

The hair/wig designers for Broadway musicals design how everyone's hair will look in the show . . . including their facial hair. Like all the other designers, they read the script and consult with the director (and especially the costume designer who often hires the hair designers) to confirm the tone of the show, the time period, the look, and the style.

REMEMBER

Hair, like costumes, helps an audience know about the character without the character saying a word. The old chestnut of an uptight person with her hair in a bun versus a free spirit with long hair a–flowin' is an easy example of how quickly the audience make judgments based on hairstyles. And like most designers, hair designers have to be aware of the budget. Each wig can cost around $3,000! Some hair/wig designers have their own shops where they create the wigs whereas others send them out to be created. After they're created, the director approves them, and the actor starts wearing them in the show, the backstage hair crew takes over their upkeep and maintenance (see Chapter 10).

REMEMBER

Wigs have become more and more popular for a few reasons:

>> **Wigs reduce the wear and tear of performers' hair.** Making a performer's natural hair turn into the character's hairstyle can cause hair damage, especially if a show runs a long time. A way to save people's hair from the effects of nonstop hair drying, curling, and dye-jobs is to have the performer wear a wig. And, P.S., it's definitely not just women who wear wigs. When I was doing *Grease!!!* in the '90s, some of the men wore wigs for that very reason. It was hard on their hair to put product in and blow dry it into a '50's pompadour every night, so on went the wig!

>> **Wearing wigs is more time-efficient.** Wigs take around five minutes to put on correctly, instead of the time it would take to do an elaborate hairstyle like an updo. Furthermore, say the plot of a show moves forward or backward in time, a great way to indicate that a scene takes place in a different year is to have a completely new hairstyle. That can be achieved quickly by taking off one wig and plopping on another.

>> **Wigs can really transform a person as well . . . sometimes more than a costume or makeup.** Look at Edna's (Harvey Fierstein) wig at the beginning of *Hairspray*. Her "hair" isn't only in a horrific flat style; it also looks dirty and greasy. Then, when Edna is transformed during "Welcome to the 60s," she comes out in a brand-new colorful costume . . . but the biggest transformation is the bright, glorious wig that suddenly makes Edna beautiful (see Figure 8-4).

FIGURE 8-4:
Nina West as
Edna Turnblad In
the frumpy and
glamour wigs
in *Hairspray*.

Peeking behind the lace-front curtain

One of the ways wigs have progressed is indicated by the *lace front*. The wigs many people know from their childhood dress-up days were just plunked on their heads. Nowadays, good wigs slip over a person's head with a bit of see-through fabric (the lace part) in front. The fabric is glued onto the forehead and makeup is applied so the lace matches the skin tone. To the audience, the effect looks completely natural, as if the hair is growing directly from the hairline.

**SETH
SPEAKS**

If you want to see a great use of wigs, check out the different looks Patti LuPone had for *Evita*. And that lace front wig she wore with the bun in the back during "Don't Cry For Me, Argentina" became such an iconic look for her and was so realistic looking that when she was doing a TV show a few years later, she mentioned to the costume person that her costume should go with her brunette hair. The costume person balked when Patti said she was brunette. Patti told her she was indeed brunette but the costume person *insisted* that Patti was blonde! Seriously!

TIP

When you see your next Broadway show, bring a pair of binoculars. Focus on the forehead of the actors. There may be plenty of performers that you think aren't wearing a wig, but when you look through those lenses, you'll see the lace front going across their forehead. Sometimes it's fun to peek behind the curtain and see how theatre magic is created!

THE CREATOR CREATED WIGS

SETH SPEAKS

I always credit wigs with helping Victoria (Vicki) Clark originate her first starring role on Broadway. Vicki had heard about a new musical called *The Light in the Piazza*. The score was by a fellow Yale alumni named Adam Guettel and, because Vicki knew Adam, she called and left him a message that she would like to be seen for the role of Margaret. Well, he called back and said something that many actors yearn to hear, "You are way too young for the role." Margaret was the Mom of Clara (eventually played by Kelli O'Hara), and Adam felt that Vicki was too young to look believable as a Mom of someone in her late 20s.

Vicki is also a director and she knows all the tricks employed to change someone's look. Instead of accepting Adam's pronouncement that she wasn't right for the role, she called him and left him this message about her looking too young, "Adam, that is why God invented wigs." Yep, she knew that the right wig (and costume) would age her up . . . and she was right! She eventually got the role . . . and won the Tony Award. Thank you, lace fronts!

Chapter **9**

"Being Alive" — The Performers

The Peter Allan song called, "When I Get My Name in Lights!" from *The Boy from Oz* is all about the dream of achieving stardom. Yes, seeing your name spelled out in lights, or with lights around it, is a clear sign you've made it as a star on Broadway. Of course, nowadays, seeing names on a marquee isn't that common because producers want the *show* to be the star. That's so the show itself is driving the ticket sales and not the star, which hopefully prevents sales from plunging after the name on the marquee leaves the production.

SETH SPEAKS

Regardless, having your name on the marquee isn't all it's cracked up to be, especially if you're in a David Merrick show. In the 1960s, Anita Gillette took over the lead role in *Carnival* for two weeks when Anna Maria Alberghetti went on vacation. Gillette's agent negotiated that her name appear above the title on the marquee, and producer David Merrick arranged for a photographer to come and take pictures. Gillette told me she posed on a ladder next to the new marquee that now read, "Anita Gillette in *Carnival*." Unfortunately, her agent wasn't specific enough. Yes, she got her name above the title, but two weeks later Merrick sent her a bill from a New Jersey sign company for $200! That's right, *Gillette* had to pay for the new marquee! Classic Merrick.

No matter how much it cost, her name above the title meant Gillette was indeed a leading lady. I explore that term and many others in the rest of this chapter.

Naming the Leads and Featured Performers in Lights

When musicals were coming into their own, their stories almost always followed a formula: a romantic couple constituted the leading man and leading lady, and another couple (usually comedic) were considered the secondary leads. For instance, Laurey and Curley are the romantic leads in *Oklahoma!* with Ado Annie and Will Parker as the side comedic couple. In *Guys and Dolls*, Sky and Sarah are the main romantic couple with Nathan Detroit and Miss Adelaide as the side comedic couple, and so on and so on. The side characters are also called *featured* or *supporting*, so I use those terms interchangeably.

The lead couple/side couple combo was *de rigeur* in the early days of the Golden Age and all musicals followed that format. As a matter of fact, the two couples were so expected that, in the early '50s, Alan Jay Lerner and Frederick Loewe put off writing *My Fair Lady* because the main characters in the story of the play *Pygmalion* by George Bernard Shaw (the source material) didn't fit the romantic leads/side comedic couple format. Lerner and Loewe felt they couldn't shoehorn Shaw's characters into the accepted standard, and they didn't know how to turn his play into a musical. But by the mid-50s, musicals began to evolve and Lerner and Loewe realized they could write *My Fair Lady* with main characters who didn't fit the two-couple formula. You can read all about this in Lerner's fabulous book *The Street Where I Live* (Norton).

The following sections look closer at these performers and what's involved with being a lead and featured performer.

Identifying the lead(s)

Most musicals to this day have at least one leading actor or actress. But who are they? An easy way to find out who's the leading lady or leading man is to check out the title of the show. If the character's name is in the title, they're the lead! Charity in *Sweet Charity*, Evan Hansen in *Dear Evan Hansen*, Evita in *Evita*, Kimberly in *Kimberly Akimbo*, Fiorello in *Fiorello!*, Mame in *Mame*, Pippin in *Pippin*, and so on. Those are the easy ones! Benjamin Barker in *Sweeney Todd* seems trickier to figure out. (*giggle* In the musical, you find out that Sweeney Todd's real name is Benjamin Barker. #SondheimFanJoke.)

TIP

Sometimes the lead's actual name isn't in the title, but the title *refers* to the lead. *Funny Girl* is about Fanny Brice, *Waitress* is about Jenna the waitress, *A Man of No Importance* is about Alfie. So, if someone asks, "What's it all about?", you can answer, "Alfie." #1960sMusicFanJoke #YoungReadersAreConfused

In musicals that have a leading man and a leading lady, the love interest of the leading person is usually the other lead. So Mrs. Lovett is the leading lady of *Sweeney Todd*, Aldonza is the leading lady of *Man of La Mancha*, Oscar is the leading man of *Sweet Charity*. But, like all the annoying idioms I had to learn in Ms. Harnick's high school French class, not everything in life follows rules. Take *Evita*. Yes, Evita is married to Perón, therefore Perón is her love interest, but Evita's nemesis Ché is actually considered the leading man. Why? Basically, because his role is bigger. I guess size *does* matter.

Back in the Golden Age, voice types and dance ability delineated leads versus featured roles. Those leading men/women sang legit/operatically, and the featured actors/actresses sang belty/vaudeville-y *and* they often danced. Examples?

>> In *The Most Happy Fella,* Tony and Rosabella sing with a legit/operatic sound ("My Heart Is So Full of You") while Cleo and Herman belt and do the dance numbers, like "Big D."

>> In *Kiss Me, Kate*, Frederick and Lilli sing in legit/operatic style ("So in Love") while Bianca and Bill belt and dance up a storm in "Tom, Dick, or Harry" and "Too Darn Hot."

SETH SPEAKS

THE LEADS DON'T DANCE . . . USUALLY

As a rule, leading men/women don't dance. Take it from me and my years as an audition pianist, there's nothing more devastating than playing piano at a dance audition featuring leading men and having to watch handsome guys with amazing voices crash and burn on a simple grapevine. #StillTraumatized.

The late, great Jan Maxwell was an incredible performer in both leading roles and featured. She told me that she was once playing the leading lady of Reno Sweeny in *Anything Goes* in summer stock and sang the title song but didn't do the dance. One day the choreographer told her he thought she *should* dance in that big tap number. The problem? It was opening night, and he told her 30 minutes before the show began. Even more problematic: Jan did *not* tap dance! Taking that info in stride, the choreographer told her to simply try her best and most importantly, to look confident by smiling up a storm. After the show, Jan saw her boyfriend and asked how her dancing was. He said, "I don't know, but I've never seen you happier!"

After *My Fair Lady* broke the mold in the mid-50s, there were many permutations in terms of the leading man/leading lady/side couple formula. For instance, musicals are now "allowed" to have *two* leading men or leading ladies:

>> *Chicago* is about Roxie and Velma.

>> *The Producers* is about Max and Leo.

>> *War Paint* is about Elizabeth Arden and Helena Rubinstein.

The leading men and leading lady roles in these shows are equal.

But what about shows where multiple roles are equal? Those musicals are called *ensemble shows*. An example is *You're a Good Man, Charlie Brown*. Charlie Brown's name is in the title, but Lucy, Schroeder, Linus, Snoopy, and Sally all basically have equal roles. Same thing with *The Drowsy Chaperone* or *A Day in Hollywood/A Night in the Ukraine*.

Being a lead or featured performer

Even though featured roles aren't as big as leading roles, they're usually the audience favorites. Yes, "I'll Know" is a pretty song sung by Sky and Sarah in *Guys and Dolls*, but "Adelaide's Lament" and "Sue Me" are the songs that bring down the house. That brings me to the question, why does it matter who's a lead and who's featured? There are a couple of answers, and a big one is the Tony Awards, followed by dressing rooms, and the title of Lauren Bacall's first musical: *Applause*.

The awards

As of this writing, the Tony Award categories are Best Actor, Best Actress, Best Featured Actor, and Best Featured Actress. (Yes, these awards are still separated by genders, but I think that will soon change.) A show's producers submit their cast list to the nominating committee and place each actor in the category to be considered. You'd think who goes where would be obvious, but gurl . . . !

Some roles have gray areas, and producers try very hard to place actors in categories where they'll have a better chance of winning. Sometimes it works perfectly. For instance, *The Producers* had two leading men (Matthew Broderick and Nathan Lane) playing Leo and Max, but triple threat Cady Huffman played Ulla in the show. In one sense, Cady could have been considered a leading lady because she was the only woman with a large role in that show, but her character didn't come on until the middle of Act One. The show's producers asked the Tony committee to consider her as Best Featured Actress. That meant *The Producers* didn't have a leading actress. The show's producers could have fought to have her considered as a lead actress, but they probably looked at who else was likely to be nominated in both categories and went with featured because they thought she'd have a better chance at winning. They made the right choice! Broadway favorite Christine Ebersole won Best Actress in a Musical for *42nd Street* that year and Cady won Best Featured Actress for *The Producers*.

The flip side of that story happened during the 1995 Tony Awards. The hi-larious and high-belting Megan Mullally was starring as Rosemary opposite Matthew Broderick in *How to Succeed in Business without Really Trying*. Rosemary is arguably the leading lady; after all, she's the romantic interest of the leading man and Smitty, her sassy best friend, is definitely the featured actress. Now, it can be opined that *How to Succeed* is a show with a leading man and *two* featured actresses, but in my opinion, the role of Rosemary is more leading lady and less featured actress. But this is where producers jockeying for a Tony Award can get in the way. Why? Well, this is my understanding of what happened: You see, 1995 was also the season of Andrew Lloyd Webber's giant *Sunset Boulevard*. After that show opened, *everyone* knew that Glenn Close would win Best Actress in a Musical. She had a string of wonderful reviews from all the critics and audiences were going crazy for her.

Well, the producers of *How to Succeed* thought Mullally was fabulous in her role and deserved a chance to win a Tony Award. They knew if she were nominated as Best Actress, she wouldn't win because Close had that award in the bag. Instead, they asked the Tony nominating committee to consider her in the Best Featured Actress category because that would mean she'd actually have a chance of winning. The Tony committee agreed, and she was put in the Best Featured Actress category. *Smokey Joe's Café*, an ensemble (all the roles are equal) opened that same season and instead of submitting all four *Smokey Joe's* women in the Best Actress category, the producers submitted them to be considered in the Best Featured Actress category. And guess what? Three were nominated and the fourth slot went to Gretha Boston for *Show Boat*. That meant there was no room for Mullally! #Backfire!

Close indeed won Best Actress, but that category only had *two* nominees: Close and the late, great Rebecca Luker, meaning there was room for *two more* nominations. If the producers had left Mullally in the Best Actress category, she wouldn't have won, but no doubt she would have at *least* been nominated. So, because of getting her moved into the Featured category, she not only didn't win a Tony Award, but she also wasn't even nominated! As Max Bialystock yells at Leo in *The Producers*, "Don't help me!" P.S. Don't cry for the multitalented Mullally. It all worked out in the end because she soon had *two* Emmy Award wins for her amazing and hilarious portrayal of Karen Walker on *Will & Grace*.

WHEN FEATURED PERFORMERS ARE LEADS

A famous Tony Award misfire happened in 1969 (when the Best Featured Actor/Actress category was called Best Supporting Actor/Actress). Before producers could lobby for whom they considered leading and featured, the Tony Awards nominating committee only considered actors whose names were above the title of a show as eligible for Best Actor/Actress. In the musical *1776*, *no one's* name was above the title. So William Daniels, who played John Adams and who was *clearly* the leading man, was nominated as Best Supporting Actor. It really didn't make any sense. He supposedly asked the producer of the awards, "My dear, whom am I supporting?" and then declined the nomination!

Even though this book is about musical theatre, I want to tell you about a very similar thing happening with Rita Moreno in a play. She played Googie Gomez in Terrence McNally's hilarious farce, *The Ritz*. Again, because of Tony Award rules, she was nominated as Best Supporting Actress despite the fact that her role was huge. She didn't decline the nomination (like Daniels did), but she used her acceptance speech to comment on the situation. She apologized to the other women in her category who truly had supporting roles because one of them should have won Best Supporting Actress. She went on to clarify that she was *not* a supporting actress in the play, she was the leading lady. Brava!

What about leading men? A musical can have two leading men as I mentioned. But what about one leading man . . . played by multiple people? Or more accurately, one leading *boy*. When the musical *Billy Elliot* opened in London, three boys rotated performances in the title role throughout the week (due to British child labor laws). And the creative team kept that same system when the show opened on Broadway. So, when the Tony Award nominations happened, *all three* boys (David Alvarez, Trent Kowalik, and Kiril Kulish) who played the title role were submitted for *one* award, Best Actors in a Musical. And all three won!

Odd versions of that type of thing occurred twice before, in 1959 and in 1998:

>> The first is one of *the* most bizarre nominations (and a precedent for the next one). As most people know, *The Sound of Music* had seven Von Trapp children: Liesl, Gretel, Marta, Brigitta, Kurt, Friedreich, and Luisa. If you can't tell by the names, that's five girls and two boys. *All* the Von Trapp kids got *one* Tony nomination . . . as Best Featured *Actress!* Seriously!

>> In the musical *Side Show*, Emily Skinner and Alice Ripley played real-life conjoined twins Daisy and Violet Hilton. They both gave fantastic performances and, in my opinion, definitely deserved Tony nominations. However, Best Actress has usually only four spots, and the producers didn't want one to

be nominated over the other; they submitted them both for *one* nomination and they were both nominated, meaning Emily Skinner and Alice Ripley were together up for Best Actress in a Musical.

To me, it doesn't quite make sense. They were playing *two different people.* Yes, the characters were conjoined and stood together onstage for the majority of show, but they sang different parts during their songs and, during a dream sequence at one point in the show, they weren't together. And when does being next to each other onstage equal one role? I'm actually thrilled they were nominated, but it would have made more sense had there been five nominees allowed, so they each would have had their own.

The dressing rooms

Another reason for why it matters who's the lead is real estate. Backstage real estate is at a premium. I'm talking dressing rooms. On Broadway, not every dressing room is created equal — not by a long shot!

There's an episode of *The Judy Garland Show* where a young Barbra Streisand is the guest alongside Judy and Ethel Merman. Streisand mentions that she's coming to Broadway in a new show called *Funny Girl,* and Merman warns her about how horrific Broadway dressing rooms can be. "Careful!" she says. "They'll give you a hook!" meaning, her dressing room will just consist of a hook on the wall to hang her costume! The good news is the dressing rooms given to the leads are the largest and usually the closest to the stage. Streisand wound up getting a good one during *Funny Girl* at The Winter Garden Theatre, and it's still called the "Barbra Streisand" dressing room. That room was then given to Betty Buckley when she played Grizabella in *Cats* and more recently, Sierra Boggess when she starred in *School of Rock.*

THE SMALL WORLD OF LIVE THEATRE

In England, children aren't allowed to do eight shows a week because of child labor laws. That meant when Andrea McArdle went to London to reprise her role as Annie, instead of doing eight shows a week like she did on Broadway, she had to divide the performances with another girl. Here's some fun trivia for you when you're at a party: When Andrea was doing *Annie* in London, the youngest orphan, Molly, was played by a future Oscar winner Catherine Zeta-Jones!

When Barbra was promoting one of her albums, CBS *Sunday Morning* did a piece on her where they filmed her visiting her old dressing room. When Barbra walked into her *Funny Girl* dressing room from 1964, she saw six of her albums on the wall. She was mystified until she found out that the dressing room's current inhabitant Sierra Boggess was a *huge* Barbra fan! Sierra even had a Barbra candle. Sierra was so happy when she found out that Barbra didn't think the Barbra decorations were a setup. That's just how Sierra always decorates her dressing rooms. All those items were there legitimately because of Sierra's fan level. Sierra had so much Barbra paraphernalia in the dressing room that, when she filmed her segment afterward for CBS *Sunday Morning,* she looked at the camera and thanked Barbra for not being creeped out! P.S. Imagine how elated Sierra was that night when she came back to her dressing room and found a personalized note from Barbra ending with, "P.S. Love the candle."

By the way, sometimes a leading man dressing room is *not* what the (literal) doctor ordered. Michael Rupert told me that when he was starring in *Pippin* on Broadway, he began to get very depressed and couldn't understand why. It didn't make sense. After all, he was starring in the title role of a hit Broadway show. He finally went to a therapist. Now, if you don't know, *Pippin* is about a group of people, basically a cult, who try to convince Pippin to die by suicide by the end of the show. Michael was in the star dressing room and the only interaction he had with the ensemble was on stage . . . where they were trying to manipulate him into doing something horrible. His therapist helped him to realize that the stage inter-action was feeling too real. He needed to connect with his fellow actors offstage, so *onstage* he would realize they were just acting. But how? He only saw them onstage because they had their own dressing room, and he was by himself. Well, he solved it by moving out. Yep, he vacated his star dressing room and moved into the men's ensemble room. This way he could be with his fellow actors offstage, get to know them, laugh and joke during breaks in the show, and then when he was onstage, he would be able to separate the offstage actor from the evil cult member. It worked, and his depression lifted!

The applause — Entrance and bows

The third big perk of being a lead is, as Lady Gaga sang, "Applause, applause." Actually, this is a Broadway book, so I should say as Bonnie Franklin sang, "Applause! Applause!" I don't mean the applause one gets after a song. I'm talk-ing about something called *entrance applause.* That's what happens when a famous lead enters the stage. These stars are being applauded because the audience is excited to see them.

That can be a problem when a leading actor comes onstage and they're supposed to say their line immediately, but they can't talk because the applause is drowning them out. Yes, getting recognition and adoration is nice, but in a situation like that, it ruins the show's rhythm. Most directors know what roles will get entrance applause, and, if they're smart, figure out a way to make it a seamless part of the performance.

For instance, *The Producers* had an opening number where the ensemble played theatregoers talking about producer Max Bialystock. At the end of the song, someone was standing center stage, reading a newspaper that covered his face. When the whole ensemble did the final moment referencing Max Bialystock ("What a bum!"), the number ended. That moment also directly coincided with the person holding the newspaper quickly lowering it and revealing his face: Nathan Lane! That way Lane got his entrance applause, but it coincided with the applause for the song, so it didn't stop the flow of the show.

Same thing with the show *Hamilton*. Right after "What's your name, man?" Lin-Manuel Miranda was revealed and he sang "Alexander Hamilton." You may notice there's no music right after that moment. That way the show could pause comfortably while he got applause and then resume when he was ready, or if there was a less famous person playing Hamilton, the song could continue without anything seeming amiss.

Even though a show is *frozen* when it opens (meaning that there are no more changes), sometimes a show is rearranged for entrance applause. When I was playing in the pit for the 1994 revival of *Grease!!!*, there was a moment in the opening number when the characters would identify themselves by name. The final moment was Rosie O'Donnell saying "And . . . RIZZO!" She'd get huge applause during a musical transition. When Jon Secada took over, he became the name star of the show and Rosie's replacement wasn't famous. Of course, Jon was *not* playing Rizzo . . . he was playing Danny. So, the order of the introductions changed so the applause would still go over the musical transition. Rizzo's introduction was now in the middle of the lineup where Danny originally was and at the end Jon would say "And . . . DANNY!" and, again, *that* moment got the applause.

As opposed to entrance applause, the lead also gets applause at the end of the show during the bows. Bows usually go in order from the smallest roles to the final bow, which is reserved for the lead, the *star bow*. Usually, when it's a male and female lead, the man does the old-school chivalrous chestnut of letting the female lead take the final bow. And sometimes when leading roles are equal, the final bow goes to the more famous or celebrated star.

You may have noticed something different at *Wicked*. When the show opened, Elphaba was played by Idina Menzel who had a Tony nomination for *Rent* but no win, and Glinda was played by Kristin Chenoweth who had a Tony Award win for *You're a Good Man, Charlie Brown*. If bows go according to who is more celebrated, then Kristin should have had the final bow. But if you look at the story of *Wicked*, it's more about Elphaba's journey, and she's more the leading lady; by that theory, she should have the final bow. Well, they solved that conundrum by having both women bow *together*. That's right, *Wicked* has no final solo bow!

AFTER YOU . . . NO, AFTER YOU!

I have a related end-of-the-show bowing story, but I have to leave out identifying details. One musical had two very famous and very celebrated leads. They each felt they should get the final bow based on their previous credits. As far as I know, the order of bows was never worked out before the first preview because they ran out of time at the final run-through. So, that night, during the first preview, the show ended, and one of them gestured to the other, "graciously" implying they should take a solo bow. But that meant the person gesturing would get the *final* bow, the star bow. The person being gestured to wasn't having it, so they did a *back atcha* move and "graciously" gestured to the other star to bow.

Nothing. Neither bowed.

The first star gestured again with an "After you!" head nod.

The other star did the same. "After you!"

This literally went back and forth and, as far as I know, neither of them bowed for that performance! If you ever meet me in person, maybe I'll tell you who they were!

Introducing the Ensemble — Side by Side

"I was *never* in the chorus!"

Vera Charles in *Mame* haughtily said that line twice and is meant to imply she was always too good for the chorus. But as anyone who has ever done a Broadway show knows, being in the chorus often requires *more* talent that playing a lead. This section explores why that's so and explains why shows often have a chorus.

"So many people in the world" (of a musical)

Here I discuss the point of the chorus, or as it's called now, the *ensemble*. The ensemble serves many purposes and is vital to many musicals. The reasons are as follows:

>> Shows are often about a few main characters, but those characters interact with other characters. These other characters may only have a few lines, but they're still needed to advance the plot.

>> A show takes place in a town or city, on an ocean liner, in a big office, or . . . you get the idea. The point is, the main characters need to be surrounded by townsfolk, people on a cruise, various office workers, and so on. Yes, often they're just walking by, or sitting at a desk or a lounge chair, but there has to be actual people available to play those people.

>> In terms of aural aesthetics, musicals often have big group numbers because it's exciting to hear a big ensemble of people singing harmony.

>> Same thing with dance numbers. Watching a fabulous dance solo is enjoyable, but there's another type of enjoyment from watching a group of people dance in unison. Or to watch a group of people doing various steps at the same time.

Recognizing who's in the ensemble

So, who's in the ensemble? My answer is different now than it would have been if this book came out in the 1950s because, back then, musical casts were much larger and there wasn't as much training easily available as there is today. Because not everyone had access to dancing and singing lessons, shows had a specific singing chorus and a specific dancing chorus. Neither had to do the job of the other. The singing chorus sang up a storm and moved around a *little*. Often, you'd see them standing in the back singing while the dancing chorus danced in front. And while the dancers were dancing, they'd move their mouths and sing along, but they weren't relied upon to make the big choral sounds known on Broadway.

Nowadays, because a lot more training is available to performers and because cost is often the bottom line of producing a musical, the ensembles are much smaller than they were during the Golden Age. Ensemble members are often expected to sing *and* dance. For example, listen to the original cast album of *A Chorus Line.* You'll definitely hear some fantastic singing (Priscilla Lopez, Donna McKechnie, Pam Blair, Ronald Dennie, and Sammy Williams to name a few), but the album also has a lot of singers on it who have heart but who don't have voices suited for a leading singing role. After you've heard a few songs, listen to the 2006 revival cast album of *A Chorus Line.* Most of the singing in that production is fantastic. It's a clear example of how the skills of ensemble people have increased dramatically over the years.

Even though the character of Vera Charles eschews chorus work, a real-life, two-time Tony Award winner, Chita Rivera, constantly talks about how important it was for her to have begun in the chorus. She feels that when you perform in the chorus you learn to work together, to move as part of a unit, to be aware of the people you're performing with, and to really feel you're one part in a whole piece.

When the Show Must Go On: Understudies, Standbys, and More

"At this performance . . . " is the beginning of the small note put into programs when there's a cast change. It usually says, "At this performance, the role of ___ usually played by ___ will be played by ___." Why is another person playing a role? Because theatre is *live* and stuff happens!

Like what? Well, traffic jams, a parent has a child who suddenly needs them, a subway gets stuck, a car breaks down, someone gets sick, someone oversleeps (yes, that's definitely happened), they forget what time a show begins (yes, that's also definitely happened when a show schedule changes), or whatever else prevents someone from getting to the theatre. Sometimes, they get to the theatre with their best intentions to perform but realize halfway through, they're too sick to continue, or they get injured, or . . . *anything!*

Luckily, Broadway has a plan for when people can't perform. Welcome to the wonderful world of the understudies, subs, standbys, and more!

Understudies — "I know it! I can go on!"

An *understudy* is someone who's in the show eight times a week *and* covers another role. For instance, if you listen to the *Wicked* cast album, you'll hear Kristy Cates in the opening number sing "No one cries 'They won't return.'" Her regular role was to sing that solo eight times a week — *unless* she had to go on for Elphaba, the green witch. So, Cates was the understudy for Elphaba, but she did her regular ensemble role if she didn't have to go on. That's classic understudy — an ensemble person who covers a main role when needed.

Sometimes people who have a fairly substantial role also understudy other roles. For instance, in the 1980's *Sweet Charity* revival, Bebe Neuwirth won the Tony Award for Best Featured Actress for playing Nicky, but she understudied the title role of Charity. And during the 2021 revival of *Company*, Jennifer Simard was nominated for a Tony Award for her performance of Sarah, but she also understudied (and went on for) Patti LuPone as Joanne!

Informing the audience

Does an audience know when an understudy is going on? Yes . . . ish.

A production definitely has to inform the audience when an understudy goes on. Here are the most common methods of informing the audience (which ones and how many are used depends on the contract of the production):

>> The "at this performance . . ." slip of paper in the Playbill that I mention at the beginning of this section

>> An announcement before the show begins

>> An "at this performance" placard placed in the lobby

REMEMBER

Recently, I've noticed a trickier way to do it where the audience doesn't know who's an understudy. Instead of having a cast list printed in the Playbill, the full cast for that performance is listed on a loose insert, so it's difficult to know who's an understudy or not. An audience is often annoyed when an understudy goes on because they think that the understudy isn't as good as the person they're understudying. That assumption is unfair and often untrue. In fact, it takes a *lot* of talent to understudy because you have to be ready to go on for a role with minimum rehearsal. And, if you look at a list of people who have understudied on Broadway, you can see so many former understudies who went on to win Tony Awards!

Some former Tony Award–winning understudies include the following:

>> Norbert Leo Butz (understudied Mark and Roger in *Rent*)

>> Billy Porter (understudied Four-eyed/No/Little Moe in *Five Guys Named Moe*)

>> Victoria Clark (understudied Adelaide in *Guys and Dolls*)

>> Lillias White (understudied the gym teacher in *Carrie*. Yes, it only ran for four performances, but still . . .)

>> Rachel Bay Jones (*Women on the Verge of a Nervous Breakdown* . . . she understudied Patti LuPone!)

SETH SPEAKS

Megan Mullally was reminiscing with me about when she was first asked to cover Rosie O'Donnell as Rizzo. When the show opened, Megan played Marty ("Freddy, My Love"), but a few months into the show, the producers asked Megan to also cover Rizzo. Rosie told her to take the job because, "I'm never going to miss a show." A few days later, Rosie got sick and was out! Megan was an innocent and didn't know to turn off her *squawk box*, the intercom in every dressing room where you can hear what's happening onstage as well as the sounds of the audience. Megan told me she was putting on her makeup when she heard the announcement, "At this performance, the role of Rizzo, usually played by Rosie O'Donnell, will be played by Megan Mullally." Megan claims her squawk box picked up everything, and she heard the audience reactions in detail. She hilariously described to me the sound of them throwing their Playbills to the ground while yelling "@#&$!" And then she heard the sound of feet stomping up the aisle to get refunds. *Note:* You can only get a refund on a Broadway show when an understudy is on if the person who is out has their name above the title. *End of story:* Megan kept the squawk box in her room turned off from then on. *Further end of story:* Those people who stormed out would now pay *full price* to see two-time Emmy Award winner Megan Mullally go on for *any* role on Broadway!

The life of an understudy

Being an understudy means going to understudy rehearsal every week. During the understudy rehearsal, a stage manager might play all the other roles or a few understudies rehearse together, playing the various roles. Those regular rehearsals begin after a show has opened. Interestingly, the period when understudies are needed most is during previews because that's a prime time when actors often get sick. During previews, the cast is rehearsing during the day to make changes and then doing the show at night. That's a lot of hours a day. *Everyone* is run-down. Unfortunately, that's also the time period before understudy rehearsals begin! There are too many rehearsals for the regular cast so there usually isn't time to teach the understudies the parts they're covering. However, understudies know they might be asked to go on so they learn the best they can without any formal rehearsal.

SETH SPEAKS

During *Thoroughly Modern Millie* previews, leading lady Sutton Foster got sick. Understudy Catherine Brunell was ready to go on even though she hadn't had any official rehearsals. The bigger issue was that Catherine didn't have *any* costumes! They had to cancel an entire performance while they went shopping and found her outfits to wear for the following performance. And during *Jekyll and Hyde*, star Linda Eder lost her voice and couldn't sing. Understudy (and future Tony Award nominee) Emily Skinner hadn't had any rehearsal, and it was deemed too dangerous for her to go on because the stage was constantly covered in fog and she could have easily had an accident. Instead of cancelling the performance, like they did for *Thoroughly Modern Millie*, Linda did all of her scene work and Emily was backstage with a mic to sing the songs while Linda lip-synched. Talk about the show must go on!

Standbys — The Vera Charles of understudies ("I was never in the chorus")

The fancier understudies are the standbys. Why fancier? Well, instead of toiling in the ensemble eight times a week, a *standby* goes on only for the role(s) they're covering. Usually, a show can cast someone with more theatre cred to be a standby because people who have played roles on Broadway usually don't want to be in the ensemble.

Standbys are used in shows that have a very difficult leading role or in a show where a huge star is playing a leading role. For instance, Chita Rivera was the star of *The Visit* and her standby was *A Chorus Line* Tony Award winner Donna McKechnie. The producers knew if the audience was disappointed Rivera wasn't going to be in the show, they'd still be thrilled to see a huge star like McKechnie take the role.

SETH SPEAKS

EVEN UNDERSTUDIES HAVE UNDERSTUDIES

Understudies aren't always told they're going on before a performance begins; often it happens after the curtain goes up. Andréa Burns was the understudy for Belle in *Beauty and the Beast* and had a two-week period scheduled for when she'd finally be playing the role. She began on a Friday night, and her whole family came up from Florida to see her, but they wanted to give her a chance to play the role at least once, so they went out to dinner and planned to attend the show on Saturday. Her mom, however, said, "There's no way my daughter is going to be starring on Broadway, and I'm going to be sitting in a restaurant," so she bought a ticket for Friday.

Andréa did her first Act One performance as Belle without a hitch . . . until the very end. Right before "Be Our Guest," she got her heel caught in a track on the stage and fell. *Tracks* are literally grooves in the stage where sets move. Andréa got right back up but knew something was wrong. Through adrenaline and denial, she miraculously got through "Be Our Guest" and actually did the kickline even though she had *broken her ankle!* She went offstage for intermission and told the stage manager she was injured. What to do? Well, even understudies have understudies! She remembers that her Belle wig was snatched off her head and immediately put on the other woman who understudied the part. The *second* understudy then prepared to go on for Act Two.

She needed to go to the ER, but she wanted to first tell her mother who was in the audience. However, this was in the 1990s before cellphone use was common, and she had no idea how to reach her mom because she didn't know what seat she was in. Stage management told her not to worry; they had a plan. They made the new understudy announcement and watched the audience. As soon as they said, "The role of Belle . . . that *was* being played by Andréa Burns . . . will now be played by . . ." they saw a woman in the audience immediately stand up frantically. Yep. There was Andréa's mom! Luckily, she healed and has done lots of Broadway shows since, including originating the role of Daniella in one of my favorite shows ever: *In the Heights!*

Megan Hilty told me that when she was a standby for the role of Glinda in *Wicked*, she didn't have to be at the theatre during the show. Yes, she had to be available to go on, but the requirement was that she just be within ten blocks of the theatre and have a beeper (it was the early 2000s). Megan decided to use that free time every night for important projects. One of them was figure out what restaurant had the best chocolate cake in the Times Square area (Her answer: Ruby Foo's).

Of course, a standby may not go on, even when one thinks they will. Hugh Jackman was the star of *The Boy from Oz*. The show didn't get great reviews, and many thought the audience was mainly coming to see Hugh give his brilliant performance, and not to see the show itself. Well, at one point during the run, Hugh had to film a movie, which meant he had to miss a week of performances. Instead of putting on his standby, the powers-that-be thought it made more sense to literally close the show for the week! I don't know if it was a financial reason or simply to save the cast from performing to a half-empty house, but everyone got a week's vacation while Hugh filmed *X-Men!*

Alternates — Guaranteed two shows a week

Alternates are something developed on the West End (London) and not that common on Broadway except for West End transfers. The role of *Evita* is definitely extremely vocally demanding, so the original star Elaine Paige only performed six shows a week on the West End. She had an alternate who did the other two shows each week. Being an alternate is often considered a better gig than being a standby because you're guaranteed to go on every week, instead of waiting days, weeks, and even months before you perform the role. The same system is in place for *The Phantom of the Opera*; whoever is playing Christine Daaé only does six shows a week, and an alternate does the additional two.

Back to *Evita* — when Patti LuPone was cast as Eva, she was told they were going to follow the West End protocol of only having her do six shows a week and letting her alternate, Terri Klausner, do two performances per week. Patti wanted to do all eight shows but didn't have a choice in the matter. To show people she had the vocal stamina to do more than six performances a week, she booked her own act at the club Les Mouches that she would do on Friday nights! Yes, she was starring as Evita and, after belting it out on Broadway, she'd do a late-night club act every week. P.S. Her act was recorded on an album called *Patti LuPone at Les Mouches,* and you can hear that she sounded vocally amazing!

Swings — So many parts!

A *swing*'s job is to cover multiple people in the ensemble and is arguably the hardest performing job on Broadway. Usually, each show has at least one male and one female swing. Say a show has 14 ensemble people, seven men and seven woman. That means each swing has to know seven different roles.

You may think, "Eh, ensemble is ensemble. What's the hard part?" Well, even if an ensemble is basically doing the same thing, they're not *singing* the same thing. A swing has to know all the different harmony lines as well as all the different ensemble solo lines each person might have. And, yes, everyone may be doing the same dance steps, but they're not doing them in the same place onstage. They're *all over the place!* A swing has to know where they need to be onstage for *every single part* they cover.

TIP

A swing is called a swing because they're "swung on" for various roles. Swings are super-organized people and usually have a show bible where they write out each individual part they cover, so they can look at their notes before they go on. My friend Paul Castree was the original male swing in *Disaster!*, the show I co-wrote on Broadway. Figure 9-1 shows his notes for every part he covered — he color-coordinated them as well to make it easier to keep track.

FIGURE 9-1:
A swing's
detailed notes.

Printed with permission from Paul Castree

Swings must mind their numbers

How do swings know where they should be while they're performing? And more generally, how does anyone know where to stand onstage so as to not bump into someone, or be in their light, or not get hit by a set? Sometimes staging is done visually, which means an actor is told to do their solo line a little to the left of center, or as far stage right as they can while still feeling the light on their face. But most shows have numbers written on the front of the stage; 0 is in the center, and then it goes 2, 4, 6, 8, 10, and so on, to the right and the same to the left. These numbers give a much more specific way to help all cast members know onstage placement.

The choreographer tells a performer to start the grand jeté on 4 stage right, land on 6, do a fast run all the way to 8 stage right, and hit the final pose on 5 stage right. When a performer is learning the *blocking* (or *staging* or *choreography*), they memorize those numbers so they remember where to be during those moments of the dance. But imagine being a swing! Say those dance steps and numbers I just mentioned are for Gary. What happens when a swing is on for Barry who's dancing right next to Gary? Yes, it's the same steps, but now the swing starts the grand jeté on 5 stage right, lands on 7, does a fast run all the way to 9 stage right, and hits the final pose on 6 stage right. *So many numbers!*

Three things that can go wrong for swings

Swings have a bible for each person they cover in the show to keep track of everything. The first few times they go on, they quickly check those numbers before they enter. If they don't, they're more likely to fall prey to the three main things that can go wrong when people are on their wrong numbers:

» **Blocking someone:** Say three rows of ensemble people hit their last pose. Everyone is in a *window,* meaning an open space where the audience can see them. Consider you're a swing and you're on for the person in the front row. You hit your last pose on number 2. But you were actually supposed to be on number 3 because the person in back of you is on number 2. That means you're now standing directly in front of the person in back of you and blocking them from the audience. Guess who's not happy? The person being blocked during the applause for that song.

» **Traffic jam:** You run directly to number 4 to start the dance. Wait! You're supposed to be on 5! Right when you get to 4 you do an awkward "Sorry! I'm moving" maneuver, which the audience gets to witness. I'm not saying the show is ruined . . . but your reputation as a swing ain't so great amongst the others in the show!

» **An actual collision:** This definitely happens when people don't check their numbers before they go on! My friend Jim Borstelmann was a swing for *Jerome Robbins' Broadway* and was so excited to go on. He was actually *so* excited that he didn't check his numbers during "The Rumble" in the *West Side Story* section, and when he turned his head, he hit his mouth on a set piece, knocking out his tooth!

And, because he wasn't in the correct area, he also missed catching someone who was supposed to jump into his arms, resulting in that dancer breaking his wrist! Jim told me he still finished the dance, even though his tooth was missing, *and* he was bleeding up a storm. As a matter of fact, when he got offstage, his white T-shirt was completely red (with blood)! Jim went to the hospital during intermission and told me he heard two audience members talking about the show outside the theatre, and one said, "Wow! The Rumble tonight was *so* realistic!" Um, yeah, it was. *The blood was real!*

SETH SPEAKS

For the late 1990s revival of *A Funny Thing Happened on the Way to the Forum,* the numbers onstage weren't written out 2, 4, 6, 8, 10. They decided to be clever and number the stage as it would have been done in ancient times. Yes, all the numbers were written onstage as I, IV, V, VI, and so on. The star of the show, Nathan Lane, quipped, "In order to do this show, you need a degree in Greek!"

Orchestral and backstage understudies

Just like everyone onstage, everyone backstage (and under the stage) has someone to cover for them. Stage managers, dressers, sound people, musicians, hair/wigs, I mean everyone! But these types of understudies are called *subs,* short for substitutes. When you're an actor, the director hires your understudy, but backstage/musician personnel can hire their own sub, which is a nice way to pay it forward or pay it back.

For example, say you're working on a Broadway show and you know someone who just graduated from college and wants to break into the business . . . *you* can ask them to be your sub and give them their first Broadway credit! Or say someone hired *you* to be their sub, but then that show closed . . . and then *you* got a full-time gig on a new show. You can hire the person who hired you the last time and pay them back for the last gig they got you!

I'm going to focus on subbing as a musician because that's my world! I was a piano sub on around 15 Broadway shows. I loved it . . . *and* it was terrifying! I understudied as an actor on Broadway and I subbed as an orchestra member, and the orchestral one is definitely more scary. When you're an understudy on Broadway, the stage manager trains you. You have rehearsal onstage where you're taught the staging, and you get to run the show (sometimes numerous times) before you go on. Occasionally, an understudy has to go on with no rehearsal, but the intention is to fully rehearse an understudy before their first performance.

When you're an orchestral sub, the preparation is up to *you!* And gurl, there ain't no rehearsal. You prepare by yourself . . . and then you're on Broadway! Here's the process:

1. You watch the book.

The book refers to the music that the instrumentalist plays. *Watching the book* means you sit next to the person playing the instrument you're planning to sub for and watch the show. It gives you an idea of the style of music, the conductor's technique, what sections are difficult, and so on.

2. You get a copy of the book to take home and practice.

When I used to sub, I'd record the show in the pit, and then I'd play along with the recording. I could have played along to an original cast album, but albums of shows don't have all the music. They're usually missing scene change music, underscoring, short reprises — the stuff folks listening at home won't miss. Near the end of my subbing career, when phones got more advanced, I'd *film* the show from the pit. Not the actual show, but the conductor. That way, when I practiced at home, I could play the video and watch the conductor so I could really feel like I was in the pit.

Another trick I'd do, specific to the instrument I subbed on, was something I discovered for *changing patches*. Backstory: A Broadway orchestra pit very rarely has a real piano. Almost all keyboard work is done on a synthesizer that plays multiple sounds. Usually you adjust the volume with a volume pedal, *and* you change the sounds or *patches* by stepping on a patch change pedal. The sheet music contains notations for when to change volumes or change patches. Sometimes it's choreographed within a beat, meaning you play a phrase on the harp sound, hit the patch change pedal on a specific beat, and then play a phrase on the organ sound, one beat later. To get used to my foot jutting out and hitting these pedals, I put small cans of vegetables next to my piano at home, so I could physically contact something, which prepared me for the real thing!

3. Practice in the pit.

Doing so isn't important to all instruments. For most instruments, like strings, brass, and others, practice can happen anywhere, and then the musician can play the show. For keyboard, practicing in the pit is important for me because not only do I need to get used to the touch of the keyboard (they don't all feel the same), but the keyboard in the pit also has all the sounds pre-programmed in the order they're used in the show. I had to graduate from cans of vegetables in my apartment to pushing the actual volume pedal and patch change pedal.

Same thing for drummers and percussionists: They don't bring their own instrument to the pit. They want to try the one used for the show, so they can see where their chair is positioned and how far the various instruments are from where they're positioned.

4. PLAY THE SHOW!

I capitalized this because I'm emphasizing there is *no* rehearsal! You don't get to run through the show with the orchestra before you're on. You rehearse by yourself — and then you're ON BROADWAY! The assumption is, you've learned how to play through the score note-wise, and you know the tricky parts, like when to make sure to watch the conductor, when the solos happen, when you have a fast page turn, and the list goes on. So once you're ready, you're on!

What's even more nerve-wracking is that you don't have the job. When you're an understudy for an actor, you're hired and you hope you do a great job the first time you're on. If you have any problems, you're given notes and rehearse to improve anything. When you're a sub, you're hired only for that first performance, which doubles as your audition. Yes, you get paid for that performance (⅛ of what the musician makes for the week, because it's for one performance out of eight), but if you don't do a fairly perfect job, you're never asked back! So not only are you stressed because it's your first time playing, but you're also being judged. Yay?

Every time I played a show for the first time was definitely stressful, but I loved subbing because after the scary part was over, I had so much variety in my life playing for various shows! Instead of playing the same musical eight times a week, I'd play *How to Succeed in Business* one night and then *Grease* the next night. Or sometimes I'd do a matinée of *Phantom* and that night I'd be playing *Les Miz!* I was always with different casts and different musicians. I definitely recommend subbing, but take your high blood pressure pills first!

SETH SPEAKS

MY VERY FIRST PUT-IN REHEARSAL

When learning a book for a Broadway show, I always reached a point when I knew I was ready to play the show. I'd practice and practice and would suddenly get to a place where I felt confident to do the show. Well, when I was learning the book for *Kiss of the Spider Woman*, my friend, Jeff Saver, whom I was subbing for, told me they were going to have a run-through of the entire show with full orchestra and asked if I wanted to play. It was a *put-in rehearsal* for a new leading man (a run-through of the show in the afternoon) and would give me the opportunity to play the show with the full orchestra before my first performance. (Chapter 12 discusses put-in rehearsals in greater detail.)

I said *yes*, of course. Looking back, I realize I wasn't at the point in my learning process when I was actually ready to play the show. I still needed a few more days of practice, but I didn't know I wasn't ready until after the run-through began, and I panicked! Even though it was just a rehearsal, it didn't feel like a rehearsal where I could make mistakes: It was a full run-through with the whole cast (including icon Chita Rivera) and Hal Prince, the director, in the audience. They wouldn't think it was charming if they had to stop because the keyboard sub played the wrong notes. AH! *Get me outta here!*

Soon after my panic set in, the conductor, Ted Sperling, started looking at me askance. He whispered to me that there was a weird vibrato coming from my keyboard. Apparently, every note I played had a wide wobble. I was too nervous to worry about it and just kept playing. Soon, sound people came into the pit and tried to adjust my keyboard. They poked and prodded, but there was nothing wrong with the mechanisms. What could it be, everyone wondered? Then I discovered that I was *so nervous* my foot was shaking uncontrollably on the volume pedal! My wobbling was making it go from no volume to 100 percent volume. And back and forth!

In other words, *I* was the one causing the problem! I lifted my foot off the volume pedal without telling anyone, and suddenly Ted looked over at me and happily said with a smile, "It stopped!" I didn't tell him why it magically stopped . . . and I'd appreciate if you kept my secret!

IN THIS CHAPTER

» Meeting some of the backstage crew

» Discovering who keeps the dances up to snuff

» Taking care of the costumes

» Noting the hair and wig pros

» Recognizing the stage management crew

» Conducting the show

» Playing the music

Chapter **10**

Introducing the People Who Work the Show Night after Night

Musical theatre is extremely collaborative because so many people work on all the various aspects of a musical. And I don't mean just musicals with huge casts. A small musical has the same number of people behind the scenes as a large musical does. Go to www.ibdb.com (the Internet Broadway Database) and look up the musical *I Do! I Do!* and see the number of people listed on the production staff. Essentially, it's the same number on the staff as for a show like *Jerome Robbins' Broadway,* which had a cast of 50, compared to the cast of two for *I Do! I Do!* (Mary Martin and Robert Preston).

Many of the people listed on the production page, especially the director and choreographer, are heavily involved with the show during the rehearsal period and, naturally, become close with the cast. But when the show's run begins, many of those people move on to other projects (I discuss many of these people in Chapters 7 and 8).

After productions start performance, a bunch of behind-the-scenes people are there side-by-side with the cast at every single performance, and new relationships are cemented. Who are they? Keep reading!

"Another (Almost) Hundred People" — The Backstage Crew

Here's an expression I'm sure you've heard: There's an app for that. Well, the Broadway version I've coined is, there's a crew member for that. Yep, there *is* a crew member for every aspect of backstage needs. Here's an overview of some of those specific duties that people have who work backstage and a few unusual examples of backstage gigs.

Keeping track of props — The prop crew

When I was doing *Disaster!* on Broadway (see Figure 10-1), I played a "Disaster expert" and entered with a beaker of (supposed) water from the Hudson River. Where did I get it from? I certainly didn't bring a beaker that I had saved from my 10th grade biology class and use it to scoop up Hudson River water. No, ma'am.

FIGURE 10-1:
With my beaker.

Published with permission by Seth Rudetsky

That beaker, which was scientific looking and filled with dirty-looking water, was created by the head of props. After the director approved it, the beaker found its nightly home on the backstage prop table, right next to a label that said "beaker." I grabbed it right before the show began, used it during the opening number, and afterward, the production prop person would be waiting for me where I exited stage right and I would hand it off to him. He'd then make sure it was put back in its proper place. There's a system set up with every prop in a show: either a *hand off* or a place where the actor can set the prop and then the production prop person puts it back on the prop table before the next performance.

However, there isn't a system to make sure the actor has the prop. That's up to the actor . . . and there have been plenty of times when actors have forgotten their props, and plot points make no sense or actors have had to improvise on the spot to try to rectify a missing/wrong prop.

**SETH
SPEAKS**

My pal Robin de Jésus played Sonny in the original production of *In the Heights* and had a prop mishap because he wasn't paying attention. At one point in Act One, he hands Usnavi (Lin-Manuel Miranda) a cup of coffee to give to Vanessa (Karen Olivo). She sips it and says that it's sweet with a little bit of cinnamon — like her grandma used to make. That connection leads to Usnavi getting a date with her. Cut to one performance: Robin picked up his prop but didn't look down to check what it was. Instead of handing Usnavi a cup of coffee, he gave him a can of Coke! Usnavi had no time to change it, so he handed Vanessa the Coke. She sipped it and ad-libbed: "Oh, my Grandma used to like these." Huh? And yet it still led to him getting a date with her!

The Sound of Music — The sound crew and sound board operator

During my run in *Disaster!*, I'd get into my costume and then, around 15 minutes before the show began, the *sound crew person* (called the *A2* by the rest of the crew) came to my dressing room and put my body mic on me. I'd then talk into the body mic so the *sound board operator* (called the *A1*) would hear it and confirm it was working.

The sound board operator, also called the *board op*, is different than the *sound designer* who's present at all the tech rehearsals and chooses all the sound levels (and creates the sound effects if there are any in the show). After everything's been solidified and turned into cues, a crew member *runs the board* (theatre talk for operates the sound board) during every performance. They sit in the back of the theatre and are in charge of making sure the show sounds like what the designer designed (Chapter 8 discusses what a sound designer does). And, because theatre is *live*, they often have to make changes on the fly. For example, an actor's body mic is usually only unmuted when they have a line. If someone skips a line or two (or many pages!), the board operator has to figure out who's talking next and unmute that microphone before someone says a line with their mic off.

SETH SPEAKS

My friend, the hilarious Chris Fitzgerald (who's also a Tony Award nominee) was the original Boq in *Wicked*. One night, during the show, he lost his footing, fell down the stairs, and landed flat on the stage. He *immediately* stood up and said something he thought was witty in the moment. He was later mortified to tell me that his "witty" quip was, "I meant to do that!" He knows it was *barely* a joke, but any slight titter he would have received had no chance of happening because he wasn't supposed to have a line at that point, so the board operator had his microphone off. Instead of a prat fall, hilarious line, and uproarious laughter, the sequence of events was the audience saw him fall down the stairs, quickly stand up, and then say — barely decipherable —"I m**** t* d* *th***."

Suffice it to say, the reaction was stunned silence.

The flip side of the story is: I was doing *Disaster!* and during the musical introduction of the song "Feelings," I'd say, "I don't need her!" Kerry Butler would enter and say, "I don't need him," and Adam Pascal would then enter and say, "I don't need her." One night, the audience heard the first two lines . . . but soon Kerry and I realized Adam wasn't onstage to say his line. Turns out, he had gotten caught up in a conversation offstage and missed his cue. But, because body mics are turned on when it's an actor's turn to speak, a perfect storm occurred: Adam's body mic was turned on *exactly* at the moment he realized he missed his cue so that night the audience heard this:

SETH: I don't need her.

KERRY: I don't need him.

ADAM (silence then . . .): *SH*T!!!*

My friend Paul Castree made me laugh after that performance because as we discussed what had happened, I said, "Ugh. I feel bad for Adam! He didn't know his mic was on." Paul asked, "Um . . . did he know the *show* was on?"

Shining the spot — The spotlight operator

If you want to see crew members at work, you need to visit backstage during a performance. But you don't have to have a backstage pass to see them in action. From your seat in the audience, look up to notice the crew member who is *high* above your head, operating the spotlight. This crew member is often known as the *spotlight operator*. Descriptive, if not terribly creative.

The spotlight is a great way to bring focus to a specific area onstage, especially if it moves! Meaning, if there's a line of dancers and one soloist in front doing steps across the stage, a spotlight operator can shine the spotlight on the soloist and keep it aimed as the dancer crosses from stage left to right.

Handling set changes — On- and offstage crew members

The bulk of crew work happens backstage or above or behind the audience, but you can *sometimes* see a crew member onstage. Even though many sets today are automated, plenty of shows have crew members that physically move sets, parts of sets, or pieces of furniture on- and offstage. Usually, they're dressed in black so the audience doesn't see them, but sometimes the lights have to stay on for various reasons and you'll see the crew at work. Certain shows want to keep the focus off these crew members, so the crew who comes onstage is dressed in some sort of costume related to the show so they don't stick out.

SETH SPEAKS

During the musical *Chess*, giant towers moved throughout the show. They created spaces for the actors to perform in. If the actors were walking down a hallway, the towers would move to make a hallway. If the actors were suddenly in a small room, the towers would create the walls of the room. Judy Kuhn, who starred as Florence, told me that each tower had a crew member inside. They each had a headset, a map of the stage, and a compass. They'd get cues through their headsets and, using the compass, move the towers where they needed to be. Kuhn said the crew members inside got attached to these giant behemoths; sometimes she'd be walking through Shubert Alley and a big, burly guy would shout out, "Hey Judy! It's me! Tower seven!"

Flying in lights, scenery, and more — The fly rail crew

Scenery isn't lowered and lifted on Broadway — it *flies!* Lights, scenery, and even people use something called the *fly rail*, which is a system of rope lines, pulleys, counterweights, and other similar devices within a theatre that enable crew members from the carpentry department to lower and lift scenic components like sets pieces, lights, scenery, and even people (I'm talking Peter Pan). And not only do these crew members fly all the aforementioned things, but, just like an old MGM movie, sometimes someone is in charge of pulling the curtain open and closed (see the nearby sidebar).

AN EXTREMELY CREATIVE USE OF A CURTAIN

What's fun to note, and what I hope creators realize, is that you don't need fancy special effects to dazzle an audience; sometimes something simple can take your breath away. In the show *42nd Street,* the curtain would be down when the audience would enter. The overture would start to play and then, while the curtain was still down, the audience would hear dialogue about an audition that was about to begin for the "new Julian Marsh show."

The music would change to the well-known song "42nd Street" and soon the audience would hear the sound of many feet tapping up a storm — all while the curtain was still down. Then, instead of the curtain going up to reveal the dancers dancing, the curtain came up just enough to see *only* everyone's feet tapping. It would stay that way for some time, and audiences *loved* seeing what amounted to a closeup of all those tapping feet. It wasn't a fancy special effect; yet that moment has gone down in theatrical history as one of the most iconic beginnings of a show. And that moment was facilitated every night by a crew member!

Broadway stage manager Linda Marvel helped me with this chapter, and she added more to this story:

She said, "This iconic moment was brought to you by the Letter M for Mistake! The curtain cue was actually called early (oops), and the production stage manager (PSM) stopped it. At that point the curtain was at the level that revealed the tapping feet. While the PSM was deciding whether to bring it back up and wait for the right timing or to just continue taking it out for that run-through rehearsal, he decided not to go back and eventually raised it. The director/choreographer Gower Champion liked it so much that he told them to keep it.

"I like this anecdote because it shows people especially young people who are growing up in a perfectly curated social media world that mistakes or at least happy accidents can be good and shouldn't be feared."

Odd crew job example 1: Onstage

Crew members are sometimes assigned very show-specific jobs. Here's an example from my show *Disaster!*: In Act Two, multiple tidal waves are predicted to flip the boat upside down around eight times. Right before the tidal waves hit, the audience would see a bunch of the cast crowded together, bracing for the boat to flip again and again. Then they'd hear the noise of the tidal wave approaching; that was followed by a blackout and then immediately a loud roar accompanied by flashing lights as the supposed tidal wave flipped the boat over and over. The audience would hear us screaming as we were flipped upside down, right side up, upside down, right side up, again and again . . . and it was hilarious.

Of course, the actors weren't flipped upside down relentlessly. Instead, during the blackout, we'd all run offstage as a kind of Ferris wheel came onstage. Attached all over the wheel were dummies dressed in our exact clothes. The wheel would turn, and the audience would see the bodies flipping and flailing over and over again. How did it turn? A crew member turned the wheel again and again while we were offstage, screaming into our body mics. Flipping bodies on a Ferris wheel isn't a specific job description, but that's what *Disaster!* needed, and so that's what a crew member did!

Odd crew job examples 2 and 3: Under the stage

In the fantastic show *Xanadu* (My family and I saw it four times and then on tour as well), the song "Suddenly" happens early in Act One. Cheyenne Jackson's character (Sonny Malone) goes into a phone booth and sits down to make a phone call while he's singing. Halfway through, Kerry Butler (she also was involved in the *Disaster!* body mic clunkfest mentioned in the previous section), who played the muse Kira, puts a spell on him and he exits the phone booth wearing roller skates (see Figure 10-2).

FIGURE 10-2:
Kerry Butler and Cheyenne Jackson perform in *Xanadu* at the 62nd Tony Awards.

Andrew H. Walker/Getty Images

The moment was magical because the audience saw him enter wearing sneakers and then exit in skates! While he was sitting in the phone booth singing, a trap door opened underneath him, and a crew member below the stage took off his sneakers while he was singing and replaced them with roller skates! Result: theatre magic! You guessed it — "sneaker-remover/roller-skate-replacer" isn't a specific job, but crew members are available for whatever has to be done.

SETH SPEAKS

A similar trap door was used in the musical *Carrie* on Broadway. This time the audience could see the trap door but not what was underneath. In the thrilling song "And Eve Was Weak," Betty Buckley (who should have won a Tony Award for one of the most brilliant performances on Broadway) played the religious zealot/abusive mother of Carrie, played by 17-year-old Linzi Hately (who is now a West End star). In the middle of the song, Betty opened the cellar door and forced Linzi inside who was half underneath the stage and desperately clawing onto the stage while Betty aggressively pushed her down. In order for Linzi not to fall down, a few crew members held her up. Betty said it was a riot to push Linzi downward and sing this crazy song while seeing these burly men — whom the audience couldn't see! — holding her up.

Odd crew job example 4: Side of stage

My close friend Paul Castree was one of the stars of *Saturday Night Fever* on Broadway. He played Bobby C, and as most people familiar with the film know, Bobby C falls (or does he jump?) off the Brooklyn Bridge. In the musical, he climbs the Brooklyn Bridge set, higher and higher. When he gets super high, he holds onto the sides and then, at the end of the scene, he lets go and the audience sees him plummet to the stage. *Right* before he hits the ground, there is a blackout.

You may ask: How was that done without him being smashed on the stage? Well, he was wearing a harness underneath his costume that the audience couldn't see and the harness had a heavy-duty cord attached. That cord ran from his body, up to the rafters, and down to the crew member who was holding it backstage. When Paul would let go of the sides of the bridge, the crew member would also let go of the cord. Paul would plummet toward the stage, and the crew would watch the cord as it ran through his hands. As soon as the crew member saw a specific mark that was on the cord, he'd grab it. That mark coincided with the point where Paul was a few feet above the stage. When the crew member grabbed it, it would stop Paul in the air (and the blackout would happen at the same time). Again, what a specific job to have!

The people who created that effect used the kind of cord used in musicals like *Peter Pan* for people to fly. Unfortunately, the cord wasn't created to be aggressively *stopped* eight times a week, and so months into the run of the show, the crew member pulled the cord to stop Paul from falling one night . . . and it snapped! So scary! Paul said he was onstage and thinking his character's thoughts: "I'm dying . . ." and then when the cord snapped, his thoughts changed to "Wait, I'm *actually* dying!" The good news is, when the cord broke, he was about six feet from the stage, which *is* high, but he cushioned his fall on his hands and knees. Amazingly, he didn't hurt himself too badly. He took off a few shows to heal and was soon back in the show. And by that time, they got a much more secure cord!

Even though he wasn't hurt, that wasn't the case all around. When the cord snapped, the poor crew member holding it was completely thrown backward and broke his wrist! Yikes! Live theatre is thrilling but sometimes dangerous.

"Go into Your Dance" — The Dance Captain

A *dance captain* is a performer in the show who makes sure all the choreography looks like what was originally choreographed. Why is there that position? Musicals are performed eight times a week, and anyone who's ever done a show knows that choreography gets modified over time . . . usually by accident. A dance move doesn't stay as precise, someone's positioning moves slightly to a different spot on the stage, or a new cast member hasn't learned a section correctly. The list goes on. These modifications to the original choreography are often minute, but they all need to be addressed to keep a show in superior shape. Does a choreographer watch the show every night and give notes constantly? No. After a show opens, the choreographer's day-to-day job is over, but they leave someone in charge, and that's the dance captain.

REMEMBER

The dance captain knows the choreography for every single person in the show and is in charge of keeping the dances up to snuff. The dance captain is *in* the show as well, so they can see what's happening around them, but they obviously can't see everything from their vantage point onstage. So, often a dance captain is *swung out,* meaning they take off a show and the *swing* (the ensemble understudy — see Chapter 9 for more about swings) goes on. But the dance captain doesn't take off a show to go for a spa day; they're watching the show from the audience and taking notes on everyone. That's the only way they can truly see what's happening throughout the show to keep it clean. Often, the dance captain gives notes throughout the week . . . usually by talking to the performer in question backstage. Brush-up rehearsals also take place where the dance captain can work on larger sections of the show and fix them. Or the choreographer sometimes comes to see the show and gives the dance captain notes to address in a brush-up rehearsal. (*Brush-up rehearsals* are short rehearsals that happen after a show opens. They're held to keep the singing/acting/dancing at the level of opening night. For more info, see Chapter 12.)

The dance captain is also often responsible for "putting in" new cast members. When someone joins a musical after it's opened, they usually don't rehearse with the choreographer. They learn the choreography from the dance captain.

SETH SPEAKS

Back in the mid-70s, when Priscilla Lopez took over the role of Fastrada in *Pippin*, she was thrilled! Fastrada is a wonderful, featured role with a great song, and she got to dance some amazing Bob Fosse choreography although Fosse wasn't the person who taught her the show. The dance captain taught her.

She said that process was *grueling*, and the dance captain was incredibly specific, and didn't allow her *any* freedom at all. And when she started performing, it was *still* a nightmare. The dance captain would give her notes all the time . . . like telling her to move her index finger more to the right or roll her shoulders in a slightly smaller circle. Priscilla told me that she prayed Fosse would come and "rescue" her — that is, give her permission to dance the choreography without focusing so specifically on every tiny part of her body. Fosse did finally come, and twist ending . . . he was a *million times* more specific about exactly how he wanted each move to look. Turns out, the dance captain was doing Priscilla a favor by being so meticulous! It saved her from being completely annihilated by Fosse! The dance captain is there to maintain the choreographer's steps and intentions, and this dance captain knew *exactly* what Fosse wanted!

REMEMBER

Depending on the choreography, a dance captain doesn't have to be an amazing dancer. Empirical evidence: In the Broadway revival of Terrence McNally's *The Ritz* starring Rosie Perez, the dance captain was *me!* Let me just say, my dance training ended in college, but I had enough knowledge to keep the dancing in the show as Christopher Gatelli first choreographed it. Let me also say, I'm glad it was only a three-month run. #NotAGreatDanceCaptain. #SkinOfMyTeeth #DontAskAgain

"Dress Has Always Been My Strongest Suit" — The Costumes Crew

Costumes are usually a fairly expensive aspect of a musical's budget, especially a musical that has multiple costume changes and/or glamorous costumes like *The Phantom of the Opera*. Even a show where cast members wear one costume for the whole show needs an entire crew to handle those singular costumes.

The head of it all is the *wardrobe supervisor*, the person who's in charge of all things costumes, not just supervising how they're put on and off the performers, but every aspect of the upkeep. The washing, the dry cleaning, the steaming, the ironing, the hanging up after the show, the mending, the this, the that. The wardrobe supervisor has many people working backstage to help with all these aspects. Those helpers are *dressers*. These sections focus more on the crew who handle all aspects of the costumes during a show's run.

Taking care of show underwear and cleanings

One of the fun things for me about being an actor in a Broadway show is getting my show underwear and show socks. Putting on these assigned underthings makes me feel like I'm leaving my daily life and becoming the character. And you know how sometimes you hold up your underthings and think, "Uh-oh. These haven't been washed . . . but I don't have any time today, so I guess I'll wear them again." (Wait. I'm the only person who does that? Okay, let me qualify that unhygienic-ness and say it *mainly* happened during my teenaged years. And only twice a year since then.) Regardless, that never happens on Broadway.

If you're in a show, right after you return to your dressing room after bows, a little mesh bag is placed in your room. When you take off your costume, you take the bag and put in your show underwear, show socks, and for men, show undershirt and/or show dance belt. And, the women put in their show bra, show stockings, and so on. Then your dresser collects the bag. The bag is back in your dressing room with everything clean for the next show! *Fantastic!*

And for those people who hate hanging up clothes neatly, you are usually allowed to just lay out your costumes after the show and when you come back, they're magically hung up! And not just hung up but *cleaned*. The washable clothes are washed and the dry clean-only ones are sent out as often as necessary. And every day, the possible smelly areas are sprayed so they don't smell. I was shocked when I saw what they're sprayed with: *Vodka!* I thought it was a joke label on the bottle, but dressers deodorize clothes with vodka to clean them! #IdLikeToProposeAToast

Helping with the quick change

Dressers do what their name states: They help performers dress. It's not like *Downtown Abbey* where you have a valet putting you in your entire outfit while you stand and talk about your latest suitor and whether or not Mummy will approve. If your costume is easy to get on, you do it yourself. But sometimes, one needs help, like getting zipped up in the back. Example: the first costume I had to wear in *Disaster!*, a full-on wetsuit!

A QUICK-CHANGE DEBACLE

One of my favorite Broadway quick-change debacles happened during the 1990s musical *Side Show*. Emily Skinner and Alice Ripley gave incredible Tony-nominated performances playing real-life conjoined twins, Daisy and Violet Hilton. When the show first began performances, they would often have to wake up super early to do morning shows, even though they were doing the musical at night. I was working on *The Rosie O'Donnell Show* at the time, and I remember them singing, "Who Will Love Me As I Am?" and right after that, Emily discovered she had burst a blood vessel on her vocal chords! She had to take off a few shows to repair it, and her understudy, the fabulous Lauren Kennedy, went on for her.

On the day Emily came back, she and Alice finished the song, "Leave Me Alone," and then backed into a door that opened in the set where the set closed in front of them. While they were hidden from view, they'd completely change their costumes and wigs in a *very* short amount of time and then reenter for the next number. During the change, vaudeville boys were onstage singing and dancing their introduction. At the end, the two would be revealed inside a sarcophagus for the big Vaudeville Egyptian Number. Well, on the night of Emily's return during the quick change, she couldn't get her costume on. AT ALL. She jokingly thought, "Could I literally have gained this much weight in two days?" Then she saw her dresser's face go white.

Turns out, the dresser had laid out Lauren's costume, which was a smaller size! The conductor, David Chase, saw the sarcophagus wasn't opening, so he started the intro music again, and the onstage dancing boys continued singing and dancing the same section one more time. The dresser had to run up three flights to Emily's dressing room to get her correct costume. The introduction music onstage started again! And again. Finally, the dresser came back, Emily got into her costume, and the two actresses entered the sarcophagus. *But* right before it opened they realized they had rushed into the sarcophagus and wound up on the wrong side of each other! It was as if they had gotten the operation to separate conjoined twins and then got sewn back together on opposite sides. Alice screamed, "There's no way I'm reversing this choreography!" so they got out of the sarcophagus and changed sides. It *finally* opened, and they saw ten chorus boys, wildly panting with a glazed look of "What the **** just happened!?"

Dressers become MVPs when they facilitate one of the most exciting/scary things in a show: the quick change. A *quick change* is when an actor has to switch costumes in an extremely short amount of time. Usually, the actor leaves the stage, gets to the quick-change area ASAP, and simply stands still. A dresser (or multiple dressers depending on the difficulty) is there to take off the actor's costume and get them into the new one. Because backstage is fairly dark, the dressers hold flashlights in their mouths. Sometimes an actor has certain moves they must do;

for example, a dress is laid on the floor and the actor steps into it and then the dresser pulls it up and fastens it. Or sometimes the actor puts on their shoes while their bustle is being fastened or a hat is being secured. Regardless, these quick changes are choreographed within an inch of their life because the actor has only so much time before making their next entrance.

Dressing the star

Usually, multiple actors share a dresser unless the actor is the star of the show. Then they get a *star dresser*. That dresser handles dressing *only* that actor. The star dresser is also usually much more than a dresser because they're constantly with the actor and they become a confidante, a cheerleader, and a problem solver. Most stars have a specific dresser that they take with them to every show they do! See the nearby sidebar for how a star dresser became a problem solver!

SETH SPEAKS

A STAR DRESSER/PROBLEM SOLVER

A live TV show quick change is the same as a theatrical quick change. My friend Ana Gasteyer was a cast member on *Saturday Night Live* and, just to give her some theatre street cred, I must mention that she then played Elphaba in *Wicked*. Anyhoo, after she left *SNL*, she was invited back the week Betty White hosted. Her first sketch was "The Delicious Dish," the NPR show she would do with Molly Shannon. In this sketch, Betty White touted her pastry called a "dusty muffin" (hilarious!). After that sketch was a commercial and then Fred Armisen's "Manuel Ortiz Show" sketch. Ana said that during the commercial break, she ran to the quick-change area in SNL underneath the audience bleachers. She took off her entire NPR outfit and went to put on her next dress, but it wouldn't go on.

The dress has an internal slip, and she started to rip it as she was putting it on. Back when she had done the show in the '90's, she had an unflappable dresser who could do *anything*. This dresser had been in the business a *long* time, for instance she had been Jessica Tandy's dresser for *A Streetcar Named Desire*. The original run! (I know that literally sounds like a joke — remember that Simpsons episode where an extremely old woman mentions that she was Eubie Blake's nanny? — but it's true.)

When Ana made her reappearance on *SNL*, her dresser had *finally* retired (Note: *A Streetcar Named Desire* opened in 1947. That's a long career!) The new dresser assigned to Ana saw her standing in just pantyhose, a strapless bra, and a wig cap with her dress crumpled on the floor and, according to Ana, screamed in panic and fell to the floor. She was *out!* Ana adopted the tone she uses with her two children and calmly

(continued)

(continued)

stated, "I need you to stop yelling now, so we can fix this." Suddenly, the commercial break was over, and the sketch had begun! Ana had around 90 seconds before her entrance. The dresser kept keening, so Ana asked for her wig so she could be partway dressed. The wig person put it on and then tried to help by giving Ana the shirt off her back. Literally! She took off her own T-shirt and handed it to Ana so she'd have *something* to wear in the sketch. Ana was appreciative, especially since her wig person was now standing in only a bra. However, Ana didn't want to go on television wearing a T-shirt over pantyhose, which she thinks is *the* most unflattering thing in the world to wear. (Cut to: Elaine Stritch won a Tony Award in that same outfit.)

Amazingly, the dresser's nonstop screaming paid off because it attracted Donna Richards. Who's Donna? She is a *star* dresser; I know her because I was a comedy writer on *The Rosie O'Donnell Show* and Donna was Rosie's dresser. On *SNL*, she is the host dresser. Whoever the mega-star host is, Donna is their dresser. She is cool as a cucumber — nothing fazes her. Ana said that Donna always has a small flashlight in her mouth, so she can see in the dark and have both hands available. She approached Ana calmly, picked up the dress, and *ripped* the entire lining out of it. She quickly put the lining on Ana with the dress still attached and hanging off of it. Turns out, the lining looked sort of like sexy lingerie and the dress, which was dragging, looked like an amazing fashion statement. Ana actually made her entrance on time! Ana said the slip was *super* short although she confirmed "no one could actually see my pubic triangle."

Aftermath: A month later, a fan approached Ana on the subway, telling her that she was in the audience for that show. The woman then dropped her voice to a vocal range/soft volume one uses to discuss the horrors of war and darkly intoned, "We saw your quick change." She then walked away, dead eyed, apparently still traumatized, vicariously. Ana then realized the *entire* bleacher section was able to see her trying to get into the dress! I'm talkin' the screaming, the wig cap, the pantyhose, the wig woman in just a bra, and Donna shredding the original dress. Yay? And look . . . I found the sketch! https://www.youtube.com/watch?v=KUx0Yu1gmo0&t=92s.

"Long Beautiful Hair" —The Hair Supervisor and Hairdressers

The show is now in performance. The wigs have been designed and fitted. The various hairstyles have been perfected. Now the hair supervisor really takes over. The *hair supervisor* is in charge of keeping the wigs in pristine condition as well as making sure each performer's hairstyle stays consistent. Like the wardrobe supervisor, the hair supervisor is on duty for every performance and has people helping in many ways. (The hair designer and/or wig designer actually create the styles before the show's run — Chapter 8 discusses what this professional does.)

SETH SPEAKS

One of my favorite stories is about Jackie Hoffman, who is hi-larious; this story nicely depicts what the hair crew does for Broadway actors. Jackie had done a string of Off-Broadway plays; she finally got her first Broadway show, *Hairspray*, when she was 40 years old. She (memorably) played three roles: Penny's mom, the gym teacher, and the prison warden. Naturally, all three had a different look and, for this show, that meant different wigs. Putting a wig on perfectly and so it looks natural takes skill, and Jackie knew there was *no* way she could do it herself. She was basically in tears when she asked a cast member, "How am I going to get these wigs on!?" The cast member, who was a Broadway vet replied, "Don't worry, Jackie. The show has someone who will put the wigs on you." Jackie then replied, through tears, "*Every day?*"

Jackie was used to the Off-Broadway do-it-yourself low budget show and was shocked to have people whose job it was to help with her hair. Those people are the *hairdressers*. They not only put on your wig, but they also style your natural hair if need be and, my favorite part, they give you a haircut whenever you need it! One of the most important jobs of the hairdressers is helping during the quick change. When actors run into the wings for a panicked quick change, they are not only changing costumes, but also often changing wigs! Their wig is snatched off and another one put on and styled in seconds.

All hail the hair department!

STUFFED WIGS, SUPPRESSED LAUGHS, AND A "LITTLE FALL OF RAIN"

SETH SPEAKS

Here's my favorite wig story and one of my favorite onstage mishaps! It involves Priscilla Lopez (Morales in *A Chorus Line*) and one of her first Broadway shows, *Her First Roman*. To wear a wig in this show, the chorus girls would pin their wig caps to their hair, and because Priscilla's hair was short, it was hard to attach the caps. She found out if she stuffed some clothes underneath the wig cap, it would give something for the cap to be attached to. She'd stuff anything she could find — underclothes, socks, whatever — it all worked. Once she saw how well it worked, she told this trick to the other chorus women while they were applying the leg paint to themselves that made them look more Egyptian. Act Two featured a funeral procession where all the ladies walked in a solemn line around a coffin. Priscilla happened to look up at the dancer in front of her during the procession and saw that she had taken her advice. Unfortunately, as Pricilla

(continued)

(continued)

marched in the solemn funeral, she saw that the dancer didn't tuck all the clothes in securely, and swinging freely from underneath the dancer's wig was a large white bra. OMG!

Priscilla wanted to laugh, but she couldn't because it was a sad scene. Literally a funeral. She tried to suppress it, but all that did was cause incredible pressure inside, which resulted in her *peeing onstage!* She couldn't stop and was mortified that it was also causing her leg makeup to run in rivulets to the stage. Soon she was even more horrified because the stage was raked. A *raked* stage means that the back of the stage is tilted up and lays in a diagonal toward the audience. What comes down must go farther down, apparently, because soon the pee was running downhill and overflowing from the front of the stage to the pit! I'm obsessed thinking about those poor musicians sitting in the pit wondering what was dripping on them. Hopefully, they felt some comfort in knowing it was from a future Tony Award winner!

"You Can Always Count on Me" — The Stage Manager

First question: What is a stage manager? Well, first of all, what are they *not?* They're not members of the crew. They *are* backstage, but they're considered the stage management team. Second question: What does a stage manager do? Well, the stage manager does *everything.* Or maybe I should say, the stage manager is *in charge* of everything. Everyone involved in the day-to-day show has to report to the stage manager after the show is running: the conductor, the crew, the actors, *everyone.* And the stage manager is often the liaison between the producers and the cast, the director and the cast, a specific actor and another actor, you get the idea. If someone in the show has a problem, they go to the stage manager first. But that's not all stage managers do. Not by a long shot! These sections point out the stage management team and explain their different responsibilities.

Introducing the stage managers

Stage managers actually have some hierarchy. Here it is in a nutshell in order of importance:

>> **Production stage manager (PSM):** This person is the big cheese, and there's just one PSM on a show. Suffice it to say they run rehearsals, do scheduling, call cues, and are responsible for keeping the show running smoothly as well as maintaining its artistic integrity. And they oversee all the stage managers.

Because they're also responsible for running rehearsals and giving notes to actors, they'll sometimes watch the show from the audience.

>> **Stage manager (SM):** This person reports to the PSM whereas the PSM reports directly to the producer(s) and general manager. The SM helps the PSM do many of their responsibilities, but during the performance the SM is in charge of *running the deck* — in other words, organizing the crew in various departments to do all the things needed for the show to run. They organize many of the technical and backstage aspects of the show — where the props get placed, where the scenery lives, where the quick changes happen, where entrances and exits of the performers happen, and so on. Most importantly, because musicals have lots of moving set pieces and people running around, SMs are in charge of keeping people safe in the wings.

>> **Assistant stage manager (ASM):** This person also does many of the tasks of the SM, but handles the more, shall I say, mundane tasks . . . like clerical duties (typing up notes) and doing the *stuffers* and *sliders* (meaning printing and distributing the pieces of paper that state an understudy is going on and get stuffed into a Playbill as well as making sure the cast list in the lobby has the correct sliders stating who is performing that night). They also visit each dressing room before the show to collect valuables. These valuables are stored in a safe so they're not left in an empty dressing room to be stolen . . . or in the West End, *pilfered*. When the PSM is out, the SM becomes the PSM and the ASM becomes the SM (and a sub ASM is brought in).

Broadway musicals usually have one PSM, one SM, and one ASM.

Managing everything during rehearsals

During the rehearsal period, the stage managers are usually the first to show up and the last to leave. The duties of the team are enormous; the following sections focus on their main responsibilities.

Taping the stage

The stage managers have to lay out the floor of the studio with tape to indicate what the stage looks like. As I discuss in Chapter 11, shows aren't rehearsed on Broadway stages with the set already built. They're rehearsed in rehearsal studios that are bare. So, if you visit a rehearsal while a show is first being put together, you'd see taped lines everywhere on the floor that indicate where the wings are, where the edge of the stage is, where set pieces begin and end, and so on.

My friend Dick Scanlon (who wrote the book/lyrics to *Thoroughly Modern Millie*) loves to pretend to be a stage manager, constantly correcting people for not acknowledging taped areas. Back in the days when we were just starting out, we did a comedy show together with my comedy partner Dick Scanlon. During our "Annoying Stage Manager Sketch," we'd be pretending to be rehearsing a new Broadway show, Dick would see step to the left and, because that's where the stairs will be eventually on the set, he'd say matter-of-factly, "You just fell down a flight of stairs."

Scheduling everything

Stage managers have to enjoy games. Well, not literally, but they're in charge of putting together the dreaded rehearsal schedule, which is like a combo of Wordle, Tetris, and being a therapist (gently telling the music director there aren't six hours to rehearse the altos). Anyone who's ever tried to schedule a musical with scene, song, and dance rehearsal knows what a *Nacht mare* that is. Trying to figure out the timing of which actors to call and which scenes to do and which dances to work on choreography and which songs to learn and who needs a brush-up and what needs to be re-rehearsed because it changed is worthy of a Mensa membership.

Keeping detailed notes

Stage managers keep copious notes of everything in the rehearsal room. They watch rehearsals with an eagle's eye and a . . . wait. What's an animal reference for good hearing? A bat's ear? Anyhoo, they have to note *everything* that happens during rehearsal like:

>> All the staging

>> Line changes

>> Lyric changes

>> Anything to do with the props and the set

>> Sound cues, projection cues, quick changes

>> Lots more!

They take clear and thorough notes, and eventually create an up-to-date script with all the new cues written in it — meaning all the cues for set changes, lighting changes, and sound cues. Why? Because the stage manager is on a headset during the show calling every single cue with any crew person who has cues! And that script is used when the stage manager subs go on. And P.S., many of these cues are musical. For example:

After 10 and a half bars of the dance break, call the cue for the set change from school to ballroom.

The stage manager has to count all those beats. Stage managers not only have to be organized, but they also have to have musical chops. And not just for musicals. Lots of plays have music in them as well!

In terms of calling cues, what does that sound like? If you're in the wings of a theatre during a show, you'd constantly hear the stage manager saying things like, "Lights Cue 37 . . . GO! Lights Cue 38 . . . GO!"

SETH SPEAKS

Speaking of Cue 37, GO!, one of my favorite stunt casting stories involves cue calling. I won't say who, but a famous woman (not famous for any aspect of performing) was cast in a long-running musical. On her opening night, as a responsible person, she got to her spot early to stand in the wings, awaiting her first entrance. Her responsible nature backfired because she was in the wings *way* before she was supposed to be. Standing there, anxious to make her Broadway debut, she was near the stage manager and could hear the cues being called. She heard "GO!" and naturally, she went! And she walked onstage during a scene that had *nothing* to do with her. The audience was like, "Who is that awkward person who just stumbled onstage? She's famous! Wait. Why is she slowly slinking off?" Anyhoo, that show has since closed, but that story lives on!

Keeping to the director's vision

After a show opens, the stage manager is not just calling the cues every night (also known as *calling the show*), but they're also keeping the show in the shape the director intended. After every performance, the stage managers issue a show report to all the powers-that-be that mentions any problems that happened during the show or any issues that need to be addressed. (Again, after *every show*. The work never ends!) If they see an actor making a change, they give a note to the actor. Or if the director comes back to watch the show, the director usually gives the notes to the stage manager to give to the actor.

The stage manager also is in charge of teaching the understudies the show and then running understudy rehearsal. *And* they're in charge of teaching the replacements the show. Often, a replacement comes into a Broadway show that was directed by somebody famous, but the new person barely even meets the director. The stage manager actually directs them, and the director usually comes on their opening night to give any notes. And in long-running shows, the director sometimes *never* sees a replacement. That's why the stage manager's role is so important; their job is to keep the show running exactly as it did on opening night.

Setting the Performance's Tone — The Conductor

The conductor's job is to conduct the orchestra *and* the performers of a musical. Let me note that the conductor is often the music director, so they've been through the rehearsal period and have a deep understanding of how the songs should be performed. (Chapter 8 discusses what the music director does.) These sections focus more on what the conductor does.

Keeping track of cues

One of the main aspects of conducting is starting each song as per the cue line. Some songs begin based on a visual cue that the conductor has to watch for. But shows are live and mistakes happen! Sometimes people skip a line cue, and the conductor has to know the show well enough to know to start the song. Or sometimes an actor skips a verse within a song, and the conductor has to communicate with the orchestra to cut to the end or to the middle or to the second verse or wherever (it happened to me).

The conductor also sets the emotional tone for the performers. If an actor looks down and sees someone with their eyes locked to the music on their podium or someone waving their hands with a blank face, it can set a pall over the show. If an actor looks down and sees someone energized and excited, it adds sass to what could otherwise be just another performance.

ALL OR NOTHING

As a veteran of 15 Broadway orchestras, I can say there are two types of conductors who annoy me. The conductor who is cueing every performer onstage even when these actors have zero need for a cue. And the conductor who cues *nothing*! I've been in orchestras and seen both at the same time! In one show, the conductor was cueing singers every eight bars once the song began. Why? The tempo didn't change. There was no way the actors didn't know to keep singing. It was really him just having fun and enjoying the music . . . but it didn't help the show.

Meanwhile, I was a sub who hadn't played the show very often, and I definitely needed help from the conductor about when to come in. I would look up after resting for 30 bars, wanting confirmation I should play, and I'd see him watching the stage and cueing the actors who'd been doing it since opening night and didn't need any help! Infuriating!

Setting the tempo

Another important job a conductor has is setting the tempo for each song. This always panicked me whenever I conducted a dance show; what if I took the big dance number a little too fast? The dancers onstage aren't able to stop and say slow down! They have to keep going, and I was always scared I would cause them to injure themselves. *Or* perhaps I took the big belty number too slowly, forcing the lead to hold the last note too long and therefore causing a vocal injury.

Even though I was always slightly in a panic about the damage I could do with that baton when I was conducting on Broadway, I must also say it's so much fun! I felt so much a part of the timing of a show; for instance, I would be the one to decide when to bring in music after a laugh line. Or one of the most fun things: I'd be the one to bring in scene-change music after a song ended so the actor would have to stand there and receive much-deserved applause until I began the next song.

SETH SPEAKS

One of my favorite moments was during my *Dreamgirls* concert for the Entertainment Community Fund. Lillias White played Effie and after her song "I Am Changing," the audience applauds and then another song begins and Effie exits. Lillias was so fantastic in "I Am Changing" that she got an incredible amount of applause. I knew that starting the next song would cue the audience to stop applauding, and I knew they wanted to *really* praise Lillias, so I just held off beginning the next song. That meant Lillias couldn't exit. Watching her stand there, receiving tons of applause, was so great. If I had started the next song, she wouldn't have been able to bask as long in that love!

"76 Trombones" — The Orchestra

The orchestra consists of musicians who play the show eight times a week. Often times, they're located in the orchestra pit and in view of the audience.

When a show is getting ready to open on Broadway, the orchestra first runs through the score with the conductor and no actors. This happens so the musicians can figure out how to play the show and also because the music is being played for the first time and the orchestrator needs to hear it to make sure it's what they heard in their head, and the composer has to sign off on it. Also, there might be mistakes! The *copyists* are the people who write out what the orchestrator orchestrated, and a wrong note or two can definitely slip into the score because of human error. This early read-through provides an opportunity for corrections to be made. Soon, the orchestra is at *tech rehearsals,* the days before the first public performance where the cast is onstage and every technical aspect is perfected. (See Chapter 11 for more about tech rehearsals.) Next comes the regular eight-show-a-week performance schedule. Often, the actors don't get to hang out with the orchestra because the actors are onstage while the orchestra is playing and never the twain shall meet.

The only orchestra member the actors usually know is the keyboard player because they're at understudy rehearsals and put-in rehearsals. That's why I'd often know so many of the cast members of shows I played, but the cello players wouldn't recognize them if they passed each other on 9th Avenue. The biggest difference between the orchestra and actors' jobs is that an orchestra member can take off 50 percent of their performances as per their union. The actors can only miss for sickness or for a personal day. A musician, however, doesn't need a reason to miss.

It may sound unfair, but an audience is definitely upset if the actor they wanted to see is out of the show. But they're usually not devastated if the orchestra is missing its piccolo player. The other difference is the musician is in charge of picking and training their understudy (called a *sub*), whereas the show's director picks the understudies for each actor. After a sub has been trained and approved by the conductor, the musician is in charge of booking their own sub. Subs become pretty valuable during the holidays because so many orchestra members want to be with family. I remember the time I got the flu and realized at around 6 p.m. that I couldn't play *The Producers* that night. I had to call the regular keyboardist and tell him that I was too sick to come in and he'd have to play. On Christmas Eve! I still feel guilty.

Here I identify what you need to know about the orchestra.

Wearing all black in the pit

Because the audience can often see into the pit, the musicians are told to wear black so they don't distract from the stage.

However, not all black outfits are deemed acceptable. Each orchestra pit has their own requirement. I could wear a black T-shirt in many shows I played in the orchestra for, but at *The Phantom of the Opera*, my black shirt had to have a collar. #Fancy

On the flip side was *The Full Monty*. The score had a pop feel and because the music wasn't highfalutin, we were allowed to wear *whatever* we wanted. I'd be in that pit in a tank top and shorts! I loved coming right off the street in whatever I was wearing and planting it in the pit.

For your information, one of the things I don't love about playing in a pit is having to change into a black outfit. You arrive at the theatre in your street clothes and you have to put on an all-black outfit. Or you were wearing an all-black outfit during the day and get a reputation for being a downer, for acting cool, or for trying to be a Fosse dancer.

When I was playing *Les Misérables,* a certain violinist didn't want to change out of what he was wearing to put on black pants. He was notorious for sitting in the pit in whatever he was wearing and draping a large black blanket over his legs. #ProblemSolved

Living in the pit

Usually, the orchestra is in the pit for the entire act, but if a musician *has* to run to the bathroom, they can leave. However, some pits allow the orchestra more freedom. When I was doing the revival of *Grease,* we were allowed to leave the pit between songs, whether to chat with the actors or get a cup of coffee at the community coffee machine. I loved it and definitely took advantage! I still remember, however, talking to someone by the sugar and hearing the beginning of "Mooning" and *running* back to the pit.

Grease traditionally was a lax show in terms of being allowed to leave the orchestra pit (the original and the revivals). My friend, David Friedman, who conducted the show on Broadway in the '70s told me that the bass player had an extra-long cord made for his bass, so he could leave the pit whenever he wanted, walk around backstage, and then play from wherever he was! He'd be chatting near the wig room downstairs, hear a cue line and, because he knew the show so well, he'd play the entire thing without coming back to the pit! Have bass, will travel!

**SETH
SPEAKS**

Speaking of *Grease,* Steve Marzullo was the regular pianist for the revival of *Grease!!!* (I was his sub). At one performance, he was drinking a cup of coffee during the show. Suddenly, it spilled — *on the electric keyboard!* Was it short circuited? Would it work? Amazingly, it worked perfectly. *For a while.* It wasn't until Act Two when it acted up. Steve went to play the opening chord of "There Are Worse Things I Could Do," and the keyboard transposed what he was playing, meaning it changed the key. That first chord was suddenly up four steps, making the song *much* higher to sing. And, spoiler alert, Rosie O'Donnell is *not* a soprano. She somehow got through the number, but Kristin Chenoweth didn't have anything to be jealous about!

Being in a community

Being in the pit is akin to living in a small community. You're all sitting very close to each other, and you learn what you need to do to get along. Sometimes you have to lean to one side to let the violinist do a bowing section that takes their arm all the way to the left. Or you may bring candy to share with the string section because they all have a sweet tooth. Or you know the oboe player always has a runny nose and forgets to bring tissues, so you bring extra.

TIP

The next time you're at a Broadway show, lean down and say hello. We musicians love to look up and see a smiling face!

3

The Blood, Sweat, and Tears of Theatre Life

Chapter **11**

Understanding How an Idea Becomes Broadway Gold

I'm always mystified when I hear a song on the radio because I don't know how that song went from the recording studio to being played on the radio. Of course, I know someone or some people wrote the song and then someone recorded it, but how did it eventually get to the point where a radio station would play it? Did the radio deejay hear it in a club and think, "My listeners will love this?" Did the deejay's boss say, "You have to play this song. It's gonna be *the* summer song." I don't know! That's why this book isn't called *Pop Music For Dummies.* I ain't the author for that. But it is *Musical Theatre For Dummies.* And that's because I know how a musical gets developed and lands on Broadway. And I'd love to tell you the details!

Finding Inspiration for Musicals

A musical begins with someone thinking "What if there was a musical about . . . ?" If those people were Tom Kitt and Brian Yorkey writing *Next to Normal*, they possibly said, "What if there were a musical about how a bipolar mother and her family deal with grief?" Those two writers thought of an original idea for a musical. If they were Jim Jacobs and Warren Casey, they probably asked each other, "What if there were a musical about the kids we went to school with who weren't the straight A students? A musical about the kids who wore leather jackets and ratted their hair and drank and smoked a little? And what if it focused on how they interact with a new goody-two-shoes girl who transfers to the school her senior year?" *Grease* was another original idea.

But what about ideas for musicals that aren't totally original? What are the source materials that turn into Broadway musicals? The following sections focus on the various types of categories that have given us many great musicals.

The Bible — Talk about old school

The oldest source material for musicals is from the oldest book. A bunch of Broadway shows are based on the written word from around 5,000 years ago. *The Apple Tree* has an entire first act called "The Diary of Adam and Eve." Andrew Lloyd Webber and Tim Rice became world-wide successes with their first two musicals: *Joseph and the Amazing Technicolor Dreamcoat* and *Jesus Christ Superstar*. And like Lloyd Webber, Stephen Schwartz was in his early 20s when he wrote his first Bible-themed musical *Godspell*. More recently, *The Book of Mormon* became a hit and it's based on . . . you guessed it . . . The Book of Mormon.

Speaking of biblical books, The Book of Matthew was the inspiration for *Your Arms Too Short to Box with God*, which was such a hit that it came back to Broadway only two years after it closed. The revival didn't run as long as the original production, but that revival was the first Broadway musical to feature Jennifer Holliday. In her Broadway debut, she was known as Jennifer Yvette Holliday. Two years later she dropped the Yvette and created the character of Effie Melody White in *Dreamgirls*, the role for which she won a Tony Award. So thank you Bible for bringing her to Broadway.

FYI: God or goddess or higher power doesn't bless every musical coming from religious doctrine. Case in point: Schwartz wrote another musical based on the Bible that has been around for a while, but it still hasn't debuted on Broadway. It's called *Children of Eden*, and it has a fabulous album that includes two of my favorite

Schwartz songs: "Lost in the Wilderness" and "Spark of Creation." And the musical *Two By Two* was based on the story of Noah and the Ark. That show didn't exactly flop, but it sure didn't run for years like its Bible brethren. But, fun fact, it featured Madeline Kahn in her first Broadway musical, so all is forgiven.

Shakespeare

Another source for material from ye olden days is The Bard. *Kiss Me, Kate* is a version of *The Taming of the Shrew* and has had two revivals on Broadway *and* a film version. And as many people know, *Romeo and Juliet* was turned into the tragedy of Tony and Maria in *West Side Story*, which has had *three* revivals on Broadway and *two* film versions. *Romeo and Juliet* is also the inspiration for the 2022 Broadway musical *& Juliet*. A lessor known musical, but one that I *love*, is *All Shook Up*, which is based on *Twelfth Night*. Listen to the album featuring Cheyenne Jackson's first lead role: www.youtube.com/watch?v=MXbETZvTCVI&t=676s. #sogood

Other plays

During the Golden Age, plays were being musicalized (stage) left and (stage) right. Here are some of the more notable ones:

>> *The Matchmaker* became *Hello, Dolly!*

>> *Pygmalion* became *My Fair Lady*.

>> *They Knew What They Wanted* became *The Most Happy Fella*.

>> The musical that started The Golden Age, *Oklahoma!* was based on the play *Green Grow The Lilacs*.

This trend was common in the early decades of musical theatre, but I can't think of a musical from the last 20 years that's been based on a play. That's probably because back in the day, three times as many plays were on Broadway as compared to now. Why? Well, Broadway ticket prices have sky-rocketed (for reasons I'll let other people explain) and, because of that, it seems ticket buyers reason if they're going to spend a lot of money to see a Broadway show, they want to see their money onstage. That usually translates to people singing and dancing, hence not a play. So, with fewer plays to mine for material for musicals, creators have turned to the modern-day play — the film, which I discuss in the next section.

Films and TV shows

The trend of turning films into musicals really took off in the 2000s. Before that, there was *maybe* one or two musicals every ten years based on a film. Off the top of my head I can only think of these few:

>> *Carnival* based on *Lily* in the early '60s

>> *Promises, Promises* in the late '60s based on *The Apartment*

>> *The Wiz* based on *The Wizard of Oz* in the '70s

>> *Singing, in the Rain* in the '80s and *Big* in the early '90s

But by the late 1990s, starting with *Footloose*, Broadway audiences saw the number of musicals based on a film increase enormously. Now, there's *at least* one musical based on a film *every* season. Some of the more recent ones have been *Legally Blonde, Mean Girls, Almost Famous, Some Like It Hot,* and *Beetlejuice.* Chapter 2 discusses other examples where movies have inspired musicals.

What's interesting is that many producers think that a musical based on a hit film will automatically translate into a long-running musical. That has decidedly *not* been the case, and yet the faux reasoning persists. In my research, I've noticed that musicals based on smaller films have been the musicals that have become box office successes. Examples include *The Producers, Hairspray, Once, The Full Monty, The Band's Visit, Kinky Boots,* and *Waitress.* All were based on lesser-known films and all became Broadway hits!

Mythology and fairy tales

Turning a film into a musical means paying for the rights to the film. Basing your musical on something like the Bible or Shakespeare is much more economical. Add to that list of free source material myths and fairy tales. The most successful musical to be based on mythology is *Hadestown,* which won the 2019 Tony Award for Best Musical.

The most successful musical based on a fairy tale is actually based on fairy tales, plural. Stephen Sondheim and James Lapine took a multitude of famous fairy tale characters, including specific ones like Cinderella, Rapunzel, and Jack from Jack and the Beanstalk, and combined them with famous tropes like the handsome princes and the evil witch and wrote an entire story including them all called *Into The Woods.*

The story of *Cinderella* herself was turned into a musical by Rodgers and Hammerstein and is titled, you guessed it, *Cinderella.* There's also a modernized version of Cinderella in Act Three of *The Apple Tree* called "Passionella," where, instead of helping her go to the ball, the fairy godmother makes her a movie star. And the classic fairy tale of "The Princess and the Pea" was turned into *Once upon a Mattress*, which not only was written by Broadway family royalty (Mary Rodgers, daughter of Richard Rodgers), but it also made Carol Burnett a star!

History and biographies

There's an expression that truth is stranger than fiction. I don't know if truth is *stranger*, but anyone who's a fan of musicals based on history or biographies can say that truth is as least as *interesting* as fiction.

Here are a few musicals that have been based on historical events:

>> *1776:* The struggle that finally led to the signing of the Declaration of Independence

>> *Parade:* The hanging of Leo Frank by a mob

>> *Come from Away:* What happened when 38 planes had to land in a small Canadian town on 9/11

>> *The Scottsboro Boys:* The horrific crime of sending a group of young black men to jail for a crime they didn't commit

In terms of musicals based on events that really happened, there have definitely been more biographical musicals than historical ones. You're probably familiar with these:

>> *Annie, Get Your Gun* (the story of Annie Oakley)

>> *The Sound of Music* (the story of Maria Von Trapp and the Trapp family singers)

>> *Call Me Madam* (based on the American ambassador to Luxembourg)

>> *Féla* (about the life of musician and activist Fela Kuti)

>> *Grey Gardens* (the story of Little and Big Edie Bouvier)

>> *Evita* (the life and death of Eva Perón)

>> *Gypsy* (how Gypsy Rose Lee became Gypsy Rose Lee)

A few lesser-known biographical musicals include the following (with more in the works):

>> *Scandalous* (about Aimee Semple McPherson)

>> *Gold* (focusing on the Mizner brothers)

>> *Diana* (the story of Princess Diana)

And, of course, you can't forget the mother lode: *The* most universally lauded show of today, *Hamilton*, which is a combo historical *and* biographical musical. Best of both worlds!

Books

Many books have been turned into Broadway musicals like *South Pacific, Fiddler on the Roof,* and *The King and I*. There's also:

>> *The Pajama Game* (based on the book *Seven and a Half Cents* by Richard Bissell)

>> *Cabaret* (based on the play *I Am a Camera,* but the play is based on the book *The Berlin Stories* by Christopher Isherwood)

>> British mega-hits *Les Misérables* (by Victor Hugo) and *The Phantom of the Opera* (by Gaston Leroux) are *both* based on books.

Some musicals are based on books that people mistakenly think were based on films. For instance:

>> *The Color Purple* was a fantastic film, but it was a book first by Alice Walker.

>> *Auntie Mame* was a Hollywood hit with Rosalind Russell and then a musical (*Mame*) with Angela Lansbury, but it was first a book by Patrick Dennis.

>> *Bridges of Madison County* was a bestselling page turner (by Robert James Waller) *before* the film version with Meryl Streep and Clint Eastwood. The musical was the third version of that story.

>> Even though *Wicked* is the backstory of *The Wizard of Oz,* the musical is based on the book *Wicked: The Life and Times of the Wicked Witch of the West* by Gregory Maguire.

>> As of this writing, Ingrid Michaelson has turned the bestselling *The Notebook* by Nicholas Sparks into a musical, which played Chicago in 2022.

>> *The Devil Wears Prada* by Lauren Weisberger is hitting Broadway (yes, it was a book first).

So as long as books keep selling, they'll keep being turned into musicals!

Jukeboxes

Ain't Misbehavin' featured the music of the great Fats Waller. *Crazy For You* interpolated Gershwin songs into its plot. 1980's *42nd Street* used songs by Harry Warren and Al Dubin that were written 50 years earlier. All of these musicals had the bones of a jukebox musical, but that term hadn't been invented yet.

REMEMBER

A *jukebox musical* contains songs that have already been written. The term didn't come into vogue until the early 2000s when Broadway began to see the rise of the jukebox musical. There are three types of jukebox musicals so far:

>> **A revue of an artist's songs:** Like *Movin' Out* (the music of Billy Joel) or *Come Fly Away* (the songs of Frank Sinatra).

>> **An original story made up around a music group's or time period's songs:** The songs are interpolated into the script to advance the plot like *Mamma Mia!* (the songs of ABBA) or *& Juliet* (the songs of Max Martin).

>> **The story of an artist's (or group's) rise to fame (and sometimes fall):** Only the songs of that artist are used, such as *The Cher Show* (Cher), *Beautiful: The Carole King Musical* (Carole King and friends), and *Ain't Too Proud* (the story of The Temptations).

The interesting part is that jukebox musicals almost didn't make it! Around the time of *Mamma Mia!*, a few shows didn't do well:

>> *The Look of Love* (the music of Burt Bachrach)

>> *Good Vibrations* (the songs of the Beach Boys)

>> *All Shook Up* (the songs of Elvis Presley; P.S. this musical is *fantastic!*)

Then, around 2005, the creators of a jukebox musical were trying to get funding, and I heard that it was hard for this one particular show to find investors and producers because the prevailing thought was that nobody was interested in jukebox musicals anymore based on the fact that these three shows didn't do well. Therefore, getting this new jukebox musical produced was nearly impossible. Finally the producing team called The Dodgers decided to take a chance on the show, and, boy, did it pay off. The jukebox musical nobody wanted won the Tony Award for Best Musical! What was the show? It's the story of The Four Seasons, and it's called *Jersey Boys* (see Chapter 2 for more details)!

Illustrations (cartoons and animation)

Characters that are drawn have been the inspiration for some extremely success-ful musicals. The undisputed king producer of this type of musical is, of course, Disney, which has had great success with *Beauty and the Beast* and *Aladdin* and *enormous* success with *The Lion King*. (Chapter 2 examines how Disney films have inspired musicals.) But Disney characters aren't the only drawn characters to have taken bows on Broadway.

The 1950s saw the very successful *Li'l Abner*, based on the newspaper comic strip. The next musical based on a comic strip wasn't as successful; the mid-1960s brought audiences *It's a Bird, It's a Plane, It's Superman* . . . which didn't do fabu-lously, but introduced Linda Lavin singing the fantastic "You've Got Possibilities." Check out www.youtube.com/watch?v=pR3Hb-FiGqE.

Then there was the Off-Broadway musical based on a comic strip that ran for years and has since played all over the world, including Broadway: *You're a Good Man, Charlie Brown*.

SETH SPEAKS

In the late '90s, Kristin Chenoweth was guest starring in my weekly comedy show at Rose's Turn in the Village. We knew each other because I was the sub piano player/conductor on *A New Brain*, which she was in. After my comedy show, I asked her what was happening career-wise, and she told me she was offered a role in the upcoming revival of *Annie, Get Your Gun* starring Bernadette Peters. I was so excited! She also told me about another role she was offered that would conflict, but I didn't think that show would do very well. I told her to take *Annie, Get Your Gun* because it was a sure thing. I mean: a huge show, a huge star, right!? Well, she did *not* take make my advice and accepted the other show. In one sense, I was right: That show she decided to do didn't last very long at all. However, Andrew Lippa wrote her special material and that show wound up being the musical that made her a star *and* got her a Tony Award. Yes, I advised her against taking Sally Brown in *You're a Good Man, Charlie Brown*, and I'm thankful she completely ignored me! Here's her Tony Award performance that would nay have happened had she listened to me: www.youtube.com/watch?v=2ix8TfqtNis.

The biggest hit musical based on a drawn character (before *The Lion King* became the behemoth is) opened on Broadway in 1977. It was the backstory about how an orphaned little girl came to live with the richest man in the world. *Annie* was based on the comic strip *Little Orphan Annie* and became a worldwide sensation with two Broadway revivals and numerous films.

Here are some other musicals based on the world of drawn characters:

>> *SpongeBob SquarePants*

>> *Spider-Man: Turn off the Dark*

>> *Anastasia*

>> *Fun Home,* the only musical so far to be based on a graphic novel, and it snagged the Tony Award for Best Musical

I'm still waiting for my two favorite animated series to be on Broadway: *Bugs Bunny* and *The Simpsons.* Someone start writing both of them ASAP!

Moving from the Page to the Stage — The Birthing of a Show

So, your show is written! Or a lot of it is written. Or the first act is written. At a certain point, you have to move past words written on a page (or computer screen) and the notes and lyrics written on manuscript paper (or on a fancy music writing program like Finale or Sebelius) and hear them out loud so they can eventually get to a theatre. The following sections discuss how ideas and words become a musical on stage.

Readings — "I See Possibilities"

Usually, the next step is a *reading*. That's when the composer/lyricist/book writer (or producer if one is already attached) get together with a bunch of actors and a music director to read the show out loud, hence the term "reading."

REMEMBER

Readings don't have any specific rules. They help people involved with the show gain a sense of what the show is, what works, and what doesn't. Sometimes they happen just for the creative team and their friends or sometimes they occur just to entice possible producers/investors.

In Sondheim's book *Finishing the Hat* (Penguin/Random House) he talks about presenting the show *A Funny Thing Happened on the Way to the Forum* to Jerome Robbins who was being asked to direct/choreograph it. It was just the script and the songs — no staging, costumes, scenery, or anything else. During the Golden Age of Broadway, musicals were written, rehearsed for around six weeks, and then toured a few cities referred to as *out-of-town tryouts* before opening on Broadway (see Chapter 4). These out-of-town tryouts were used to make changes to the script and score. Sondheim writes that hearing the show read out loud, unadorned by scenery or costumes or choreography, laid out what was good — and what was bad — with the script and music.

That production changed the way musicals were developed because, by doing this reading, the creatives were able to make changes *before* rehearsals even began, which saved them all that time out of town. Rehearsals began with an improved script! This was the first reading I've heard of, and nowadays almost every musical begins this way.

Readings happen a few different ways, including the following:

» **Table read:** A *table read* is what it sounds like. Actors sit around a table and read a script out loud. It's usually done *only* for the writers (and possibly the director and producer) to hear the show for the first time read by people other than the writers. Often the composer or composing team performs the songs. No one else is in the room.

» **29-hour reading:** The most common reading is a *29-hour reading* (a union term that means the actors can rehearse for 29 hours spread out over days). The cast of a reading usually sits at music stands and a director gives general direction (about acting as well as suggestions for script changes to the creators) and a music director play the music on a piano, so the actors can learn the songs and sing them.

» **Staged reading:** The next step is to get it on its feet in something called a *staged reading*. The three different levels of staged readings are usually as follows:

- Sometimes the actors use scripts the entire time and, even though they're moving around, they have minimal staging.

- Sometimes they have scripts for the scenes but put them down for the musical numbers so it's more like a performance.

- Sometimes they have scripts for much of the script and the songs, but the songs have some minimal choreography with a few fully choreographed moments . . . like a tap break in one song in Act One and a partnering romantic dance in Act Two.

Workshops — Much more than readings

Like a reading, there's nothing specific about what a *workshop* exactly has to be, but it usually has a higher staged/production value level than a staged reading. And sometimes a workshop is at a *really* high level, production-wise — workshops often have a sound system, a band, costume pieces, and fully choreographed numbers.

REMEMBER

Workshops are done for the same reason as readings, but with the emphasis more on attracting investors. What was once called a *backer's audition* is now usually called a workshop. Actors in a workshop don't make very much money, but they divide a percentage of the profits of the Broadway production and future productions (if it makes a profit, that is!). And they're guaranteed their roles on Broadway or the producers pay them four weeks' salary.

Labs — A new (controversial) version of workshops

As things evolve in terms of show development, something very similar to a workshop is now an option for producers. This is called a *lab,* and it's a *very* new addition to the development of the show. Labs are basically the exact same thing as a workshop but with an important difference: The cast gets a higher weekly salary than what they're paid for a workshop.

That might sound like a good thing, but the trade-off for that higher salary is that the actors don't get points (which leads to money after the show is profitable) in future productions and no guarantee they have their roles if the show moves to Broadway. Actors' Equity started a hashtag #NotALabRat because they wanted a more equitable share of show profits. If you want more info, go to the Actors' Equity website (www.actorsequity.org/) STAT!

The post-reading, pre-Broadway world

The show has been written and is in a shape that the lead producer(s) think(s) is ready for Broadway. As the show moves toward its big destination, various things must happen. There's no chronological order of these events, they just have to happen before Broadway rehearsals begin.

Hiring the creative team

One of the most important next steps is the producer(s) has to hire the creative team. Readings and workshops often have a director, choreographer, music director, and so on, but when the show is ready for Broadway, a producer might want a director with a bigger name to attract bigger stars. Or the show may require a choreographer who has more experience in the show's particular kind of dance, or the composer always works with one particular music director when their shows come to Broadway. That means that sometimes members of creative teams are let go right before the show hits Broadway.

The time between workshops and Broadway is also when the costume, sound, set, and lighting designers, stage managers, orchestrators, vocal arrangers, and other behind-the-scenes staff are chosen. Basically, the entire creative and production team has to be hired in the period before Broadway rehearsals begin. But wait? How can you hire people if you don't know what you're going to pay them? Enter the next very important person.

Hiring the general manager

Before a producer can hire anyone for a Broadway production, they must engage a general manager. General manager is a fairly generic title. For Broadway shows, the *general manager (GM)* really should be called the *financial manager.*

The GM creates the budget and the producer approves it. That budget is then shared with investors in the hopes that they see the possibility of the show making money. And that investment money (hopefully) gets raised.

REMEMBER

The GM has to decide where all the money goes. One of the most important aspects is negotiating everyone's salary. How does a GM decide what to pay, you ask? The unions set certain minimums for mostly every person on a show, but often people with experience are paid above or *way* above the minimum — especially stars! And there are star designers as well.

Even if the GM knows how much a particular set and costume designer's salary is, you may wonder how they figure out how much money should go toward the actual sets. Costumes. Wigs. Marketing and publicity. The opening night party . . . everything! Well, if it's a *big, splashy* musical, why not spend millions for every single aspect? Because the money going out has to ideally be made back to pay off the initial investment and then the show can start paying investors a profit.

REMEMBER

The budget has something called a *recoupment schedule,* which shows how long it will take investors to get their money back, and it's based on ticket sales. For example, if a show sells at 100 percent capacity, it will take X number of weeks to recoup the initial investment. If it sells at 90 percent, it will take XX number of weeks, 80 percent at XXX number of weeks, and so on.

The GM (and producer) has to have a vast knowledge of Broadway, including the answers to these types of questions:

>> How will tickets sell during previews? How do certain types of shows normally sell in previews? A revival compared to a new show? A show with a star compared to a show with an unknown cast?

>> What if the reviews wind up being bad? Do they estimate the show can continue to run based on positive word of mouth?

>> Is it the kind of show that will last no matter what the reviews are for as long as the mega-star is in it?

>> Can the show last after the mega-star's departure with a regular Broadway star taking over? Or will another mega-star have to be willing to replace in order to keep the show running?

>> Should the tickets be discounted to spark word-of-mouth? For how long?

>> How will the show sell in the summer? How about the winter?

>> What kind of show schedule should it have? A four-show weekend because it's for out-of-towners who visit New York City on weekends? Or a schedule with extra matinées to get more kids to come?

The GM must consider all of these and more when creating the budget.

Finding a Theatre

Locating an available theatre is a tricky and bizarre balancing act.

There have been *many* shows on Broadway over the years, but there are only 41 Broadway theatres (as of 2022), so there are only 41 Broadway shows at any one time. *Note:* A theatre is considered a Broadway theatre if it has more than 499 seats.

Does this mean 41 new shows debut on Broadway every year? No. Some shows plant it on Broadway for four, five, six years or more, making their theatres unavailable for other shows. And some shows have made theatres unavailable for decades. Nothing has been in the Gershwin since *Wicked* took it over in 2003, the same year *Chicago* moved to the Ambassador. *The Lion King* opened at the New Amsterdam Theatre in 1997 and then moved to the Minskoff in 2006, and it doesn't look like it's leaving.

When a producer wants to bring a new show to Broadway, they can count out opening at the Ambassador, Minskoff, or Gershwin, as well as any theatres where the current shows are probably going to run for a few more years. The producer then looks at all the other theatres on Broadway and narrows down the theatres in a variety of ways. Here are just two key considerations:

>> Does the upcoming show need an intimate space? That means perhaps the Helen Hayes or Circle in the Square is the right theatre.

>> Does this show need a big stage? And will it hopefully sell lots of tickets each night? In that case, a large theatre like the St. James or the Imperial is right.

I discuss some of the factors that come into play and the decisions that have to be made to find a Broadway theatre in the following sections.

Narrowing down theatre options

After the producer has a few theatres in mind, they then have to answer these questions and employ other methods to further narrow down where they can open:

1. Is there a theatre owner who's a fan of this show and wants it in one of their theatres?

2. If so, does this theatre owner have a theatre that's appropriate in size?

3. If so, is that theatre available?

4. If not, and here's the hard part, is the show running in that theatre looking like it's going to close soon-ish?

   The producer will probably look at weekly ticket sales (available online). If those numbers aren't looking great, they'll probably talk with the theatre owners and ask how long the show will last. Why the theatre owners? Well, even though a producer gives the word to the cast and crew that a show is closing, they aren't the only ones making the decision.

If the show isn't profitable, a producer can still decide to keep it running if the budget has the money or they have the hope that ticket sales will increase. Perhaps they want to keep it running so when it closes, they can say it stayed on Broadway for X number of years in order to give it some cachet to be produced around the world more often. A theatre owner can tell a show it has to close. *However*, a producer can't close a show for completely arbitrary reasons.

Usually, the contract has a clause between the producer and the theater owner that states if a show isn't selling a certain percentage of tickets, a theatre owner can tell a show to close. Why? Consider this example: A show has mediocre ticket sales, but the show's producers can keep it running for the next three months. What if the producers of a new Broadway show approach the theatre owner and say they want to open their show in two months? And the theatre owner predicts this new show will run for at least a year (based on facts like a star name attached or a workshop that had great word-of-mouth)?

The theatre owner would want the new show because that show will pay rent for the theatre for at least a year. If the theatre owner kept the current show as its tenant, they'd have rent paid to them for three months but then the theatre could sit empty for a long time — with no one paying rent — until another show came knocking.

Picking the right time to open

Here's another producer problem: They find a theatre that's perfect, but it's availability starts in July. Lots of producers don't want to open shows in July. Spring is an ideal opening time because the show can build momentum and then get the publicity that comes with awards season. All this keeps tickets selling. If they open in July, they have to have the money to run for almost a year without any of the big national attention that awards season brings (talk show appearances for nominees, newspaper and magazine articles about award predictions, the Tony Awards TV broadcast, and so on).

January and February are notoriously difficult months to sell tickets. The show might not make it through the winter, which means it would be closed before the next Tony Awards — a big national advertisement for Broadway. So don't open in July, many think. But, if the producer doesn't take up the theatre's offer to open in July, the theatre may not be available the following spring, so the show won't be able to open this year at all. There are so many balls to juggle!

REMEMBER

Another important consideration when to open is the availability of a star to do the show. What happens if the star is only available from this September for a year? Only one theatre is available starting in September, but it's wrong for the show. It's way too big, and this show is an intimate, two-person musical. Does a producer take a chance that the theatre space doesn't matter that much? Or do they postpone and hope the star will somehow be available at a later date? Welcome to the headache of finding a theatre!

Recognizing What Happens Way before Opening Night

As I discuss in the section, "Moving from the Page to the Stage — The Birthing of a Show," earlier in this chapter, most musicals have readings and workshops before they open on Broadway. But then what?

These sections walk you through what occurs with the production side of the show, starting with auditions, offers, rehearsals, run-throughs, and previews . . . and finally opening.

Auditions — Finalizing the cast

When a show is slated for Broadway, some roles have already been cast, usually based on the final workshop, meaning the producer and creative team have seen certain actors play the roles and liked their performances enough to bring them to Broadway. But other roles and ensemble parts still need to be cast, which means the creative team needs to hold more auditions.

Sometimes, even though someone did a good job at all the readings and workshops, the creative team might think, "Well, let's just see who else is out there." They'll hold auditions, and maybe they'll see someone who is more suited to the role. Or sometimes someone new can seem like an exciting choice just because they're fresh and new. It's kind of like when you're married and you meet someone cute and nice and, even though you don't really know this new person, a part of you thinks "Should I leave my husband for this person? *They* seem amazing!" And don't pretend you don't know what I mean!

SETH SPEAKS

My point is, doing the final workshop doesn't guarantee anything. Yes, an actor has to be offered the part on Broadway — *or* they have to be paid four weeks' salary. The "or" happens a lot! Kerry Butler laughs all the time about the year she starred in the workshops of *The Wedding Singer*, *The Little Mermaid*, and *Legally Blonde*. She said she was so anxious thinking about having to decide which show she should do on Broadway if they all opened at the same time. Turns out, she didn't have to worry because she wasn't offered *any of them!* But then, that same season, she was offered the role of Kira in *Xanadu*, which led to her first Tony Award nomination. So *phew!*

Sometimes the reverse is true: Anika Larsen had done lots of readings of *Beautiful: The Carole King Musical*, but she wasn't offered the final workshop. After the workshop, they brought her in to audition for the Broadway production, but she felt it was just a courtesy call, as a "thank you" for doing the early presentations. (Ugh. The business is so hard.) She decided she had *had* it with theatre. She was going to move away from acting. She started researching new careers and in the middle of Google searching, her agent called. "You got the part!" he told her. Well, in her head, she had so moved on that she replied, "*What* part?" She didn't know what he was talking about! End of story: She originated the role of Cynthia Weil in the Broadway production of *Beautiful* and got her first Tony Award nomination!

And sometimes, after the final workshop, an actor is indeed offered the Broadway production, but the timing is wrong. Kristin Chenoweth played the Madeline Kahn part in the workshop of *Young Frankenstein*, but when they offered her the role on Broadway, she had to turn it down because she was contracted to do the TV show *Pushing Daisies*. (It all worked out. The role went to Megan Mullally who got to come back to Broadway after winning two Emmys for *Will & Grace*, and Kristin won an Emmy for *Pushing Daisies*.)

A show usually has a few days of ensemble auditions and *Equity Principal Auditions* (EPAs), where union members audition, and actors agent appointments (procured by the casting director). These auditions usually have a dance audition as well. (Chapter 13 discusses the various types of auditions from an actor's standpoint.)

Offers — Negotiating . . . and signing on the dotted line

After the auditions, dance calls, callbacks, and the chemistry reads are all done, offers are made. This doesn't, however, mean all offers are *accepted*. What if the show is going out of town for months? Some actors don't want to leave their families and decide to pass on the offer. What if the contract won't allow performances off from the Broadway run if someone is offered a TV show? Sometimes actors want to know they aren't locked into something that could hurt their more lucrative TV/film career so they decide against accepting the gig. What if a performer is offered *two* different shows at the same time? All of these issues can come up after offers are made. And either compromises are made on one or both sides *or* an actor passes on the show and offers then go to second choices.

Eventually, offers are accepted, contracts are negotiated and signed, and rehearsals begin within a few weeks. Of course, exceptions do happen: When *Merrily We Roll Along* had its final callback, Hal Prince announced to the very young cast (all in their teens and early 20s) that they were all cast. Yay! Everyone was *freaking out* with happiness. Then he announced he had to direct a new opera, so rehearsals wouldn't begin for the next *nine months*!

SETH SPEAKS

In one sense, that was a letdown, but original cast member Liz Callaway told me it was amazing for her career. She was suddenly seen for tons of roles because her agent was able to say, "She's going to be in the new Sondheim/Prince musical." She wound up working up a storm during those nine months, including filming the TV movie *Senior Trip* that also featured Mickey Rooney as well as fellow *Merrily We Roll Along* cast member Jason Alexander. And after those halcyon days, she began what every Broadway musical has. . . (see the next section).

Rehearsing for six to eight weeks

The road to opening night really starts moving when rehearsals begin. That first day is often called "the first day of school" in theatre parlance because that's what it feels like. You're meeting a whole bunch of people whom you're going to be with for a while. And like in high school, you might be with some of these people for years!

The first day of rehearsal is often the day when *everyone* shows up: not just the cast, but everyone from the creative, design, and producing teams, plus the people who do publicity and marketing. Rehearsals happen in a studio space at another location, not in the theatre where the show will be performed. Everyone mills around introducing themselves and greeting old friends all while noshing on breakfast treats. Then they all quiet down, and the director often shows a small model of the set and describes how it works. Costume and wig designs are shown as well.

The actors then often do a read-through of the script. Refer to the section, "Readings — 'I See Possibilities,'" earlier in this chapter. Everyone (hopefully) applauds and laughs in all the right places and gets excited for what's coming and then the work begins! Chapter 13 gives more specifics about rehearsals from an actor's perspective.

Tech rehearsal — Working in the actual theatre

At this point, the show is ready to start *tech rehearsal*, which is focused on figuring out how the show works on the actual set — in the theatre, not in the rehearsal space. These rehearsals last one to two weeks. Adjustments to the staging and choreography are constantly made throughout these rehearsals. What seemed like an exciting idea . . . having a soloist climb the stairs for their big high note . . . now makes the soloist too distant from the audience, so the staging is changed. During this period all the props are added and there's often a *costume parade*, where actors model their looks onstage, and the director approves or adjusts the costumes.

The sitzprobe

This is the part of rehearsal most people love the most: the *sitzprobe. Sitzprobe* is a German word that means "seated rehearsal" because the performers aren't doing any of their *blocking* (the movements that go with spoken dialogue or sung lyrics). They're simply singing the score all the way through with the orchestra, so both groups can get used to each other (all while being led by the conductor), and the creative team can hear what it's going to sound like. And, yes, they'll make changes if need be — more percussion is needed during the dance breaks so those accents really pop, or the trumpet orchestration is drowning out the singer at the very end of the song. No matter what, musical casts *love* the sitzprobe. It's so exciting to go from singing with just a piano or a piano and drums to suddenly hearing the orchestrations for each song.

The 10 out of 12s

The term *10 out of 12s* stands for the union rule that if actors are called in for 12 hours of rehearsal, they may work for only 10 of those hours. This type of rehearsal happens at the end of the tech rehearsal period, and it's when all the final meticulous tech work — sound, lighting, and so on — happens. An actor might make their first entrance and, before they say their line, stand onstage for 10, 15, 20 minutes while the lighting is adjusted. It takes incredible patience and, suffice it to say, I'm always the one being yelled at for talking/fidgeting when I've been explicitly told to stand and not move. #AlmostFired. These rehearsals are exhausting for *everyone* and there is a current movement to have them modified or completely eliminated!

The run-through — Including everything

After all the pieces have been perfected as well as they can be, a show usually conducts a full run-through with sets, lights, and orchestra but no costumes or wigs and makeup. After that, they then do a few run-throughs with every aspect of the show — lights, sound, costumes, props, wigs, makeup, quick changes — *everything!*

Sometimes tech rehearsals get behind schedule, leaving no time for a full final run-through. I've been there. It's the end of the rehearsal process and instead of doing a run-through to make sure everyone knows what they're doing and everything is working, there just isn't time for it. Tickets have been sold and, instead of a full run-through to fix any glitches, the show must face its first preview!

Previews — Having a live audience

The theatre is unique in that a show can be running on Broadway . . . stars, costumes, orchestra, set, full-priced tickets, and so on . . . yet not be open. How is that possible? Movies don't run in cinemas unless they're open, right? This theatrical contrivance occurs because the final rehearsal process takes place during the *preview period.* A show *has* to have a live, paying audience in order for the creative team to really understand what needs to be changed. What's funny to fellow performers in the rehearsal room (or to friends/family invited to a run-through) can lay an egg in front of a paying crowd. If that happens, the director and creative team must figure out what to change.

This process is much more difficult when a show starts previews directly on Broadway without an out-of-town pre-Broadway tour. Previews only last a few weeks, and the show has to be perfected in that time. The best way to get a show into shape is to have it tour a few cities before Broadway. This way, the show is in front of paying audiences for months, giving more time to make changes before the Broadway preview process begins.

Out-of-town tryouts, as they're called, were once how musicals always came to Broadway back in the day. Nowadays a lot of those changes are done in the work-shop phases. Out-of-town tryouts still happen, but usually just in one city. The most common are Chicago, Seattle, D.C., Denver, and Boston.

My favorite out-of-town tryout story is *Hello, Dolly!* It opened in its first out-of-town city and it clanked. Director/choreographer Gower Champion counted how many weeks the show had to play out of town before it got to Broadway and told everyone he was going to make one big change per week. And he did! One of the biggest was at the end of Act One: Dolly is the lead character and it seems obvious to musical theatre fans now that she should have the big Act One finale, but when the show was being written, the big song went to Horace Vandergelder. Thankfully, they realized (from the audience reaction) that the end of Act One wasn't working and soon Carol Channing was singing that showstopper "Before the Parade Passes By."

Actors need to have stamina! When the show is in previews every night, rehearsals happen during the day with changes being made. Often, the changes being made during the day go into the show that night! Nancy Opel told me about learning "It's Hot Up Here," the opening of *Sunday in the Park with George*'s second act. She recalled that the cast rehearsed the song for the first time in the afternoon, and it was then put in the show that night. If you don't know, the song has all these random solos, and Nancy said the performers wrote their words on pieces of paper and taped them to all parts of the set, so they'd know what the heck they were singing! Imagine learning that song in one day: www.youtube.com/watch?v=zQ36LCcSx5o.

Being Ready — Right before Opening

When you think of a Broadway musical, the most exciting thing is probably the opening night. You need to know a few things that must happen *before* the big opening. I'm talking about freezing the show and preparing for critics.

Freezing a show

When the preview period is nearing its end, the show is *frozen*, meaning there can't be *any* more changes from the director/creative team. During previews, changes are made every day, which is exhausting, and most people involved with a show look forward to the moment when all the changes have been made. A famous Ethel Merman story sums it up with sass: Apparently, she was doing a musical where they kept making changes. Finally, she had *had* it. When someone told her something new was being put into the show, she retorted, "Call me Miss Birdseye, this show is *frozen!*"

You may ask, why does a show get frozen? That's so the cast can get comfortable with what's in/what's out and get ready for the next major part of a Broadway show opening: critics nights, which I discuss in the next section.

Preparing for critics

For the first few decades of Broadway, opening night was *the* night when all the critics came. The show would begin at an earlier time than usual, generally 6:30 p.m. to give the critics time to write their reviews and submit them that night so they'd be in the next day's newspaper. That all changed in the 1980s. Now, after a show is frozen, the actors perform it a few times to paying audiences, but no critics. Then critics are invited to four to six performances, ending the night before opening. Most opening nights are on Thursday because producers think theatre lovers read the Arts sections on Friday; therefore, a Friday review will have the most eyes looking at it. Of course, that was more true when online news didn't exist, but theatre traditions don't go away quickly. Critic invites start around a week before opening and end on the performance before opening night.

The good part about critics coming over a period of time is: The reviews still come out on the day after opening, but the critics don't have the frantic rush to get the review written in a few hours. Furthermore, not every single review is riding on one performance. Say you crack on your high note. Phew! No need to think you ruined the show's reviews for everyone. Only three reviewers were there that night instead of every reviewer in the entire city!

TIP

If you want to be part of Broadway history, go see a show at one of the final performances before opening night. You'll be at one of the performances that critics review, and your applause and laughs will be part of what that critic experiences!

Finally, opening night

By having critics come *before* the official opening night means that the opening performance can be a true celebration. Instead of a night filled with anxiety, it's a night to perform the show for a theatre of your nearest and dearest . . . plus A-list stars who are invited, so their photos can get online and into papers to help publicize the show.

After the show, everyone involved (plus their family and friends) attend the opening night party to dance, eat up a storm, laugh, take photos, reminisce about the entire process, get praise, and generally just feel a wonderful sense of relief and joy.

BETTY BUCKLEY WAS A SCAREDY-CAT!

The trend of critics' nights started in the 1980s, and not everyone knew things had changed. Betty Buckley told me that when she was doing *Cats*, she was nervous about opening night because she hadn't done an opening night on Broadway since 1969 (when she played Martha Jefferson in *1776*). Now it was 1982, and she was returning to Broadway after spending years in L.A. filming the TV show *Eight Is Enough*. She had a whole plan for the day the critics came that included things like taking a luxurious shower, having a voice lesson, getting a massage, and really employing techniques to relax. Well, she was backstage the night before opening night right before her entrance to sing "Memory," and she told someone how she was going to prepare for all the critics coming on opening night. The other person told her that the following night was indeed opening night, but *no* critics come on opening night anymore.

As a matter of fact, they told her that the *New York Times* critic was there that very night! WHAT!?! Betty was decidedly *not* prepared! She hadn't done any aspect of her relaxation routine. While she was freaking out, she was suddenly approached by a sound person who told her the mic she was wearing completely stopped working! Argh! She took off her cat bodysuit and had a whole new mic attached. She was getting very close to going out to sing her big *11 o'clock number* (the bring-down-the-house song that happens near the end of Act Two) when the sound person ran up one more time; turns out, *this* mic wasn't working either! *What!?* Too late to get a new one! What to do? Someone in the wings who knew her told her to get as far downstage as possible near the audience and sing like she sang when she was a little girl.

She knew what that meant. Yes, she didn't have a mic, but she was a belter from way back. Her belting must have been loud because the *Times* review stated that her delivery "rattled the rafters." As for the busted mics, Betty feels that her body chemistry got so thrown by her nerves that it shorted out her mics! Regardless, she wound up winning the Tony Award! And well deserved. Her Tony night performance is immortalized at www.youtube.com/watch?v=5ml11RdIfqw.

Until the moment when the reviews come out. Those reviews can often decide the fate of the show and therefore the income of everyone associated with the show. Sometimes the reviews start coming out and the party gets even more joyous . . . and sometimes a pall sets over everyone and the party breaks up.

But up until that moment when those reviews are printed . . . it's time to celebrate.

Why?

Another Broadway musical has opened!

Chapter **12**

"Hi-Ho, the Glamorous Life" (of a Broadway Performer)

Wen you're trying to have a career in the theatre, so much of it is spent at taking lessons — voice technique lessons, voice coaching, dance classes, acting classes — auditioning, and often working a day job. The reality is, it's very difficult to be cast in a Broadway show, and it's an even bigger miracle if your show has a long run. But say the miracle happens; you have a great audition, a great callback, and you get the part! The show opens to rave reviews and you're in a hit. What's your day-to-day life as a working performer on Broadway? Well, this chapter gives you a clearer idea!

Rehearsal Makes Perfect

I touch on rehearsals in Chapter 11, where I describe what happens leading up to a show's big opening — not only the rehearsals for the Broadway production, but the initial workshops and labs, tech rehearsals, previews, and more. Here I give you the full scoop on what rehearsal is like for the performers, including the understudies and replacements.

Diving deeper into the nitty-gritty of rehearsals

Rehearsals for a Broadway show usually are scheduled for around six weeks. The stage manager and the creative team schedule the first week of rehearsal, which takes place in a rehearsal space, not at the theatre where the show will eventually run but a separate space just for rehearsing. This space usually has two to three rooms so everyone can be rehearsing something. One room is for staging scenes, another for teaching music, and another for choreography.

Rehearsals generally take place six days a week (Mondays off) from 10 a.m. to 6 p.m. with a lunch hour and a union-required five-minute break every 55 minutes or a ten-minute break after 80 minutes. Throughout these earlier days of a show, performers are taken out of rehearsal for short periods of time to do costume fittings and adjustments.

Usually, after around eight days, the director has a run-through of Act One . . . and then after another eight days or so, a run-through of Act Two. Actors usually hold scripts through these run-throughs; they aren't required to be *off book* (their part fully memorized) until the third week of rehearsals. P.S. Even though the script and score are usually completed by the first day of rehearsal, changes are being made every day.

After about 16 days, the director has an initial run-through of the whole show. Unlike the later run-throughs that occur, this early one comes with lower expectations and is often referred to as a *stumble-through*. After the stumble-through, the show undergoes more changes, and finally a more polished run-through happens in the rehearsal space — usually called the *designer run* — for the lighting and sound teams to give them a sense of the staging of the show so they can start fully designing the lighting and sound. Finally, after about four weeks, the show leaves the rehearsal space for tech rehearsals (see Chapter 11); the show can move to the Broadway theatre or a theatre outside of New York where the show will begin.

Brushing up — "Put 'Em Back The Way They Was"

The show has finally opened, and it's going well. According to the performers, that is. According to the music director, the choreographer, and the director, the show is *horrendous!* That's an exaggeration, but it's true that as a show is running, cast members forget certain things and bad habits creep in; Musical cut-offs or entrances aren't crisp, comedy is exaggerated, harmonies are modified, extra lines are added that aren't in the script, and so on.

Usually, the director or stage manager gives notes throughout a run, but some-times it's just easier to get the whole cast together and do a *brush-up rehearsal.* For example, remind people that the choreography in a certain section has to be extra-precise, or the cutoff for the finale has to be on the *and* of three, or everyone onstage has to keep their lines moving extra-fast in the madcap comedy scene.

Brush-up rehearsals don't happen all the time, usually every few months, but they reinvigorate the show. They're also responsible for the origin story of Mandy Gonzales's nickname: Mandy played Nina in the original cast of *In the Heights* and, as can be heard on the album, has an incredible voice. And it's a voice that sounds like she can sing *anything.* Perfectly. Well, one day there was an *In the Heights* music brush-up rehearsal. Someone noticed that Mandy wasn't there. She might have had a conflict or maybe she wasn't called in, but whatever the reason, a cast member who noticed her absence asked, "Where's Mandy?" Karen Olivo (who played Vanessa) immediately responded, "The beast don't need no music brush-up rehearsal." And from then on, Mandy was known as *The Beast!* Here she is telling the origin story with me: www.youtube.com/watch?v=00gvWToON4Q.

"Welcome to Our House on Maple Avenue" — Put-ins

Although being in a long running show is definitely a blessing, not everyone stays from opening night to closing night. Performers leave because they get other jobs, their contracts expire and they feel it's time to move on, they're still loving it but they want to leave before they *have* to leave, and so on. When the original cast learns their roles, they have a long rehearsal period because the show is being created, but when a replacement comes in, it's a different story. Replacements usually rehearse for two weeks maximum and are trained by the stage manager, the dance captain, and the music director or rehearsal pianist.

REMEMBER

The stage manager/dance captain teaches the staging and the dances and plays all the other roles in the scene work or dance sequences. This happens for a while, but the new performer eventually needs a chance to do it on the stage with the other bodies to see what it really feels like to be in the show. Plus, they need a chance to perform everything in full costume and wigs. So, right before the performer's first performance, the cast is called for a *put-in rehearsal*, so named because the performer is being *put into* the show. The entire cast shows up to run the whole show, although it's a very disparate stage picture: The regular cast wears their street clothes, but the new cast member is in *full* costume/wig/makeup. It definitely feels like showing up for a jeans-only lunch, only to find you're wearing an evening gown.

Put-ins are important because the new performer not only needs a chance to run the entire show on stage, but they have to know what it's like doing the show, in terms of "Is it hard to bend over in these pants?", "Can I kick in these heels?", "Where is the pocket in this jacket for my prop?", and so on. Also, being in full costume/wig is especially important if they have quick changes (which I discuss more in Chapter 10).

SETH SPEAKS

One thing the replacement actor usually doesn't get during a put-in rehearsal is the orchestra. Paying every single musician to be there for this rehearsal costs more money than producers want to pay, so usually the put-in rehearsal just features a pianist. I've done a *lot* of these rehearsals in my time on Broadway, and they're always fun because it gives the cast a way to meet their new cast member and vice versa. One of the sweetest stories I know is when Audra McDonald went into her first Broadway show *The Secret Garden*. They rehearsed a group number onstage and right after everyone sang, the late great Rebecca Luker turned around and asked Audra, "And who is this wonderful singer joining our show?" Rebecca was a huge star, and it made the very young Audra feel so welcome and relaxed her for the rest of rehearsal.

HOW A PUT-IN REHEARSAL LEAD TO THE FIRST BELTING BELLE

Andrea McArdle, Broadway's original Annie, was featured in the Leading Ladies concert at Carnegie Hall in the late 1990s. Bernadette Peters was originally booked for one song but had a conflict for the day, so Scott Ellis, the director, asked Andrea if she would fill in. He wanted her to do a combo of "Look for the Silver Lining" into "Tomorrow," but he wanted a large portion sung non-belty. Andrea is known for belting, but she softened her voice, and it came out great! Check it out at www.youtube.com/watch?v=vFc-1-6M_QA.

That one performance led to Disney calling and asking her if she wanted to do *Beauty and the Beast*. Andrea was in her 30s at the time and hilariously assumed they wanted her for Mrs. Potts, the Angela Lansbury role from the movie! Turns out, they wanted her for Belle, and she told them a resounding *yes*. During all the rehearsals, she sang with the sweet sound she used for the Carnegie Hall concert and sounded very Disney ingenue-ish. Finally, she had her put-in rehearsal.

Because she's a star, they splurged to have the entire orchestra there! After she ran the show, she saw Michael Eisner in the audience and called him over. She knew there was still time left for rehearsal because she had finished the show quickly without a hitch, and she asked if she could try something. What, you ask? She wanted to show him how she would sing the score in her signature McArdle Broadway belt, instead of a pretty Disney voice. He gave her the go-ahead to try it once, and she *belted* that shizz. As soon as she stopped, he came over and said, "I don't ever want you to sing it the other way again," and she wound up being the first Belle to belt the whole show! Listen www.youtube.com/watch?v=H9e3t23rPAk.

Focusing on the understudies

Understudies/swings/alternates are a vital part of every Broadway show and sometimes get their own rehearsal. They all do the same type of thing . . . but different. Chapter 9 focuses on them in greater detail; here's just a quick overview of them:

>> **Understudy:** They perform in the show eight times a week and cover a larger role or roles.

>> **Swing:** They don't perform in the show unless they're on. They cover the ensemble roles.

>> **Alternate:** They don't perform in the show unless they're on. They cover one lead or various leads.

As Covid taught, understudies are often the only thing keeping a show open! A show can't go on if key characters are missing, and *understudies* step in at a moment's notice to make sure the show is complete. How do they learn their parts? During initial rehearsal, they're watching and taking notes. That's in case they have to go on during previews, which definitely happens. Official understudy rehearsals usually don't begin until after opening, so understudies going on during previews really proves the superheroes they are!

Why aren't there understudy rehearsals during previews? Well, changes happen almost every day, and a show doesn't have time to rehearse the understudies because the cast is rehearsing the actual show. But after a show opens, the understudies officially learn their roles from the stage manager, music director, and dance captain, and then begin a weekly understudy rehearsal. These rehearsals usually happen on Thursdays, and as soon as all the understudies know their roles, the Thursday rehearsal is a run-through, just so the understudies can stay up to speed. Sometimes actors understudy multiple roles, so they may do a run-through one week in one role and in a different role the following week. If those characters aren't in the same scenes ever, they can play multiple characters during the run-through.

"A LITTLE FALL OF RAIN" . . . A MASSIVE SPAN OF YEARS

SETH SPEAKS

Understudy rehearsals help prepare the understudy to go on. Of course, sometimes the person who the understudy is covering doesn't get sick, so the understudy never gets to perform the role. And according to this story, years can pass and those understudy rehearsals can still pay off!

Jenna Russell is an Olivier Award–winning West End Star and was Tony Award–nominated for her Broadway performance as Dot in *Sunday in the Park with George*. Her first big West End show was *Les Miz* where she was in the ensemble and understudied Eponine. She loved it, but she never went on for Eponine. She eventually left the show and, out of the blue, they called one day and told her that the woman playing Eponine was sick, and the understudy wasn't feeling well. This was *four years* after she had left the show! They knew it was odd, but they wanted to know if Jenna would be willing to go on if the understudy couldn't.

Jenna asked who the understudy was and when she heard, she knew that woman would definitely go on because she never missed a show. So Jenna said yes, of course, she would go on if she had to, but she knew she wouldn't have to. That afternoon, she went out shopping with her mom, and they went to dinner around 6 p.m. She ordered a pint, as they say in Britain, and before the drink or the food came, Jenna thought "Blimey!" I'm assuming that was the word she thought. Then I know for a fact she did indeed think, "I better check in with *Les Miz* just to be responsible." She moseyed over to the restaurant pay phone and called the stage manager . . . just to confirm she wasn't on. He responded, quite calmly, "Oh, hello. Yes . . . you're on." *She was on!* For the role of Eponine. A role she never performed. In a show she did four years earlier. Her next thought was, "Well, I'd better not have that pint."

Jenna got to the theatre and, as it turned out, the show went great, and she had the best time! There probably isn't a specific British Equity rule for someone going on in a role who isn't officially in the show anymore — and hasn't been for four years — and won't be going on ever again. She told me at the end of the night, as she was leaving the theatre, they just handed her an envelope with 200 quid in it, and off she went. #YourMoneyIsontheDresser

Arriving for the Big Show

In Chapter 5 I recommend that audience members get to the show around 30 minutes before the performance begins. You need to have time to use the restroom and find your seats, and you don't want to miss a minute of the show! But when do the performers get to the theatre? How early do they have to be there? Keep reading to find out.

Showing up — Half-hour call

Every actor has to sign in by *half hour* (the time performers have to arrive at the theatre — 30 minutes before showtime). This assures the stage manager that everyone is accounted for and an understudy doesn't have to go on. If someone is sick, they've already notified the stage manager so the understudy/swing/alternate is prepared to go on.

Sometimes, though, an actor doesn't show because a subway breaks down or something else unforeseen and immediately understudy protocol breaks into action. The stage manager decides who's going on (certain roles have multiple understudies) and, if multiple actors are out, the stage manager/dance captain decides how the show will be altered so it can still be performed with fewer people than normal — like a dance being modified to three couples instead of four. Sometimes there's an awkward moment when a stage manager tells an understudy they're going on at half hour and they start getting into the costume when suddenly the regular actor arrives. The stage manager usually decides whether to have the regular actor or understudy go on at that point.

Even though half hour is the time everyone has to be there, certain circumstances like the ones in the following sections require that some performers arrive earlier.

Rehearsing the fisticuffs — Fight call

Certain shows have fights. It may just be a punch that knocks someone out, or a few punches, kicks, and then someone climbs on someone's back. These fights are staged during rehearsal, but if one of the actors is in the wrong position, the fake punch can become *not* fake and land on someone's face. So in order to make sure everyone remembers where everything goes, a *fight call* takes place every performance around ten minutes before half hour so the players can go through the fight. The fight captain (like the dance captain, a member of the ensemble) usually leads the fight walk-through. The fight is first practiced in slow motion and then at regular speed.

SETH SPEAKS

Practicing fights before a performance is a great way to assure no one gets hurt. There isn't, however, a "teeth" call. *What?* Well, I was thinking about getting injured, and I remember talking to Cheyenne Jackson when he understudied Gavin Creel in *Thoroughly Modern Millie*. In one scene he's hiding in a small area with Millie played by Sutton Foster, and they're both quickly turning their heads back and forth. Cheyenne said that he and Sutton were super close to each other and not used to knowing what the proper distance should be for each other. When they turned their heads toward each other, their teeth collided! He said they were *really* close and they "both have big teeth." Broadway is dangerous!

Getting all dolled up — wig/makeup call

If a show requires a lot of wigs, some actors are scheduled earlier, sometimes as long as 90 minutes before curtain because 30 minutes isn't enough time to get everyone into a wig. If a character has heavy-duty makeup, they'll also have to arrive earlier than just 30 minutes, although *usually* the actor applies the makeup.

Whoever is playing Elphaba in *Wicked* needs at least 30 minutes to get all the green applied. The actress has her green face makeup applied by the show's makeup expert, and then a sort of air brush is used to apply the green to other exposed body parts. You can scrub the green makeup off, but I've heard from various Elphabas that they'll go to a routine checkup and their doctor will say gravely . . . "The insides of your ears are green." It takes *years* to come off! Of course, the most famous makeup on Broadway that requires an actor to arrive before half hour is the Phantom in *The Phantom of the Opera!* Whoever's playing the Phantom has to arrive with enough time to complete the two-hour (!) makeup process. *And* they don't get to run out after the show either. It takes 30 minutes to take off!

STAGE DOORING ON HIATUS

One of the greatest thrills for an audience member used to be meeting a Broadway performer after their show. Almost every fan has a story about *stage dooring* — standing in line after a show at the stage door to get an autograph, photo, video, or one-on-one encounter with their favorite star. I still remember waiting at the stage door of *Annie* when I was a kid and getting Laurie Beechman's autography. I've often told people that when she came out, I was able to peer into the stage door and see into the backstage area. I've described it as if I were seeing into Narnia . . . a magical world. I treasured that autograph. I'd take the Playbill out of my dresser drawer all the time and stare at the autograph. It was proof that I had met someone on Broadway with whom I was obsessed!

Today the act of stage dooring has stopped. Covid is still contagious so fans don't line up at stage doors to meet stars because doing so is just too dangerous. But hopefully things will get under control at some point so fans can once again meet the people who bring them so much joy!

Setting That Alarm for TV Appearances

TV performances are often on morning shows. And, let me remind you, Broadway shows happen at night. *And* furthermore, before a morning TV show goes on the air, there's a camera blocking rehearsal where the number is performed full-out in order for the TV director to choose the camera angles. So, for most performers, the typical Broadway show ends between 10 and 11 p.m.; by the time they go to bed, it's midnight (if they can fall asleep with all that show adrenaline), and then they have to be at the TV show for rehearsal at around 7 a.m.

Often when a performer is tired, they can take some liberties and not do every difficult thing at 100 percent. Maybe they modify a high note, or not hold it as long, or not quite kick their face during the dance — but this TV performance is going on record and YouTube! So, they *want* to give their best performance even though they're *so tired!* The good news is that TV performances don't happen all the time. The bad news, they usually happen either:

>> When the show first opens, so everyone has been rehearsing for weeks. This includes rehearsing in the daytime during previews, so they're hitting maximum exhaustion.

>> During award season, which often coincides with the show first opening. Again, they've been rehearsing nonstop and are exhausted. And they can't call out of the show at night to save their health. Tony voters might be there, and they want to be there to be seen *plus* to ensure the show is at its most perfect. (The alternative is to have understudies or swings go on for the first time, which isn't ideal because rehearsals for them haven't begun in earnest.)

Thanks to YouTube, your performance of a song from a Broadway show on a TV show is public record for all current and future generations to see. I equate it with giving birth; it's so great to have a child and when you look at your child, you often forget what a nightmare it was to give birth. Yes, being able to watch your performance from said TV show is fun, but, holy cow, it was *hard*.

Even with all that to deal with, in the long run, it's wonderful to have a Broadway performance immortalized on TV so keep them coming!

A DAY IN THE LIFE OF A NATIONAL TOUR PERFORMER

National tours are wonderful for people who don't live in New York City. Instead of having to fly to Broadway, the entire musical is brought to your town. From a performer's perspective, the hard part about being on a national tour is the traveling. Doing the first national tour of a show is easier for performers because the show has only been on Broadway and therefore plenty of people in other cities want to see this new musical. As a result, the tour spends a week, two weeks, a month, or more in one city. That's delicious.

Doing *split weeks*, meaning the show spends a few days in one city and then picks up the whole show (and cast) and moves it to another city, is harder. Besides all the travel, tours are also difficult because the show has to do mini-tech rehearsals in every new city. Usually, that means getting onstage and singing through some songs for sound check . . . as well as getting fully situated in a brand-new dressing room.

The amazing part about doing a national tour is the people in these cities are so thrilled that Broadway is coming to them. Instead of having an opening on Broadway and then running for a year, the tour lasts for a year and every three weeks or so is another opening night! TV appearances, newspaper articles, and screaming fans out front is a common occurrence in each city. That kind of thrill makes up for the lack of sleep on travel days and the loneliness of missing your dog (or kitty or family).

Participating in One-Night-Only Events

After a performer is ensconced in the New York theatre scene, they're probably going to be asked to participate in a slew of wonderful events that the city has to offer. Here's a quick rundown of some of the incredible events that are special events.

The Red Bucket Follies/The Easter Bonnet Competition

Twice a year, Broadway Cares/Equity Fights AIDS (BCEFA; https://broadway cares.org) does a six-week fundraising drive. Usually a curtain speech is made to explain that the BCEFA raises money for organizations across the country that help people with HIV and AIDS — not with medical research, but with basic things like food, medicine, and housing. Cast members then stand in the audience holding red buckets and collect money. Often fun things are offered for sale like autographed Playbills and posters, and sometimes the cast auction off items from the stage, like the white T-shirt Hugh Jackman wore during that particular performance or Harvey Fierstein leaving your outgoing message on your voicemail. Thousands of dollars *per night* from each show can be raised from these one-of-a-kind auctions!

When I did *Disaster!* on Broadway, we asked audience members to donate to come onstage and watch our cast members perform songs from previous shows they had done. Faith Prince sang "Adelaide's Lament" from *Guys and Dolls*, Adam Pascal had Daphne Rubin-Vega join him for "Light My Candle" from *Rent*, and here's Kerry Butler joined by lots of *Hairspray* original cast members (and the composer Marc Shaiman) doing "Without Love" — www.youtube.com/watch?v=eozwr74TA_k.

To celebrate all the money that's raised after those six weeks, the Red Bucket Follies happens in December and The Easter Bonnet Competition in April. Broadway and Off-Broadway casts put together sketches, parody songs, dances, serious songs . . . whatever they want. All of these acts are performed in one big variety show to a sold-out audience of other cast members, theatre insiders, and people from the public lucky enough to snag a ticket. Some of the comedy acts have been hilarious, like when *Fiddler on the Roof* teamed up with *Ave Q.* and performed *Avenue Jew.* Check out www.youtube.com/watch?v=1Oq97zaBhko.

Celebrity judges give out awards for best act and, in April, best Easter Bonnet (each act in April ends with an Easter Bonnet designed with the show's theme).

Then big celebrities come out at the end and announce how much money has been raised for BCEFA. It's always in the millions, and the whole show is thrilling. And when I say big celebrities, let me just say that I've been hosting the Red Bucket Follies since 2009, and a typical year was when I shared my dressing room with Hugh Jackman and Daniel Craig. P.S. I still haven't recovered.

MCC's Miscast

This is a super fun yearly event that raises money for the MCC Theater Company (https://mcctheatre.org), which is a nonprofit Off-Broadway theatre. The idea of Miscast is so fun that it always attracts a bunch of big stars. Broadway stars perform songs from roles that they'd never be cast in, like Tony Yazbeck dancing and singing *A Chorus Line*'s "Music and the Mirror" and Kristin Chenoweth performing Effie's "And I Am Telling You" from *Dreamgirls*. You can view many of these performances on YouTube. Here's Jonathan Groff singing and dancing the entire title song that Sutton Foster performed in *Anything Goes* (www.youtube.com/watch?v=YQv_hZwyz5Q).

Concert versions of musicals

The 1985 concert of *Follies* was one of the first concert versions of a Broadway show. A concert version means that the performance isn't fully staged. Sometimes the actors hold scripts the whole time, sometimes they put them down for the songs, sometimes half of the songs are choreographed. Since *Follies*, there have been some incredible concert versions of shows.

Most notable is The Encore Series in New York City where they do around three musicals that run for less than three weeks. These musicals use a full orchestra, and they've evolved from everyone holding scripts when they first began to basically having the same performance level as a Broadway show. And some have been so amazing that they've transferred to Broadway — most recently, *Into The Woods* with Sara Bareilles and previous shows like *Violet* with Sutton Foster and the behemoth *Chicago*, which is now the longest running American musical on Broadway!

Waiting on Pins and Needles for Awards Season

Almost everyone involved with Broadway deep down wants to win a Tony Award. But almost everyone knows how arbitrary awards are. Before I get into the specific awards, think about it. For instance, consider best actress in a musical. What factors are the committee members considering? Is it based on the fact that the role isn't well-written, yet this actress does a brilliant job with the given material? Is it because the material is extremely difficult to perform and, compared to the other roles from other shows that year, this one needed the most skills?

Usually not. It's really hard to say what the award decisions are based on.

The Tony awards would *maybe* be fair if everyone on Broadway was playing the exact same role and you could say, "Out of all the interpretations, this one is universally considered the best." But the reality is, everyone is playing a different role. How can anyone decide why someone who acts Dolly Levi is better than the person who acts Fanny Brice? Well, they did. It was decided Carol Channing was the best actress that year over Barbra Streisand. But again . . . why? Was she more believable? Was her role harder? Was her singing prettier? (I can answer that particular question — no.)

Awards are a mystery. Even though I think awards are dubious for many reasons, I sure do love watching the amazing performances that are featured and the wonderful speeches that have been televised throughout the years. And I'm so happy for people who win! Here I examine the biggest theatre awards out there.

The Tony

The Producers has a moment where Max Bialystock played by Nathan Lane is trying to convince Roger DeBris played by Gary Beach to direct his musical, *Springtime for Hitler*, and nothing is working. Finally, he says, "Think of the Tony!" Everyone onstage stops moving while they all sing, "Tony! Tony! Tony! Tony!" That's a stage version of what most of us involved in theatre act like when anyone mentions the Tony. It's considered the highest theatrical accolade.

Yes, there's the Kennedy Center Honors and various Lifetime Achievement Awards, but the Tony Award (www.tonyawards.com/) holds a special place in the heart of almost everyone in the biz. Named after actress/director Antoinette (hence, Tony) Perry, the Tony Awards (see Figure 12-1) were first awarded in 1947, not long after what was considered the first modern day musical, *Oklahoma!* (which opened in 1943).

They continued each year but took national prominence in 1967. Soon producers realized that not only could a show winning a Tony Award help sell tickets, but the exposure a show received by performing on the Tony Awards was also invaluable. A Tony Award win has always been important, but now it's equally important, if not more important, to be nominated because that nomination guarantees a televised spot on the show.

FIGURE 12-1:
A Tony Award.

Lev Radin/Shutterstock

The nominations are first decided by an ever-changing Tony Awards Nomination Committee made up around 50 theatre professionals. After the nominations happen, the actual awards are voted on by around 800 New York theatre professionals. What does it mean to win?

SETH SPEAKS

Having a Tony Award in any category means that your peers respect your work, which (I'm told) is a wonderful feeling. As a matter of fact, Marissa Jaret Winokur, who won Best Actress in a Musical for playing Tracy in *Hairspray* has her Tony Award on a platform in her house. She also has lights aimed right at it. The lights are activated by a Clapper (you know, the sound-activated light switch? *Clap on!*). She told me that anytime she's in a bad mood, she claps twice, and her Tony Award is suddenly illuminated!

SETH SPEAKS

Besides a good feeling, winning a Tony Award doesn't guarantee anything else. After Audra McDonald won her first Tony Award for *Carousel*, I was doing a concert with her near the end of *Carousel*'s run. Audra mentioned the show was closing and how she wasn't sure what was next. She quipped, quite honestly, "Just because you have a Tony Award doesn't mean you have a job!"

However, actors often enjoy increased salary for work they do after winning any acting awards. In fact, Broadway contracts are often initially negotiated with a *Tony bump* clause, meaning an actor gets a certain increase in salary if they're nominated in their role and a bigger increase later if they win.

For the viewing audience, whether in the theatre or at home, watching the Tony Awards is one of the best nights of the year. It's wonderful to see all your favorite artists in one place, doing their thing, getting awarded for their work, and supporting each other.

The incredible performances are the best part of the evening. Besides the Best Musical performances, there have been some wonderful other performances. In 1981, the Tony Awards featured five actresses from the past best musical winners: Priscilla Lopez singing "What I Did for Love" from *A Chorus Line*, Andrea McArdle singing "Tomorrow" from *Annie*, Nell Carter singing "Honeysuckle Rose" from *Ain't Misbehavin'*, Angela Lansbury singing "By the Sea" from *Sweeney Todd*, and Patti LuPone singing "Buenos Aires" from *Evita*. Each performance was *incredible!* Check out www.youtube.com/watch?v=0pmxc4iWYtc.

However, sadly, the time allotted for the Best Musical nominee performances has greatly been reduced. Every year, news articles appear in newspapers and online about viewership for the Tony Awards and how the ratings aren't very high. So the people who run the telecast have tried many ways to attract more viewers, and sometimes that includes having more well-known people making appearances and/or performing — which has taken away time from the Best Musical performances. When the Tony Awards were first airing, Best Musicals segments were usually eight minutes. Nowadays, they're around five minutes. The good news is, as of this writing, there seems to be a pullback to honoring theatre and not obsessing about ratings and there have been fewer TV/film/recording artists on the Tony Awards and more Broadway artists honoring Broadway. Here's hoping it stays that way!

Olivier

Broadway has the Tony Awards, and the Brits have the Olivier award, named after famed British actor, Lawrence Olivier. The categories for the Oliviers (https://officiallondontheatre.com/olivier-awards/) are basically the same as the Tony Awards, but the similarity ends there.

Interestingly, a show that wins the Olivier doesn't mean it's guaranteed to win The Tony . . . and vice versa. *Groundhog Day* won the Olivier for Best Musical, but it didn't win the Tony . . . and wound up not running very long on Broadway. And *Rent*, which swept the Tony Awards (and won the Pulitzer!), lost the Olivier best musical crown to *Kat and the Kings*.

Back in the day, one had to be firmly situated in England to watch the Oliviers, but now you can find plenty of fabulous clips online to enjoy. Get thee to YouTube, stat to watch Olivier winner Gavin Creel in *The Book of Mormon* at www.youtube.com/watch?v=udAfi1GnSaw and the amazing opening number from *Everybody's Talking about Jamie* at www.youtube.com/watch?v=__mmb2WVA-o.

Speaking of Gavin, if you get a chance, watch the clip of him when they announce Best Actor at www.youtube.com/watch?v=oXKeNG2CkV0. He had a knee injury in *Thoroughly Modern Millie*, and it really flared up again on the day of the Oliviers. It was *killing* him. He had physical therapy *and* a massage that day, but the pain was still extreme. He told me that when he was sitting in the audience, he actually hoped he wouldn't win! Why? Because he thought he wouldn't be able to walk up the stairs from the audience to the stage. Cut to — they called his name, and the joy he felt provided a miraculous healing! If you watch, you can see him spring up higher than a Jack-in-the-box and run up those stairs quicker than you can say, "You won't be able to walk tomorrow!"

Obie

The Obie Awards (https://obieawards.org) are strictly for Off- and Off-Off Broadway shows. *The Village Voice* started the Obies in the 1950s, right when Off-Broadway was coming into its own. Interestingly, actors and actress awards are all noted as "performance" awards; there are no fixed categories.

Nominations aren't announced beforehand, and not all categories are awarded each year. The awards themselves have the essence of many Off-Broadway shows: experimental, nonlinear, and more about the art than the glory.

Outer Critics/Drama Desk

The Outer Critics Circle Awards (est. 1949) and the Drama Desk Awards are more egalitarian, in a sense, than the Obies or Tony Awards because they honor both Off-Broadway *and* Broadway, and many of the categories are combined. An Off-Broadway actress who's starring in a theatre with an audience capacity of 300 can be nominated for a Best Actress award opposite a well-established Broadway star who's in a theatre that sells out all 1,100 seats every night!

Here's who does the voting:

>> **Outer Critics:** The New York theatre writers who write for out-of-town papers (hence: outer critics) as well as digital and national publications.

>> **Drama Desk Awards:** The committee is made up of theatre critics, editors, journalists, and broadcasters.

Both awards are often seen as precursors to the Tony Awards. But's that's literally what they are. A *precursor* just means something that comes before another thing to which it's similar. Yes, the Outer Critics Awards and Drama Desks are given out before the Tony Awards ceremony, but they don't predict what will win (or even be nominated for) a Tony Award. Off the top of my head, Steve Kazee won the Tony Award for Best Actor in a musical when he starred in *Once*. Not only did he not win a Drama Desk, but he also wasn't even nominated! *Young Frankenstein* was nominated for ten Outer Critics Awards, leading the pack with the most nominations of any show that year, *and* it won Best Musical. When it came to the Tony Awards, *Young Frankenstein* got three nominations and definitely didn't win Best Musical because it *wasn't even nominated!* Yet, every year, people see these awards as a way to predict Tony nominations.

REMEMBER

The other thing you can count on is seeing people *rage* on theatre message boards. "Why wasn't so-and-so nominated for a Drama Desk or Outer Critics!? Why are they being snubbed?!" The reason that happens is that a lot of Off-Broadway shows move to Broadway. You can only be Drama Desk or Outer Critics nominated for a role *once*. So, if your show began Off-Broadway and you got a nomination, when your show moves to Broadway, you won't be nominated again. So, everyone, please *chill out!*

Drama League

The Drama League Awards (https://dramaleague.org/awards/) are the oldest awards to honor theatre in North America (est.1922). The membership consists of many members of the New York theatrical community. This award doesn't have as many categories as the other awards, but there are two fun aspects: *Everyone* who is nominated each year for the "Distinguished Performance Award" makes a two-minute speech. It's the only awards show where the nominees all make a speech instead of just the winner. And speaking of winners, after you win a "Distinguished Performance Award," you can never be nominated again!

The Grammy

The Grammy Award (www.grammy.com) has certainly changed a lot . . . although it's a little like someone who says, "Do you like my new outfit?" and all they've done is changed their dark brown belt to darker brown. The Broadway Grammy category was first Best Original Cast Album (Broadway or TV) and then Best Broadway Show Album, Best Show Album (original Cast), Best Original Cast Show Album, Best Score from an Original Cast Show Album, Best Score from the Original Cast Show Album, Best Cast Show Album, Best Musical Cast Show Album, and now . . . Best Musical Show Album.

I'll tell you where I don't want to be: in a Grammy Award meeting deciding the new name of the Broadway album category. The one change I love is that now the primary vocalists on the album get a Grammy Award, too! The Grammy Award in the Broadway category used to only go to the composer/lyricist and producers, but starting in 2012, the primary vocalists won the Grammy Award as well. So, the composer/lyricists and producer of *The Book of Mormon* won the Grammy in 2012, and so did the two principal vocalists Andrew Rannells and Josh Gad.

SETH SPEAKS

This rule should apply retroactively, and I support anyone who agrees. For instance, the 1977 cast album of *Annie* won the Grammy Award and whenever I do a concert with Andrea McArdle, I introduce her as a Grammy Award winner because if today's rules applied back then, she would have a Grammy!

The Pulitzer Prize

Journalist Joseph Pulitzer established the Pulitzer Prize (www.pulitzer.org) in his 1904 will. Pulitzer specified four awards in letters and drama (that's us!), four in journalism, one for education, and four traveling scholarships. Most of the drama awards have been for plays, but musicals have won a few times. *Of Thee I Sing* was the first, followed by *South Pacific*, *How to Succeed in Business without Really Trying*, *A Chorus Line*, *Sunday in the Park with George*, *Rent*, *Next to Normal*, *Hamilton*, and *A Strange Loop* (see Figure 12-2). The Pulitzer doesn't have a television ceremony, which could help ticket sales for the winners, but being a musical to win the award is considered extremely prestigious because the prize usually goes to a play.

FIGURE 12-2:
A Strange Loop won both the Pulitzer and the Tony Award for Best Musical in 2022.

Marc J. Franklin

Bigger than the honor of winning the Pulitzer Prize is the mystery of: How the heck do you pronounce it? Is it puh-lizter or pew-lizter? Answer: It is PUH-LITZER!

Legacy Robe

The Legacy Robe is a very inside award, and every Broadway musical has a winner. Once called The Gypsy Robe, this honor is given on opening night to the ensemble member who has done the most Broadway shows. It began in 1950 when an ensemble member of *Gentlemen Prefer Blondes* sent a dressing gown to a friend in the ensemble of *Call Me Madam*. A feather rose from *Call Me Madam's* star Ethel Merman was added to the robe and then it was sent to an ensemble member of *Guys and Dolls*. And thus the tradition began!

Rules were added, and the ritualistic ceremony has stayed basically the same since the late '50s:

1. **On opening night, the entire cast and crew gather onstage with an Actors' Equity rep and the cast member (from the last Broadway show that opened) who received the Legacy Robe (see Figure 12-3).**

2. **The past recipient is wearing the Legacy Robe, which is decorated with drawings and mementos from previous shows that have opened.**

    Once space runs out, a new legacy robe is created, and the previous robe is either given to the New York Public Library, Actors' Equity, or The Smithsonian.

3. **A representative from Equity reads the history of the robe and then announces the new recipient.**

4. **The old recipient puts it on the recipient who then circles the stage three times counterclockwise while everyone touches the robe for good luck.**

FIGURE 12-3: I'm pictured with Paul Castree after he received his Legacy Robe.

Printed with permission from Paul Castree

What's fun is that the new recipient supervises the mementos and drawings that are added to the robe to represent the recipient's show. They're then required to be at the next Broadway show opening to give the robe to the next recipient!

That tradition happens on opening night. Whenever a cast member leaves a Broadway show, there's a tradition of singing them a farewell, not with a classic Broadway song, but with a cowboy song. Yes, if someone is giving their final performance, you can bet there's a little gathering to say goodbye while the whole cast sings "Happy Trails."

Chapter **13**

Landing a Role (Paying or Not!)

H ave you thought about being in a musical? Good! You may therefore wonder whether being in a musical is easy? The answer is *yes!* You may also wonder whether being in a musical is hard? The answer is also *yes!* As contradictory as that sounds, it really is both. Certain things are required for performing in a musical that are intuitive to many people and don't require training. However, other things are difficult to do without proper training. And no matter what, the more training you have, the more musicals you'll be cast in. This chapter looks at what you should work on so you can get to do the thing you love.

Identifying Skills You Need to be Onstage

Being in a play requires the ability to act. Being in a musical requires the abilities to act, sing, and often dance! But before you get to act, sing, and possibly dance in a musical, you have to win over the powers-that-be at the audition. I explain how to do all these things in the next sections.

"The Music of the Night" — Singing (Yes! You can sing!)

When you think of musical theatre, the first thing you think of probably is the performers onstage breaking into song. Therefore, being able to sing is an important skill to have before auditioning for a show.

"Well," some of you are saying, "I guess I'll never do a musical. I really can't sing." Okay, let me say you really don't have much of what anyone would call a beautiful singing voice. Yes, you're relatively on pitch, but often it sounds like you're yelling — and yelling in a way that sounds like you smoke a pack a day. Great! Maybe you'll have the career similar to that of Tony Award winner Elaine Stritch. If you don't know what I'm talking about, listen to her version of "The Ladies Who Lunch" at www.youtube.com/watch?v=slvaecBozmQ.

Or maybe you can speak well with good diction and great volume, and you have internal rhythm, but all you can do is *barely* match pitch and you just don't have the ability to sustain a note very long. Great! You can star in the Broadway, London, *and* film version of *My Fair Lady* like Rex Harrison did.

If you're still unsure that you could ever be in a musical, keep reading. Here I discuss what you can do to work on your singing chops.

Discovering your natural voice

Find out what your natural voice is. The best way to do that is go to a vocal coach who will have you sing some scales. If you don't want to commit to that just yet, then sing along with some classic singers and see what's comfortable. Here are some examples of basic ranges:

>> **Soprano:** If Audra McDonald's (Carrie Pipperidge) songs in *Carousel* or Kristen Chenoweth's (Glinda) songs in *Wicked* are easy for you, you're probably a soprano.

>> **Belter:** If you can easily sing along with Sutton Foster, Lillias White, Idina Menzel, or Barbra Streisand, you're a Broadway belter.

>> **Tenor:** If you can hit the notes of Colm Wilkinson (Jean Valjean) in *Les Miz* or Lee Roy Reams (Billy Lawlor) in *42nd Street*, welcome to the world of the tenor.

>> **Baritone:** If you're most comfortable with Brian Stokes Mitchell's (Fred/Petruchio) songs in *Kiss Me, Kate* or Victor Garber's (Antony) songs in *Sweeney Todd*, you're a baritone.

>> **Bass:** If you can hit the low notes that the great Paul Robeson can in "Ol' Man River" (www.youtube.com/watch?v=1xDIK_cvl_c) or you're vocally

comfortable with anything Patrick Page (Hades) sings in *Hadestown,* then you are Bea Arthur — and/or a bass.

TIP

Whatever your range, go to a voice teacher and develop it. Look up songs online that are right for your voice and learn them for auditions and because you might want to play those roles one day.

I've worked as a music director for many years, and I've often heard people say, "I don't sing." The reality is that anyone can sing. When you search online for "tone deaf," you discover that only 2 to 5 percent of the population is, so, you can safely assume you aren't in that very slim margin. But just because everyone can sing, that doesn't mean everyone's singing is right for every role. Think about Barbara Cook's soaring soprano, which is perfect for those shows with beautiful high soprano songs, like *The Music Man* and *Candide.* But would you want to hear that voice belt it out as Mimi in *Rent?*

And, vice versa, would you want to listen to the hard-rock, raspy voice of Daphne Rubin-Vega hitting that final high E flat above high C in "Glitter and Be Gay" from *Candide?* No, and no.

Both of them are fabulous singers, but their voices are more suited for certain roles than others.

Developing other parts of your voice

You should also focus on developing *other* parts of your voice. If you're a soprano, study how to belt. If you're a belter, study how to soar up to those high notes. If you're a classically trained singer, learn how to riff. If you're a pop singer, learn how to sound good on classic Broadway scores. The more types of singing you can do, the more opportunities will be available to you.

Many people have expanded their singing styles and can sing in different ways. For example, Patrick Wilson made his first splash on Broadway singing the pop score of *The Full Monty,* but then he showed his "legit" voice as Curly in *Oklahoma!* Audra McDonald has a gorgeous soprano voice that she used in *Carousel* and *Ragtime,* but she also belted up a storm in my production of *Dreamgirls.* Check out www.youtube.com/watch?v=-wJWPCnAZ24. She also sped up her vibrato and almost sounds vocal-damaged for her Tony Award–winning performance as Billy Holliday in *Lady Day at Emerson's Bar and Grill* (www.youtube.com/watch?v=TZTwdR3C6_E).

TIP

The more different ways you can sing, the better. And you don't necessarily have to take tons of singing lessons to do this. See if you can change your sound to be like a singer you're listening to. That's *not* to say you should sound like anyone besides yourself; but a lot of great Broadway singers I know did this exercise when they were starting out. Through trial and error, they learned phrasing, how to riff, how to add or not use vibrato, how to control their breath, and so on by listening to great singers. Then they developed their own style.

Taking voice lessons to "protect the gift"

The main goal of singing lessons is to expand your voice, learn how to sing without injuring yourself, and learn how to sing so you have the stamina to do eight shows a week. Don't avoid lessons because you think you don't have a pretty voice or a "Broadway" voice. There's no one type of singing on Broadway and everyone's voice can be improved by technique. Perfect whatever you can have. If you don't want to commit to lessons, do any of the following:

>> **Join a local chorus.** It's a great way to get some regular singing in your life and improve your musicality.

>> **Go to piano bars.** Get up and sing.

>> **See if your house of worship has a choir.** Join and audition for the solos.

No matter where, sing whenever you can.

GET ME MY 16 BARS: WHAT A VOICE COACH CAN DO

A *voice teacher* helps with technique, whereas a *vocal coach* helps with the performance of the song. How? In many ways! They're used very often to help with auditions; they'll find you material that suits your voice/the roles you want. Furthermore, they'll put the songs in the right key for you, and, often very importantly, they'll help you make the song shorter.

Auditions often ask for 16 bars, which means 16 measures of music. Most songs have many more measures than 16 so a coach can find the best 16 bars that highlight you as a performer and *still* make the song enjoyable, even though it's shorter. I do a lot of master classes as a coach and have a short video highlighting some of the tips I teach when I coach: www.youtube.com/watch?v=J2AZJQTsNTY&t=2s.

"Doin' What Comes Natur'lly" — Acting (There's a reason why it's called a play)

The question: What is acting? The answer I love is from the great acting teacher Sanford Meisner: "Acting is living truthfully under imaginary circumstances." That's it. Just act as if something is really happening.

Yes, acting has other elements, but that definition demystifies the basics of it. Literally just pretend something is happening. Isn't that what everyone did as kids? Remember? You'd be with friends and have tea parties or move your toy monsters around and give them voices or dress up and play different characters in a story. You weren't self-conscious back then. The trick as an adult is to get out of your own way. You know what it's like to brush your hair, but suddenly when you have to do it in a scene, you become self-aware. *Wait. Is that where the brush goes? Where do I look? What do I do with my other hand?*

TIP

Recreate that lack of self-consciousness when you're given a scene to perform. Just pretend it's happening. And don't think you don't have any professional acting experience. You already got all the experience you need pretending when you were a kid! You're a veteran. However, you can always improve. These sections delve deeper into what acting skills can help you as a musical theatre performer.

GET THEE TO AN ACTING TEACHER

An acting teacher/coach can help you in various ways:

- They can show you how to get rid of your self-consciousness so it's easier for you to perform naturally.

- They can help you access your emotions so the audience believes you when you're playing someone angry, grief-stricken, guilty, traumatized, jealous, — you name the emotion.

- They can also notice helpful tricks that you fall back on when you're nervous or aren't really in the moment.

Just make sure you don't go to the kind of acting teacher who thinks they have to break you down to build you back up again. And avoid the know-it-all Svengali who won't allow discussions to happen. It's best to remember; if you're feeling bad about yourself after a few classes, this isn't the right teacher for you.

Using your voice effectively

Acting isn't just physical movement. It's speaking the lines so everyone in the theatre can hear you. Yes, performers on Broadway have body mics, but performers shouldn't rely solely on amplified sound to fill the theatre. Figuring out how to use your voice effectively is important to anyone who sings or speaks onstage. A singing teacher can help teach you how to open up your singing voice, and an acting teacher can help you learn how to get the most out of your speaking voice when you're acting.

Speaking with an accent

If you're auditioning for a character who comes from a different country or region or the musical is set in another country, you need to know how to speak (and sing) with an accent. A dialect coach can help. You can also find plenty of online videos to teach you the basics of the most common accents that are needed for theatre.

Discovering comic timing

Comic timing basically means knowing how to say the setup to a joke, knowing how to land the joke and knowing how long to ride the following laugh. It's important to have because even musicals with serious themes (*West Side Story*) have comedy moments ("Gee, Officer Krupke"). Comic timing *can* be learned. Watch great comics (on YouTube) and see how they milk a laugh, or build to a laugh, or make a side comment. Better yet, take a scene study class, work on a comic scene, and then perform it for the class.

TIP

The best way to figure out comic timing is in front of an audience. When I first did stand-up comedy, I entered a comedy contest at The Duplex in the Village. I had beginner's luck and reached the semifinals right away. I was *thrilled!* However, when I performed my same act that got me into the semifinals at the semifinals, I bombed *so badly!* A few days later, I saw one of the other comics who had been there at my clunkfest, and he jokingly said, "I thought you quit the business!" Well, I swallowed my pride and kept going back to the initial contest week after week, even though I had to face those comics who had seen me bomb. I'd tape record my performances and listen to see what got a laugh and what didn't. I realized that yes, sometimes it's the material, but often it was the comic timing. For instance, a joke might not get an immediate laugh . . . but if I said and then didn't say anything . . . my pausing facial expression would lead to audience laughter. Finally, after I understood timing better, I made it back to the semifinals and this time, I made it to the finals! And then . . . *I won the grand prize!* My point is (besides bragging) that practice really helps, so keep trying!

Acting while singing

Knowing how to act during scene work in a musical and being comfortable singing the songs in a musical are important skills. However, singing isn't just carrying the tune. It's acting the words *while* singing the melody. Doing both is the real skill it takes to have a role in a musical.

TIP

Some people have beautiful voices, but when they sing, the audience isn't moved *at all* because no story is being told. Basically, they're just hearing a pretty tone . . . the same effect can be achieved by an oboe playing the melody. David Craig has a wonderful book called *On Singing Onstage* (Applause), which can help you learn how to not just create beautiful sounds onstage. For instance, he talks about learning how to "act on the air." That means to act between the lyrics when there's just music. Instead of "Maybe this time" (pause for music) "I'll be lucky" (pause for music) "Maybe this time he'll stay . . ." (2,3,4 . . .) you have *thoughts* during those musical interludes.

> "Maybe this time" (*It could happen, couldn't it?*) "I'll be lucky" (*I deserve it!*) "Maybe this time he'll stay . . ." (*Maybe we'll have children!*)

Yes, the audience doesn't know what you're thinking, but they see your *face*, which reflects what you're thinking. Because they see you experiencing these thoughts, they believe they're witnessing your emotional journey.

"I Could Have Danced All Night" — Dancing (Don't skip!)

I know what many of you are thinking, "I don't have to read this section. I definitely don't dance, and I'll never do a show where I have to dance."

That's not true!

For all those folks who tell me, "I don't sing!" there are double the amount who tell me, "I don't dance." Guess what? You dance better than you think *and* you should learn how to dance better!

I'm not saying you have to rival Baryshnikov's skills or have the dance moves to be in an Andy Blankenbuehler choreographed musical. But you have to know how to move your body comfortably onstage.

"But Seth!" you cry, "I'm planning on being a lead. The ensemble dances, the leads act and sing. Right? Right? *Please!??*"

Guess what? Lots of musicals have megamixes (see Chapter 3) at the end where *everybody* does some choreography. So accept it and just take some dance classes — just like the title of the book I bought six years ago (but haven't read yet . . .): *Feel the Fear and Do It Anyway* by Susan Jeffers.

"Well, where do I begin?"

TIP

Start with a beginner dance class. I recommend everyone begin with ballet class. Ballet training is the basis for every kind of dance you'll ever do. And the other styles that can help you in musical theatre: jazz, modern, tap, hip hop, and show dance, which is geared more toward musical theatre.

And you can definitely start any type of class at a later age. Cheyenne Jackson was cast in *Thoroughly Modern Millie* (his first Broadway show), and he needed to learn how to tap as soon as possible. He signed up for a beginner's tap class. He told me the dichotomy was crazy! — just imagine his over-six-foot self and a bunch of 8-year-old girls. But he did it! *And* even though he started tap class in his mid-20s, he learned it quick and well enough that he didn't get fired from *Millie!*

If you're too scared to take any of those types of classes, which I know might seem daunting, take an aerobics class at your local gym — or any kind of group fitness class. Getting used to having someone in front of you demonstrating a move that you can replicate with your body is important. And, like everything else, the more you do it, the more comfortable you'll feel, and you won't panic during a dance call!

"I Hope I Get It" — Auditioning

Lots of shows hold an initial audition and then callbacks and then hopefully, you get the role. But that's not often the case. There can also be a dance call after the first audition, or another kind of call, like *Meet Me In St. Louis*, which had an ice-skating audition. (Yes, the Broadway show had an ice rink for Act Two!)

Here's what those terms mean:

>> **Initial audition:** This is the first time you're auditioning for the show. The audition requirement might be to sing something from the show, something in the style of the show, or perhaps just sing something that shows your abilities. If a whole bunch of people are being seen, perhaps the casting office is just asking for 16 *bars* of music (16 measures — around one minute; see the nearby sidebar).

The creative team might be at this audition or perhaps just the casting director or casting associates are. It's very rare that anyone is offered the job after this audition *unless* it's an audition for a role in a show that's running and they're bringing in people whom they know are right for the role. That usually means the creative team is at the audition and they decide that day who gets the gig.

>> **Callbacks:** This is the audition *after* the first audition. Often there's more than one callback. And sometimes there are lots (like more than five!). Multiple callbacks happen for various reasons:

- Sometimes you're given additional material to learn.

- Sometimes you're given an acting note to work on and come back.

- Often, as they whittle down the final candidates for the role, more and more powers-that-be are brought in to watch the audition like the producers, the writers, and so on.

>> **Dance calls:** For ensemble dance roles, auditions usually begin with a dance call. You audition in a group by learning a dance taught by the choreographer or an associate. After that, they usually call out the names of those whom they want to stay and show more. Everyone else knows to leave. Sometimes you're asked to stay and sing or sometimes you're asked to dance a different combination.

This is for the ensemble who are labeled as "dancers who sing." The reverse happens for ensemble members who are "singers who dance." You come in and sing, and if they like what they hear, you're asked to come to a dance call. The same audition process happens with roles that have some dancing. You audition with a song (and maybe a scene) and then you may be asked to return and do a dance call specific for that role. Often it's with a bunch of other people auditioning for that same role!

TIP

No matter the temptation, don't pull a *Showgirls*. #StaircasePush

>> **Chemistry calls:** Sometimes a show holds chemistry calls, which I touch on again in Chapter 11, where two people audition together to see if they connect well onstage.

As you can see, there's no set number of auditions one can have for a role.

Peeking inside the audition room

Though the amount of auditions vary, the majority of them look basically the same. They're usually held in a rehearsal room at a rehearsal studio. A pianist is present with the people leading the audition sitting behind a table. Sometimes one person is behind the table, but usually a few. Typically you'll see the casting person, director, and music director. The further along the audition, the more people. Depending on the role, final auditions can have many people there to give their approval — 10, 15, 20!

TIP

If you have an audition time, you sit in the area outside the rehearsal room with other people who are also waiting to audition. If it's an *open call*, meaning anyone can audition, you usually line up and wait — sometimes for long periods of time. The process of waiting can be tedious, but you can chat with the people around you, which is how friendships are formed. Just don't be the annoying person who can't take a hint and chats nonstop as a fellow auditioner is trying to prepare and don't be the blowhard that keeps talking loudly about their various amazing auditions and upcoming gigs. #Shunned

After your name is called, you walk in, make small talk with the people behind the table, and hand the pianist your music. You then sing, make more small talk, and then sometimes you're asked to sing another song you have with you or perform your own monologue. Sometimes, you'll be asked to read something from the show that you received in advance. If it's not a monologue, you'll do the scene with a reader. A *reader* is an actor who's hired to perform various scenes with everyone auditioning. P.S. These readers are *good*. Santino Fontana began as a reader before he won his Tony Award for *Tootsie!*

After you're finished, you'll usually be thanked, and you'll find out later whether or not you got a callback. Sometimes you'll be asked on the spot if you're available later for a callback. It's always a delicious feeling to walk out of an audition room knowing they want to see you again! But try not to smirk *too* much when you walk by the other peeps auditioning.

Dance auditions are similar in terms of being in a rehearsal studio with a pianist. The studio has walls with mirrors so you can watch yourself as you learn the dance.

THE AUDITION THAT'S SOMETIMES NOT AN AUDITION

The most frustrating type of audition is one where you don't get to actually audition. That's when the powers-that-be *type* you. This happens during auditions where there are lots and lots of hopefuls. They bring in groups of around 10 to 20 people who stand in a line, and the person in charge of the audition looks at everyone and decides what types look right for the show. Those people who pass the physical test are asked to stay . . . and everyone else is asked to leave — without ever having auditioned!

When that happens, it means you've been *typed out*. You've waited for hours just to have someone look at you and say no . . . in around 20 seconds. It happened to Priscilla Lopez when she auditioned to be one of the young girls in the original production of *Gypsy*. But years later, she won a Tony Award so there!

Focusing on these tips for auditioning

Preparation is key. Here are some quick tips for auditioning, no matter what level of musical theatre you're doing:

>> **Have a few great go-to audition songs.** Have a song (or songs) that shows who *you* are. It doesn't have to have incredibly specific lyrics. A general song about happiness or love can be great because *you* can bring your specific self to it. The way you express the lyric makes you unique. Think about how you would say "I love Paris in the Springtime" and think about how your mom would say it. I bet it's totally different. My point is, if you express the lyrics as you really would in real life, you'll be special. And always be thinking when you're singing and when you're not singing. (I discuss *the air* of the song in the section, "'The Music of the Night' — Singing (Yes! You can sing!)" earlier in this chapter.)

- • **Do:** Make sure you're always thinking and it shows in your facial expressions. "What good is sitting alone in your room?" (Thought: Here's a great idea for you to cheer yourself up!) "Come hear the music play!"

- • **Don't:** Avoid going blank-faced between phrases. "What good is sitting alone in your room?" (Blank-faced) "Come hear the music play."

The way you look when you're thinking or expressing that thought in the air is uniquely you, and *that's* what will make you stand out at an audition.

REMEMBER

>> **Know exactly in what key you sing your audition song.** You may sound fantastic on a sustained belted A, but the sheet music you have ends on a C. Change the key! Find the key that fits *your* voice. P.S. You can do this if you're singing an audition song *not* from the show you're auditioning for. But if you're auditioning for a specific part in the show, the music you sing should be in the key of the show. It's not that common for a theatre (except Broadway) to transpose the key of a song from a show that already exists.

TIP

No matter what, *always* run your audition song with a pianist in advance. I've played piano at so many auditions where people bring music they've never rehearsed. They buy the sheet music thinking it's the same as the recorded version they've sung along with . . . and it's not! They wind up singing something that doesn't suit their range at all — too low or too high — or it's a version of the song with a different ending than what they know. The result is the same: a bad audition.

>> **You *can* sing from the show if you want, but you don't have to.** I suggest you bring a song that's similar to the role you want to get. After you're done, the people behind the table making the casting choices may ask you if you know a song from the show, and if you do, that gives you another opportunity to sing for them!

>> **Remember that the people behind the table have a problem, and they want you to solve it.** They need to cast this show, and it would be great if *you* were the person they could cast. Then they can move on to the next phase of the show.

So, don't think they're sitting there thinking, "How dare this person think they can be in our show?" They *want* you to succeed. The meanness of the judges on *American Idol* isn't how Broadway (or other theatres) is. Yes, there has been the random hostile director, casting director, music director, or whatever, but it *isn't* the norm! So go in there confident that you're the person they want.

EVEN AUDITIONS STRESS OUT SUCCESSFUL ACTORS

SETH SPEAKS

Auditioning is a skill unto itself. I know many super-famous and successful actors who loathe them. I mean, truly loathe them. They often talk about how *horrible* they are at auditioning. Read those last sentences again and take in that information because most people think, "I'm a nervous wreck at auditioning, but I'm sure that people who are really talented are always amazing. They never get nervous!"

Really? How about this? I played piano for an audition for Audra McDonald, and she was so nervous, she passed out! #TrueStory!

Auditions will always be stressful, but I highly recommend going to Jack Plotnick's amazing website (www.jackplotnick.com/) where he has a free acting e-book to download. The book has a section called Actor Affirmations where you can find tips to help with nerves. He believes that, when you're nervous, you fight with your "vulture" (your negative voice). Before you audition, you'll think "I really hope I hit that note!" and your vulture says, "You're going to crack!" and you say back "No, I'm going to hit it!" and your vulture says, "You are not!" and it goes on like that. He therefore believes it's important to "release and destroy your need" so your vulture has nothing to argue about. Instead of "I really hope I hit that high note!" you think "I release and destroy my need to hit that high note." Silence. There's nothing to go back and forth about with your negative inner voice and it frees you up. And you can use it for anything! "I release and destroy my need to get a big laugh," "I release and destroy my need to remember my lyrics," and so on.

Sutton Foster heard about these affirmations and when I visited her backstage at *Thoroughly Modern Millie,* she had them hanging up in her dressing room! Try it and see what happens.

Being nice — The most important skill

What is the most important skill to have wherever you wind up performing? Is it best to be known as a great singer, a great actor, or a great dancer?

None of the above. (Trick question!)

The most important skill is one that requires no training. And no actual talent. (No, not being a pop singer who lip-syncs.) Being known as a nice person is the *most important* skill.

Seriously.

Show business is such a small community, and everybody knows everybody. If you have a fit during rehearsal, you can bet every person in the cast, crew, and orchestra will know about it later that day even if they weren't there. And people in other shows will also know because all the people in your cast are friends with everyone else around town.

And, often, details of your fit will live on for years. Theatre people love telling a good story! Like that one that happened 20 years ago — those of us who were on Broadway back then still know all about that leading lady who kicked a hole in the drums because the new drummer missed her drum accents during her big number. Don't be the subject of a story that won't be forgotten!

Why be nice, you ask?

Directors, stage managers, music directors, choreographers and everyone else in a position to hire want to hire and work with people who are fun to hang out with and people who are respectful to others around them.

The concept of being nice is so basic. And yet, some performers yell at others or brazenly upstage their fellow performers or act out in other ways because they think, "the show can't survive without me." That may be true . . . for that particular show. But guess what? Shows close, and then you're back looking for another show just like everyone else. And that next show will be able to survive without you because *you won't be cast*!

Having a reputation as someone great to work with is the most important skill you can cultivate.

Talking like an Insider

It's the first day of rehearsal. Uh-oh. They're going to find out that you've never been onstage before. I actually know an actress who was cast in a college play, and on the first day, they staged the opening scene. The director told her to say her first line while walking across the stage, listen to the other actor while she drank her tea, and then sit on the couch and deliver her monologue. On the second day of rehearsal the director asked everyone to run the scene they had staged the day before. My friend was completely confused. She had *no idea* that the purpose of the first rehearsal was to teach her the staging she'd be doing when she performed the show. She didn't write anything down because she didn't know she was ever supposed to do those moves again. End of story: She didn't know what a show was!

So, don't despair because I'm here to help. Here's a list of terms, so you can go into your first rehearsal with a much greater knowledge than the aforementioned actress: Tony Award winner Debra Monk!

>> **Stage left/right:** *Stage left* is the left of the stage as you're standing on the stage looking at the audience. Why is it stage left? Because when the director is in the audience, or the *house,* the director's left is the opposite, or *house left.* *Stage right* is just the opposite — the right of the stage as you're standing on the stage looking at the audience. So don't confuse what the director or choreographer means when they tell you to go *stage left, stage right, house left,* or *house right*!

>> **Downstage/upstage:** Think of the stage as being lifted up in the back. So when you're downstage, you're close to the audience. When you're upstage, you're near the back.

>> **The pit:** The *pit* refers to the orchestra pit, the big hole in the front of the stage. When you're doing a show, make sure you're aware of the pit. There are many stories of actors falling into the orchestra pit, and it ain't fun for the actor and/or the oboe player they land on.

>> **Wings:** The *wings* are the sides of the stage that are offstage. Right before an entrance, an actor usually positions themselves there, hence the expression, "Waiting in the wings."

>> **Chemistry calls:** This happens to see how two people who have to play opposite each other in the show connect when performing together. Sometimes one role is cast and various people come into audition opposite whomever that actor is, and sometimes certain actors up for both roles and the creative team pairs them up in a mix-and-match sort of way. The hope is to see two people who have a wonderful rapport when auditioning together.

>> **Half hour:** This is the call time that actors have to be at the theatre. Each show has a sign-in sheet that an actor must sign so the stage manager can make sure everyone is present and an understudy doesn't have to go on. (Chapter 12 discusses this call time and other call times in greater detail.) This is also the time I was always late for when I was doing my last Broadway show and why the stage manager threatened to call Equity. #oops

>> **Button:** A *button* is the last beat of a song. For example, listen to "It's Today!" from *Mame.* The chorus holds the last note, there is a trumpet riff, and then everyone yells "HEY!" The "HEY" is the button.

>> **Vamp:** A *vamp* refers to a repeated phrase of music played by the orchestra. Kander and Ebb are known for their amazing vamps. Listen to the beginning of "All That Jazz" from *Chicago* or the songs "Cabaret" and "Wilkommen" from *Cabaret.* That repeated musical phrase at the beginning of each song is a vamp.

This term can also refer to a phrase that's repeated and repeated and repeated until a cue. That kind of vamp is employed sometimes when dialogue appears in the middle of a song. Dialogue can't always be timed exactly, so a vamp plays underneath. When the actor gets to a specific word, the conductor then cues the orchestra to move on.

>> **16 bars:** Preliminary auditions try to have as many people come in as possible. Instead of everyone singing a full 3-to-5-minute song, the people casting the show usually request 16 bars. That means 16 measures of music, which lasts around one minute. This gives the people behind the table an essence of each person, and they can bring the promising ones back for the next round. (Refer to the section, "Peeking inside the audition room," earlier in this chapter for more about what happens during an audition.)

>> **Peas and carrots:** Sometimes if you whisper "peas and carrots" onstage, it looks like you're having a conversation in the background of a group scene. You can also substitute "Hub bub, hub bub." Or, my tip, you can have an actual conversation! If you're supposed to act a conversation, then act a conversation!

"I'm the Greatest Star" — How Broadway Actors Become Stars

Children are often asked what they want to be when they grow up. Sometimes the desired career has a clear path, like a doctor, teacher, or firefighter. Sometimes a particular career seems more difficult to achieve, like an astronaut, president of the United States, or a vampire.

And sometimes kids talk about wanting to be a performer. To parents who have nothing to do with the arts, this dream may seem impossible to realize. As Donna McKechnie's parents said (which was later turned into an actual lyric in *A Chorus Line*):

> Listen to your mother. Those stage and movie people got there because they're special.

Well, yes, you have to be special — that is, have talent — to be successful, and that's something you can't control. But you can control many other things that I discuss in the following sections that can help make it possible for you to be a professional performer. And I promise you they're more fun than taking those horrific upper-math classes you need to be an astronaut.

Getting a degree

I can hear you asking, "Do I really need a degree to be onstage?"

Short answer: No.

Longer answer: In the *Saturday Night Live* sketch about Jewess jeans, the voice-over states: "You don't have to be Jewish to wear Jewess Jeans," and then Gilda Radner ends with, "But it wouldn't hurt!"

That's the case with a musical theatre degree. It doesn't hurt to have a degree, and it can definitely help in the following ways:

>> **You can make professional connections.** There are people on Broadway from theatre schools all over the country who want to help fellow alums. Maybe you can't get an audition for a new show, but then you find out the director went to your school. Send them a message on Twitter or Instagram, and you may end up getting an audition because of school spirit.

>> **You're surrounded by up-and-comers like yourself at school.** When you graduate and start navigating the business, you can help each other. Need someone to dog-sit when you go to that open call? Call your first-year roommate. Or maybe your old scene partner from your Shakespeare class is now the assistant director on a new show. They can recommend you to the director and get you seen!

>> **You get training for four years.** Some theatre programs are definitely amazing and can give you incredible training for a career in the arts. That can only help, right?

Well, yes and no.

REMEMBER

I've definitely heard my share of stories about theatre schools that give you wrong information ("Never sing fill-in-the-blank at an audition") or schools that make you pay full tuition every year but don't allow you to take full advantage of the program.

For example: I know a Broadway star who did a four-year theatre conservatory program and *never* got a role in one of the school shows. How is that worth tuition? I say to these schools; if there aren't enough roles to go around, then have fewer students admitted to the program or do more shows! #Ripoff

TIP

The bottom line is this: You don't need a theatre degree to work professionally. And in some sense, having a degree in something else may help so you're more well-rounded as long as you can train while you're in college. I was a piano major at Oberlin, but I was still able to take ballet class and do musicals, both acting and music directing, for all four years. So, investigate before you commit!

Is Broadway the only place I can make "Money Money Money"?

(Tip o' the hat to *Mamma Mia!*)

In theatre, the most money to be made *weekly* is usually in a Broadway show. For example, here's an idea what the weekly pay may be:

>> **Ensemble:** The base salary on Broadway is a little more than $2,100 a week. Ensemble members make at least that, and they get extra money for things like *extraordinary risk* (for example, the bottle dance in *Fiddler on the Roof* with real glass that could break) or from understudying roles.

>> **Roles:** In terms of salary, usually the bigger the role, the more money the actor makes. The salary is negotiated (usually with an agent) when the actor signs the contract. The producer/general manager is basing the salary on how large the role is *and* how much experience the actor has on Broadway. An actor can also make more money from things like Tony Award bumps: An actor gets a raise if they're nominated and another raise if they win. A leading person on Broadway can make between $4,000 to $20,000 a week.

>> **Star salary:** This can be *a lot* of money if the producer deems the actor a star that will sell tickets. From $10,000 to $100,000 per week and that's just the base salary. Many stars have provisions in their contract that give them a percentage of the box office sales. So, if their name is truly selling tickets, they get a cut. This can make their weekly salary go to $500,000!

Money is delicious, and it's good to know that Broadway isn't the only way to get a salary as a musical theatre performer. You can make money performing in other ways. Sometimes you can get a gig that pays as much as you'll make doing a few months of a Broadway show. These sections break down what's out there for the theatre professional who isn't located in the New York City theatre district.

Summer stock

One of my favorite jobs was summer stock, and I can't recommend it enough. Summer stock theatres are in towns that are vacation places, so already you're in a lovely area. The performers in summer stock usually all live in the same house or the same housing area, so you can bet everyone hangs out together after the show. It feels like being in musical theatre summer camp! The pay really varies from a couple of hundred dollars a week (plus room and board) to Broadway salaries.

I recommend summer stock because it really teaches you how to focus during rehearsal. You usually only get a handful of rehearsals, and then you're perform-ing it in front of an audience. Trust me. If you have a chance to do summer stock, take it!

SETH SPEAKS

The best ones to work at are the summer stocks that keep one cast for multiple shows. I did *one week stock*, which was an incredible learning experience. I worked at Surflight Summer Theatre (which is still around) for three years, and when I was there, there was one cast and we did a different show *every week*. That means we got there the first week of June and rehearsed our first musical *Promises, Promises*. We began performances on the following Tuesday . . . and never had another night off! While we performed *Promises, Promises* at night, we rehearsed *Grease* during the day. Then the next week when we did *Grease* at night, we rehearsed *Sweet Charity* during the day. The next week we did *Sweet Charity* at night and rehearsed *Applause* during the day. This went on for three months — 12 shows in 12 weeks.

National tours

National tours are a great way to do a musical with high production values that are often put together by the original creative team. Here are some different levels of national tours:

>> Ones that spend weeks or months in one city comprise the highest level of tours. Those are the first-time tours of hit shows. The tour cast rehearses for weeks in New York and then flies to a city, checks into a nice hotel or a nice apartment complex, and plants it for a few weeks or months. After the tour finishes in that city, the cast flies to the next city and moves into another great

hotel or apartment and then starts performances for another extended period of time.

» Lower down on the comfort level are bus and truck tours. They often do one-nighters or *split weeks,* meaning two cities in seven days. After the cast finishes their performance, they don't go back to their hotel. They get on the bus and travel to the next town. Overnight. They're sleeping *on* the bus! These tours are a good way to pay your dues in terms of not being comfortable, yet still do a show with a talented cast and nice production values.

The pay varies on tours because there are various tiers of minimum salaries. There are ten types of touring contracts and the salaries get smaller depending on what the presenter (the theatre where the tour is playing) guarantees in ticket sales. The good news is, tours were completely on their way out in 2000 (down around 40 percent), but because of these new contracts, they are back. Sadly, though, the days of making good money as a performer doing national tours seem to be over.

SETH SPEAKS

One of the best things about tours, no matter what the salary level, is having a chance to see the country. TV/film/Broadway star Peter Gallagher was in the Broadway revival of *Hair* and singing "Electric Blues" and understudying Claude. Right when previews began, he was offered the role of Danny on the tour of *Grease.* He went to the *Hair* producers and asked to leave the production. *Leave a Broadway show? Why* they asked? Well, he was from upstate New York and had never seen America. He thought it would be a wonderful chance to see the entire country. They understood and kindly let him out of his contract. But before he left, they asked if he wanted a chance to go on for the lead. He politely declined. He didn't have enough rehearsal and didn't feel prepared. Peter wound up playing Danny and seeing parts of the country he never would have seen if he hadn't been on a tour!

Regional theatre

Regional theatre is like doing a national tour, but in just one city. Sometimes performers who live in the city are cast in the show, but often people from other cities, especially New York, are flown in for the bigger roles.

Usually, regional theatre produces shows that have been hits in New York; doing regional theatre is a nice way to play a role you've always wanted to play, but know you'll never get a chance to do on Broadway. Maybe because it's a show that will never be revived or maybe you've aged out of it or you're still too young. But the regional theatre thinks you'd be great! Nathan Lane was young when he played Nathan Detroit in a regional production, but he got experience playing the role and when he was the right age, he was able to play Nathan in the highly successful Broadway production of *Guys and Dolls!*

Regional theatre salaries vary, depending on the size of the role and the experience or name recognition of the actor, but they aren't on the level of Broadway. Often, people who live in the cities where they perform in regional theatre have a day job to sustain them.

Regional theatres not only do established shows, but they also premiere new pieces. And you never know where that will lead. James Monroe Iglehart wanted to play Jimmy Early in a regional production of *Dreamgirls*, but after he auditioned, they cast him in a smaller role. Right after he was offered the *Dreamgirls* role, he got an offer to do a regional production of a new musical. He wound up taking the role in the new musical and eventually that musical left its regional home, moved to Broadway, and won the Tony Award for Best Musical! Instead of *Dreamgirls*, Early took the regional production of *Memphis*, which led to him playing his first original role on Broadway!

Theme parks

Opryland, Great American, Hershey Park, Cedar Point, Six Flags, Disney, and other theme parks have many more opportunities for performers. They offer a wide array of opportunities: elaborate musical shows based on famous films, revues that are like mini-juke box musicals, close harmony singing groups, and so much more. These high-quality shows are a great way for performers to learn the ropes and, if they want, make their career. These types of shows often combine improv skills, singing, and dancing, learning various roles, difficult harmony, and so on.

So many incredible people began in theme parks and wound up on Broadway (Jason Danieley and Paul Castree), have TV/Broadway careers (Wayne Brady), and have won Tony Awards (Betty Buckley, Kristin Chenoweth, and Stephanie J. Block). Salaries in many parks are so good that you don't need a day job. Actually, it often *is* your day job because you sometimes work day and night. Many performers love the security and benefits and wind up staying for years and years.

Industrials

Some big corporations do events for their best clients or their workforce. These special events often include a show, which is known as an *industrial*. Sometimes it'll be a variety show, or sometimes the show will have classic songs, but with lyrics changed to be about the product the company makes.

These gigs are great because they pay *a lot* and are usually in incredible locations like Hawaii or Puerto Rico. I just got back from doing one, and we were at the five-star Four Seasons on the island of Nevis in the Caribbean! Performers can easily make $10,000 for just one performance. Sign me up!

"Another Opening, Another Show" — Performing for the Love of Theatre

You say, "I have a career in an unrelated field, but I still want to perform." And I say, "If you love theatre, you should keep it in your life even if it's not your full-time job." You're not going to make much money, if any, but these are some ways to scratch that theatre itch!

Joining community theatre

Many cities and towns have nonprofessional theatres where they put on multiple musicals per year. And nonprofessional doesn't mean amateurish. I'd guess you've seen a community theatre production and thought, "That's as good as any musical I've seen on Broadway!"

And if you have a family, community theatre is a great way to get your kids to love theatre. Audition for the role of Marion Paroo and have your son audition for Winthrop in *The Music Man.* And then just make sure you have money for your own therapy bills when he lands the role and you get cast as River City Townsperson.

Putting together a cabaret act

Do you love Gershwin? Billy Joel? Songs from the '50s? Sondheim tunes? Put together an evening performing the songs you love and string them together with patter. You'll be performing your first cabaret act. Most cities have clubs where you can book your own act and doing so isn't expensive. You usually have to pay for a tech person (and, of course, your music director) and often you have to guarantee people will come. But it's worth it for a chance to do the songs that bring you joy for an hour or so. Hopefully the money you make from ticket sales will cover all your costs. And you might even make some money on top of it!

Why do a cabaret if you're already a performer in theatre? Well, cabaret is a way to sing songs from roles you might never get to play. Too old for Eponine? Who cares! Close your cabaret act with "On My Own." It's *your* show!

Reading through scripts with friends

Do you have a gang of people who love theatre? Get together every few weeks and read through a script. Assign everyone a role beforehand and get your theatre fix in. When you get to the song in the script, play the album and lip-synch! Or, better still, if you have a friend who plays the piano, have them play and sing the songs when you get to them.

Volunteering at your local fill-in-the-blank

Maybe your local high school stopped doing musicals, but you know kids who would love to perform. Or maybe your place of worship has never done a show, and you know there's an audience that would buy tickets. Put on a show!

Volunteer to be the director at your local school. Or tell whatever religious institution you're affiliated with that you want to put on a musical. Who knows? You may start a tradition that grows and grows each year. P.S. When they can't find a local person who can sing the high notes of *Evita*, guess who'll volunteer to direct *and* star?! Answer: you!

Going Pro

You've had the leads in all your high school or college shows. Or you know you could if just given the chance. You've brushed up on your singing, dancing, acting, and being nice skills. How do you start making money? Three ways: audition, audition, audition. Really. You're going to spend your life auditioning. And that's even after you've been on Broadway and won a Tony Award. It never ends! See the section, "'I Hope I Get It' — Auditioning" earlier in this chapter on how to audition.

TIP

When you get a chance, go to Backstage.com and see what auditions are out there and go to them *all*. It doesn't have to be a role you're perfect for. You just need the experience of auditioning, so it gets more comfortable for you.

But what are the other ways that help you be a pro? Keep reading.

Getting an agent

Just so you know, there are no set ways to get an agent. But many different ways have worked, and here are a few:

>> Have a nice photo postcard printed and send it to every agent in your city asking for a meeting. Print your contact and a link to your website that has your resumé and hopefully some clips of you performing.

>> Do a local production and invite agents to come see it.

Ask other people in the cast if they invited agents. If any have seen the show, send them a friendly email or letter or call them and let them know who you played in the show and ask for a meeting.

>> Ask your friends with agents to recommend you.

>> If you auditioned for a show and got an offer (YAS!), call an agent and ask them to negotiate the contract. That can start your relationship.

You can also check out the second edition of *Breaking into Acting For Dummies* by Larry Garrison and Wallace Wang (John Wiley & Sons, Inc.) for more information.

REMEMBER

The main jobs of an agent are as follows:

>> To get you auditions

>> To negotiate your contracts

Often, an agent is just trying to convince a casting director to see you. So, don't fret if you can't get an agent right away. If a casting director already likes you, you can eliminate the middleman. That means go to as many auditions as possible and get those casting people to like you! The casting people will start to know and call you in, and you won't need an agent to beg them. Again, it comes back to learning how to audition well.

SETH SPEAKS

Getting an agent can help, but it's ain't easy. The good news? It's not a necessity. Don't despair if you can't get one. My friend, the aforementioned Debra Monk, co-wrote and co-starred in the Broadway musical *Pump Boys and Dinettes*. The show was nominated for a Tony Award, and she was one of the four people in the show who performed at the Tony Awards. But she still couldn't get an agent!

Becoming a member of Equity

Joining the actors union (Actors' Equity) used to be almost more difficult than getting an agent. However, a movement called open access is beginning May 2023, so go to ActorsEquity.org and see what the requirements are these days. Besides open access, if you're a member of certain sister unions, you're eligible to join.

REMEMBER

Sometimes people don't want to join the union too early. Maybe they're getting tons of non-Equity regional shows, and they want to make money and hone their craft before they join the union. After you have your Equity card, you won't be allowed to work in a non-Equity show.

So why join? Because a union protects you. A non-Equity show can rehearse with no breaks, make you sleep anywhere they want, have no air conditioner, heat, or running water backstage, and the list goes on. They may even stop paying you, and you'd have to hire your own lawyer to get your money. Of course, that can all happen in an Equity production (and it has), but when the show is an Equity show, the union will take on your complaint and hopefully solve it!

All hail the theatrical unions!

Working a side job

You're a professional actor! That means you make all your money performing, right?

Wrong. No matter how pro you are, sometimes you won't be working. Performers, no matter how successful, often have side jobs. Theatre work simply isn't consistent. Really, *all* of show business work isn't consistent. As a matter of fact, Chandra Wilson was starring as Dr. Miranda Bailey on *Grey's Anatomy* and kept her side job for the first two seasons, "just in case!"

You can usually always find work as a restaurant server, a receptionist, or a nanny. They're all great ways to make money because they pay well and they provide flexibility so one can leave for auditions. If you have some office skills, register with a temp company! You can get work on the days you don't have auditions. If you can, become friendly with the people who employ you. It's wonderful to have a side job that lets you take a few months (or years) off when you get a show and then come right back.

SETH SPEAKS

Christine Ebersole was working as a waitress in her early 20s when she was suddenly offered the role of the maid in *Angel Street*. *Angel Street* is the play the film *Gaslight* was based on, and the maid was played by Angela Lansbury in the film. Christine told me that she bid farewell to "all you little people" at her restaurant she was going to be in a Broadway show. Well, the show closed *very* quickly, and Christine admits that two weeks later she was at the restaurant once again, *begging* for her job back!

The best kind of side job is when you have a skill you can use to make money and therefore you can control your own hours. Taking photos, doing hair and makeup, acting coaching, and teaching piano are all wonderful skills to cultivate. And, most importantly, don't be ashamed of having a side job. Theatre notoriously doesn't pay well, and side jobs provide us performers the funding so we can continue to make art!

The Part of Tens

Read about ten careers in the theatre (besides being onstage) and how you can get hired.

Discover ten popular songs that you probably don't know are from musicals.

Recognize ten celebrities who started in musical theatre before moving onto music, TV, and movies.

Chapter **14**

Ten (Plus) Songs You Didn't Realize Came from Musical Theatre

M any a Broadway song have ear-wormed their way into people's brains, becoming solid fixtures in popular culture. Many people have heard "Sunrise, Sunset" at a wedding and thought of their high school production of *Fiddler on the Roof* or when they hear someone at a karaoke bar haul out "All That Jazz," they immediately think of Chita Rivera (or Bebe Neuwirth or Catherine Zeta-Jones) in *Chicago*.

However, the songs in this chapter have become part of many people's lives not realizing that these magical lyrics and melodies started on Broadway! I'm here to rectify that, for at least the songs that made it onto my list . . .

"My Funny Valentine"

Most people think of it as an American standard love song written for Valentine's Day. But it's by Rodgers and Hart and originated in the musical *Babes in Arms*. It's indeed a love song, but not written specifically for February 14th. Instead, one of the female leads, Billie, sings it to the male romantic lead, Val. Why the title of the song? Because his full name is Valentine!

"All the Things You Are"

This is another songbook classic but not written for a 1940s crooner. It was actually written for the Broadway musical *Very Warm for May*.

Anybody?

Nobody. It ran less than two months in 1940, but it gave audiences this gorgeous song!

"Edelweiss"

Yes, most people know it's performed in *The Sound of Music*, but many people think it's actually a famous Austrian folk song that was added to the show. It isn't. Rodgers and Hammerstein composed it for the musical. Sadly, it was the last song Hammerstein wrote.

"As Time Goes By"

The world knows it from the film *Casablanca*, but this song was first introduced on Broadway in a short-lived musical called *Everybody's Welcome* that featured a score by Sammy Fain and Irving Kahal. *However*, they didn't write this classic song! The show had "additional material" by other composers, and one of those songs was "As Time Goes By" by Herman Hupfeld.

"I'll Never Fall in Love Again"

Yes, you can hear a great recording of the Burt Bachrach/Hal David sung by Dionne Warwick on the radio (specifically SiriusXM's '70s on 7), but it was first performed in *Promises, Promises* in Act Two. Chuck (Jerry Orbach) discovers Fran

(Jill O'Hara) in his apartment after she attempts suicide because her heart has been broken by a married man (who uses Chuck's apartment for his liaisons). Chuck helps Fran feel better, she picks up a guitar, and they sing the pretty duet!

"And I Am Telling You"

You would think a lot of people know this song is from *Dreamgirls*, but a lot of people don't! And even the people who *do* know it's from Broadway might not know why the title of the song begins with an "And." "And"? It's the first word of the sentence! Why begin a sentence with "and" when there's nothing before it to which the singer is adding?

Well, in fact, the character of Effie *is* adding to something. At the end of Act One, she's kicked out of the group for acting out. Various characters have a long fight, all of which is completely sung and, near the end, Effie sings, "For seven years I sung with you, I was your sister! And now you're telling me it's all over." They agree. "And now we're telling you it's all over." She counters with, "And now I'm telling you I ain't going!" Which leads to "And I am telling you I'm not going . . .!" Hence the "and"!

"Send in the Clowns"

Judy Collins made the song famous, but it was first sung by Glynnis Johns in *A Little Night Music*.

SETH SPEAKS

While *A Little Night Music* was in rehearsals, Stephen Sondheim still hadn't written the 11-o'clock number for leading man Len Cariou. Len and Glynis Johns felt that their characters would act differently than what was in the original script because the show had evolved during rehearsals, so director Hal Prince suggested that they improvise a scene and have Sondheim watch it because that might help him finally write Len's big number. Sondheim came to the studio and watched the two do the scene they had made up. The next day, Sondheim came in and gave good news and bad news: The good news was he finally wrote the big 11-o'clock number. The bad news (for Len) was that the song was now for Glynis. Ouch! Yes, it was "Send in the Clowns," and became Sondheim's most well-known song!

"Aquarius"/"Let the Sunshine In"

"Aquarius" is the very first song in *Hair* and "Let The Sunshine In" is the very last. The wonderful group "The Fifth Dimension" had the amazing idea to combine *both* songs and their version became an international hit!

"Come Rain or Come Shine"

While researching what songs would surprise people to find out were from Broadway shows, *I* discovered that "Come Rain or Come Shine" is from a Broadway musical. Who knew? I always thought it was an American classic like "It Had to Be You" or "Witchcraft." Turns out, it's from *St. Louis Woman*. Writing this book has been educational for me!

"Til There Was You" . . . and a Few More

Here are a few more songs that I promised you in the chapter's title. I feel *a lot* of people know these songs are from musicals, but I keep hearing from people who were shocked when they found out:

>> "Til There Was You" wasn't a Beatles song first. It's from Meredith Willson's *The Music Man*.

>> "Give My Regards to Broadway" isn't just an old chestnut; it's from George M. Cohan's *Little Johnny Jones*.

>> "Put on a Happy Face" isn't just a precursor to men walking by you and aggressively asking you to "Smile. Why don't you smile?" It's a joyous song by Charles Strouse and Lee Adams and was sung by Dick Van Dyke in Broadway in *Bye Bye Birdie*.

>> "One Night in Bangkok," which I saved for last because it does *not* scream Broadway on any level. It was constantly on the radio in the '80s and was super hip because it had singing *and* rapping. Back while I was doing the robot to it in college, I had no idea it was from the musical *Chess* by Benny and Bjorn (from ABBA) and Tim Rice. "I get my kicks above the waist . . ." Classic!

Chapter 15

Ten Celebs Who Started in Musical Theatre

So many stars have begun their careers singing and dancing on Broadway that I couldn't possibly include all of them. You may have known about a few of these already, but I'm guessing you wouldn't guess all of them . . . or am I underestimating your musical theatre/TV star knowledge? Read on to find out!

Nancy Walker

Yes, I'm going old school. Those of you who grew up in the 1970s remember *The Mary Tyler Moore Show* and Mary's best friend Rhoda Morgenstern. Rhoda's mom, Ida Morgenstern, was played by Nancy Walker. You may also remember her as Rosie, the waitress, who did those paper towel commercials. This TV stalwart got her big break on Broadway in 1944 when she was one of the three female leads in *On the Town* by Leonard Bernstein and Betty Comden and Adolph Green. I was shocked when I first heard what a sassy singer she was! And, amazingly, her performance is preserved on YouTube www.youtube.com/watch?v=uAxxGJ1Yesk.

Valerie Harper

On *The Mary Tyler Moore Show*, Valerie Harper who played Mary's best friend Rhoda also began her career on Broadway. She was in the dancing chorus when shows had singers in one group and dancers in another (see Chapter 9 for more about that division). Harper danced in shows like *Take Me Along*, *Li'l Abner* (as well as the film), and *Wildcat* (with Lucille Ball). As a matter of fact, around ten years after that show, Harper won the Emmy Award for her portrayal of Rhoda, and Ball presented it! You can watch the clip on YouTube at www.youtube.com/watch?v=qwRDdCKgtr0. It's so sweet! She warmly reminds Ball that she was in her ensemble.

One of the most impressive things I found out about Harper was what she did when she was in the show *Subways Are for Sleeping*. The actors playing the porters in that show were white, even though the real-life porters on New York trains were Black. Casting them as white took away opportunities from Black actors and, because of that injustice, there were protests in front of the theatre. One of the people protesting was Harper — even though she was in the show and could have been fired. Remember, this was in the days before *just cause*, which requires a show to provide only union-approved reasons for firing an actor. This was when an actor could be fired for any reason. Harper would hold signs in front of the theatre . . . and then go in at half hour and do her show. I love that she protested for something she believed in even though she could have lost her job over it!

Christian Slater

Before he was in films, Christian Slater was in a Broadway musical. Not a long running musical but a musical that was featured on the Tony Awards. Yes, you can see him center stage in the Tony Award segment from *Merlin*. The show starred Broadway legend Chita Rivera and soon-to-be Broadway superstar Nathan Lane. And Merlin himself was played by world class magician Doug Henning. Watch! Check out www.youtube.com/watch?v=0fiS_MZ-26o.

SETH SPEAKS

ABRACADABRA — MAGIC GONE AWRY

Nathan Lane told me a story I love: One night, during the run of *Merlin,* magician Doug Henning was regaling Nathan with magic-gone-awry stories. Doug had been doing a Vegas show, and the final act was turning his wife into a tiger. He finished the trick but noticed that the chain attached to the tiger . . . was broken! He told Nathan that the rest happened in slow motion. The tiger started prowling toward the audience who then began screaming. Also, because it was a New Year's Eve show, the audience was packed with celebrities. This took place in the 1970s, so I'm imagining an audience filled with hysterical Loni Andersons, Bonnie Franklins, and Gabe Kaplans. Doug grabbed onto the tiger's chain and started yanking the tiger backward.

Naturally, the tiger turned and started to advance on Doug. Suddenly, the tiger leapt on top of him . . . and licked his face. I, of course, thought that part was adorable until Nathan explained that tigers clean their food before they eat it. OMG! The tiger then put Doug's entire head inside his mouth! Doug was so petrified that he fainted and because what the tiger considered prey suddenly seemed so limp and odd, it let go of his head. Doug told Nathan that the next thing he remembered was waking up in his dressing room with Bob Hope standing above him saying, "That's the best finale I've ever seen!"

Sara Ramirez

I knew Sara Ramirez for years as a musical theatre actress, but my daughter is a *Grey's Anatomy* fan and was shocked when I told her Ramirez was from Broadway. So, if you only know Ramirez as Grey Sloan Memorial Hospital's Dr. Callie Torres or as Che Diaz on the *Sex and the City* reboot, *And Just Like That*, you may be shocked to know that she did her fair share of musicals on Broadway. However, for the first ten years of her career, she was cast in Broadway shows that didn't run very long: *The Capeman, Fascinating Rhythm,* and *A Class Act* were her first three shows.

Finally, she had had it. She was sick of struggling and living in an apartment with a bathroom down the hall and was quitting the biz. She didn't want to stress about money anymore. I was so upset because I knew she was a super talent. Well, lo and behold, just like the "As soon as you don't want a boyfriend, you'll get a boyfriend" maxim, as soon as she thought about leaving the business, she got cast as The Lady of the Lake in *Spamalot* and then won the Tony Award. And that immediately led to her joining *Grey's Anatomy.* TV has now had her for years so I demand she come back to Broadway. She is missed!

Sarah Jessica Parker

Carrie Bradshaw from *Sex and the City*, also known as Sarah Jessica Parker, began on Broadway in the musical *Annie*. Interestingly, she was first just a kid in the audience watching the show with her dad who told her, "You're not Annie material." A little while later, she was playing the role! #FatherDoesntKnowBest.

Parker was initially cast as July (the orphan who doesn't have much to do, according to her) as well as the Annie understudy. The big blizzard of 1978 hit on her very first performance as July, and many cast members weren't able to make it to the show. She was getting ready to go on for the orphan who "doesn't have much to do" when she was told she was instead going on as Annie — the title role. She hadn't even done the show in her regular role! However, they decided to hold the curtain to see if Andrea McArdle's train would make it from Philly, and thankfully it did, so Parker didn't play Annie that performance. But the show must go on, as they say, and it did with half the orphans missing.

Later in the run while Parker was still playing an orphan, Sandy Faison (who played Grace) gave her notice. Shelly Bruce, who had taken over the role of Annie after McArdle left, was sick on Faison's last show, so Parker, her understudy, went on. The timing was perfect because all the creative team happened to be in the audience to bid Faison farewell and therefore saw Parker's performance. They thought she was great, and that's how she became the third Annie.

Also, FYI, Parker was the oldest Annie (14) when she landed the role. It worked because she's super short. But, like most adolescents, she began to grow. In her case, she grew two inches really quickly. She remembers one of the stage managers telling her, not that long after she began playing the role, that they were going to start looking for her replacement as soon as possible. However, after he dropped that bomb, he told her to just "put that on the back burner." Yay! It's easy to play a role knowing that you're on the verge of being replaced because your own body is betraying you.

SETH SPEAKS

I asked Sarah during a concert we did in Provincetown if she was devastated when her run ended, and she said she actually wasn't. Her hair had been dyed red for the show, and she said that she immediately went out and dyed it back to her "natural dark brown color." She then looked at the audience, mortified, and said, "I mean . . . blondish brown."

John Travolta

Before his TV fame in *Welcome Back, Kotter*, John Travolta was on Broadway in *Over Here!*, a musical that starred The Andrews Sisters. As a matter of fact, you can see him dancing (in a number featuring the late, great Ann Reinking) on the 1974 Tony Awards (www.youtube.com/watch?v=5K9GP8zNgII).

Even before that, he was cast in the national tour of *Grease* where he played Doody, the sweetest of the Greasers, who sings "Those Magic Changes." He was only 18 years old, and the cast remembers thinking, "It'll never happen" when he told them, "One day, I'm going to play Danny Zuko." It happened all right!

Ariana Grande

I was playing in the pit of *Mamma Mia!* off and on, and I met one of the ensemble members named Frankie Grande. I thought he was so talented and so funny, and we became pals and worked together on a lot of benefits. He told me that his sister was trying to break into singing, and I thought it was "cute." He was super excited when she got cast in a Broadway show that featured only teenagers as the cast, and I remember seeing her photo on the promotional material. The show was *13*, and it became a launching pad for a bunch of the leads who went on to various Disney shows. Ariana Grande was cast in the show *Victorious*, and it led to her incredible recording career. But she hasn't forgotten Broadway. She returned to her Broadway roots when she played Penny in the *Hairspray* live performance on NBC and as of the writing of this book plays the role of Glinda in the film *Wicked*!

Nick Jonas

Nick Jonas began as a typical Broadway actor kid, going from show to show. He was a Gavroche in *Les Misérables*, a Chip in *Beauty and the Beast*, and one of the kids in the Bernadette Peters revival of *Annie, Get Your Gun*. After his recording fame, he came back to Broadway and replaced Daniel Radcliffe in the revival of *How to Succeed in Business without Really Trying*. And he came back to *Les Miz*, but as an adult! You can see him as Marius in the London filmed version (www.youtube.com/watch?v=vMZQXhg4MWQ).

Hair: The Show, Not a Performer

Yes, *Hair* is indeed the name of a show, but the show has been the launching pad for so many stars that I put them together in one entry. If you listen to the original cast album and hear the song "Black Boys," you'd be hearing it sung by Annie Hall! Yes, Diane Keaton was in the original production of *Hair*. And "Two Out of Three Ain't Bad" and "Paradise by the Dashboard Light" singer Meat Loaf was also in *Hair* before he hit the airwaves. And, for you *Love Boat* fans, Ted Lange was in *Hair*. Yes! Isaac the bartender! And before *Sex, Lies, and Videotapes, American*

Beauty, and *The O.C.,* Peter Gallagher made his Broadway debut in the 1970s revival of *Hair.*

Fun Reveal: An Almost Was

Let me qualify by saying that although this person *almost* had her start on Broadway, I still think she belongs on this list. Back in the early 1980s, there was a Broadway musical called *Rock 'N Roll: The First 5,000 Years.* It was a jukebox musical before the current trend of jukebox musicals, and it told the story of rock 'n' roll juxtaposed with what was happening in history. Every great singer from the radio was represented, and Tony Award winner Lillias White played Gloria Gaynor and Aretha Franklin and she told me this story.

SETH SPEAKS

The cast member who was going to sing the Janis Joplin hits decided to quit the show during rehearsals. Why? She wanted to have a recording career. Lillias told me that everyone in the cast was basically asking, "Why would you quit a Broadway show for a recording career that hasn't even begun?" But this person was insistent. She quit the show to become a recording artist. End of story: *Rock 'N Roll: The First 5,000 Years* was ahead of its time and only ran a week, and the person who quit the show got rid of her last name and is known as simply Madonna. For rizzle!

Index

A

Aaron, Hank, 25
ABBA, 103–104, 137, 203, 303, 368
Abbott, George, 36, 227
Acito, Tim, 220
acting skills, 343–345
acting teachers and coaches, 343
Actors' Equity, 34, 93, 154, 307, 337, 361–362
Adams, Lee, 57, 207, 368
Addams Family, The, 214
Adelaide Cabaret Festival, 150
Adler, Richard, 36–37, 227
Aduba, Uzo, 59
Africa, 149
agents, 360–361
Ahrens, Lynn, 84, 88, 207–208
Aida, 96, 203
Ailey, Alvin, 38
Ain't Misbehavin', 10, 211, 303, 333
Ain't Too Proud, 13, 303
Aladdin, 47, 93, 109, 160, 185, 204, 304
Alberghetti, Anna Maria, 243, 249
Aldredge, Theoni, 235
Alexander, Jason, 82, 313
All about Eve, 57, 97
All Shook Up, 299, 303
Allen, Debbie, 12, 52
Allen, Peter, 115, 249
Allesendrini, Gerard, 48
alley stages, 173–174
Almost Famous, 13, 206, 300
alternates, 264, 323
Alvarez, David, 254
Ambassador Theatre, 309
American Graffiti, 60
American in Paris, An, 27, 147
Anastasia, 208, 305
& Juliet, 137, 299, 303

Anderson, Benny, 203–204, 368
Anderson-Lopez, Kristen, 207
Andrews, Julie, 38, 44, 86–87
Andrews Sisters, The, 372
Angel Street, 362
angels, 239
Angels in America, 114
Annie, 65–67, 127, 136, 195, 207, 220, 235–236, 243, 255, 304, 327, 333, 336, 372
Annie Get Your Gun, 211–212, 301, 304, 373
Anything Goes, 30–31, 33, 213, 251, 330
Apartment, The, 54, 300
Applause, 57–58, 97, 157, 207, 212
Apple Tree, The, 298, 301
Applegate, Christina, 52
Arlen, Harold, 38
Armisen, Fred, 283
Armstrong, Louis, 49
Arthur, Beatrice, 51–52
Ashman, Howard, 94, 109, 204–205
Asia, 147–148
assistant stage managers (ASMs), 287
Astin, Skylar, 107
auditions, 312–313, 346–350
Australia, 149–150
Avenue Q, 100, 105–107, 133, 206–207, 209, 329
Avian, Bob, 54
awards, 330–338
Azaria, Hank, 101

B

Babes in Arms, 210, 365
Baby, 133, 211
Bacall, Lauren, 57–58
Bachrach, Burt, 54–55, 152, 303, 366
Back to Broadway, 47
Back to the Future, 141
backer's auditions, 307

backstage understudies, 267–269

Backstage.com, 360

Bad Cinderella, 83

Bailey, Pearl, 49, 53

Baker, Josephine, 27

Baker's Wife, The, 151, 196, 201, 226

balconies, 176, 178–179

Ball, Lucille, 51, 206, 370

Ball of Confusion, 1

ballad operas, 21

ballads, 130

Ballard, Florence, 77

Ballard, Kaye, 156

Banderas, Antonio, 69

Band's Visit, The, 98, 102, 300

Barbeau, Adrienne, 61

Bareilles, Sara, 115, 213, 330

Barrett, Brent, 199, 221

Bart, Lionel, 47

Beach, Gary, 331

Beach Boys, 303

Bean, Shoshana, 59

Beane, Douglas Carter, 102

Beatles, 368

Beautiful: The Carole King Musical, 111–112, 303, 312

Beauty and the Beast, 93–95, 160, 204–205, 263, 304, 323, 373

Bechdel, Alison, 115

Beechman, Laurie, 71, 327

Beef & Boards Dinner Theatre, 158

Beetlejuice, 235, 300

Beggar's Opera, The, 21

Belafonte, Harry, 38

Bells Are Ringing, 201

Benanti, Laura, 47

Benjamin, Nell, 101

Bennett, Michael, 42, 54, 56, 76–77

Berlanti Family Foundation, 121

Berlin, Irving, 9, 210, 212

Bernstein, Leonard, 10–12, 32–33, 40, 125, 229, 369

Best Little Whorehouse in Texas, The, 9, 201–202

Big, 102, 300

Billy Elliot, 103, 254

Birch, Pat, 224

Birdcage, The, 78

Bishop, Kelly, 65

Bissell, Richard, 302

Black Crook, The, 24, 26

Blair, Linda, 90

Blair, Pam, 259

Blake, Eubie, 27

Blankenbuehler, Andy, 108

Blickenstaff, Heidi, 149

Block, Stephanie J., 159, 358

blocking, 265

Bock, Jerry, 47–48

body microphones, 68, 243, 273–274

Boggess, Sierra, 255–256

book (libretto; script), 8, 10, 28–29

Book of Mormon, The, 110–111, 206–207, 235, 298, 333, 336

book writers, 14

Boone, Debbie, 90

Booth Tarkington Civic Theatre, 161–162

Borstelmann, Jim, 266–267

Boston, Gretha, 253

Boublil, Alain, 146, 210

Bowen, Jeff, 149

bows, 137, 257–258

box seats, 177

Boy from Oz, The, 249, 264

Boyfriend, The, 69

Brady, Wayne, 159, 358

Breakfast at Tiffany's, 170

Brenner, Yul, 34–35, 191

Brice, Fanny, 24

Bridges of Madison County, The, 196, 302

Brigadoon, 208

Bring It On, 221

Broadway, 140–142

Broadway Album, The, 39, 68

Broadway Cares/Equity Fights AIDS (BCEFA), 2, 329

Broderick, Matthew, 90–91, 98, 111, 136, 252–253

Brooks, Mel, 98

Brooks Atkinson Theatre, 38

Brown, Georgia, 46

Brown, Jason Robert, 1, 214

Bruce, Shelly, 372

Brunell, Catherine, 262

brush-up rehearsals, 279, 321

Bryson, Peabo, 204

Buckley, Betty, 72, 80, 86, 141, 153, 159, 255, 278, 318, 358

Bullets over Broadway, 120

Bundy, Laura Bell, 101

burlesque, 24

Burnett, Carol, 24

Burns, Andréa, 263

Burstein, Danny, 118

Burton, Richard, 44

Busker Alley, 91

Butler, Kerry, 205, 274, 277, 312, 329

button, 353

Butz, Norbert Leo, 261

Bye Bye Birdie, 43, 131, 136, 207, 368

C

Cabaret, 50–51, 88, 91–92, 113, 126, 145, 192–193, 195, 209, 302, 353

cabaret acts, 359

Cagney, James, 26

Caird, John, 74

Call Me Madam, 212, 301, 337

Callaway, Cab, 83

Callaway, Liz, 47, 103, 313

callbacks, 347

Camelot, 44, 127

Cameron Crowe, 208

Can-Can, 35–36, 62, 213

Candide, 125, 341

Cape Playhouse, 157

Capeman, The, 101, 371

Capitol Theatre, 149

Cariou, Len, 57, 68, 367

Carnegie Hall, 322–323

Carnegie Mellon University, 163

Carnival, 54, 243, 249, 300

Carousel, 97, 109, 111, 202, 332, 340–341

Carrie, 261, 278

Carroll, David, 199

Carroll, Diahann, 46, 49, 86

Carter, Nell, 211, 333

Casablanca, 366

Casey, Warren, 298

cast albums, 168

casting directors, 218–219

Castree, Paul, 91, 159, 265, 274, 278, 337, 358

Catch Me If You Can, 205

Cates, Kristy, 260

Cats, 25–26, 64, 70–72, 83, 121, 141, 145, 203, 243, 245, 255, 318

Cavanaugh, Michael, 104

cell phones, 186–187

Cerveris, Michael, 85, 143

Champion, Gower, 76, 136, 276, 316

changing patches, 268

Channing, Carol, 48–49, 316, 331

Charley's Aunt, 34

Charnin, Martin, 66, 207, 220

Chase, David, 282

chemistry calls, 347, 352

Chenoweth, Kristin, 55, 150, 159, 257, 293, 304, 312, 330, 340, 358

Cher, 303

Cher Show, The, 303

Chess, 13, 59, 203, 275, 368

Chicago, 11, 25, 50, 52, 61–63, 75, 84, 90, 127, 142, 150, 160, 177, 209, 236, 252, 309, 330, 353

Children of Eden, 201, 298–299

choreographers, 14, 221, 223–224

choreography, defined, 10

Chorus Line, A, 4, 11, 60, 62–65, 70–71, 83, 90, 121, 123, 126, 129–130, 141, 143–144, 147, 163, 194, 235, 259, 263, 285, 330, 333, 336, 354

Christie, Agatha, 145

Christmas Story, A, 209–210

Chronicle of a Death Foretold, 87

Cilento, Wayne, 85

Cinderella, 235, 300–301

Circle in the Square Theatre, 115, 174, 309

City of Angels, 82–83, 125, 206

Clark, Petula, 86

Clark, Victoria, 91, 235, 248, 261

Class Act, A, 101, 371

Close, Glenn, 86, 253

Closer Than Ever, 211

clothing, 170–171

Coco, 57

Cohan, George M., 26, 368

Coleman, Cy, 52, 82–83, 125, 206

Collette, Toni, 214

Collins, Judy, 367

Color Purple, The, 196, 302

Comden, Betty, 32–33, 57, 115, 197, 207, 212, 369

Come Fly Away, 303

Come from Away, 160, 301

comic timing, 344

community theatre, 161–162, 359

Company, 12, 56, 58, 113, 132, 171, 215, 260

company managers, 15

composers, 14, 197–198, 202–216, 220

concept albums, 59, 69

concert versions, 330

conductors, 14, 229, 290–291

Connell, Jane, 51

Connick, Harry, Jr., 36

Contact, 8

Cook, Barbara, 39, 47

Cooper, Lilli, 107

copyists, 291

Cordero, Nick, 120

costume designers, 15, 221–222, 232–235

costumes crew, 280–284

Covid-19, 83, 117–118, 120–122, 323, 327

Cradle Will Rock, The, 74

Craig, Daniel, 330

Craig, David, 345

Crawley, Brian, 207

Crazy for You, 27, 303

creative team, 307–308

Creel, Gavin, 47, 143, 326, 333–334

crews, 15

Criss, Darren, 44

Criswell, Kim, 130

critics, 317

Crowe, Cameron, 13, 206

cruise ships, 159–160

Cry Baby, 121

Crystal, Billy, 205

Cumming, Alan, 92, 193

Curry, Tim, 101

Curtains, 195

D

Daly, Tyne, 4

d'Amboise, Charlotte, 52

Damn Yankees, 37, 52, 127–128, 245

dance, 10–12, 31

dance breaks, 129

dance calls, 347

dance captains, 279–280

Dancin', 104

dancing skills, 345–346

Daniele, Graciela, 84, 88

Danieley, Jason, 358

Daniels, William, 254

David, Hal, 54–55, 152, 366

Davis, Bette, 57

Davis, Ossie, 38

Dawes, Dominique, 90

Day in Hollywood/A Night in the Ukraine, A, 135, 198, 252

de Jésus, Robin, 273

De Shields, André, 66

Dear Evan Hansen, 10, 59, 116–117, 121, 160, 201, 209, 235, 250

degrees, 354–355

Dennie, Ronald, 259

Dennis, Patrick, 51, 302

designer runs, 320

Devil Wears Prada, The, 302

Diana, 302

Díaz, Justino, 130

Dickens, Charles, 47, 79

Die Fledermaus, 22

Different Worlds, 23

Diggs, Taye, 87, 214

Diller, Phyllis, 49

dinner theatre, 158

Dion, Celine, 204

directors, 14, 220–223

Disaster! 265, 272–274, 276–277, 281, 329

Disney, 93–96, 159–160, 304, 358
Do I Hear a Waltz? 202
Doctorow, E. L., 88
Dogfight, 209
Don't Tell Mama, 2
downstage, 352
Downtown Abbey, 281
Drama Desk Awards, 334–335
Drama League Awards, 335
Dreamgirls, 54, 77–78, 133, 211, 229, 234–235,
    241–242, 291, 298, 330, 341, 358, 367
dressers, 281–282
dressing rooms, 255–256
Drowsy Chaperone, The, 145, 252
dry tech rehearsals, 239
Du Prez, John, 101
Dubin, Al, 303
duets, 131
dummy versions, 205
Duplex in the Village, The, 344

E

Easter Bonnet Competition, 329
Easton, Sheena, 90
Eastwood, Clint, 302
Ebb, Fred, 17, 23, 42, 50–51, 85, 92, 192–193, 196,
    208–209, 353
Ebersole, Christine, 253, 362
Edelman, Gregg, 130
Eder, Linda, 262
Edinburgh Fringe Festival, 165
Educational Theatre Association, 165
Edward, Blake, 86
Edward, Sherman, 55
Eisner, Michael, 323
Electric Light Orchestra, 102
electronic tickets, 184
11 o'clock numbers, 41, 135–136
Elliman, Yvonne, 59
Elliot, T. S., 204
Ellis, Scott, 322
Encore Series, 90, 142, 330
ensembles, 16, 258–259, 355

Entertainment Community Fund, The (Actors Fund),
    54, 77, 121–122
entr'acte, 134
entrance applause, 256–257
Equity. *See* Actors' Equity
Equity Principal Auditions (EPAs), 313
Errico, Melissa, 143
Esparza, Raúl, 143
Esplanade Theatre on the Bay, 148
Eternal Sunshine of the Spotless Mind, 4
Europe, 145–147
Evans, Harvey, 29, 35
Everybody's Talking about Jamie, 333
Everybody's Welcome, 366
Evita, 14, 50, 59, 68–69, 145, 162, 203–204, 232, 247,
    250–251, 264, 301, 333
exit music, 137
Eyen, Tom, 211

F

Fain, Sammy, 366
Faison, Sandy, 372
Falsettos, 10, 14, 131, 142, 196
Fame, 164
Fantasticks, The, 54, 142
Fascinatin' Rhythm, 27, 101, 371
featured actors, 15
Féla, 301
Ferguson, Jesse Tyler, 33
Fiddler on the Roof, 48, 82, 133, 160, 196, 199, 302,
    329, 355
Fields, Dorothy, 52, 211
Fields, W. C., 24
Fierstein, Harvey, 78, 100, 196, 246–247, 329
Fifth Dimension, The, 53, 368
fight directors, 221
film adaptations, 160
filmed live performances, 160
film-to-musical genre, 97–103
finales
  Act One, 132–133
  Act Two, 136–137
Finn, William, 10, 195
Fiorello! 250

Fiorello H. LaGuardia High School, 164

Fisher, Joely, 90

Fitzgerald, Chris, 274

Five Guys Named Moe, 261

Flaherty, Stephen, 84, 88, 207–208

Flavin, Tim, 130

Flower Drum Song, 202

fly rail crew, 275

Foa, Barrett, 59

Follies, 56, 131–132, 156, 225, 330

Fontana, Santino, 348

food and drinks, 169, 185–187

Footloose, 300

Forbidden Broadway, 48, 92, 238

Ford Foundation, 155

Forever Plaid, 142

Forrest, Robert, 198

42nd Street, 76, 129, 276, 303, 340

Fosse, Bob, 34, 36–37, 50, 52, 60, 62, 193, 227, 280

Foster, Sutton, 30, 52, 99, 143, 161, 186, 220, 262, 272, 326, 330, 340, 350

Four Seasons, The, 105, 303

Franklin, Bonnie, 57

freezing, 316–317

Friedman, David, 293

fringe events, 164–165

Frozen, 207

Full Monty, The, 98, 102, 156, 196, 242, 292, 300, 341

Fun Home, 99, 114–115, 174, 207, 305

Funny Face, 26

Funny Girl, 24, 80, 125, 128, 133, 135, 141, 162, 202, 243, 250, 255–256

Funny Thing Happened on the Way to the Forum, A, 42, 45–46, 82, 126, 200, 215, 267, 305

G

Gad, Josh, 110, 336

Gallagher, John, Jr., 107

Gallagher, Peter, 60, 357, 374

Garber, Victor, 59, 340

Garland, Judy, 61

Garrison, Larry, 361

Gaslight, 362

Gasteyer, Ana, 283–284

Gattelli, Christopher, 54, 280

Gay, John, 21

Gelbart, Larry, 45

Gemignani, Paul, 81, 229

Genarro, Liza, 40

Genarro, Peter, 40

Genée, Richard, 22

general managers (GMs), 14, 308–309

Gentleman Prefer Blondes, 202, 337

Gentleman's Guide to Love and Murder, A, 156

Gere, Richard, 60

Gershwin, George and Ira, 26–27, 29, 303

Gershwin Theatre, 309

Ghost, 102

Gigi, 208

Gilbert, W. S., 22

Gilford, Jack, 45

Gillette, Anita, 249

Girl Crazy, 29

Gleason, Jackie, 196

Godspell, 59–60, 298

Gold, 302

Gold, Andrew, 38

Golden Age musicals, 12–13, 22, 31–42

Goldsberry, Renée Elise, 120

Gonzalez, Mandy, 223, 321

Good Vibrations, 303

Goodman Theatre, 155

Gordon, Ruth, 50

Got Tu Go Disco, 13

Goulet, Robert, 44

Graff, Randy, 83

Grammy Awards, 335–336

Grand Hotel, 198–199, 221, 237

Grande, Ariana, 373

Grande, Frankie, 373

Gray, Gilda, 24

Grease, 59–60, 70, 108, 157, 201, 224, 243, 269, 293, 298, 356–357, 372–373

Grease!!!, 89–90, 99, 172, 246, 257, 293

Green, Adolph, 32–33, 57, 115, 197, 207, 212, 369

Green, Amanda, 206

Green Grow the Lilacs, 151, 299

Grey, Joel, 26, 50–51, 193

Grey Gardens, 301

Griffin, Kathy, 30

Griffith, Bobby, 227

Groff, Jonathan, 107, 330

Grossman, Larry, 201

Groundhog Day, 145, 333

group numbers, 132

Guettel, Adam, 202, 248

Guevera, Ché, 68–69

Guthrie Theatre, 155

Guy, Jasmine, 90

Guys and Dolls, 12, 34, 62, 88–89, 128, 130, 134, 136, 143, 215, 233, 250, 252, 261, 329, 337, 357

gypsies, 64

Gypsy, 16, 24, 31, 40–41, 82, 125, 128, 135, 161, 192–194, 201–202, 301, 348

H

Hackaday, Hal, 201

Hadestown, 66, 300, 341

Haffner, Karl, 22

Hair, 9, 13, 43, 53–54, 108, 141, 243, 357, 368, 373

hair artists, 15, 245–248

hair supervisors, 280–284

hairdressers, 284–286

Hairspray, 99–100, 102, 129, 143, 160, 195–196, 205, 246, 285, 300, 329, 332, 373

half-hour calls, 325–326, 353

Hall, Carol, 202

Hamilton, 9, 14, 20, 29–30, 39, 64, 75, 95, 108–109, 118–120, 130, 141, 153, 160, 177, 181, 213, 224, 257, 302, 336

Hamlisch, Marvin, 126, 131, 203

Hammerstein, Mary, 202

Hammerstein, Oscar, II, 20, 28, 30–31, 33–34, 46, 92, 144, 151, 194, 202, 210, 215, 300, 366

Haney, Carol, 36

Hanks, Tom, 47

Hanson, Grey, 152

Harburg, Yip, 38

Harnick, Sheldon, 47–48

Harper, Valerie, 206, 370

Harrison, Rex, 38, 51, 340

Hart, Lorenz, 210, 365

Hately, Linzi, 278

Hayes, Sean, 55

Headley, Heather, 77, 95–96

Hedwig and the Angry Inch, 115, 142

Helen Hayes Theatre, 309

Hello, Again, 214

Hello, Dolly! 48–50, 53, 132, 152–153, 198, 215, 235, 299, 316

Henner, Marilu, 60

Henning, Doug, 370–371

Hepburn, Audrey, 38

Hepburn, Katherine, 57

Her First Roman, 285–286

Hercules, 82

Herman, Jerry, 42, 48–49, 51, 76, 78, 135, 198, 215

Herscher, Sylvia, 61

Hershey Park, 159

Hibbard, David, 245

Hilty, Megan, 264

HIV/AIDS, 77–78, 87, 94, 97, 121, 199, 204, 211, 329

H.M.S. Pinafore, 22

Hoffman, Jackie, 285

Holiday Inn, 160

Holliday, Jennifer, 77, 90, 211, 241–242, 298

Hollywood Bowl, 143

Holmes, Rupert, 79

Holzman, Winnie, 192–193

hooks, 199

Hope, Bob, 24, 371

Horne, Lena, 38

house seats, 182

House Un-American Activities Committee, 45

How to Succeed at Business without Really Trying, 30, 44–45, 90–91, 132, 153, 215, 253, 269, 336, 373

Hudson, Jennifer, 54, 160

Hudson Scenic Studio, 239

Huffman, Cady, 252

Hugo, Victor, 73, 302

Humphries, Barry, 46

Hunchback of Notre Dame, The, 93

Hupfeld, Herman, 366

I

I Am a Camera, 302
I Am Harvey Milk, 214
"I am" songs, 127
I Do! I Do! 271
I Remember Mama, 195
"I want" songs, 126–127
Idle, Eric, 101
Iglehart, James Monroe, 143, 358
Imperial Theatre, 61, 310
"In one" songs, 128
In the Heights, 75, 102, 108, 132, 160, 213, 263, 273, 321
in the round, 173–174
industrials, 358
Inspector Calls, An, 8
inspiration, 298–305
intermissions (intervals), 133–134
Internet Broadway Database, 271
Into the Woods, 16, 80–82, 142, 156, 160, 196, 215, 220, 300, 330
It's a Bird, It's a Plane, It's Superman, 304
Ixion, 24

J

Jackman, Hugh, 220, 264, 329–330
Jackson, Cheyenne, 102, 277, 299, 326, 346
Jackson, Chris, 95, 120, 223
Jackson, Michael R., 197
Jacobs, Jim, 298
Jacques Brel Is Alive and Well and Living in Paris, 142
Jagged Little Pill, 117, 121–122
Jamaica, 38
James, Brian d'Arcy, 214
Janki, Devanand, 54, 220
Janney, Allison, 102
Jarreau, Al, 90
Jeffers, Susan, 346
Jekyll and Hyde, 59, 147, 262
Jenkins, Capathia, 59
Jerome Robbins' Broadway, 82, 266, 271
Jersey Boys, 13, 105, 303

Jesus Christ Superstar, 13–14, 58–59, 69, 123, 147, 203, 298
Jeter, Michael, 221
jewelry, 171
Joe Allen restaurant, 169–170
Joel, Billy, 104, 198, 303
John, Elton, 95, 103, 203–204
John-LaChiusa, Michael, 214
Johns, Glynnis, 367
Jonas, Nick, 44, 373
Jones, Davy, 46, 90
Jones, Rachel Bay, 171, 261
Joplin, Scott, 88
Joseph and the Amazing Technicolor Dreamcoat, 14, 70–71, 132, 137, 203, 298
Joseph Jefferson Award, 143
jukebox musicals, 13, 21, 103–105, 111–112, 118, 197–198, 303
Julia, 46
JumpStart Theatre Program, 165

K

Kael, Pauline, 42
Kahal, Irving, 366
Kahn, Madeline, 299, 312
Kail, Tommy, 223
Kander, John, 17, 23, 42, 50, 85, 92, 123, 192–193, 196, 208–209, 353
Kane, Brad, 47
Karimloo, Ramin, 239–240
Kat and the Kings, 149, 333
Kaufman, George S., 29
Kaye, Judy, 60, 103
Keaton, Diane, 373
Keller, Helen, 25
Kennedy, Jackie, 44
Kennedy, John F., 44
Kennedy, Lauren, 282
Kennedy Center, The, 143, 151
Kern, Jerome, 28, 202
Kerr, Deborah, 38
Kidd, Michael, 36
Kiley, Richard, 46, 49

Kimberly Akimbo, 99, 207, 250

King, Carole, 59, 111, 303

King and I, The, 34–35, 38, 82, 92–93, 191, 194, 202, 302

Kinky Boots, 113–114, 159, 196, 300

Kismet, 11, 198

Kiss Me, Kate, 12, 33, 130, 200, 213, 251, 299

Kiss of the Spider Woman, 50, 85, 196, 209, 222, 269, 340

Kitt, Eartha, 214

Kitt, Tom, 13, 206, 298

Klausner, Terri, 264

Kline, Kevin, 23

Korie, Michael, 206

Kowalik, Trent, 254

Krakowski, Jane, 47, 72

Kretzmer, Herbert, 146, 210

Krieger, Henry, 211, 229

Kritzer, Leslie, 59

Kron, Lisa, 207

Kuhn, Judy, 115, 123, 143, 174, 237, 275

Kulish, Kiril, 254

L

La Cage Aux Folles, 78, 105, 196, 215

La Jolla Playhouse, 81, 155

labs, 307

Lady Be Good, 26, 28

Lady Day at Emerson's Bar and Grill, 341

Lady Gaga, 118, 256

Lane, Nathan, 34, 78, 98, 136, 161, 252, 257, 331, 357, 370–371

Lange, Ted, 373

Lansbury, Angela, 4, 51, 204, 302, 323, 333, 362

Lapine, James, 10, 76, 78–80, 195–196, 220, 300

LaPook, Jonathan, 121

Larents, Arthur, 78

Larsen, Anika, 112, 312

Larson, Jonathan, 87, 228

Last Five Years, The, 124, 200, 214

Last Ship, The, 115

Laurents, Arthur, 40, 192–194

Lavin, Linda, 304

Lawrence, Gertrude, 34

Lazarus, Frank, 198

Leachman, Cloris, 30

leads/featured performers, 15, 250–257

Lear, Norman, 57

Lee, Baayork, 63

Lee, Michele, 30

Legacy Robe, 337–338

Legally Blonde, 101–102, 153, 185, 300, 312

Legs Diamond, 115

Lena Horne: The Lady and Her Music, 38

Lena Horne Theatre, 38

Lerner, Alan Jay, 12–13, 37, 44, 208, 250

Leroux, Gaston, 302

Les Misérables, 2, 14, 70, 72–75, 83, 121, 132, 143, 145–146, 148, 210, 236–237, 293, 302, 324–325, 340, 373

levelers, 244–245

Levi, Zach, 47

Levy, Eugene, 59

Lewis, Marcia, 50

Lewis, Norm, 77, 85, 102, 160, 214

librettists, 192–197, 220

Light in the Piazza, The, 202, 248

lighting designers, 15, 221, 240–242

Li'l Abner, 131, 304, 370

Lily, 97, 300

Linden, Hal, 83

Lindsay, Robert, 30

Lindsay-Abaire, David, 207

Lion, Margo, 205

Lion King, The, 88, 93, 95, 103, 185, 203, 304, 309

Lippa, Andrew, 214, 304

Little Johnny Jones, 368

Little Mermaid, The, 93, 127, 160, 204, 312

Little Night Music, A, 56, 131, 215, 367

Little Shop of Horrors, 47, 204

Little Theatre Movement, 155

Little Women, 99

Llana, José, 93

lobbies, 185

Loesser, Emily, 130

Loesser, Frank, 34, 37, 45, 130, 215, 227

Loesser, Jo Sullivan, 37

Loewe, Frederick, 13, 37, 44, 208, 250

Look of Love, The, 303
Lopez, Priscilla, 170, 259, 280, 285–286, 333, 348
Lopez, Robert, 206, 209
lottery sales, 181
Loudon, Dorothy, 66–67
Love Never Dies, 147
Love! Valor! Compassion! 196
Lucille Lortel, 142
Luker, Rebecca, 253, 322
LuPone, Patti, 4, 69, 74–75, 86, 161, 196, 204, 226, 229, 247, 260–261, 264, 333
Lyceum, 144
lyricists, 14, 199–200, 202–205, 212–216, 220
lyrics, 9–10

M

Macchio, Ralph, 153
MacDermot, Galt, 53
Mackintosh, Cameron, 70, 145
MacLaine, Shirley, 36, 52
Madonna, 69, 374
Maguire, Gregory, 302
makeup artists, 15
makeup designers, 245
Maltby, Richard, Jr., 210–211
Mame, 51–52, 136, 215, 250, 258, 302
Mamma Mia! 13, 74, 103–104, 137, 160, 232–233, 303, 373
Man of La Mancha, 46, 251
Man of No Importance, A, 250
Mann, Barry, 111
Mann, Terrence, 94
marketing teams, 15
Marlowe, 13
Marshall, Rob, 80, 86, 160, 192–193
Martin, Andrea, 59
Martin, Jesse L., 87
Martin, Mary, 41, 161, 271
Martin, Max, 303
Martin, Ricky, 69
Martin Short's Fame Becomes Me, 205
Marvel, Linda, 276
Marx, Jeff, 206, 209–210

Mary Poppins, 158, 160
Mary Poppins Returns, 99
Marzullo, Steve, 293
Massey, Daniel, 47
Master of Ceremonies, 51
Masteroff, Joe, 192–195
Matchmaker, The, 48, 299
Matilda, 160
Maude, 52
Maxwell, Jan, 251
McAnuff, Des, 85
McArdle, Andrea, 65–67, 72, 195, 243, 255, 322–323, 333, 336, 372
MCC Theater Company, 330
McClelland, Kay, 83
McCollum, Kevin, 228
McCormick, Maureen, 89
McCraken, Joan, 227
McDonald, Audra, 4, 27–28, 42, 77, 89, 143, 161, 322, 332, 340–341
McDonald, Zoe, 42
McGovern, Maureen, 23
McKechnie, Donna, 54, 64, 129, 156, 259, 263, 354
McNair, Barbara, 83
McNally, Terrence, 121, 196, 254, 280
Me and My Girl, 70
Me Nobody Knows, The, 240
Mean Girls, 185, 300
Meat Loaf, 373
Meehan, Tom, 195
Meet Me in St. Louis, 171, 346
megamixes, 137
Memphis, 160, 358
Mendes, Sam, 192–193
Mendez, Lindsay, 59
Menken, Alan, 94, 204–205
Menzel, Idina, 87, 257, 340
merchandise, 185
Merlin, 370–371
Merman, Ethel, 4, 29–31, 41, 49–50, 53, 161, 170, 255, 316, 337
Merrick, David, 46, 49, 69, 76, 96, 151, 226, 249
Merrily We Roll Along, 4, 78, 124–125, 200, 313
message boards, 161, 164

mezzanines, 176–177

Michaelson, Ingrid, 302

Michele, Lea, 107

Michener, James, 33, 194

Midler, Bette, 49, 205

Mikado, The, 22

Miles, Ruthie Ann, 35

Miller, Ann, 24, 49, 156

Mills, Stephanie, 65

Minelli, Liza, 50, 84, 145, 193

Minskoff Theatre, 309

minstrel shows, 23

Miranda, Lin-Manuel, 26, 75, 102, 106, 108, 115, 119–120, 161, 181, 206, 208, 213, 223, 257, 273

Miscast, 330

Miss Saigon, 14, 70, 75–76, 103, 210, 236

Mitchell, Brian Stokes, 121–122, 340

Mitchell, John Cameron, 115

Monk, Debra, 352, 361

Montalban, Ricardo, 38

Monty Python and The Holy Grail, 101

Moore, Douglas, 212

Moore, Melba, 53

Moore, Tom, 61

Moreno, Rita, 86, 254

Morgan, Helen, 24

Morisette, Alanis, 117

Morrison, Matt, 102

Morse, Robert, 44

Most, Donny, 90

Most Happy Fella, The, 14, 37, 123, 132, 215, 251, 299

Mostel, Zero, 45–46, 196

Moulin Rouge, 13, 117–118, 120, 185, 198, 232

Mousetrap, The, 145

Movin' Out, 104, 198, 303

Mr. Saturday Night, 214

Mrs. Doubtfire, 121

Mueller, Jessie, 111, 116, 143

Mulan, 82

Mullally, Megan, 91, 150, 163, 253, 261–262, 312

Murney, Julia, 214

Murphy, Donna, 16, 92

music, as component of musicals, 9

Music Circus, 157

music directors, 14–15, 228–229

Music Man, The, 38–39, 177, 192, 215, 220, 341, 359, 368

musical comedies, 12, 22

musical theatre
  anatomy, 123–137
  attendance, 167–187
  components of musicals, 8–12
  defined, 8
  hatred for, 11, 13
  production, 297–318
  professionals, 14–16, 191–229, 231–294
  testing your knowledge of, 16–17
  types of musicals, 12–14
  venues, 139–165

musical theatre history, 19–122
  early precursors, 20–27
  1920s-1930s, 28–31
  1940s-1950s, 31–42
  1960s, 42–56
  1970s, 56–69
  1980s, 69–83
  1990s, 83–96
  2000s, 96–108
  2010s, 109–120
  2020s, 120–122

My Fair Lady, 12, 37–38, 44, 51, 131–132, 160, 208, 250, 252, 299, 340

My Life on the D-List, 30

My One and Only, 27, 195

Myers, Pamela, 58

Mystery of Edwin Drood, The, 79–80

N

Natasha, Pierre and the Great Comet of 1821, 172

Nathan, Anne, 113

National Actors Theatre, 118

National Endowment for the Arts, 155

Nelson, Tracy, 90

Neuwirth, Bebe, 52, 260

New Amsterdam Theatre, 185, 309

New Brain, A, 304

New Girl in Town, 52

New York International Fringe Festival, 165

New York, New York, 50, 208

New York Theatre Workshop, 142

New York Times, The, 42, 47, 89, 158, 318

Newman, Phyllis, 156

Newsies, 196, 204

Next to Normal, 30, 59, 108, 111, 206, 298, 336

Niblo's Garden, 24

Nice Work If You Can Get It, 27

Nights of Cabiria, 52

Nine, 160, 198, 201

Nine To Five, 102

9/11 terrorist attacks, 98

Nixon, Marni, 38

No Strings, 46, 49

Norman, Marsha, 196

Northstage Dinner Theatre, 158

Northwestern University, 143

Norton, Elliot, 143

Notebook, The, 302

Nouri, Michael, 86

Nunn, Trevor, 72, 74, 204

Nunsense, 142

Nyro, Laura, 59

O

Oberlin College, 163

Oberlin Conservatory, 123

Obie Awards, 334

O'Connor, Carroll, 30

Odd Couple, The, 98, 118

O'Donnell, Rosie, 89, 257, 261, 293

Of Thee I Sing, 29–30, 336

Off-Broadway, 141–142

Off-Off Broadway, 141–142

Oh, Kay! 26

Oh! Calcutta! 24, 53

O'Hara, Jill, 367

O'Hara, Kelli, 36, 131

O'Hara, Paige, 130

O'Keefe, Lawrence, 101

Oklahoma! 12, 16, 20, 28, 31–32, 40, 127, 130, 134, 151, 194, 202, 250, 299, 331, 341

Old Globe, 156

Oliver! 46–47, 69, 158, 237

Olivier, Lawrence, 333

Olivier Awards, 333–334

Olivo, Karen, 273, 321

O'Malley, Rory, 111

On a Clear Day You Can See Forever, 208

on- and offstage crew members, 275–279

On the Town, 32–33, 82, 115, 147, 212, 369

On the Twentieth Century, 10, 125, 131, 200, 206

On Your Feet, 13

On Your Toes, 210

Once, 102, 113, 142, 300

Once on This Island, 84–85, 208

Once Upon a Mattress, 202, 301

one-night-only events, 329–330

onstage seating, 172

Opel, Nancy, 316

open calls, 348

opening night, 317–318

opening numbers, 126

operas, 13, 20–23

operettas, 22, 125

Orbach, Jerry, 54, 366

orchestras, 15, 291–294

orchestra pits, 175, 352

orchestra seats, 175–177

orchestral understudies, 265–267

orchestrators, 14–15

Orfeh, 103

Orso restaurant, 169

Osmond, Marie, 153

Outer Critics Circle Awards, 334–335

out-of-town tryouts, 150–152, 305, 316

Over Here! 372

overtures, 124–125

P

Pacific Overtures, 56

pacing, 222

Page, Patrick, 341

Paige, Elaine, 69, 86, 264

Pajama Game, The, 36, 83, 129, 134, 201, 227, 302

Pal Joey, 210

Panko, Tom, 158

Papermill Playhouse, 156

Papp, Joseph, 141

Parade, 131, 214, 301

Parker, Sarah Jessica, 91, 371–372

Parker, Trey, 207

Pascal, Adam, 87, 96, 153, 274, 329

Pasek, Benj, 116–117, 209–210

Passion, 143, 196

Patinkin, Mandy, 69, 150, 214

Patio Players, 161

Patti LuPone at Les Mouches, 264

Patton, Lauren, 117

Paul, Justin, 116–117, 209–210

peas and carrots, 353

Pedi, Christine, 4, 84, 162

Perez, Rosie, 280

performers, 15, 250–257, 319–362

perfumes and colognes, 171

Perry, Antoinette, 17, 331

Peter Pan, 82, 278

Peters, Bernadette, 4, 66, 78, 80–81, 150, 161, 304, 322

Phantom of the Opera, The, 25, 50, 62, 70, 73–75, 80, 83, 100, 103, 113, 133, 142, 145, 147, 153, 160, 203, 232, 236, 239–240, 264, 269, 280, 292, 302, 326

Phillips, Lou Diamond, 35, 92

photography, 187

Pierce, David Hyde, 101

Pippin, 60–61, 66, 127, 250, 256, 280

Pippin, Donald, 58

Pirates of Penzance, 22–23

Piscopo, Joe, 90

Pitre, Louise, 74, 103

Plain and Fancy, 196

Platt, Ben, 117

Playbill, 141, 186

Playwrights Horizons, 142

Plotnick, Jack, 350

Pocahontas, 93

Porgy and Bess, 9

Porter, Billy, 28, 47, 60, 77, 113–114, 163, 261

Porter, Cole, 9, 12, 31, 33, 35, 212–213

Pose, 114

Poseidon Adventure, The, 23

Presley, Elvis, 43, 303

Preston, Robert, 39, 271

Pretty Woman, 153

previews, 315–316

Prince, Faith, 34, 89, 92, 329

Prince, Hal, 16, 36–37, 42, 47, 50, 58, 68, 78, 85, 96, 192–193, 221–222, 227, 269, 313, 367

producers, 14, 225–228

Producers, The, 12, 98, 102, 136, 144, 195, 244, 252–253, 257, 300

production stage managers (PSMs), 276, 286–287

production values, 232

Prom, The, 160

Promises, Promises, 54–55, 152, 157, 194, 300, 356, 366

prop crew, 272–273

proscenium stages, 172–173, 175

Public Theater, The, 115, 141, 174

publicists, 15

Pulitzer, Joseph, 336

Pulitzer Prize, 336

Pump Boys and Dinettes, 361

punctuality, 172, 185

put-in rehearsals, 269–270, 321–322

Pygmalion, 37, 250, 299

Q

quartets, 132

quick changes, 282–284

Quinn, Anthony, 196

quintets, 132

R

Radcliffe, Daniel, 44, 373

Radner, Gilda, 59, 354

Rado, James, 53

Ragni, Gerome, 53

Rags, 207

Ragtime, 4, 88–89, 121, 126, 196, 208, 341

Rainey, Ma, 23

Ralph, Sheryl Lee, 77

Ramirez, Sara, 101, 130, 371

Rand, Sally, 24

Randall, Tony, 118

Rannells, Andrew, 110, 336

Rapp, Anthony, 35

readings, 305–306

Reams, Lee Roy, 340

recitative, 21

Red Bucket Follies, 329–330

Red Shoes, The, 202

Reddy, Helen, 59

Redhead, 52, 211

regional theatre, 155–156, 357–358

rehearsals, 313–314, 320–325, 352–353

Reichard, Daniel, 105

Reinking, Ann, 372

Rent, 30, 35, 87–88, 135, 160, 181, 228, 261, 329, 333, 336, 341

reprises, 135

resellers, 182

restrooms, 184

revues, 10

rhyming, 9–10, 200

Rice, Tim, 14, 58–59, 68, 70, 94–95, 203–204, 298, 368

Richards, Donna, 284

Richardson, Natasha, 193

Riley, Charles Nelson, 43

Ripley, Alice, 85, 108, 254–255, 282

Ritter, Thelma, 57

Ritz, The, 196, 254, 280

Rivera, Chita, 36, 40–41, 43, 62–63, 85, 129, 136, 177, 222, 229, 235–236, 259, 263, 269, 370

Roar of the Greasepaint, The Smell of the Crowd, The, 200

Robbins, Jerome, 33, 40, 45–46, 48, 82, 126, 227, 305

Roberts, Tony, 86, 156

Robeson, Paul, 27, 340

rock musicals, 13, 87

Rock 'N Roll: The First 5,000 Years, 374

Rock of Ages, 13, 197–198

Rocky, 102

Rodgers, Mary, 301

Rodgers, Richard, 28, 30–31, 33–34, 41, 46, 92, 144, 151, 202, 210, 215, 300–301, 365–366

Rodriguez, Krysta, 107

Roger, Elena, 69

Rogers, Ginger, 50

Romeo and Juliet, 39, 299

Rondstadt, Linda, 23

Rooney, Mickey, 24, 26, 313

Rose, George, 23

Rosemary's Baby, 50

Rose's Turn, 304

Ross, Diana, 77

Ross, Jerry, 36–37, 227

Royal Shakespeare Company, 72–73, 146

Rubin-Vega, Daphne, 87, 329, 341

Ruby Foo's, 264

Rudetsky, Seth, 2–4

Runaways, 202

run-throughs, 315, 320

Runyon, Damon, 34

Rupert, Michael, 256

Russell, Bill, 211

Russell, Jenna, 324–325

Russell, Rosalind, 302

Ryan, Meg, 47

Ryskind, Morrie, 29

S

salary, 355–356

Salonga, Lea, 75–76

Sarafina! 149

Sardi's, 170

Sarich, Drew, 147

Saturday Night Fever, 103, 278

Saver, Jeff, 269

scalpers, 182

Scandalous, 301

Scanlon, Dick, 99, 207, 288

Scarlet Pimpernel, The, 186

scene change music, 128–129

Schaffer, Paul, 59

Schlesinger, Adam, 121

Schonberg, Claude-Michel, 146, 210
School of Rock, 255
school productions, 164–165
Schwartz, Stephen, 56, 59–60, 100–101, 151, 192, 207, 298–299
Scott, Jeff, 162
Scott, Sherie Rene, 85, 96
Scottsboro Boys, The, 23, 301
seating, 175–179, 184
Secada, Jon, 257
Secret Garden, The, 196, 322
Seesaw, 211
Seff, Richard, 51
Seller, Jeffrey, 228
Senior Trip, 313
Serber, Cara, 158
set changes, 275
set designers, 15, 221, 236–240
Seurat, George, 78
Seussical, 208, 222
1776, 55–56, 195, 200–201, 254, 301, 318
sextets, 132
Shaiman, Marc, 99, 204–205
Shakespeare, William, 39, 299
Shannon, Molly, 55, 283
Shaw, George Bernard, 37, 250
She Loves Me, 47–48, 160, 194–195, 200–201
Sheldon, Cathy, 161
Shelton, Reid, 67
Shenandoah, 131
Shevelove, Burt, 45
Shields, Brooke, 89
Shire, David, 210–211
Shop around the Corner, The, 47
Short, Martin, 59
Show Boat, 20, 28–29, 131, 194, 253
Shrek, 115
Shuffle Along, 27–28
Shuffle Along, or the Making of the Musical Sensation of 1921 and All That Followed, 27–28
Sia, 118
side jobs, 362
Side Show, 211, 254–255, 282

Signature Theatre, 143
Simard, Jennifer, 260
Simon, Carly, 59
Simon, Lucy, 196
Simon, Neil, 54, 194
Simon, Paul, 59
Sinatra, Frank, 303
Singing in the Rain, 212, 300
singing skills, 340–342
Sissie, Noble, 27
Sister Act, 204
sitzprobes, 314
Six, 132, 160
16 bars, 342, 346, 353
skills, 339–346
Skinner, Emily, 150, 254–255, 262, 282
Slater, Christian, 370
Smalls, Charlie, 202
Smith, Bessie, 23
Smith, Rex, 23
Smokey Joe's Café, 253
Snoopy, 201
Some Like It Hot, 10, 205, 300
Sondheim, Stephen, 16, 40, 45, 56, 58, 68, 76, 78–82, 126, 192, 195, 202, 208, 215, 300, 305, 313, 367
Sondheim, Steven, 9
Song and Dance, 134
Songs for a New World, 214
Soo, Phillipa, 120
sound board operators, 273–274
sound crew, 273–274
sound designers, 243–245
Sound of Music, The, 41–42, 46, 147, 153, 194, 202, 254, 301, 366
South America, 149
South Pacific, 30, 33, 130, 194, 200, 202, 235, 244, 302, 336
South Park, 110, 207
souvenir programs, 185
Spamalot, 12, 101, 130, 371
Sparks, Nicholas, 302
Sperling, Ted, 90, 270
Spider-Man: Turn off the Dark, 305

split weeks, 328

SpongeBob SquarePants, 304

spotlight operators, 274–275

Spring Awakening, 107–108, 142, 172

SRO (standing room only), 178

St. James Theatre, 310

St. Louis Municipal Opera Theatre (The Muny), 157

St. Louis Woman, 368

stage dooring, 327

stage left/right, 352

stage managers (SMs), 15, 286–289

stage mothers, 40

stage types, 172–175

staged readings, 306

standbys, 16, 262–264

star bows, 257–258

star dressers, 283–284

star salary, 355

star vehicles, 220

Starlight Bowl, 157

Starlight Express, 72

Stars in the House, 121

Starting Here! Starting Now! 211

Stein, Joseph, 48, 196

Sting, 115

Stone, Matt, 207

Stone, Peter, 55, 195

Strange Loop, A, 30, 197, 336

Strauss, Johann, II, 22

StreamYard, 121

Streep, Meryl, 3, 80, 302

Streetcar Named Desire, A, 283

Streisand, Barbra, 39, 47, 49, 68, 80, 92, 141, 203, 208, 243, 255–256, 331, 340

Stritch, Elaine, 58, 171, 340

Strouse, Charles, 43, 57, 207, 368

stumble-throughs, 320

Styne, Jule, 40, 125, 192, 196, 202–203

subscriptions, 155

Subways Are for Sleeping, 370

Sugar Babies, 24

Sullivan, Arthur, 22

summer stock, 156–158, 356

Summer Stock, 156

Sunday in the Park with George, 78–79, 142–143, 195–196, 201, 215, 316, 324, 336

sung-thru musicals, 13–14, 21, 59, 69, 73

Sunset Boulevard, 85–86, 203, 229, 237, 253

supertitles, 146

Supremes, The, 77

Surflight Summer Theatre, 156, 356

Swados, Liz, 202

Swan Lake, 8, 191

Sweeney Todd, 50, 56, 68, 113, 144, 160, 215, 250–251, 333, 340

Sweet Charity, 52, 136, 194, 206, 211, 250–251, 260, 356

Sweet Smell of Success, 131

swings, 16, 265–267, 279, 323

Sydney Lyric Theatre, 149

Sydney Opera House, 149

T

table reads, 306

Take Me Along, 196, 370

Taming of the Shrew, The, 33, 299

Tandy, Jessica, 283

Tap Dance Kid, The, 211

Taylor, Elizabeth, 44

Taymor, Julie, 95, 123

tech rehearsals, 291, 314–315

Temptations, 303

10 out of 12s, 314–315

Tesori, Jeanine, 99, 115, 207

Tharp, Twyla, 104

Theatre Development Fund (TDF), 180

Theatre du Chatelet, 147

Theatre Royal, Drury Lane, 144

Theatre Tokens, 180

Theatre-By-The-Sea, 157

theatres, 140–141, 309–311

theme parks, 159, 358

They Knew What They Wanted, 299

They're Playing Our Song, 194

13, 160

Thompson, David, 23

Thoroughly Modern Millie, 99, 131, 207, 262, 288, 326, 334, 346, 350

thrust stages, 172–173

tickets, 179–182, 184

Time of the Cuckoo, The, 194

Titanic, 195, 237–238

[title of show], 132, 149

TKTS ticket booths, 179–181

TodayTix, 181

Tommy, 85, 149

Tony Awards, 252–255, 331–333

Tootsie, 348

Torch Song Trilogy, 196

touring productions, 153–154, 328, 356–357

transportation, 168–169

Travolta, John, 60, 372–373

trios, 131–132

Truman, Harry S., 27

Tune, Tommy, 7, 83, 91, 198

Tunick, Jonathan, 58

Tunie, Tamara, 77

Turning Point, The, 194

TV appearances, 327–328

TV commercials, 60–61, 66

Tveit, Aaron, 118

Twelfth Night, 299

12 tones, 197

29-hour readings, 306

Two By Two, 299

typing, 348

U

Uggams, Leslie, 161

Ulvaeus, Björn, 203–204, 368

underscoring, 129–130

understudies, 16, 260–263, 265–267, 323–324

university productions, 162–163

Unprotected, 114

Unsinkable Molly Brown, The, 215

upstage, 352

uptempos, 130–131

Urinetown, 165

V

vamps, 353

Van Dyke, Dick, 43, 136, 368

Vance, Vivian, 31

vaudeville, 24–25

Verdon, Gwen, 35–37, 52, 62, 177

Vereen, Ben, 60

Very Warm for May, 366

Via Galactica, 13

Viagas, Robert, 63

Victorious, 373

Victor/Victoria, 86–87

videography, 187

Vigard, Kristen, 195

Village Voice, The, 334

Violet, 207, 330

Visit, The, 263

vocal arrangers, 14–15

voice teachers and coaches, 342

volunteering, 360

Vosburgh, Dick, 198

W

Waissman, Ken, 61

Waitress, 59, 102, 111, 115–116, 120–121, 130, 134, 213, 250, 300

Walker, Alice, 302

Walker, Nancy, 33, 369

Waller, Fats, 10, 303

Waller, Robert James, 302

Wallis, Shani, 158

Walsh, Thommie, 63

Wang, Wallace, 361

War Paint, 252

wardrobe supervisors, 280–281

Warner, Jack, 38

Warren, Harry, 303

Warwick, Dionne, 366

Watanabe, Ken, 35

watching the book, 268

Waters, Sarah, 80

Watson, Susan, 43

Way We Were, The, 194

Webber, Andrew Lloyd, 14, 56, 58–59, 68, 70–73, 75, 82, 85, 203–204, 253, 298

Wedding Singer, The, 312

Weede, Robert, 37

Weil, Cynthia, 111–112

Weisberger, Lauren, 302

Weissler, Barry and Fran, 89–90

Weitzman, Ira, 81

West End, 143–145

West Side Story, 10–12, 36, 38–41, 62, 82, 109, 129, 132, 160, 163, 193–194, 227, 229, 235, 299

Where's Charley? 34

White, Betty, 52, 283

White, Lillias, 77, 90, 261, 291, 340, 374

Who, The, 85

Wicked, 29, 66, 100–101, 107, 121, 126, 129, 132, 148, 153, 185, 192–193, 201, 225, 237–238, 245, 257, 260, 264, 283, 302, 309, 326, 340, 373

wig designers, 221–222

wig prep, 170

wig/makeup calls, 326

Wild Party, The, 201, 214

Wildcat, 125, 206, 370

Wilder, Billy, 86

Wilder, Thornton, 48

Wilkinson, Colm, 75, 340

Wilkof, Lee, 47

Will Rogers Follies, The, 125, 195, 206, 212

Williams, Robin, 78

Williams, Sammy, 259

Williams, Schele, 96

Williams, Vanessa, 168

Willson, Meredith, 38–39, 192, 215, 368

Wilson, Chandra, 362

Wilson, Patrick, 98, 242, 341

wings, 352

Winokur, Marissa Jaret, 99–100, 129, 332

Winter Garden Theatre, The, 26, 255

Wittman, Scott, 99, 204–205

Wiz, The, 65–66, 136, 201–202, 300

Wizard of Oz, The, 38, 65, 100–101, 160, 300, 302

Woman of the Year, 58

Women on the Verge of a Nervous Breakdown, 261

Wonderful Town, 212

Wood, Natalie, 38

workshops, 306–307

Wright, George, 198

X

Xanadu, 102, 172, 277, 312

X-Men, 264

Y

Yazbeck, David, 98

Yazbeck, Tony, 330

Yeston, Maury, 198–199

York, Rachel, 86

Yorkey, Brian, 206, 298

Young Frankenstein, 312, 335

Your Arms Too Short to Box with God, 298

You're a Good Man, Charlie Brown, 132, 172, 214, 252, 257, 304

You've Got Mail, 47

Z

Zaks, Jerry, 60, 220

Zanna, Don't! 220

Zbornik, Kristine, 1

Zellweger, Renée, 160

Zeta-Jones, Catherine, 160, 255

Ziegfeld Follies, 25

Zien, Chip, 81–82

Zippel, David, 82

Zorba, 196

About the Author

When Broadway shut down in 2020, **Seth Rudetsky** and his husband James Wesley started the livestream "Stars in the House," which raises money for The Actors Fund (now The Entertainment Community Fund). They've had reunions of Broadway shows like *A Chorus Line*, *Ragtime*, and *The Producers* (with Nathan, Matthew, and Mel!) and TV shows like *Grey's Anatomy*, *Taxi*, and *ER* (with George Clooney). So far they've raised more than $1.1 million dollars and recently celebrated their two year anniversary of the show.

Before that, Seth spent many years on Broadway as a pianist and conductor starting with *Les Misérables* and then many other shows including *Grease!!!*, *Ragtime*, *The Phantom of the Opera*, and *The Producers*. He also spent two years as a comedy writer on *The Rosie O'Donnell Show* (three Emmy nominations with his co-writers), which led to him writing two opening numbers for the Tony Awards, the first featuring Patti LuPone, Betty Buckley, and Jennifer Holliday singing their signature songs.

He is now the afternoon deejay on the SiriusXM Broadway channel as well the host of the talk show *Seth Speaks*. He's performed his show *Deconstructing Broadway* in London, Boston (Irne Award winner), and Los Angeles (with Barbra Streisand in the audience!). He co-wrote and co-starred in *Disaster!* (a *New York Times* critics' pick) on Broadway, which was licensed by Music Theater International and is being performed around the country. He's written the books *Seth's Broadway Diary Volumes 1 and 2* (Dress Circle Publishing) and two young adult novels: *My Awesome/Awful Popularity Plan* and *The Rise and Fall of a Theater Geek* (Random House).

Seth and James co-produced the "What The World Needs Now Is Love" recording with Broadway Records (number one on iTunes), featuring amazing singers like Idina Menzel, Audra MacDonald, Lin-Manuel Miranda, and so many more to help the victims and families of the Orlando Pulse Nightclub shooting. He and James also produce and host the yearly "Voices For The Voiceless" concert to benefit You Gotta Believe, which helps older foster kids find families (stars have included Tina Fey and Jessie Mueller) as well as producing/hosting 13 Concert For America benefits that help nonprofits like National Immigration Law Center and NAACP (stars have included Audra McDonald and Chita Rivera).

Contributors: Ryan M. Prendergast is an Assistant Teaching Professor in Drama and Music at Carnegie Mellon University. He was formerly a lecturer at the University of Texas at Austin. His research focuses on music theatre, opera production, and opera recording. He received his doctorate in theatre from the University of Illinois, Urbana-Champaign.

Bill Jenkins is a Full Professor and the Department Chair of Theatre and Dance at Ball State University in Muncie, Indiana, where he has been since 2000. He's an active member of the Society of Directors and Choreographers and regularly directs both professionally and on campus. An active scholar and practitioner, Bill loves to expose students and audiences to the history and power of the musical theatre form.

Dedication

This book is dedicated to those who created musical theatre and those who continue to keep it alive — onstage, backstage, and in the audience.

Authors' Acknowledgments

I must thank the following incredible people for not only doing such an amazing and meticulous job putting this book together, but for being so kind and patient as I missed a few (many, *many*) deadlines: Chad Sievers, project manager/development editor (Chief of Patience); Nicole Sholly: Dummifier (Grand Dame of Patience); William Jenkins and Ryan Prendergast, contributors; André Garner, technical reviewer; Imani Sidney Wright Brissett, art assistant; Eric Myers, my long-time book agent for always pushing me; James Wesley, my loving husband for being there no matter what; and Juli, my daughter, for always seeing Broadway shows with us — even though she's not *obsessed* like I am.

And a special thanks to Linda Marvel: The Broadway stage manager extraordinaire for her amazing editing and insight into the backstage world of Broadway; Tom Viola: From Broadway Cares/Equity Fights AIDS for being so willing to help with photos; Lin-Manuel Miranda: The one and only for reading the chapter that was killing me and giving me tips; Tobin Ost and Alexander Dodge: The Broadway diva set designers for their set design insight; and Steve Hayes: And an extra big thank you! Steve reached out to me in the first place and asked if I'd write the book. And a *bigger* thanks to his daughter, Matilda, who recommended me to her dad in the first place. Matilda, thanks for the gig! I owe ya.

And finally, thank you to every single theatre professional I've interviewed throughout the years who opened their hearts and lives to me — and whose stories fill this book.

Publisher's Acknowledgments

Executive Editor: Steve Hayes

Project Manager/Development Editor:
Chad R. Sievers

Senior Managing Editor: Kristie Pyles

Dummifier: Nicole Sholly

Technical Editor: André Garner

Production Editor: Tamilmani Varadharaj

Cover Image: Courtesy of Booth Tarkington
Civic Theatre, Photographer –
Zach Rosing; Author photo courtesy
of Lauren Kennedy Brady

Inspiration: Matilda Hayes and
Kimberly Ruse Roberts

Special Help: Imani Sidney Wright Brissett

Take dummies with you everywhere you go!

Whether you are excited about e-books, want more from the web, must have your mobile apps, or are swept up in social media, dummies makes everything easier.

Find us online!

dummies.com

dummies
A Wiley Brand

Leverage the power

Dummies is the global leader in the reference category and one of the most trusted and highly regarded brands in the world. No longer just focused on books, customers now have access to the dummies content they need in the format they want. Together we'll craft a solution that engages your customers, stands out from the competition, and helps you meet your goals.

Advertising & Sponsorships

Connect with an engaged audience on a powerful multimedia site, and position your message alongside expert how-to content. Dummies.com is a one-stop shop for free, online information and know-how curated by a team of experts.

- Targeted ads
- Video
- Email Marketing
- Microsites
- Sweepstakes sponsorship

20 MILLION
PAGE VIEWS
EVERY SINGLE MONTH

15 MILLION
UNIQUE
VISITORS PER MONTH

43%
OF ALL VISITORS
ACCESS THE SITE
VIA THEIR MOBILE DEVICES

700,000 NEWSLETTER
SUBSCRIPTIONS
TO THE INBOXES OF
300,000 UNIQUE INDIVIDUALS EVERY WEEK

# of dummies

Custom Publishing

Reach a global audience in any language by creating a solution that will differentiate you from competitors, amplify your message, and encourage customers to make a buying decision.

- Apps
- Books
- eBooks
- Video
- Audio
- Webinars

Brand Licensing & Content

Leverage the strength of the world's most popular reference brand to reach new audiences and channels of distribution.

For more information, visit dummies.com/biz

PERSONAL ENRICHMENT

Staying Sharp
9781119187790
USA $26.00
CAN $31.99
UK £19.99

Facebook
9781119179030
USA $21.99
CAN $25.99
UK £16.99

Guitar
9781119293354
USA $24.99
CAN $29.99
UK £17.99

Investing
9781119293347
USA $22.99
CAN $27.99
UK £16.99

Beekeeping
9781119310068
USA $22.99
CAN $27.99
UK £16.99

Digital Photography
9781119235606
USA $24.99
CAN $29.99
UK £17.99

Meditation
9781119251163
USA $24.99
CAN $29.99
UK £17.99

Pregnancy
9781119235491
USA $26.99
CAN $31.99
UK £19.99

Samsung Galaxy S7
9781119279952
USA $24.99
CAN $29.99
UK £17.99

iPhone
9781119283133
USA $24.99
CAN $29.99
UK £17.99

Crocheting
9781119287117
USA $24.99
CAN $29.99
UK £16.99

Nutrition
9781119130246
USA $22.99
CAN $27.99
UK £16.99

PROFESSIONAL DEVELOPMENT

Windows 10
9781119311041
USA $24.99
CAN $29.99
UK £17.99

AutoCAD
9781119255796
USA $39.99
CAN $47.99
UK £27.99

Excel 2016
9781119293439
USA $26.99
CAN $31.99
UK £19.99

QuickBooks 2017
9781119281467
USA $26.99
CAN $31.99
UK £19.99

macOS Sierra
9781119280651
USA $29.99
CAN $35.99
UK £21.99

LinkedIn
9781119251132
USA $24.99
CAN $29.99
UK £17.99

Windows 10
9781119310563
USA $34.00
CAN $41.99
UK £24.99

SharePoint 2016
9781119181705
USA $29.99
CAN $35.99
UK £21.99

Fundamental Analysis
9781119263593
USA $26.99
CAN $31.99
UK £19.99

Networking
9781119257769
USA $29.99
CAN $35.99
UK £21.99

Office 2016
9781119293477
USA $26.99
CAN $31.99
UK £19.99

Office 365
9781119265313
USA $24.99
CAN $29.99
UK £17.99

Salesforce.com
9781119239314
USA $29.99
CAN $35.99
UK £21.99

Coding
9781119293323
USA $29.99
CAN $35.99
UK £21.99

Learning Made Easy

ACADEMIC

9781119293576
USA $19.99
CAN $23.99
UK £15.99

9781119293637
USA $19.99
CAN $23.99
UK £15.99

9781119293491
USA $19.99
CAN $23.99
UK £15.99

9781119293460
USA $19.99
CAN $23.99
UK £15.99

9781119293590
USA $19.99
CAN $23.99
UK £15.99

9781119215844
USA $26.99
CAN $31.99
UK £19.99

9781119293378
USA $22.99
CAN $27.99
UK £16.99

9781119293521
USA $19.99
CAN $23.99
UK £15.99

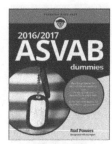

9781119239178
USA $18.99
CAN $22.99
UK £14.99

9781119263883
USA $26.99
CAN $31.99
UK £19.99

Available Everywhere Books Are Sold

dummies.com

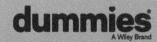
dummies
A Wiley Brand

Small books for big imaginations

9781119177173
USA $9.99
CAN $9.99
UK £8.99

9781119177272
USA $9.99
CAN $9.99
UK £8.99

9781119177241
USA $9.99
CAN $9.99
UK £8.99

9781119177210
USA $9.99
CAN $9.99
UK £8.99

9781119262657
USA $9.99
CAN $9.99
UK £6.99

9781119291336
USA $9.99
CAN $9.99
UK £6.99

9781119233527
USA $9.99
CAN $9.99
UK £6.99

9781119291220
USA $9.99
CAN $9.99
UK £6.99

9781119177302
USA $9.99
CAN $9.99
UK £8.99

Unleash Their Creativity

dummies.com

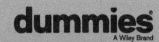